Early Ror

Blackwell Sourcebooks in Ancient History

This series presents readers with new translations of the raw material of ancient history. It provides direct access to the ancient world, from wars and power politics to daily life and entertainment, allowing readers to discover the extraordinary diversity of ancient societies.

Published

The Ancient Near East
Edited by Mark W. Chavalas

The Roman Games
Alison Futrell

Alexander the Great
Waldemar Heckel and J. C. Yardley

The Hellenistic Period
Roger Bagnall and Peter Derow

Ancient Greek Religion
Emily Kearns

Ancient Greece from Homer to Alexander
Joseph Roisman and J. C. Yardley

Early Rome: Myth and Society
Jaclyn Neel

Early Rome

Myth and Society: A Sourcebook

Jaclyn Neel

WILEY Blackwell

Registered Offices
John Wiley & Sons, Inc., 111 River Street, Hoboken, NJ 07030, USA

Editorial Office
350 Main Street, Malden, MA 02148-5020, USA

For details of our global editorial offices, customer services, and more information about Wiley products visit us at www.wiley.com.

Wiley also publishes its books in a variety of electronic formats and by print-on-demand. Some content that appears in standard print versions of this book may not be available in other formats.

Library of Congress Cataloging-in-Publication Data applied for.

Hardback: 9781119083795
Paperback: 9781119083801

Cover image: Wolf Mosaic, Aldborough Roman Town, Yorkshire, 300 AD (mosaic) / Leeds Museums and Art Galleries (Leeds City Museum) UK / Bridgeman Images

Set in 10/13pt Stone Serif by Aptara Inc., New Delhi, India

Printed in the United States of America

10 9 8 7 6 5 4 3 2 1

For my parents

The scholarly community has become increasingly aware of the differences between Roman myths and the more familiar myths of Greece. *Early Rome: Myth and Society* steps in to provide much-needed modern and accessible translations and commentaries on Italian legends.

This work examines the tales of Roman pre- and legendary history, discusses relevant cultural and contextual information, and presents author biographies. This book offers updated translations of key texts, including authors who are often absent from classical mythology textbooks, such as Dionysius of Halicarnassus and Servius. Editor Jaclyn Neel debunks the idea that Romans were unimaginative copyists by spotlighting the vitality and flexibility of Italian myth – particularly those parts that are less closely connected to Greek tales, such as the story of Caeculus of Praeneste. Finally, by calling attention to the Italian rather than Roman nature of the collection, this book suggests that Roman culture was broader than the city itself. This important work offers:

- Up-to-date and accessible translations of Roman and Italic legends from authors throughout antiquity
- Examination of compelling tales that involve the Roman equivalent of Greek heroes
- Unique view of the strength and plasticity of Roman and Italic myth, particularly the parts less closely connected to familiar Greek tales
- Intelligent discussion of relevant cultural and contextual information
- Argument that Roman culture reached far beyond the city of Rome

Fresh and readable, *Early Rome: Myth and Society* offers essential reading for students of ancient Rome as well as those interested in Roman and Greek mythology.

Jaclyn Neel is Assistant Professor of Instruction at Temple University, USA. She is the author of *Legendary Rivals: Collegiality and Ambition in the Tales of Early Rome* (2014) and several articles on Italic myth.

Contents

Preface

Students inspired me to write this book. I was teaching my first class on early Rome when I realized that the only translation of Dionysius was over 100 years old and so antiquated that the majority of the class simply refused to read it. After a few weeks, I couldn't blame them; I'd switched back to the Greek. I found myself skipping material that was interesting, but essentially unteachable: not only Dionysius, but also passages from Servius and other writers who lack any English translation.

This book cannot fill that gap, but I hope that it makes some progress in doing so by providing a selection of material that can be used to teach (or simply read) about early Rome. There is far more material than I've had space to provide, both textual and iconographic. Space restrictions inevitably mean that I've had to limit some authors (notably Dionysius and Plutarch) whose prose is more elaborate.

In selecting texts, I have tried to hew closely to two principles. The first is novelty: if two authors tell essentially the same story, and one of those two authors has a modern translation, I have translated the other. In doing so, I have omitted several of Rome's most famous authors almost entirely; this book contains little Vergil. But the world is so rich in translations of Vergil that I think the fault is forgivable. The other principle is variety: when many variants of a given tale exist, I have translated as many as possible. That has yielded a book whose organization is as imbalanced as surviving Roman narratives: there's far more Romulus than Numa, for example. Astute readers will notice that the variety diminishes in later chapters, again matching the character of the sources.

This book is intended for a rather disparate audience, ranging from advanced undergraduates to graduate students in non-classics fields. The explanatory material will doubtless be too detailed for some and not sufficient for others. I have assumed basic knowledge of Greek myth (e.g., the names of the gods and their major activities) and of Roman history (e.g., the identity of Julius Caesar).

The chapters can be read in any order, although the organization is largely chronological. As a result, there's some repetition in the explanatory material between chapters, which I've tried to limit as much as possible. Within the chapters, the sources are organized chronologically.

The "Further Reading" sections aim to be accessible and cover a range of methods. Because the scholarship on early Rome is international, I've pointed to some important arguments in the "Introductions" – but there is, of course, far more available. Advanced students will benefit from the additional bibliography maintained by Alain Meurant at the excellent Lupa Capitolina Electronica website (http://lupacap.fltr.ucl.ac.be/LCE.ang/default.htm). Instructors will want to supplement to suit their own aims; my plan was undertaken with Cornell's *The Beginnings of Rome* (Routledge, 1995) and Richardson and Santangelo's *The Roman Historical Tradition* (Oxford, 2014) in mind.

All translations are my own. Generally speaking, I have translated the Greek texts from the *TLG;* the Latin texts came from more varied sources (Loeb, OCT, and Teubner). References to Ennius always use Skutsch. For Cicero's *De Republica*, I've used the Teubner. The Propertian text is my own hybrid of Fedeli, Richardson, and Goold. Although I used Lindsay for Festus, I've referred to the lemma rather than the page; anyone with good Latin can find the original in the freely-available Mueller. When necessary, I have indicated textual problems and variants in the notes; although perhaps not strictly necessary in a sourcebook, it may inspire classroom discussion. When significant textual variances exist, I have tried to put the most common reading in the text and the variant(s) in the notes. References to ancient works always cite the original language.

Books rarely succeed without assistance. The entire team at Wiley has been unfailingly helpful; I owe particular thanks to Allison Kostka, Brinda Balasubramanian, and Denisha Sahadevan for fielding inquiries, and immense gratitude to Haze Humbert for bringing the project to publication. Alessia Argento, Stefano Anastasio, Angela Carbonaro, Stefano Casciu, Elisa Dal Canto, Maria De Francesco, Rosanna Di Pinto, Maria Daniela Donninelli, Maria Cristina Guidotti, Laura Minarini, Marco Pierini, Valentina Prestigiovanni, and Manuela Santini helped me secure permissions and photographs. The Textbook and Academic Authors Association generously covered part of the permissions costs, and I am grateful to its Executive Director, Michael Spinella, for his quick communications about the process.

Gabe Moss at the Ancient World Mapping Center was unfazed by a complete map novice, and managed to corral my list of several hundred sites, mythical and real and spanning the entire Mediterranean, into the two lovely maps found here. Rebecca Sears, Amy Russell, and Gwynaeth MacIntyre read almost the entire book in draft form, as did my former student Leah Bernardo-Ciddio; I owe them an enormous debt of gratitude for their comments and suggestions, many of which I hope they will recognize in the finished product. Isabel Köster deserves special mention: she and her students road-tested the Romulus and

Remus, Lucretia, and Horatii and Curiatii narratives, and pointed me to many areas that needed further clarification.

I am also immensely grateful to my team of student researchers, who read a textbook without a class in addition to their normal workload: Berat Barzanjee, Noah Brinder, Christina Cannavicci, Sandy Dief, Daniel Jankulovski, and Kim McCullough. Their diligence and enthusiasm for an independent project was exemplary, and I hope that they, too, will recognize some of their suggestions in the completed work. Their participation was funded by the Social Sciences and Humanities Research Council of Canada; Janet Friskney was a great resource in securing this grant. I'm also grateful to the students of my original Early Rome class at York University in 2012/2013, whose discussions helped me decide what material was most interesting to an undergraduate audience.

Finally, many friends and family outside the discipline provided fresh eyes and enthusiastic encouragement: my parents and sisters, Debbie Pollack, David Neel, Julia Abbott, and Tamar Zeffren. Garnet and Barb Wallace put up with me for an entire summer, during which most of the book was written *in otio*. As always, my most immense debts are to Chris, who knows why.

Abbreviations & Symbols

CAH²   *The Cambridge Ancient History.* 2nd ed.; 14 vols. Cambridge: Cambridge University Press, 1970–2006. Online (with subscription): https://www.cambridge.org/core/series/cambridge-ancient-history/010C506409EE858277F898C129759025

CIL   *Corpus inscriptionum Latinarum.* 17+ vols. Königlich Preussische Akademie der Wissenschaften zu Berlin, Berlin. 1893–.

FRHist   *The Fragments of the Roman Historians* (3 vols.), ed. Timothy Cornell *et al.* Oxford: Oxford University Press, 2014.

FGrHist   *Die Fragmente der griechischen Historiker.* ed. Felix Jacoby. Berlin, Weidmann. 1923–. Online (with subscription): http://referenceworks.brillonline.com/browse/die-fragmente-der-griechischen-historiker-i-iii

ILS   *Inscriptiones Latinae Selectae* (3 vols.), ed. Hermann Dessau. Berlin, Weidmann. 1892. Online: http://archive.org/search.php?query=Inscriptiones%20Latinae%20Selectae%20AND%20mediatype%3Atexts

RRC   *Roman Republican Coinage* (2 vols.), ed. Michael Crawford. Cambridge: Cambridge University Press, 1974. Online (with subscription): http://quod.lib.umich.edu/cgi/t/text/text-idx?c=acls;cc=acls;view=toc;idno=heb01433.0002.001

[...]   indicates an excerpt: material has been omitted for this book only

[lacuna] indicates text that is missing in the original Latin or Greek

[*italics*] indicates a summary of the omitted text; this is not ancient

[word] indicates an explanation that is not in the original text.

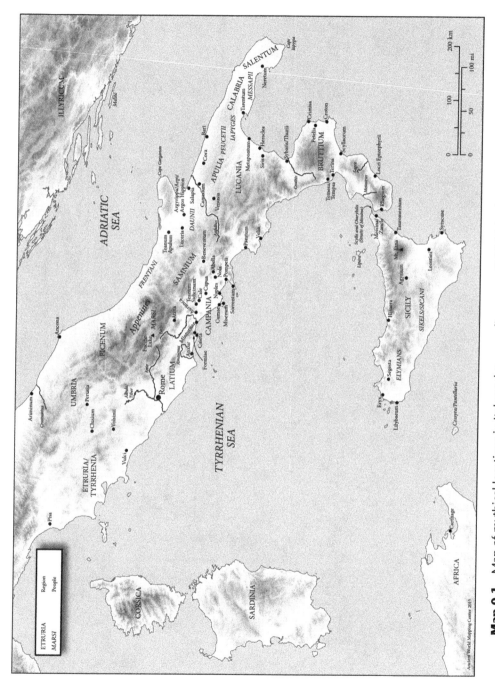

Map 0.1 Map of mythical locations in Italy and surrounding areas. © 2016 Ancient World Mapping Center.

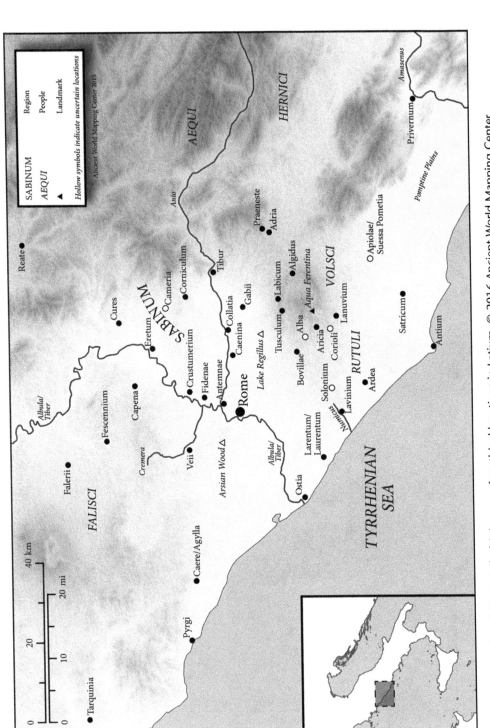

Map 0.2 Detail of 0.1: map of mythical locations in Latium. © 2016 Ancient World Mapping Center.

1

Introducing Early Rome

Introduction

In 44 BCE, graffiti appeared on the statue of Lucius Junius Brutus, the founder of the Roman Republic. It explicitly called on him for help against Julius Caesar, Rome's leader at the time, who had taken to wearing traditional royal symbols. This Brutus had received the nickname "The Liberator" for driving out Rome's kings (**7.6, 8.1**); by requesting his aid, the writer suggested that Caesar was a king too, and had to be eliminated.

> Some men scrawled 'If only you were alive!' on the statue of Lucius Brutus. Similarly, on Caesar's own statue they wrote a ditty: 'Brutus kicked out the kings and became the first consul; Caesar kicked out the consuls and then was made king.' (Suetonius, *Life of Julius Caesar* 80)

Caesar's biographer Suetonius linked the graffiti to Caesar's assassination. If you know the quote *et tu, Brute*, you might too: Brutus' descendant Marcus Brutus, a friend of Caesar's, was one of the leaders of the conspiracy. By reminding fellow citizens of a past heroic act, the anonymous writer made a statement that was politically, socially, and culturally relevant to his own day. Nor was such historical modeling limited to periods of political strife.

Myths and legends held long-term significance in many aspects of Roman society. In fact, stories about the city's past formed a backbone of *shared cultural knowledge*. These tales taught men and women, natives and foreigners how to behave, what qualities were valuable, and how to make sense of the world and their community. In addition to teaching Romans about their past, these

Early Rome: Myth and Society, A Sourcebook, First Edition. Jaclyn Neel.

stories also gave advice about the future and helped create meaning for the entire Roman community. Modern scholars study Roman myth to learn about the city's culture, customs, history, and literature.

1.1 What Is a "Myth"?

You're probably familiar with the terms "myth" and "legend" from books, movies, or previous courses. Sometimes these words are used interchangeably, but often they refer to different types of traditional stories. These differences are sometimes defined by a spectrum of truth value (Calame 2003, 9–11). For example, a "myth" can be defined as a tale that explains the origin of natural features, such the formation of mountains or cities; it does not need to have a basis in scientific fact, but is rather a divine explanation for a visible phenomenon. In contrast, a "legend" is usually based on a factual event and has been exaggerated. The elaboration of these tales may include fantastic elements such as the use of magic or the possession of special powers by the hero or his companions – but the legend still must have a "kernel of truth." A "folktale," in contrast, may or may not have a basis in fact; it more often has a basis in social standing. Myth and legends tend to retell stories of extraordinary people, often of high status; folktales focus on the lives and deeds of ordinary people.

In studying the classical world, "myth" is usually applied to traditional Greek stories about gods and heroes. Similar stories from other parts of the ancient world are called "legends." This distinction and definition are increasingly seen as problematic for a number of reasons. For one thing, we know about many Greek myths thanks to the works of Roman authors like Ovid. So "Greek" is not an exclusive category; in many ways, "Greco-Roman myth" is a better term.

But this term leads to a second problem: how do you pinpoint what is "Greek" or "Roman" about a given narrative? We do not have much information about Roman society before it had contact with Greece. Yet there are clearly traditional tales from Rome that do not appear in any surviving classical Greek evidence. Is this the best way to define "Roman" myth?

Another problem is that many Roman traditional tales do not involve gods or semi-divine humans, but rather ordinary people who do extraordinary things. This led early researchers to conclude that Romans did not have myths of their own. Instead of the anthropomorphic gods associated with Greek myth, these researchers found that early Romans believed in *numina* (divine powers). Because these powers did not necessarily have faces and names, like "Athena" or "Ares" in Greece, there was no need to develop stories about them. Later, Romans learned about Greek myths; they were captivated by the Greeks' creativity and adopted their gods and traditional tales as their own. As a result, Roman myths are simply copies of Greek mythology. This theory of Rome's "mythless society" was popular for many decades, and is now thought to be wrong.

Instead, scholars now realize that Roman traditional tales are quite different from Greek traditional tales. As Mary Beard (1993, 48) has written, "the observation (or complaint) that Rome has no myth is probably no more than an observation that it does not have *Greek* myth." In other words, "myth" has been defined in such a way that only a limited number of story patterns will match it. Greece offers the gold standard for such tales; other societies, including Rome, inevitably fall short. In order to study Roman myths, we must first understand that not all myths match the Greek model of gods with human qualities who fall in love, misbehave, cause trouble, rescue men, or otherwise interfere in human affairs.

Together with this redefinition of Roman myth, classicists are coming to realize that even Greek myth is not unitary. Not only did Greeks recognize many variations of their "standard" tales, but they also retold narratives that we do not recognize as mythic in structure. As Claude Calame (2003) has argued, the Greeks did not recognize "myth" as a category distinct from "legend," "folktale," or "fiction." These modern distinctions have been wrongly applied to the ancient material, confusing our understanding of how ancient narratives worked in context.

Some scholars have argued that Rome has a special type of mythology, which can be called "historical myth" (e.g., Fox 1996). They prefer this term to "legend," which (as we saw above) implies that the tale contains a certain amount of truth. "Historical myth," in contrast, shares the dubious reality of myth; it is true *to the culture*, but need not be true outside of that culture. Unlike the traditional category of "myth," which tells stories from a timeless past, the tales of "historical myth" take place in a concrete and historically defined period. For those studying ancient Rome, that period is called "early Rome" (see **1.5**). Roman myths take place in specific locations (in and around the city) and in specific eras. Although the dividing line between "myth" and "history" is intensely debated by modern scholars, many would agree that stories about the gods or their children are mythical, while stories that had contemporary documentary support are historical.

But there is substantial disagreement about what records were available to ancient authors. We aren't sure what records were kept before approximately 300 BCE; we also don't know how much Romans cared about preserving strict historical accuracy versus imagining the past. The debate about how to deal with the "memory" of the past through oral and visual means is ongoing in ancient history, as well as other fields. This book takes a broad view of "myth." It includes stories about larger-than-life heroes, some of whom may have existed historically. They are "mythical" because their actions are unrealistically exaggerated. By including characters who would typically be considered "legendary," this book suggests that the exact distinction between "myth" and "legend" may not be helpful for understanding Roman society. Rather, the myths that were told about early Rome can help us understand how

Romans thought about their history. Myths tell us which stories were worth retelling; what degree of variance between different versions was acceptable; how authors decided that an event was believable (or not); and how authors expected or wanted their audiences to interpret the story's outcome.

An example of how one well-educated Roman understood the city's traditional tales can be found in Cicero, *On the Laws* 1.5. Discussing the material that's appropriate for history and poetry, Cicero distinguishes two types of tale: the *fabula* (more fictional) and the *historia* (more truthful). The criteria for determining what makes a *fabula* fictional are vague, suggesting that questions of veracity were left to individual discretion, at least to a certain degree. In reading narratives in this book, you'll come across the judgments of authors themselves. Livy, Dionysius of Halicarnassus, and Plutarch are particularly prone to reflect on the likelihood of various alternative narratives, and their judgments offer modern historians the best evidence for what was credible (or not) in antiquity. But be careful: these authors often disagree, leaving modern historians unsure about how their readers would have interpreted the story. Ancient authors also include stories that they claim are false or suspicious. The inclusion of such tales in historical writing has long puzzled scholars, and there is no currently accepted boundary between "true history" and "myth." This boundary is something you should consider as you read, but don't worry if you can't find a single answer!

It is important to recognize that these terms – myths, legends, "historical myths" – are not universally recognized or mutually exclusive. Modern historians disagree on the appropriate vocabulary to use when discussing Rome's traditional tales. Some scholars will use the terms myth, legend, and folklore interchangeably; others use them to indicate different themes or truth values. It is in your best interest to read this scholarship carefully, paying particular attention to definitions. Be careful: these are sometimes found in footnotes (or endnotes).

From this point forward, this book will refer to all traditional tales about the regal period and early Republic as "myths," regardless of likely historicity. This choice underlines an important aspect of Roman traditional stories: that regardless of whether modern scholars view them as true or false, they had continuing value *to the elite Romans* who read and wrote the works we examine. In that sense, they all try to communicate some "truth" to their audience. Stories that had no value to society were not retold.

1.2 Types of Stories You Will Read in this Book

As you probably realize by now, "Roman myth" includes a variety of different stories. These can be categorized into a number of different subtypes, which are not unique to Rome (although the stories themselves may be). These labels are not mutually exclusive – a story can easily fit into two or more categories.

The point of such categorizations is not to fence in similar stories and protect them from alternative classification; rather, by identifying themes of various stories, we can better understand what interested Romans about their past and the type of question they asked (and didn't ask) about their contemporary society. You'll notice that Romans often asked different questions than we do! In understanding their questions, we can better understand how these authors understood their world, both in the past and in their own day.

Some of the uses of myth can be striking to those not used to ancient patterns of thought. Romans sometimes used tales of the city's early past as we do, to try to learn about the historical life of their ancestors. But the study of the past for its own sake (called "antiquarianism") was different from the study of the past directed towards contemporary goals. Rome's early history could be manipulated to make a new custom seem old (or older); help Romans feel proud of their city and teach them how to behave in similar situations; advertise the crucial importance of an elite family to the city; inform foreigners of basic virtues; and reinforce the importance of traditions. Other uses of historical myths were also possible – for example, orators may cite myths in legal cases – but connecting the past to the present in some way is the most common reason to (re)tell a narrative above the past.

Foundation narratives relate the establishment of cities and peoples (a term that is broadly similar to an "ethnic group" in modern usage). They require at least one founder, and it is rare to have a large group; in Italy, however, the presence of two founders seems relatively common. A single place might have multiple foundation narratives, and these narratives can be complementary (for example, Rome's foundation tales of the Lupercalia and the walls: **3.2, 3.3**) or contradictory (for example, the different accounts of Remus' death: **3.4**). We should not think that there was only one "correct" narrative. Rather, one narrative might be more or less correct for a given genre or context.

Aetiological tales are similar to foundation narratives: they relate the creation of cults, customs, and other rituals. *Aetiology* comes from the Greek word *aetia* (meaning "cause"), and answers the question "why do we do this?" A single event frequently has multiple aetiologies. As with foundation narratives, these different explanations aren't necessarily mutually exclusive. It's quite common in Rome for at least one aetiology to be traced back to the foundation. Roman society, like many traditional societies, prized ancestral custom and was suspicious of novelty. Anything associated with the city's founder, Romulus, was immediately old and therefore respectable. As a result, many customs were associated with Romulus, even if they were already attributed to another figure in Rome's history. Jacques Poucet (1985) has called this process "**Romulization**."

In this book, only aetiologies that take place in early Rome will be covered. But aetiologies could relate to any period in the city's history, including the quite recent past. A similar type of tale is the *exemplum* (plural: **exempla**). An *exemplum* can be either a person or deed, and serves as a shorthand for a particular virtue. We might say that an *exemplum* embodies that virtue. *Exempla* provided a useful way to communicate a complex cultural concept. This book opened with an *exemplum* in action: the *exemplum* of Brutus the Liberator encouraged Romans to free themselves from the "king" Julius Caesar. *Exempla* are more complex than they seem, and will be discussed further in **chapter 8**. For now, you can think of them as similar to invoking Hitler to indicate that someone is evil, with a range of associations.

Another concept that's similar to aetiologies is the **eponym**. Roman authors were interested in the names of locations, gods, and rites. They often tell stories that relate these names to a single individual. That person is the eponym of that place or ritual. You can probably find an eponym where you live: some examples named after European monarchs include Adelaide in Australia; Victoria in British Columbia, Canada; and the U.S. states of Georgia and Virginia.

Although Rome had fewer **tales of gods and heroes** than Greece, it did have some. We easily recognize heroic tales that set Greek heroes into a new location. Many Italian cities, Rome included, retold legends about the visit of Hercules on his way home from Spain. Similarly, many Italian cities claimed that they were founded or visited by heroes of the Trojan War whose ships got lost or diverted on the route between Anatolia and the Greek mainland. Early Greek colonies in central and southern Italy may have contributed to the proliferation of these tales.

Not all heroic tales go back to Greece. The hero Caeculus of Praeneste (**6.6**)) is an Italian original. Similarly, many of the stories told about the Roman kings lack convincing Greek parallels. The same can be said about the majority of Rome's tales about gods. These are relatively few in number, if you don't count the stories that take place in Greece. But when Roman gods do act in Italy, they often act in characteristically Roman ways, such as the hair-splitting dialogue between king Numa and Jupiter over human sacrifice (**5.2.3**).

Much as we all know stories about our own families that have become quasi-legendary, Roman aristocratic clans also had **family legends**. These narratives are almost never explicitly called family legends by Roman authors. Instead, modern scholars have guessed that such legends "belonged" to a group of family legends based on the prominence of a particular family in the story. A good example of such a family legend is the tale of the 306 Fabii (**8.7**), where even the name announces that it is about the Fabian *gens*. Similar tales may have explained the reason behind an individual family *cognomen* (such as Scaevola (**8.3.2, 8.3.4**) or Brutus (**5.6.5, 8.1**)) or glorified individual Roman ancestors (such as Cloelia (**7.7**) or Horatius (**5.3.2**)).

Although it is not certain, many scholars believe that such familial legends were retold at aristocratic funerals (see Polybius 6.53–54). Because some families were associated with particular cults and rites, it's also possible that these legends were publicly recounted at festivals and rituals. The average Roman may also have seen images of these tales on public buildings, monuments, or statues. Unlike the written texts that make up the majority of this book, public images were viewed by non-elite Romans. Private imagery also supplies a potential source of iconography that would be recognizable to a broader audience. Pictorial representations offer us valuable insight into the ways that Romans may have learned about their past.

Not all stories will match one of the above categories, and others will fit in to more than one. Perfect categorization of a diverse set of myths is unlikely. Instead, these categories should help you begin to conceptualize the topics Roman authors found *worthy of myth*. In other words, these tales give us answers to the questions Romans asked about their past. We can use these answers to help us reconstruct not only the questions, but also the potential reasons why such questions were important.

1.3 Literary Genres in this Book

We tend to think that history is transmitted in a limited number of ways: textbooks, primary source compilations (such as the one you're reading now), and documentary films are a few examples. In the ancient world, almost any type of material could contain information about the legendary past. Romans seemed to have used this period as a way to conceptualize their contemporary customs, struggles, and decisions in a way that is quite different from how modern historical thinking works. On the one hand, this openness means that students of Rome's mythic history have almost limitless options for understanding a particular story or theme. But we also must be careful to avoid falling into traps of genre.

Every style of writing has its own conventions. Academic books are annotated; depending on the discipline, they may use parenthetical references, footnotes, or endnotes. Memoirs are lightly fictionalized; autobiographies, ideally, are not. An understanding of the conventions of the different genres of ancient writing, both Greek and Roman, will help you determine the best way to evaluate your sources.

Narrative history is probably the most familiar genre. Writers in this category are primarily concerned with producing chronological accounts of Roman history that are more or less "accurate" in their own terms. A standard way for an ancient historian to differentiate himself from his predecessors was to accuse those predecessors of carelessness or even lies; you should be wary of such accusations. Many, but not all, narrative historians provided the reader with several potential historical scenarios. These options allow us to identify variants of a given narrative, and they should not be seen as mutually exclusive. As many modern scholars have pointed out, the beliefs of ancient historians are not the same as ours; therefore, what seems fantastic to us was not necessarily outside the realm of possibility in their view.

But historians also transmitted some stories that they didn't believe were true. Often the importance of these stories is attributed to "tradition": this tale has been part of Roman culture for so long that it *must* be retold in its chronological place. An example of such a tale is the divine birth of Romulus (**3.1**). This habit has led many modern scholars to speculate about how Romans understood their past. While this book does not attempt to provide answers, the **Further Reading** options often do.

Before their histories were written down, Romans had other ways of transmitting details about their past. These **oral** and **visual sources** continued to be consulted after written histories came into use. In addition to the funeral orations mentioned in **1.2**, we have evidence for historical painting (for example, the Esquiline Fresco of Fabius and Fannius[1]), probably similar to the plaques that were displayed in the Roman triumph (Holliday 2002). Other images were found on public statues, monuments, and reliefs. Peter Wiseman (1998) has also suggested that dramatic performance was a means of transmitting historical information, as were various forms of poetry (Cato, *FRHist* 5 F113[2]). Modern scholarship on oral traditions suggests that they're less fixed than written narratives, which may help explain why Roman myths, which were written down relatively late in Rome's history, vary so greatly in specific details.

Rome's earliest narrative histories were written in Greek, either by Greeks (such as the historian Timaeus of Tauromenium, in Sicily) or by Romans perhaps eager to communicate with a Greek audience (such as Quintus Fabius Pictor, a Roman patrician). These Roman authors are sometimes called "annalists," because their works took a year-by-year structure (see Wiseman (2007)). The group of "annalists" includes authors such as Livy, whose *From the Foundation* may be familiar to you. You'll find more information on these authors in **Appendix 1**.

Another genre that frequently draws on the legendary past is **epic poetry**. Epic poetry refers to the large-scale poems written by authors such as Vergil. Many, but not all, of these poems take place in the legendary past. Be careful not to confuse the modern word "epic" (large-scale, impressive) with the ancient genre of epic, which is based on poetic meter. All epics, regardless of their subject matter, were written in a meter called dactylic hexameter. Many epics told the stories of past heroes who were capable of deeds that could no longer be accomplished in the writer's own day. Common features of such narratives include the personal involvement of the gods in the hero's life (in the *Aeneid*, for example, the hero is the son of Venus); at least one meeting of the gods ("divine council") to determine the fate of the hero and/or his companions; a journey to the underworld (see *Aeneid* book 6); battles; and arming scenes (in which armor is described at length). Because these scenes are standard for the *genre*, they may represent authorial additions to the myth. Nevertheless, these new additions might be included in subsequent retellings.

Elegiac poetry differs from epic in both meter and typical subject matter. Just as epic poetry was defined by dactylic hexameter, elegiac poetry had to be written in a specific verse pattern called the "elegiac couplet." Although this genre started out as a funeral lament, by the Roman period elegiac poetry was typically (but not always) about the romantic failure of a high-status male. Themes of such **love elegy** include the lover's lament, often outside the locked door of his girlfriend; the motifs of love as a battlefield and the lover as soldier; the lover's inability to retain the interest of his girlfriend, despite his higher status; and gender inversion, in which the high-status male becomes subservient or enslaved to his low-status female love interest. Elegiac poets such as Propertius and Ovid used these themes to redefine the past in their own terms.

You may have had experience with the first three genres in other classes dealing with antiquity. The next three genres are often less common in undergraduate courses. Although **philosophy** is often more closely associated with the Greeks, Romans also wrote philosophical works. The most important for this book is Cicero, who often used Rome to explore political philosophy. Cicero wrote about history of the city in various works and occasionally contradicts himself, which suggests that an individual's understanding of the past was flexible and could change over time.

Didactic treatises fall into several different categories. For us, the most important are **antiquarian** literature and **commentaries** on poetic works. Antiquarian literature may at first seem hard to differentiate from historical works. One of the major differences is how the material is arranged: antiquarian works are frequently arranged by topic, whereas histories tend to be written chronologically. There may also be a difference in methodology: antiquarians may accept traditions that do not seem true enough to be historical, but are nonetheless important to Roman self-definition, tradition, or culture. Some of these distinctions are fuzzy: Dionysius of Halicarnassus, for example, writes a history that we call the *Roman Antiquities*. Both genres are valuable: Cicero (*Academica* 1.3.9) claimed that Varro's great antiquarian works (now lost) "let us recognize where and who we are."

Closely related to the antiquarian works are the commentaries on canonical literature, such as Vergil. These books are organized line by line (or sentence by sentence) and provide valuable contextual information on many topics. These commentaries were written several centuries after the works in question, and don't speak for the author. Instead, they show us how the work was understood in antiquity. Such commentaries often offer **fragments**, which are references to or quotations of earlier writers whose complete works are lost. Although any incomplete work can be considered "fragmentary," the term is usually reserved for works that can't be understood in their existing state.

Finally, **Christian apologetics** offer a variety of material relating to Roman myth. In order to defend their own religion, apologists retold Roman mythic material in order to ridicule or argue with it. Sometimes they cite an author directly, providing a fragment (for example, most of our knowledge of Varro's work comes from Augustine's *City of God*). In other instances, they cite too vaguely to identify an author or not at all. Because these works are frequently aimed at discrediting the Roman myth in question, their information must be carefully assessed. It's rarely sufficient to reject the myth because it is found in a Christian source, or to accept it simply because it is ancient.

1.4 Theoretical Approaches to Roman Myth

For a long time, Roman myth was considered derivative of Greek myth. As a result, many of the theories used to analyze Greek myth were used to analyze Roman myth. Although most modern scholars now appreciate the creativity behind Roman myth, they continue to use many of the same theoretical tools.

A very popular way to analyze Roman myth is the **historical approach**. This type of analysis sees Roman myth as a type of oral history. The more improbable aspects of the stories (such as Aeneas' and Romulus' divine parents) can be explained through narrative elaboration: generations looking back to their past inflate their legendary heroes into larger-than-life figures. Although this may seem unlikely to us because we live in a heavily documented society, scholarship on modern oral traditions has shown that it takes only a few generations for traditions to become mythicized. The historical approach is a common perspective for stories that occur from the Tarquins on (see **1.5**). A subtype of this model is **exemplary history**, which is discussed further in **chapter 8**; in brief, Romans used idealized stories about their past as models to guide present behavior.

Another common model is **structuralism**. Although the term "structuralism" derives from the theories of the French anthropologist Claude Lévi-Strauss, scholarship before Lévi-Strauss had already advocated for similar ideas in the myths of Rome. The basic model is that these myths symbolize a binary opposition in society. For Rome, the most common oppositions are primitive/civilized (also called savage/civilized), plebeian/patrician, modest/luxurious (sometimes nationalized as Latin/Sabine or Latin/Etruscan), and male/female. Because these oppositions are mutually exclusive, the myths offer contemporary audiences a way to negotiate their values in a safe space. Lévi-Strauss argued that oppositions allowed a population to negotiate the differences between ideas to produce new relationships.

Similar to structuralism in concept, but quite different in execution, is Georges Dumézil's **trifunctional** model. These three functions are, according to Dumézil, broadly applicable to all Indo-European cultures (including Roman, Greek, Vedic, and Norse myth) provided that they all appear in the same tale. Therefore trifunctionality is a form of **comparative mythology** (in which similarities between the myths of different cultures can be used to better understand the myths of a single culture or the process of cultural exchange). The three "functions" are the three areas that early societies seemed to value most: the priest, the farmer, and the warrior. Both myth and society were organized along the same lines, so myth serves to illuminate society. As Dumézil admitted, his approach did not work for *every* myth, but only those myths that featured a struggle for power between the three functions.

Romans themselves often suggest that their society is worse than the society of previous generations. This **model of decline** is also common in Greek thought, and should not be taken literally. It is a conservative way of viewing the past that seeks to preserve the *status quo* and promote traditional values. In some cases, these values had long been lost or disappearing (see especially the stories of women in **chapter 7**).

We have already seen that myths can act as **aetiologies** for customs and rituals. These explanations reinforce the local importance of particular tales. For example, in tales involving a Greek hero like Hercules, the aetiological model would emphasize connections to Roman religious rites, public traditions, or particular locations in the city. Tales that aim to record the reasons for religious rites may also have been retold at the rites, gaining a wider audience than the text. Studying this wider audience is part of the approach called **cultural memory**, which attempts to discover what Romans in general "knew" about their past and their society. You'll notice as you read that Roman authors, especially Ovid and Livy, are eager to make these connections, and that this model therefore has roots in antiquity.

It's important to recognize that although these theories are distinct, they do not need to be mutually exclusive. Current work on Roman myth often features a combination of theoretical approaches. The models outlined above are also only a selection of the most common approaches to Roman myth, and shouldn't be considered comprehensive.

1.5 Chronology of Early Rome

"Early Rome" is a loosely defined period in classical scholarship. In this book, "early Rome" refers to the years between **c. 1200–c. 390 BCE** (the abbreviation "c." means "approximately"). These boundaries cover, in terms of narrative, the years from the arrival of Aeneas in Italy to the Gallic sack of Rome. It is important to realize that these dates are our society's translation of ancient dates into our own terms. The Romans did not use the dating system BC/AD or BCE/CE; these are modern, Christian dates that use year "0" as the moment of Jesus' birth. Roman authors used a variety of dating systems which had to be synchronized in complex ways. This different system of keeping records helps explain why we are often unsure of the exact year, much less month or day, in which events in ancient history occurred.

Most authors who wrote in Latin calculated the date based on how many years had passed since the foundation of the city. But this process was complicated by the fact that there was no agreement about when the city had been founded until the first century CE. Modern scholars use the "Varronian" date (see **Varro** in **Appendix 1**) of 753 BCE for the foundation of Rome; in antiquity, however, dates ranged from 815 (Timaeus (Dionysius of Halicarnassus 1.74.1)) to 750 (Eratosthenes (Solinus 1.27); see Dionysius of Halicarnassus 1.74.2). There was slightly more agreement on the era of the Trojan War: the Hellenistic chronographer Eratosthenes (third century BCE) determined that Troy fell in (our) 1184 BCE.

After the foundation of the Roman Republic in 509, dates of events in the city could be determined by the names of the yearly consuls ("eponymous" or "consular" dating). Because these two men changed every year, the combination of the consuls' names plus the number of years that had occurred since the foundation when these two men had jointly held the consulship offered a date. As you can imagine, this system was somewhat unwieldy and required much memorization! Lists were probably maintained from an early period, but our earliest lists have been lost. There's therefore a great deal of debate, both ancient and modern, about the reliability of early Republican history. Sometimes our authors express confusion about the consular dates: either they are not sure in whose consulship an event occurred, or they are not sure about the order in which the consuls held office (see Livy 2.8 for a famous example).

Greek-speaking authors of the Hellenistic period (c. 323–31 BCE) more frequently used the Olympiad dating system, which calculated one Olympiad every four years beginning in 776/5 BCE. These dates were sometimes equated ("synchronized") with other local dating systems, such as Roman consular dates or Athenian archon dates. After the establishment of the Roman Principate, contemporary events could be dated by regnal years of the emperor; for early Rome, there were few alternatives to the consular dating system established by the very first Roman historians (for further details, see Feeney 2009 and Frier 1979).

With these cautions, we can establish a periodization for early Rome that is based on dates that are *relatively* canonical. That means that these dates would not have been considered firmly set by many people in antiquity, who were less concerned about "the actual date" than we are. With this in mind, "Early Rome" falls into three broad eras:

(1) Aeneas and Alba Longa (c. 1184–c. 753 BCE): This period covers the events of Aeneas' departure from Troy to the end of his dynasty. Although many Roman noble families claimed to be descended from Aeneas or his followers (**1.2, 3.5.7**), Aeneas' line came to an end after the death of Romulus (**3.7**). This contradiction was unproblematic for many, although Cicero mocked the pretensions of contemporary Roman aristocrats who invented or "rediscovered" important family heritage (*Brutus* 62).

After Aeneas died, his kingdom was ruled by a series of kings now known as the Alban Kings, after their capital city of Alba Longa. Little is known about Alba Longa today, and the number of kings varies; some early Roman authors omitted the dynasty altogether. It seems that all sources include the first and last kings, Ascanius/Iulus (Aeneas' son(s)) and Amulius and Numitor (the grandfather and great-uncle of the city's founder Romulus); however, even these rulers are the subjects of dispute. Because of the many discrepancies in our sources, most modern scholars now believe that this dynasty was invented (different views in Grandazzi 2008 v.2; Cornell 1995, 45–57).

Key events of this period include the arrival of Aeneas in Italy, the foundation of Alba Longa, and the Alban Kings.

(2) The Regal Period (c. 753–c. 509 BCE): This period covers the foundation of Rome itself and the seven original kings of the city. The kings may be divided in various ways; the most common methods are the division into "good" (all but the Tarquins) and "bad" (Tarquins) rulers, and the division into "Latin" (Romulus through Ancus) and "Etruscan" (Tarquin I through Tarquin II) rulers. Neither division is fully sanctioned by ancient texts or archaeological findings.

By the period of our earliest writers, these seven kings were canonical: that is, all seven consistently appear in our sources in the same order. Even in antiquity there was some dispute about which king was responsible for what; this will be discussed in more detail in **chapter 5**, where there is a detailed chronological breakdown of the different reigns. Key events of this period include the foundation of the city and many important monuments in it; the establishment of priesthoods and civic structures, such as voting divisions; and Rome's conquest of nearby cities, including Alba.

The Regal Period came to an end with the expulsion of the Tarquins and the foundation of the Republic. Ancient writers consistently associate this event with the rape of Lucretia (**7.6**) in the year 509.

(3) The Early Republic (c. 509–c. 390 BCE): This period is an invention of modern scholarship, with only limited authority in ancient writings. Roman authors conceived of "the Republic" as a single period running from the fixed date of its foundation in 509 to a variety of termination points in the late first century BCE (for detailed discussion, see Flower 2010). In contrast, modern historians have divided the Republic into three periods: early (c. 509–c. 390), middle (c. 390–c. 133), and late (c. 133–c. 27).

The rationale behind the choice of 390, the Gallic sack of Rome, can be justified by the Roman historian Livy (6.1.2): "written records, the one faithful guardian of events, in those days were short and rarely kept. And most of whatever there was, in pontifical commentaries and public or private monuments, was lost when the city burned" in the sack. Where ancient authors perceived a break in history, modern historians have been eager to follow.

Literary evidence indicates that the city was razed. The archaeological evidence for the destruction of the city in this era is less clear (Cornell 1995, 313–322). Few would deny that Italy was invaded by Gauls, perhaps numerous times, in the fourth century (contemporary evidence cited in Plutarch, *Camillus* 22: see **8.10.2c**), but invasion should not be equated with destruction. It may be the case that written records were not kept, or not well–maintained, in the city prior to the fourth century BCE. Later Romans, who found the notion of not keeping records incredible, developed the idea that all of the records had been destroyed together with the city. The relationship of archaeological remains, textual traditions, and history "as it really was" remains contentious in modern scholarship.

Conclusion

Much of the information you've read may seem confusing, contradictory, or overwhelming. Don't worry! Early Rome is a complex and exciting topic, with many opportunities for original research and ideas. No one masters this material after only a few days.

To effectively use this book, you may find it helpful to refer to the author biographies in **Appendix 1** before or after reading each selection. Particularly in cases where there are many different versions of the same tale, why might an author choose to relate only one? (Or, alternatively, why tell multiple versions?) Can you find similar themes in the stories an author chooses to tell, or which he chooses to believe? Can you make a connection with the genre of the work and variant of the story? If so, congratulations: you're well on your way to understanding early Roman myth.

Notes

1. http://en.centralemontemartini.org/var/museicivici/storage/images/musei/centrale
   _montemartini/percorsi/galleria_fotografica/affresco_con_scene_militari_da_una_
   tomba_a_camera_della_necropoli_esquilina/64857-8-eng-US/fresco_with_military_
   scenes_from_a_chamber_tomb_of_the_esquiline_necropolis_gallery.jpg
2. This standard way to cite fragmentary historians is a little complicated: the format is the author's name, identifying number in a standard work (see **Abbreviations**), and the fragment number (indicated by F).

References

Beard, Mary. 1993. "Looking (harder) for Roman Myth: Dumézil, Declamation, and the problems of definition." In *Mythos in mythloser Gesellschaft: Das Paradigma Roms*, edited by Fritz Graf, 44–64. Stuttgart and Leipzig: Teubner.

Calame, Claude. 2003. *Myth and History in Ancient Greece: The Symbolic Creation of a Colony*. tr. Daniel W. Berman. Princeton, NJ: Princeton University Press.

Cornell, Timothy J. 1995. *The Beginnings of Rome: Italy and Rome from the Bronze Age to the Punic Wars (c. 1000–264 B.C.)*. London: Routledge.

Feeney, Denis. 2009. "Time." In *The Cambridge Companion to the Roman Historians*, edited by Andrew Feldherr, 139–151. Cambridge: Cambridge University Press.

Flower, Harriet. 2010. *Roman Republics*. Princeton, NJ: Princeton University Press.

Fox, Matthew. 1996. *Roman Historical Myths: The Regal Period in Augustan Literature*. Oxford: Oxford University Press.

Frier, Bruce W. 1979. Libri Annales Pontificum Maximorum: *The Origins of the Annalistic Tradition*. Ann Arbor, MI: University of Michigan Press.

Grandazzi, Alexandre. 2008. *Alba Longa: Histoire d'un legende*, 2 vols. Rome: École française de Rome.

Holliday, Peter. 2002. *The Origins of Roman Historical Commemoration in the Visual Arts*. Cambridge: Cambridge University Press.

Poucet, Jacques. 1985. *Les origines de Rome. Tradition et histoire*. Brussels: Facultés universitaires Saint-Louis.

Wiseman, Timothy Peter. 2007. "The Prehistory of Roman Historiography." In *The Blackwell Companion to Greek and Roman Historiography* (2 vols.), edited by John Marincola, 67–75. Malden, MA: Blackwell.

Wiseman, Timothy Peter. 1998. *Roman Drama and Roman History*. Exeter: University of Exeter Press.

Further Reading

Bremmer, Jan, and Nicholas Horsfall. 1987. *Roman Myth and Mythography*. London: Institute of Classical Studies. One of the earliest works to take Roman myth seriously in its own right, this book delves into the city's major myths. The authors present a series of case studies, rather than an introduction. The scholarship is dense, but both readable and fascinating. The book is available online (with subscription): http://onlinelibrary.wiley.com/doi/10.1111/bics.1987.34.issue-S52/issuetoc (last accessed November 21, 2016).

Csapo, Eric. 2005. *Theories of Mythology*. Malden, MA: Blackwell. Introduces the different ways of interpreting myth in their historical context. Although no background in ancient myth is required, this book isn't aimed at beginners. Students who are interested in the various approaches that scholars have taken to "myth" more generally are encouraged to read it carefully; it's an excellent introduction to the academic study of mythology.

Miles, Gary B. 1995. *Livy: Reconstructing Early Rome*. Ithaca, NY: Cornell University Press. A difficult but worthwhile read. Miles analyzes how Livy's history uses memory, monuments, and myth to re-imagine lost history. He is particularly interested in the repetition of motifs through different narratives.

Rea, Jennifer. 2007. *Legendary Rome: Myths, Monuments, and Memories on the Palatine and Capitoline*. London: Duckworth. Mainly interested in the Augustan-era poets' rendition of Rome's past. Rea argues that the need to recreate Rome for the new, post-war age drove many of the legendary recreations that we now have.

Wiseman, Timothy Peter. 2008. *Unwritten Rome*. Exeter: University of Exeter Press. Focuses on what we can learn about early Rome from three sources: religious ritual (represented in texts and/or images); dramatic performances; and poetry. Wiseman is an accessible writer; this is a series of case studies, some previously published and some new, about many aspects of early Rome.

In addition to the above works, there are now "Companions" to almost every major topic in this chapter and author in this book; these offer a good starting point for further research.

2

Rome Before the City

Introduction

The Trojan War was a cultural touchstone for many societies. Some of you may already be familiar with the basic events from Homer's poem *The Iliad* or from Greek plays such as Aeschylus' *Agamemnon*, Sophocles' *Ajax*, or Euripides' *The Trojan Women*. But the significance of Troy was felt across the Mediterranean. Odysseus, in his travels home, passed by areas recognized as Sicily and the Straits of Gibraltar; other Greek warriors, such as Diomedes, were accepted as founders by Italian communities. Trojan heroes also became founders of cities in Italy and elsewhere (**6.1, 6.3**). The most famous of these heroes today is Aeneas, whose adventures are retold in Vergil's epic *The Aeneid*. Although Vergil's account is the longest, it is not the only one; many Roman writers referred back to Aeneas as the founder of the Roman people. These stories show many differences from Vergil.

According to ancient authors, Aeneas was one of several Trojans who were allowed to leave Troy after the city was sacked. The reasons for this vary: some authors say that he betrayed the city, while others note that even the Greeks recognized Aeneas' virtue (*pietas*). Aeneas departs with his father Anchises and his son, whose name varies; the most common options are Ascanius and Iulus. Sailing across the Mediterranean, Aeneas reaches Sicily and then central Italy (in Vergil and his followers, he also visits Carthage). In his travels, Aeneas encounters new and old friends, and founds several cities. However, these cities are unsatisfactory for various reasons. The journey is long enough that the aged Anchises dies en route.

The Italian mainland is Aeneas' ultimate destination. Once there, he fights against some of the natives (including Turnus, the leader of the Rutuli, and

Early Rome: Myth and Society, A Sourcebook, First Edition. Jaclyn Neel.
© 2017 John Wiley & Sons, Inc. Published 2017 by John Wiley & Sons, Inc.

Mezentius, king of Etruria) and allies with others (including Evander, a Greek exile living on the future site of Rome, and Latinus, king of the Latins). Eventually Aeneas marries Latinus' daughter and founds a city, but in many versions this marriage does not end the strife between Trojans and Italians. In these versions, Aeneas dies in battle and is worshipped as the god Indiges, while his son Ascanius concludes the war. Early authors disagreed about even this narrative because of Aeneas' long voyage. Some of them promote the adventures of Ascanius by saying that Aeneas actually died near Troy. In these versions, Ascanius and his followers undertake the journey to Italy and found a city there. The initial city founded by Aeneas and/or Ascanius is usually called Lavinium; later, a second city called Alba was added.

For the most part, ancient sources agree that Aeneas had some relationship with the city of Rome. But what exactly *was* that relationship? The answers to that question are varied, especially in the earliest Greek sources. When Greek cities sent out colonists through the Mediterranean (starting c. 800 BCE), they encountered new peoples and places. Although these peoples may have had myths of their own, the colonists tried to explain their adventures in terms that could be understood by fellow Greeks. Thus Greek authors tried to work other cultures into their own mythic universe (Bickerman 1952). Over time, these Greek myths became integrated with local tales. In Italy, many cities traced their foundation to the *nostoi* (return of Homeric heroes from Troy). In Italy, Odysseus and Diomedes were among the most common Greek founders of cities. Other cities claimed to have been founded by Hercules driving Geryon's cattle back from Spain.

Narrative accounts of Italian origin stories are considerably later than the foundation of the cities themselves. This gap between foundation and retelling means that the legends that reach us are sophisticated and developed, but they may also be contradictory or confusing. The stories often show the seams where tales have been stitched together. The variance in accounts of Aeneas thus suggests that Rome was important enough to be mentioned in even early histories of Italy, but also that there was no consensus about the city's origins. Such lack of consensus may be due to the Romans' own differing account(s) of their origins.

Modern scholars hold various opinions about the relationship between Aeneas, the ultimate ancestor of the Roman people, and Romulus, the founder of the city itself (and the subject of **chapter 3**). Older research tried to determine which foundation story was the "original" and why the "secondary" story developed. But recent studies have abandoned the attempt to determine which story came first, since our earliest accounts mention both Aeneas and his descendants. These descendants usually include Romus, who may be an early or Hellenized form of either Romulus or Remus.

Aeneas appears in Homer's *Iliad*, and was thus familiar to Greek authors. Most took Homer as a starting point, but they did not necessarily agree on what the Homeric version of Aeneas' life after Troy was. It is clear from iconographic evidence that Aeneas was known to the Etruscans as early as the sixth century,[1] and was worshipped in Lavinium, the city he founded. Yet there's substantial debate about his place in Rome's mythic history. Karl Galinsky (1969) argued that the archaic Aeneas was substantially different from the one we see in Latin literature: brave and smart, rather than *pius* (a complex virtue involving a sense of duty and respect for gods and family). Nicholas Horsfall (1987) disagrees, claiming that Homer describes Aeneas as *pius*. For Erich Gruen (1992), the Aeneas story became most important for Romans conquering Greek cities in the second century BCE. Troy offered a way to insert Rome into a Greek historical tradition, but also to emphasize the differences between Greek and (Trojan-) Roman cultures. In contrast, Andrew Erskine (2001) suggested that Troy was a particularly suitable narrative for the Greek colonists of Magna Graecia and Sicily. Romans later adopted the legend as a way to engage with the Greek world on their terms.

It's clear that Aeneas had a role in Italian myth from an early date, but his relationship to Rome in particular remains confusing. Aeneas may have been important to specific noble families before he became important to Rome as a whole. The earliest accounts of the city's foundation reveal numerous alternative founders and members of dynasties, which by the first century CE had become standardized. This canonization is due in part to the use of late first-century authors such as Vergil and Livy as teaching texts in Roman elite classrooms; however, these texts also seem to reiterate familial legends of the most powerful families in Rome, especially the family of Julius Caesar. Christopher Smith (2010) has argued that a relatively obscure member of Caesar's family may have elaborated the Aeneas legend to strengthen ties between the Julian family and Aeneas' son Iulus, as well as between the Julii and Aeneas' mother Venus. Similar family legends are known in other households. The Roman antiquarian Varro, for example, wrote a whole book that outlined the history of Rome's "Trojan Families." This work is, unfortunately, lost – but the practice of tracing one's ancestry back to mythical characters was common enough that it could be mocked by Cicero (*Brutus* 62). Such origin stories could serve a number of different functions: for example, connecting a Roman elite family with a town or region under its patronage; glorifying a family that was falling into decline; making unofficial partnerships explicit; competing with the elaborate genealogies of the Hellenistic royals; or reiterating the rationale behind a particular group's social and political power. These functions could co-exist or fluctuate, as could the particular motifs and ancestors that a family chose to emphasize. For example, the Aemilii, a prominent family of the middle Republic, claimed descent from Numa (Plutarch, *Aemilius Paullus* 2), from Pythagoras, and from Aeneas (Festus, "Aemilian family").

By the imperial period, Aeneas was established as "the founder of the Roman people," thanks both to his statue in the Augustan Forum (which was imitated locally in the West), and to Vergil's status as a school text. Aeneas appears on diverse monuments, such as the Ara Pacis in Rome, and is even satirized in

Pompeiian graffiti.[2] It's at this point, in the first century CE, that competing narratives probably started to lose ground.

Despite his canonical status, only a few Roman traditions were associated with Aeneas. The most important were the *Penates*,[3] Roman household gods, and the Palladium, the sacred statue of Troy that was kept safe by the Vestal Virgins. Aeneas was much more strongly connected with the Julii, and thus the imperial family. Over the course of the Principate, as the Julii (and other old families) died out, this connection diminished. Nevertheless, Aeneas' status as a "founder" was maintained.

For Further Thought

1. Consider the narrative of Troy told in Homer's poems *The Iliad* and *The Odyssey* (if you need more information, try the Troia Projekt at http://cerhas. uc.edu/troy/legends.html). Why do you think the Romans chose Aeneas as a founding figure?

2. Aeneas was one of many eastern heroes who came to Italy and the area around Rome (others include the Greek war heroes Odysseus and Diomedes, as well as Hercules). What do these characters add to existing legends in the area? Is there a difference between "adopting" or "adapting" a character like Hercules and "assimilating" a native god (such as Indiges) to a new figure like Aeneas?

3. What is the relationship between Lavinium, Alba, and Rome? What does Rome gain by repeating this lengthy history? What does it tell us about Roman historical thought?

TEXTS

2.1 The Earliest Italians

This section begins with the history of Italy before Aeneas arrived. These texts recall a "Golden Age" of Italy whose inhabitants were slowly pushed to the margins of the Italian peninsula. Newcomers brought civilization, but also negative qualities such as war and greed. Later generations would look back to primitive Italy as a peaceful place: Italian cultures that retained their customs proudly advertised their ancient values. The idea of a rustic "pre-Rome" was a theme in Augustan-era poetry, which emphasized the difference between the rural Rome of myths and the new marble city. This romantic view may relate to the dichotomy between savage and civilized (**1.4**) and/or the historically attested renovation of the city, which started in the second century BCE but considerably increased under Pompey, Caesar, and Augustus in the late first century.

--------------- 2.1.1 Vergil, *Aeneid* 8.315–8.335 ---------------

Evander explains the early history of Rome. In his account, the site was once home to a Golden Age civilization that has been declining for generations; the audience, living centuries later, would be still worse.

"Fauns[4] and nymphs once possessed these groves, natives to this place. There were men, too, born from tough oak branches. They didn't have laws or civilization; they didn't know how to yoke bulls or conserve resources or be sparing with what they had. Instead they ate acorns and whatever animals they hunted. Saturn was the first to come down from heavenly Olympus, fleeing the might of Jupiter.[5] He was an exile once his kingdom was stolen. He gathered that untamed group from their scattered spots on the tall mountains and gave them laws. "Latium" was his choice of name, because in this space he *lay low*[6] in safety. The golden years were under that king. He ruled the people in calm peace. But gradually, the young generations got worse and tarnished. They wanted war madly and craved possessions. Then the Ausonian[7] band and the Sicani[8] came, and the Saturnian land lost its name over and over again. Among the kings was fierce Thybris, whose body was enormous. He gave his name to the river Tiber; its real name, Albula,[9] was lost. All-powerful Fortune and inescapable fate dropped me here after I was driven out of my country and crossed the deep seas. The frightening warnings of my mother, the nymph Carmenta,[10] and divine Apollo's authority drove me on."

--------------- 2.1.2 Justin 43.1.2–43.1.10 ---------------

Towards the end of his comprehensive history, Justin offers a digression on the early history of Rome.

The first inhabitants of Italy were the Aborigines, whose king Saturn was so just that there were no slaves or private goods under his reign. Instead, all property was communal and undivided, as if everyone had inherited everything. Following his example, the Romans take pains to flatten all social distinctions at the Saturnalia, and slaves lie down next to their masters at feasts. And so Italy was named "Saturnia" after the king, and the mountain where he lived was called "Saturnius." Nowadays it's called the Capitol, as if Jupiter pushed Saturn out.[11]

They say that the third to rule after Saturn was Faunus. In his reign Evander came from the Arcadian city Pallanteum to Italy. He had a largish group of people with him. Faunus kindly granted him some land

and the hill which was later called "Palatine" [...] Faunus' daughter was raped by Hercules, when he was traveling through Italy [...][12] Latinus was the child of this affair. While he was king, Aeneas came to Italy from Troy.

------------------------ 2.1.3 Dionysius of Halicanassus, ------------------------
Roman Antiquities 1.9.1–1.10.1

Dionysius' aim was to prove that the Romans were in fact Greek. Here he traces the various peoples of Italy back as far as he can, probably drawing on lost Greek sources.

They say that very long ago, barbarian Sicels,[13] who are native to the place, inhabited the land the Romans now hold. Before them, no one can say for sure whether others lived there or it was deserted. In later times, the Aborigines captured it in a great war and lived there. Until then, they'd lived in isolated mountain villages, without walls; then the Pelasgians[14] and some other Greeks started war against their neighbors. They drove the Sicels out of their city, threw up walls, and plotted war against everyone who lived between the rivers Liris and Tiber [...] They remained in the same settlement and weren't ever ejected by any others, but this same people changed their name for themselves twice. Until the beginning of the Trojan War, they preserved the name "Aborigines." Then they began to call themselves "Latins" after King Latinus, who lived during the Trojan War. Finally, 16 generations after the Trojan War, Romulus founded the city he named for himself and the Romans changed their names to that which they now have [...] Some say that the Aborigines, from whom the Roman people are descended, were native to Italy, a people that came into being through itself alone [...] and they say their name was given to them at first because they founded families that were descended from them. As we'd say, they were "patriarchs" or "forefathers." But others say they were rootless nomads who joined up there from many lands and settled in these deserted regions by fate. They made their living by grazing and stealing herds.

------------------------ 2.1.4 Strabo, *Geography* 13.1.53 ------------------------

Strabo describes the various traditions about Aeneas' kingdom.

They say that he escaped the war because he held a grudge against Priam [...][15] and that Antenor and his sons ruled with him, due to their friendship with Menelaus [...][16] So Antenor, his children, and the Eneti who survived escaped to Thrace, where they settled in the place called "Enetic" on the Adriatic.[17] But Aeneas, his father Anchises, and his son Ascanius sailed with a group of people he'd gathered. Some say they settled in Macedonian Olympus. Others say they founded Capua in Arcadia [...] Still others say they traveled to Egesta in Sicily [...] and took control of Eryx and Lilybaeum [...] From there they went to Latium to wait, in accordance with an oracle [...][18]

But Homer seems to agree with no one, not even those who mention Aeneas' rule of Skepsis. He shows that Aeneas remained in Troy and received the throne there, and passed it down to his children's children.[19] He completely contradicts the others, who say that Aeneas wandered all the way to Italy and died there.

———— 2.1.5 Plutarch, *Life of Romulus* 2 ————

Plutarch's account of Rome's founder is elaborate and rich in variants. Many are unique to Plutarch, representing a lost Greek mythical tradition about Rome. This passage refers to characters seen in many Greek myths, who are identified in the notes.

Some say that Roma gave her name to the city. She was the daughter of Leucaria and Italus[20] (or was it Telephus the son of Hercules?) and married Aeneas (or possibly Ascanius, his son). Others say that Romanus, the child of Odysseus and Circe,[21] founded the city; or Romus, the son of Emathion, who was sent away from Troy by Diomedes;[22] or Romis the tyrant of the Latins, who expelled the Tyrrhenians from Thessaly (and the Tyrrhenians went first to Lydia and then Italy[23]). So they don't at all agree about the family of the city's founder or his name.

———— 2.1.6 Festus, "Rome" ————

Festus' dictionary entry for "Rome" includes variant founders of the city. Most details of these accounts are now unknown, but the list helps us understand how complex the tradition was before the first century BCE. The consistent presence of a Romus/Roma as the eponymous founder of the city suggests that Greeks were working Rome into their own model of foundation legends.

Cephalon of Gergitha, who apparently wrote about the arrival of Aeneas in Italy, says that ROME was named after a companion of Aeneas. This man was living on the hill that's now called the Palatine. He founded a city there and named it "Rome."[24] Apollodorus in his work *On the Black Sea* says that Maylles, Mulus, and Romus were the sons of Lavinia, and the city took its name from Romus. Alcimus says that Romulus was the son of Tyrrhenia[25] and Aeneas. Alba[26] was the daughter of Romulus and granddaughter of Aeneas, and *her* son, named Rhodius, founded Rome. Antigonus, who wrote Italian histories, says that Romus was one of the sons of Jupiter and founded a city on the Palatine, which he called "Rome" [**lacuna**] The author of *The History of Cumae* says that some Athenians [...] decided to seek out remote lands and were washed ashore in Italy. After a great deal of wandering, they were called "Aborigines" [...][27] By virtue of their unparalleled strength, they established themselves on the Palatine, where they camped very frequently. The settlement was called "Valentia"[28] after the vigor that brought them there. After Evander[29] and then Aeneas came to Italy with a troop of Greek-speaking interpreters, the site started to be called "Rome," which is Greek for "strength." Agathocles, who wrote a history of Cyzicus, says that the prophecy of Helenus[30] encouraged Aeneas to seek Italy. Aeneas took with him his granddaughter Roma, the daughter of Ascanius. After the Phrygians[31] gained control of Italy (especially the part around the current city suburbs), Roma was the first to consecrate a temple on the Palatine [...] When a city was founded on the hill, it seemed right to name it "Rome" after the first settler. And Agathocles adds that there are many writers who say that Aeneas is buried in a Phrygian city near the river Nolon. It was one of his descendants (named Romus) who came to Italy and founded Rome, naming it after himself. Caltinus, who publicized the achievements of Agathocles the tyrant of Sicily, thought that a band of Trojans escaped when Troy was captured. One of them was named Latinus and had a wife named Roma. After Latinus gained a foothold in Italy, he founded a city and named it "Rome" after his wife. Heraclides Lembos claimed that Greeks founded the city. As they were on their way home from Troy, a storm forced them ashore in Italy. Following the course of the Tiber, they came to the site that is now Rome. There, sick and tired of sailing, the captive women burned the fleet; one of the older women, named Roma, encouraged them. So they were all forced to stay there. They founded a city and named it after the woman whose advice led to the settlement. Galitas writes that, after Aeneas died, Latinus gained control over Italy. He was the son of Telemachus and Circe, and he married Roma. They had sons: Romus; Romulus, who founded a city on the Palatine and called it Rome; and [**lacuna**]...

2.1.7 (Anonymous), *The Origin of the Roman People* 9–10

The unknown author of this work relates several versions of Aeneas' journey from Troy to Italy. Some of them are harsh to Aeneas; others try to resolve the controversy noted by Strabo (2.1.4).

After Troy was betrayed to the Greeks by Antenor and other leading men, Aeneas left at night. He held his family gods out before him, his father Anchises on his shoulder, and his small son by the hand. At daybreak he was recognized by the enemy, but they were impressed by his dutiful burden. Not only they did they not stop him, but king Agamemnon let him go to Mt. Ida as he wished. There Aeneas built boats with several others, both men and women [...]

Lutatius says it was not just Antenor who betrayed his country, but also Aeneas himself, which is why king Agamemnon let him go wherever he wanted. Lutatius also says that he asked to bring only what he thought was most important on his shoulders: that is, nothing except his family gods, his father, and two young sons (as some say; others say that there was only one son whose name was Iulus and later called Ascanius). In any case, the Achaean leaders were moved by his piety and let him go home to get whatever he wanted. So he left Troy for a long journey across the sea, with a large treasure and many companions, both men and women. He traveled through different lands and eventually came to Italy. First he landed at Thrace and founded Aenus [... Then] on the island of Delos, he accepted the hand of Lavinia. She was the daughter of Anius the priest of Apollo; her name is remembered in *Lavinian shores*.[32] After that he traversed many seas and landed on a spit of land in Italy at Baiae near Lake Avernus.

2.1.8 Servius, *On the* Aeneid 1.273

Vergil's line reads: "the land will be ruled by Hector's people for 300 years, until a royal priestess gives birth to twins."

Many different traditions are told about the foundation and the founder of the city. Clinias says that the daughter of Telemachus (named Roma) married Aeneas, and the city was called "Rome" after her. Another says Latinus was the son of Odysseus and Circe, and he named the city after his dead sister. Ateius claims Rome was called "Valentia"[33] long before the arrival of Evander, but afterwards it was called "Rome," which means the same thing in Greek. Some say the city was named after the daughter of Evander; others say that it was named after a prophetess who told Evander where to establish his settlement. Heraclides says that Roma was a noblewoman, a Trojan captive who was forced here and persuaded them to settle because they were bored with the ocean. And the city was named after her. Eratosthenes calls the founder "Romulus" – but Romulus was the son of Ascanius and grandson of Aeneas. Naevius and Ennius relate that Romulus the city's founder was the grandson of Aeneas via his daughter. And the Sibyl says "Romans, children of Romus."

2.2   Inhabitants of the Site of Rome

Although Aeneas would ultimately build a new city, that city was a neighbor of Rome rather than Rome itself. The future site of Rome was inhabited when Aeneas arrived (**2.1.1**). Both the natives and the Greeks eventually came together in the Roman people, a metaphor of colonization that will be discussed further in **chapter 6**. The passages below focus on two figures who remain important throughout Roman myth: the woodland deity Picus (**5.3.2**) and Cacus, who was defeated by Hercules. The Greek demigod Hercules was a popular figure throughout Italy (**4.1, 4.2, 6.2, 7.1**). He was worshipped at the Ara Maxima in Rome's Forum Boarium (cattle market), where a statue of him dating to the sixth century has been found.[34]

————————   2.2.1   Diodorus Siculus, *Library of History* 4.21   ————————

*Diodorus relates local myths of Hercules. His version of Cacus is strikingly different from first-century Roman versions (**2.2.2, 2.2.3**), although the names of the main characters are the same.*

Hercules traveled through the country of the Ligurians and Tyrrhenians. Arriving at the Tiber, he made camp where the city of Rome is now. But this place was founded many generations later by Romulus the son of Mars.[35] At that time some of the natives lived on the hill now called Palatine, making up a teeny-tiny city. Two of the most notable men in that place, Cacius and Pinarius, welcomed Hercules with remarkably pleasant gifts and tokens of friendship and honored him. The Romans preserve mementoes of these men even now. "Pinarius" is a name still in use among the Roman nobility, as a very old leader, and the stone stairway on the Palatine called "Cacus' Steps" is named after the same Cacius (it's close to the former location of his house). And Hercules accepted the goodwill of the men living on the Palatine and told them that when he became a god they should promise to dedicate a tithe to Hercules and their lives would be exceptionally fortunate.

2.2.2 Vergil, *Aeneid* 8.193–8.272

Evander recalls the local monster Cacus and his defeat by Hercules.

"It was a cavern, tucked within the deep recesses of the cliff. The owner was Cacus, a half-man with a terrifying appearance. The sun couldn't reach back in there. His floor was always warm from freshly-spilled blood and the faces of his poor victims were nailed to his proud doors. They hung there, waxy with gore. This monster was Vulcan's son, and he lurched his great mass around, puking fire from his mouth. But time brought us the help we hoped for – time, and the arrival of a god. Our great avenger Hercules came straight from the murder of three-headed Geryon, triumphant with his spoils. Victorious, he also herded his enormous bulls here; they grazed between the valley and the river. But the savage mind of that thief Cacus never failed to do something outrageous. He left no trick or scheme untried. So he snatched four cows and four heifers from the mass that stood grazing, the most beautiful in the herd. He didn't want them to leave hoofprints in the right direction, so he dragged them by their tails into the cave and hid his theft in the gloomy rocks by this backwards path.[36] The cave offered no clue to anyone searching. Meanwhile, Hercules' cows had eaten their fill and he was ready to move them. But as they departed, the cows bellowed; their mooing and noise for the cows left behind filled the entire grove and all the hills. One of the cows returned the call and mooed within the deep cave. Cacus' hope of keeping the theft under wraps was foiled.

"Then indeed the trick sparked Hercules' fury with black bile. He snatched up his weapons, especially his heavy oak club, and ran up the steep path of the lofty hill. For the first time we saw Cacus afraid, with confusion in his eyes. Right away he ran, faster than the wind, to his cave. Fear made him fly. He locked himself in and tossed down a boulder by breaking its chain (it could hang thanks to the Vulcan-forged iron). In this way he defended himself by reinforcing the door. Imagine how Tirynthian Hercules approached, furious. He scouted every access point, sticking his face here and there, gnashing his teeth. Hot with rage, he circled the entire Aventine three times.[37] Three times he tried to rush the rocky threshold – but three times, exhausted, he returned to the valley.

"A sharp rock erupted from the side of the cave, chiseled out from the cliff on all sides and extremely tall. It was the sort of place where terrifying birds like to build nests. Hercules faced it and pulled the rock towards the right, since it tilted left towards the river out of the cliff. It took huge effort. As he loosened the rock from its deepest roots, he suddenly pulled it out. The sky roared loudly with his effort, the banks jumped apart and the river drew back with fear. But Cacus' cave lay unroofed, his castle loomed huge, and the space deep within the shady cavern was open to the sky [...] Cacus howled eerily as Hercules pelted him with spears from above. The hero used anything as a weapon, peppering Cacus with trees and boulders. But Cacus, unable to flee this peril from above, puked huge waves of smoke from his throat – amazing but true! – and covered his home with dusky shadows, blocking Hercules' view. In the cave, smoky night unrolled, mixing fire with shadows. Hercules couldn't bear it. He jumped through the fire on his toes in the thickest smoke. The immense cave roiled with dark fog. The hero grabbed Cacus in a headlock as he puked useless smoke into the dark. He choked the monster until his eyes popped out and his throat dried out from blood.

"Hercules immediately flung open the doors of the dark house. The stolen cows, Cacus' lies and his theft, were visible to everyone. He dragged the shapeless body out by its feet. Our hearts couldn't get enough of the sight: the monster's terrifying eyes, his face, his shaggy chest like an animal's, and the fires in his gut, now at last put out. Since that day we've celebrated his deed, and our descendants will rejoice when they remember it. First Potitius and Pinarius guarded the rites of Hercules. He set up this altar in the grove, which we'll always call 'greatest'[38] because it always will be."

─────────────── 2.2.3   Propertius 4.9.8–4.9.20   ───────────────

*The rest of Propertius' account of Hercules appears in **7.1.1**. The contrast between Hercules' quick defeat of Cacus and inability to defeat the sacred virgins is ironic.*

Cacus was a native bandit with a terrifying cave. He uttered different sounds from each of his three mouths.[39] To make sure that there wouldn't be clear indications of his open crime, he dragged the cows backwards into the cave by the tail. But the god[40] was still watching. The cattle mooed at the thief, and Hercules angrily knocked down the savage gates. Cacus was hit three times[41] by Hercules' club, and lay limp. Then Hercules said, "Come, cows! Cows of Hercules, come! You're my club's last labor. I went on two quests for you, cows, and twice you were my prize. Establish the cattle fields;[42] make them sacred with your long mooing. The Roman Forum will be your noble pasture."

———————————   2.2.4   Dionysius of Halicanassus,   ———————————
                  Roman Antiquities 1.31.1–1.31.4

*Dionysius' narrative of Italian prehistory (**2.1.3**) picks up in the mid-thirteenth century* BCE, *a generation before the fall of Troy. He describes the arrival of the Greek Evander ("Goodman"), the Arcadian king who symbolizes the idealized values of primeval Rome.*

Not long afterwards, another Greek fleet reached this part of Italy [...] sailing from the Arcadian city of Pallanteum. Evander, allegedly the son of Hermes and some local Arcadian nymph, was their leader [...] Faunus was king of the Aborigines in those days; they say he was a descendant of Mars, a doer with smarts to boot. The Romans worship him as a local god with songs and sacrifice. He welcomed the Arcadians with great warmth, since there weren't many of them, and gave them as much of his land as they wanted. The Arcadians [...] chose a hill not far from the Tiber, which is now basically in the middle of Rome [...] They named it "Pallanteum" after their homeland.

———————————   2.2.5   Ovid, *Metamorphoses* 14.320–14.396   ———————————

*Picus and Faunus were two of early Rome's most commonly mentioned local deities. As gods, they appear in stories from before Aeneas through the regal period (**5.2.3**). In this passage, Ovid explains how Picus was deified. The* Metamorphoses *is a book about humans changing into non-humans. Most of the stories are based on Greek myth; by retelling Italian myth in the same style, Ovid seems unconcerned about distinctions between Greek and Roman tales.*

"Picus was a descendant of Saturn, king in Ausonia. He was good at war and loved horses. Here's a picture of him. If you look closely, you can discern true beauty despite his changed shape. He hadn't turned 20, and his soul was as sweet as his face. His appearance caught the attention of the dryads born in Latin mountains. The water spirits sought him out too [...]. But he spurned most of them and favored one nymph [...]

"Picus went out into the Lauretine fields to spear a native bull. He was gripping the flanks of a warhorse and carrying two spears in his left hand while he tied back his red cloak with a tawny gold pin.

"The daughter of the sun[43] went into the same woods to collect new plants from the fertile hills. She left her name behind – the fields are called "Circean." As soon as she saw the youth from her hiding place in the bushes, her jaw dropped. The herbs she'd collected[44] fell from her hands and fire seemed to dart across her organs. As soon as she'd pulled herself together, reeling from the strong fire, she admitted what she wanted. It wasn't for him to come towards her, but to make his horse run away and force his companions to scurry off the road.

"'You won't escape,' she said. 'You'll be carried off by the wind if I know myself. If all the strength of my herbs holds steady and my spells don't fail me, it will occur.'

"These were her words. She made a specter in the shape of a boar and told the phantom to run right past the king and disappear into the trees of the dense forest. The woods were so thick that it was impossible to ride a horse there. Without hesitation, Picus jumped to chase his prey. He didn't know that it was only a shadow. Quickly he abandoned the sweaty back of his horse and pursued his goal, tracking the boar in vain through the deep woods [...]

"Circe reached the place and seized the opportunity. 'By your eyes that caught mine, by your outstanding beauty that has made me, a goddess, into a beggar, I ask you. Pay attention to my fiery love [...]' In vain she repeated her agitated prayers [...] 'You'll learn the hard way what a hurt woman can do when she's in love! And Circe is just such a woman!'

"Then she turned twice to the West, twice to the East. She touched the young man three times[45] with her wand and said three spells. He ran, but he seemed to run faster than he was used to. He saw feathers spring from his body, and suddenly there was a new species of bird in the Latin woods. Furious and offended at the change, he pecked at a hard oak, peppering the long branches. He took the purple color of his feathers from his cloak; he bit at the pin he wore and his golden clothing; he gained a plume and a neck banded with yellow gold. Nothing remained of Picus except his name."[46]

2.2.6   Ovid, *Fasti* 1.575–1.584

*Ovid's version of the Cacus story combines **2.2.2** and **2.2.3** to explain the hero's significance in multiple Roman neighborhoods.*

Hercules took charge. He picked up his knotty club and swung it into the man's face 12 times. Cacus fell, barfing smoke mixed with blood. When his chest hit the ground, he died. So, Jupiter, the winner sacrificed one of his bulls to you, and he called Evander and the people farming nearby to see. He set up an altar to himself, which is called the Ara Maxima, right here in the part of the city that gets it name from herds: the Cattle Market.[47] And Evander's mother wasn't silent: she let Hercules know that it was almost time for him to leave the earth and become immortal.

2.2.7 (Anonymous), *The Origin of the Roman People* 5–8

This rather unusual version of the Hercules tale suggests that he is a normal human rather than a hero. This type of rationalization, where a god or demigod is "really" an extraordinary human, is called Euhemerism.[48]

Evander taught the Italians how to read and write, just as he had learned before. He also showed them how to farm, which had been invented in Greece earlier, and then he taught them how to use the plow. He was the first to yoke bulls in Italy in order to cultivate the land. While he was king, it just so happened that a man named Recaranus appeared there. He was Greek, a shepherd with an immense body and enormous strength. Because he was bigger and stronger than everyone else, he was called "Hercules." While Hercules was letting his herd graze near the river Albula, a servant of Evander's named Cacus crept towards them. He was a worthless person, prone to petty theft. He stole the visitor's cattle and dragged them backwards into a cave so he wouldn't draw attention.

Recaranus searched high and low in the areas nearby and looked in every nook and cranny. Eventually he lost hope of finding his herd. Although he handled the loss with a good spirit, he decided to leave the area. But Evander was known for his outstanding justice. When he discovered what his servant had done, he punished him and forced him to give the cows back.

Then Recaranus dedicated an altar to Jupiter Inventor[49] at the foot of the Aventine. He called it the Ara Maxima[50] and he sacrificed a tenth of his herd there. Because the nymph Carmentis had been invited to the rite but didn't show up, he made it a law of the shrine that women aren't allowed to eat anything that had been dedicated on this altar. So women are totally removed from this sacrifice [...][51]

After Recaranus or Hercules had consecrated the Ara Maxima to Jupiter Inventor, he taught two Italians to care for the shrine and its rituals. The ones he chose were Potitius and Pinarius. But Pinarius arrived first and ate the organ meat, shutting Potitius out because he arrived late.[52] And this custom remains to this day.

2.2.8 Solinus, *Collected Tales* 8–10

Solinus' account of Hercules is quite different from other accounts and in many ways less flattering. Scholars disagree on how old the variant is.

Cacus was arrested by Tarchon the Etruscan[53] (he and Megales the Phrygian had been sent to Tarchon by king Marsyas[54] on an embassy). Escaping his chains, he went back to where he had come from. He seized a kingdom around Volturnum in Campania and fortified it with many garrisons. Meanwhile he dared to steal even the places which were rightfully Evander the Arcadian's. (In those days, Evander had only just reached Italy.) In return, Cacus was attacked by Hercules, the Arcadian general. The Sabines welcomed Megales and learned augury from him. That same Hercules set up an altar to his own divinity.[55] It's considered "the greatest" by the pontiffs. Nicostrata, Evander's mother, revealed to him that he was an immortal. She was also known as a "Muse"[56] from her prophecy.

2.3 Aeneas in Italy

Prophecy was an important source of information for mythical heroes. In this section, two different prophets of Apollo foretell Aeneas' future in Italy: Cassandra, a princess of Troy, and the Sibyl of Cumae.

2.3.1 Lycophron, *Alexandra* 1248–1270

The prophet Cassandra foretells the future of the Trojans after the city falls. This difficult and allusive text provides early evidence for Rome's importance.

"They will meet Tarchon[57] and Tyrsenos,[58] fierce as wolves, born from the blood of Hercules. There they will find a table full of food, which later will be eaten by his companions.[59] He will recall the memory of ancient oracles and they will found a country in the area of the Aborigines,[60] settling beyond Latinus and the Daunians. It will have 30 towers, the same number as the offspring of the black sow which sailed from the Idaean peak and Dardanian lands, nursing in its litter the same number of piglets.[61] [...] While warlike dogs entirely devour our country with their spears,[62] he wraps the gods in a toga. The enemy offers only him the option to take what he wants from his home and carry it out. Even among his enemies he is judged the most pious..."

--------------------------------- 2.3.2   Vergil, *Aeneid* 6.82–6.100 ---------------------------------

Aeneas learns about his future struggles from the Sibyl, a prophet of Apollo.
You'll see her again in **5.6.4**.

"At last you're done with the great dangers of the sea! But on land even
worse perils remain. The children of Dardanus[63] will enter the realms
of Lavinium – don't worry about that! – but they'll wish they hadn't.
I see wars, terrible wars, and the Tiber frothing with buckets of blood.
You'll have a Simois, a Xanthus,[64] a Dorian camp – even a new Achilles
awaits you in Latium, a goddess' son like you. Juno too will never be
far from the Teucrians.[65] You'll beg many peoples and cities of Italy,
going as a suppliant in need. The cause of such evils? A wife, again
foreign to the Trojans, again taken from another man's bed. Don't give
way when faced with these evils – push onwards, be daring! This much
your fortune allows you. The best path to safety is the least expected:
it lies in a Greek city."

   This was the speech that the Cumaean Sibyl gave in her shrine. She
foretold terrifying mysteries. As her words echoed through the cave,
they wrapped truths in riddles.

------------------------------- 2.3.3   Tibullus, *Elegies* 2.5.18–2.5.66 -------------------------------

Invokes the Sibyl's prophecy to Aeneas as inspiration for his own poetry.
This passage provides the first known use of the name "eternal city" for
Rome.

This fate she gave to Aeneas, they say, after he carried his father and
the *Lares*[66] which he snatched from danger. And he couldn't imagine
Rome would exist when he sadly watched Troy and his gods burning
from a high peak. (Indeed, Romulus had not yet built the walls of the
eternal city, a place where he would not live with his brother Remus.[67]
But at that time cows grazed on the grassy Palatine and humble
houses were standing on Jupiter's citadel [...] There where the Velabrum
lies open, a tiny boat used to travel, pushed through the shallow
water [...])[68]

   "Tireless Aeneas, brother of winged Cupid,[69] who carries Troy's gods
on exiled ships, now Jupiter has allotted you the Laurentine fields, now
a welcoming land calls your wandering *Lares*. There you will become
a god when the holy waters of Numicus send you to heaven as the
divine Indiges.[70]

   "Look, Victory flies above the tired fleet; finally that aloof goddess has
come to the Trojans. Look, the burning Rutulian camp shines out to me:

right now I prophesy death to you, savage Turnus. Before my eyes lie the
Laurentine camp and the walls of Lavinium and Alba Longa, founded
under Ascanius' leadership [...] Bulls, crop at the grass of the seven hills
now, while you can: soon this place will be a big city. Rome, your name
is fated to rule the world!"

2.3.4 Dionysius of Halicanassus,
Roman Antiquities 1.53.4–1.53.5

Some stories about Aeneas were less optimistic about his fate.

Some writers say that Aeneas didn't reach Italy with the Trojans, or that
it was a different Aeneas, not the son of Anchises and Aphrodite, or that
it was Aeneas' son Ascanius or someone else. And even among those
who say that Aeneas the son of Aphrodite settled his people in Italy,
some claim that he returned home and ruled the Trojans. When he
died there, he left his kingdom to his son Ascanius, whose descendants
ruled for many years.

2.4 Aeneas' Arrival in Latium

Aeneas knew what signs would mark the end of his travels: the sow with 30
piglets and the eaten tables (**2.3.1**). These prophecies were mysterious to him,
but we can at least partially understand them. The sow helps fill in the chronological gap between Aeneas and Romulus (**1.5**) by laying the groundwork for
the foundation of Alba Longa. Although there are variations on how the sow
was found, both the color and number of piglets are miraculous. Pigs' lit-
ters are typically only 8–12 piglets, and pure white pigs are extremely rare.
A Roman audience would immediately understand the 30 milk-white piglets
of the prophecy as a divine sign. The name "Alba," which means "white," connects the city to the pigs. The "tables" that Aeneas must eat may relate to cultic
customs at Lavinium.

2.4.1 Varro, On the Latin Language 5.144

*Varro explains the complex relationship between Aeneas' city Lavinium and
Rome.*

Lavinium was the first town to be established in Latium by the Romans.
In that city are the *Penates*, our gods. The place itself is named after

Lavinia, the daughter of Latinus, who married Aeneas. After 30 years in this place another town was founded: Alba. It's named after a white sow. This sow ran out of Aeneas' ship in Lavinium and gave birth to 30 piglets. Because of this miracle, a new city was built 30 years after Lavinium was founded. It's named after both the color of the sow and the shape of the site: Alba Longa, the Long White City. This is where the mother of Romulus, Rhea, came from; this is where Romulus came from; this is where Rome came from.

———————————— 2.4.2   Vergil, *Aeneid* 7.107–7.118 ————————————

Aeneas and his companions have just landed near the Tiber river.

Aeneas, the leading men, and glorious Iulus lay themselves down under the branches of a tall tree. They readied the feast and set spelt cakes on the grass under their food (so Jupiter himself inspired them[71]) and added wild apples to their flatbread. It turned out that they had eaten everything else, and in their hunger they had to resort to bites of the thin bread. So they tore the round of the fated flatbread with fierce hands and jaws, and they didn't spare a crumb.

"Hey!" said Iulus. "Are we going to eat the tables, too?" Laughing, he said no more. But his words first marked an end to their struggles.

———————————— 2.4.3   Vergil, *Aeneid* 8.43–8.56 ————————————

The River Tiber addresses Aeneas in a dream, confirming that he has reached the correct location and reassuring him about the future.

"And now, so that you don't think you've invented these nothings in your sleep: a huge pig will be found under the oaks by the shore. A sow, just given birth to 30 piglets. Milky white she'll lie there, relaxing on the ground, milky white litter around her udders. [This will be the location of the city, a certain end to your labors.[72]] Thirty years after this occurs, Ascanius will found Alba, whose name sparkles. What I say is hardly new to you.[73] But now I will tell you how you will solve the problem you're faced with. Pay attention for a few moments, victorious one. The Arcadians [...] wage war endlessly against the Latins; seek them out as allies and make a treaty."

——————— 2.4.4 Servius, *On the* Aeneid 3.390–3.393 ———————

*Servius explains different traditions about the sow (**2.3.1, 2.3.3**). He cites a line of Vergil identical to the bracketed phrase in **3.4.3**.*

About this sow: some say, following Vergil, that it was found in Italy. But others say that the Trojans brought the sow with them, following the custom of sailors, and they knew from an oracle that the city would be founded wherever the pig was found after it ran away. So it is said that it ran away into Campania and was found in Laurolavinium.[74] Ascanius later named the place "Alba" after the pig [...] THIS WILL BE THE LOCATION OF THE CITY: that is, the city will be in this area; for both Lavinium and Alba are far from the seashore.

——————— 2.4.5 (Anonymous), *The Origin of the Roman People* 12 ———————

Although the two omens about the Trojans' future seem canonical, variants existed. This passage connects the sow to Roman ritual, perhaps following a relief on the Ara Pacis,[75] and offers an explanation for the long gap between Lavinium and Rome.

Domitius says it wasn't round loaves of grain (as I said above) but rather than "tables" of food it was parsley that they were to consume. This was quite plentiful in that place. When they had eaten everything else, they ate these plants. Afterwards they understood that *these* had been the "tables" that they were supposed to eat.

Meanwhile they sacrificed the pig on the beach. It is said that Odysseus' ships happened to sail by at that very time.[76] Although Aeneas worried that he'd be recognized by the enemy and risk his life, he was also concerned about disrupting the sacrifice. This would have been the height of impiety. So he covered his head with his robe and in this way fulfilled the ritual. This way of sacrificing[77] has come down to posterity [...]

He was given 50 acres by Latinus, king of the Aborigines, who owned the land at that time. But Cato in his *Origins* says [...] Aeneas was sad because the farmland was bad. As he was resting, the images of his family gods seemed to appear to him and encouraged him to persevere and finish the foundation he had begun. After the same number of years as there were piglets, the Trojans would move to more fertile lands and richer fields, and they would found the most famous city in Italy.

2.5 War in Italy

Aeneas, like most other colonists, was not joyfully welcomed by the native inhabitants of Italy. Most accounts of his arrival feature at least one war, often brief. Other traditions spoke of a longer, intergenerational conflict between the Italians and the Trojans. Our sources agree that the Trojans eventually overcame local resistance, represented by the Latin Turnus (**2.5.1–2.5.3**), the Etruscan Mezentius (**2.5.4, 2.5.5**), and the Volscian Camilla (**7.2.1, 7.2.2**). These ethnic groups also frequently fought Rome in the fifth and fourth centuries. The myths may represent historical memories of those largely undocumented conflicts.

The timeline of Aeneas' war(s) with Italian leaders (such as Turnus) is complex. The simplest tradition, represented by Vergil (**2.5.2**), is that Aeneas allied with some Italians, defeated Turnus in a duel, and subsequently became leader of the Latins. More complex accounts agreed that Aeneas killed Turnus, but they add that he also died. Ascanius/Iulus then continued the war against the Etruscan Mezentius, Turnus' ally. When Mezentius was also defeated, some narratives suggest peace; others relate the danger of civil conflict in Ascanius' kingdom, which was eventually resolved by the foundation of Alba Longa (**2.7**).

———————— 2.5.1 Livy, *From the Foundation* 1.1–1.2 ————————

*Livy briefly describes the conflict between Trojans and Latins. His description of Aeneas as exceptionally virtuous is flattering to his Roman readers. This passage continues at **2.7.1** and **3.1.2**.*

The Trojans disembarked. After nearly endless wandering, they had nothing left except weapons and ships. So they foraged from the fields. King Latinus and his Aborigines, who owned the land, ran out from their cities and fields. They were armed and determined to force the strangers out. From this point on, the tradition splits. Some say that Latinus was conquered in battle and made peace with Aeneas. After that, they became relatives by marriage.[78]

Others say that the battle lines were drawn up, but before the trumpets sounded, Latinus and his chief advisors marched out and called the enemy general[79] to negotiate. The king asked what sort of men they were, where their homeland was and why they'd left it, and what they wanted in Laurentum. He learned that the men were Trojans, that their leader was Aeneas the son of Anchises and Venus, that they'd left their city when it was burned to the ground, and that they were looking for a place to settle and to found a city. Admiring the good qualities of both people and leader (especially their spirit, which was prepared for peace or war), he stuck out his hand. So they sealed their future friendship. The leaders made a treaty, while the armies hailed each other.

Aeneas stayed at Latinus' home as a guest. The king added a private treaty to the public one: there, before his *Penates*,[80] he married off his daughter to Aeneas. This marriage in particular confirmed the Trojans' hope that they'd at last reached the end of their wanderings: a fixed and secure homeland.

They founded a city, which Aeneas named Lavinium after his wife. Soon the new marriage yielded a son. His parents named him Ascanius. Then war came to the allied forces of the Aborigines and Trojans. Turnus, king of the Rutuli, had been engaged to Lavinia before Aeneas' arrival. He didn't appreciate being booted out by a stranger, so he waged war against Aeneas and Latinus. Neither side left the battlefield rejoicing: the Rutuli lost, and although the Aborigines and Trojans won the fight, they lost their leader Latinus.

Turnus and the Rutuli were desperate and fled to king Mezentius and the flourishing wealth of the Etruscans.[81] Mezentius ruled Caere, which was a wealthy city in those days. From the start, the foundation of a new city hadn't made him happy; he thought Troy's fortunes were increasing faster than was safe for their neighbors. So he was hardly unwilling to ally himself with the Rutuli. Faced with the horror of a huge war, Aeneas wanted to win over the Aborigines. He renamed his people "Latins," so that they shared a name as well as laws. From that point on, the Aborigines were as eager and loyal to King Aeneas as the Trojans.

─────────── 2.5.2 Vergil, *Aeneid* 7.647–7.653 ───────────

In Vergil's account, Mezentius is a pure villain with few redeeming qualities. His impiety and greed establish him as a foil for both Aeneas and his ally Evander (whose name means "Goodman"). Lausus, Mezentius' son, is a more redeemable character who doesn't survive the war.

The first to enter the war and outfit his army was harsh Mezentius, from the Tyrrhenian[82] shores, contemptuous of the gods.[83] Beside him was Lausus, his son; no one was more beautiful, except Turnus of Laurentum. Lausus, tamer of horses[84] and fighter of beasts, led a thousand men from the city Agyllina. They followed him in vain. He was quite pleasant, worthy of his ancestors' power, and Mezentius was hardly a father to him.

——————————— 2.5.3 Vergil, *Aeneid* 12.887–12.952 ———————————

Aeneas and Turnus meet for their final battle as war rages around them. Inter-preting the death of Turnus is a major controversy in scholarship, since it seems to contradict Aeneas' typical moderation. Some suggest that killing Turnus was an emotional outburst of revenge; others see it as Aeneas' only way to end the cycle of violence.

Aeneas pressed on and brandished his spear. It was as big as a tree.[85] He addressed Turnus from his furious chest: "Why this delay *now*? Turnus, why are you suddenly pulling back? A battle isn't fought by running, but by fighting up close with deadly weapons![86] Change your appearance into anything, gather anything you can get, naturally or with human skill. Pray that you can fly to the cruel stars on wings or hide yourself deep in the hollow earth."

Turnus shook his head. "Tough words, but your threats don't frighten me. The gods do, especially Jupiter if he's hostile." He spoke no more, but caught sight of a huge rock, an ancient boulder that by chance lay in the field. It had been set there to mark its boundary and forestall arguments. Twelve men couldn't have hoisted it onto their backs – not the sort of men that live today. But the hero Turnus, straining, grabbed it in one hand. He stood up tall, took a running start, and hurled it at Aeneas.

But he couldn't feel himself running, moving, lifting up the boulder, or shifting it from his hand. His legs collapsed and an icy chill hardened his blood. The rock twisted through empty space. It didn't go far enough to strike Aeneas [...] Varied emotions churned in his chest: he saw his people and city; he hesitated from fear and dreaded his coming death. He saw that there was no way to escape and couldn't see how to approach his enemy. He couldn't see his chariot or his sister[87] driving it.

As Turnus hesitated, Aeneas shook his deadly spear. His eyes darted around for an opening. Far away, he hurled the spear with his whole body. Rocks never clash like this when they're struck with catapults, and even the crash of thunder isn't as big. His weapon flew like a dark tornado, bringing painful death. It tore open the edge of Turnus' breastplate and the outer edge of his seven-layered shield. Whizzing, it passed through his thigh. As he was hit, huge Turnus' knees collapsed and he toppled to the ground.

Groaning, the Rutuli got up. The whole surrounding hillside echoed their moans deep into the woods. On the ground, Turnus stretched forth his arm and looked at Aeneas beseechingly. He begged, "Truly I've deserved it, and I won't plead with you; use your good luck. But, if a father's care means anything to you at all, I beg you to have pity. Pity my father Daunus' old age – your father Anchises was in a similar situation with you – and return me to my people. Or if you'd rather kill me, return my body. You've won. The Ausonians[88] see me conquered and stretching out my hands. Lavinia is your wife. Don't hold a grudge."

Fierce Aeneas stood with his weapons, his eyes darting. He didn't take the hand. Again and again he began to be persuaded, but hesitated. Then he saw the unlucky sword belt on Turnus' tall shoulder, which flashed with the known charms of the boy Pallas.[89] Turnus had laid him low with a wound and killed him, and now carried his enemy's spoils on his shoulder.

When Aeneas saw the reminder of his harsh grief and had filled his eyes with the spoils, furious anger ignited within him. He spoke terrifying words: "You're wearing the armor of my soldier whom you've taken from me? Pallas gives you this wound, Pallas sacrifices you, and he will exact the penalty from your cursed blood." As he spoke, he buried his sword in Turnus' chest, burning with anger. But Turnus' limbs loosened with cold death, and with a groan his unworthy life fled underground.

2.5.4 Ovid, *Fasti* 4.880–4.896

Mezentius' impiety is highlighted in the myth of the Latin vintage. Aeneas vows to dedicate the wine to the gods, showing his characteristic pietas, *while Mezentius greedily seeks it for himself. A similar deal appears in the Greek accounts of war between Locri and Croton (**6.4.6**).*

Turnus sought Etruscan aid. Mezentius was famously fierce when he'd taken up arms; if he was big on a horse, he was bigger on foot. The Rutuli and Turnus tried to win him to their side. In response the Etruscan leader said: "My bravery comes at a price. See how I've often sprinkled my wounds and my weapons with my own blood. You want help. Give me a reward (I don't need anything big): the next wine, fresh from your press. There's no need to hesitate: it's yours to give, ours to win! Aeneas will wish you'd denied me!"

The Rutuli agreed. Aeneas and Mezentius both armed up, but Aeneas addressed a prayer to Jupiter: "The enemy's grape harvest is vowed to the Etruscan king. Jupiter, it will be yours with a Latin victory." The better vow won; great Mezentius fell, and struck the earth with his unworthy chest.

2.5.5 Plutarch, *Roman Questions* 45

Plutarch's version of the vow has Mezentius try to placate Aeneas, rather than receive a reward from the Rutuli. Note the association of the story with a ritual, which may be how Plutarch came to hear of it.

Why do they pour out a lot of wine at the shrine of Aphrodite on the festival of the Veneralia?[90] Is it because, as most people say, Mezentius the Etruscan general sent to Aeneas to make a treaty in exchange for that year's wine harvest? But Aeneas spurned the offer and the king promised the wine to the Etruscans if they were victorious in battle. When Aeneas heard about the promise he vowed the same wine to the gods. After his victory he gathered up the harvest and spilled it before the temple of Aphrodite.

2.5.6 Servius, *On the* Aeneid 1.267

Servius explains the confusion over both the number of battles and the name Iulus-Ascanius. The Vergilian line reads "But the boy Ascanius, to whom now the name Iulus is given, was once Ilus."

Aeneas came to Italy with his father and fought against Latinus and Turnus after he'd invaded their territory. In this battle Latinus died. Afterwards, Turnus fled to Mezentius and sought his help in renewing war. In this battle Aeneas and Turnus both died, so the leadership in battle transferred to Ascanius and Mezentius, and they fought a duel. As Caesar[91] writes, it was after Mezentius was killed that Ascanius began to be called "Iulus" [...] But Vergil departs from this history, as he shows in other places, not because he doesn't know it, but from poetic license.[92] For example, he says "When Italy is found, you will rejoice with me all the more."[93] Here he speaks ambiguously, but he implies that Anchises came to Italy.[94] Still, everything is made up in contrast to that history, as for example when Aeneas is said to see Carthage, although it is agreed that it was founded 70 years before the city of Rome.[95] For in fact between the fall of Troy and the foundation of Rome there were 340 years.[96]

2.5.7 (Anonymous), *On the Origin of the Roman People* 13–15

Latinus makes a prudent decision: to ally his primitive troops with the sophisticated Trojans. This version draws on Livy (2.5.1), but emphasizes the divide between sophisticated East and rustic West that is often found in Greek accounts (2.1). This passage continues at 2.6.2.

Latinus the king of the Aborigines, when he got the message that a crowd of foreigners had sailed their fleet up to occupy the Laurentine field, led his men *en masse* against the new and undesired enemy. Before he could give the signal to attack, he noticed the Trojans drawn up in military formation, while his own men were armed with stones and sharpened sticks. He compared the clothing – or rather, the hides – which covered his men's left arms as they advanced. And so the battle paused to let the leaders confer. Latinus asked the Trojans who they were and what they wanted, and on what advice or whose authority they found themselves there. (He had often been advised, in dreams and via sacrifice, that he would be safer against his enemies if he joined forces with a stranger.) When he learned they were Aeneas and Anchises, who had been kicked out of their own country through war and who were seeking a place for the statues of their gods, he made a treaty with them and swore to share the same friends and enemies.

So[97] the Trojans began to fortify the spot and named it "Lavinia" after Aeneas' wife, the daughter of the king, who had previously been betrothed to Turnus Herdonius.[98] But Amata, the wife of King Latinus, was upset that Lavinia had spurned her cousin Turnus for a Trojan stranger. So she roused Turnus to arms. Soon he had gathered an army of Rutuli and spread them out in the Laurentine field. Latinus and Aeneas marched out against him together. As they were fighting, Latinus was defeated and killed. But Aeneas didn't stop fighting the Rutuli even though he'd lost his father-in-law. In fact, he killed Turnus. Once the enemy was defeated and ran away, Aeneas went back to Lavinium with his men. They unanimously elected him king of the Latins [...] After Latinus died, Amata killed herself.

Once Turnus was dead, Aeneas ruled the state. But he was still angry, and so he decided to continue the war against the Rutuli. They went to Etruria to beg Mezentius, king of Agylla, for help. They promised that if they won, they would give Mezentius everything they had. Then Aeneas, who had fewer troops, brought everything that had to be guarded into the city. He set up a camp outside Lavinium and put his son Euryleon[99] in charge. [...] When Ascanius took the throne,[100] he continued the war against Mezentius. Mezentius' son Lausus at that time occupied the hill of Lavinium's citadel. Because the town was surrounded by the troops of the king, the Latins sent an embassy to Mezentius to find out his terms for their surrender. Among many other steep penalties, he added that he wanted all the wine that the Latin fields could produce in several years. So the Latins decided to die for freedom rather than live under such servitude. Ascanius advised them to do this and gave his blessing. Afterwards the Latins vowed all of the wine they produced that year to Jupiter and publicly consecrated their city.[101] They rushed out of their city with the god's favor and assistance, killed Lausus, and forced Mezentius to flee. Mezentius later sent an embassy to the Latins seeking friendship and an alliance [...]

So the Latins believed that Ascanius was the son of Jupiter, due to his outstanding virtue. Gradually the nickname stuck and they called him first Iolus, then Iulus. This name remains in the Julian family today, as Caesar writes in his second book and Cato writes in the *Origins*.

2.6   The Death of Aeneas and "Pater Indiges"

According to literary tradition, Aeneas was deified after his death. Archaeological evidence suggests that he was worshipped as a hero in Lavinium. Many founders of Greek cities received a shrine after their death, and it is plausible that Aeneas too would have had one. Evidence for his worship, while controversial, may go back to to the fourth century BCE or earlier. The god "Indiges" may be older still, and may have become assimilated to Aeneas over time; we have a similar example with Romulus (**3.7**), as well as the equation of Greek and Roman gods (e.g., Mars/Ares: **Appendix 3**).

——————   2.6.1   Ovid, *Metamorphoses* 14.580–14.608   ——————

*Ovid describes Aeneas' change of "shape" from human to divine at the Numicus River near Lavinium. His account is very similar to his later description of Romulus (**3.7.3**).*

At last Aeneas' valor compelled all of the gods, even Juno herself, to set aside their ancient anger. So, with the well-founded fortunes of Iulus on the rise, the Cytherian[102] hero was ripe for heaven. Venus had solicited the gods and draped herself around her father's neck. "Dearest daddy," she said, "you've never been mean to me. So now please be the sweetest and make my Aeneas divine. Even just a little, as long as it's something! He's your grandson, born from my blood. It's enough that he's seen horrible Hades once, that he's crossed the river Styx[103] once."

The gods agreed, and royal queen Juno did not hold her head up stiffly, but nodded with a calm smile. Then father Jupiter said, "You are both worthy of this heavenly gift – both you who ask and your son for whose benefit you ask it. My daughter, your wish is granted!"

Jupiter had spoken; Venus rejoiced and thanked her father. Then she traveled through the light air in a dove-drawn carriage and approached the shores of Laurentum. The River Numicus, covered with reeds, twists to the nearby gulf there. She commanded the river to wash the mortality off of Aeneas, and then to drag him quietly under the water. The river god followed Venus' instructions: he purged Aeneas of anything human and sprinkled him with his waters. The best part was restored to him. Then Aeneas' mother anointed his purified body with divine perfume. She touched his mouth with ambrosia mixed with sweet nectar and made him a god. Romans call him "Indiges" and worship him with a temple and altars.

2.6.2   (Anonymous), *On the Origin of the Roman People* 14

*This passage picks up where **2.5.7** leaves off. The war between Trojans and Rutuli has been interrupted by a huge thunderstorm, in which Aeneas disappears. In the omitted sections, Iulus' important role is attributed to the Caesars, who claimed him as an ancestor.*

Afterwards both sides wanted to stop fighting. But Aeneas had been caught up in the sudden confusion of the storm and never appeared again. It's said that he had been standing near the river and fell, unseen, from the banks into the water. So the battle ended. But afterwards, when the clouds parted and disappeared and the serene sun shone out, men thought Aeneas had been taken up to heaven while still living. And so it was stated, by Ascanius and some others, that Aeneas had been spotted around the banks of the Numicus, wearing the armor and weapons that he usually wore into battle. Their statements confirmed the rumor of his immortality. And so a shrine was dedicated to him in that place and he became known as *Father Indiges*. Then his son Ascanius, AKA Euryleon, was named king by the consensus of the Latins.

2.6.3   Servius, *On the* Aeneid 4.620

Vergil's text reads, "But let him die before his time and be buried in unknown sands."

BUT LET HIM DIE BEFORE HIS TIME. Cato says that the companions of Aeneas brought their plunder close to Laurolavinium.[104] There was a battle; Latinus died, Turnus escaped. He got help from Mezentius[105] and started the war up again, but then he was defeated by Aeneas. But after the battle Aeneas himself was never seen. Later Ascanius killed Mezentius. Others say that after Aeneas won, he made sacrifices of thanks for the victory. He slipped into the Numicus River, and his body was never recovered – alive *or* dead. So Vergil says "buried in unknown sands." Later Aeneas is said to have become a god. In fact, they say that he was discovered to be without mortal blood even while he was fighting the Aborigines.

──────────── 2.6.4 Servius, *On the* Aeneid 12.794 ────────────

Servius betrays doubt about the nature of Aeneas' divinity. In later eras, deification as an honor for members of the imperial family was relatively common.

With Turnus dead, Lavinia became Aeneas' wife and he founded a city. He was sacrificing near the River Numicus (as some say) or running from Mezentius (according to others) or Messapus[106] when he died. And his body was never found. So Ascanius his son with the other Trojans believed that Aeneas had become a god, and once Mezentius was defeated they spread the word. Or maybe Ascanius wanted to deify his father and so built a shrine in his honor, and commanded that the shrine be called "Of Indiges."

2.7 Ascanius, Silvius, and Lavinia: the Alban Dynasty

Many scholars believe that the Alban dynasty was a late addition to Rome's mythic history. Although the tradition about the Alban kings is scanty, the themes we see here anticipate several other myths. The struggle for kingship, deaths by drowning and fire, and female regency will reappear in the myths of the seven kings of Rome (**chapters 3** and **5**) as well. The story of drowning also echoes the death of Aeneas (**2.6**). This repetition may suggest important themes of Latin myth more broadly. The kings themselves, while relatively flat figures, have the important role of bridging Rome's two major foundation cycles, Aeneas and Romulus.

──────────── 2.7.1 Livy, *From the Foundation* 1.3 ────────────

*Livy relates a brief account of the Alban kings. This passage continues his account of Aeneas (**2.5.1**) and will be continued as **3.1.2**. The colonization* *motif reappears here, and will be repeated again as Alban men depart their homes to found new cities.*

Aeneas' son Ascanius wasn't old enough to rule yet. But his rule remained safe until he reached puberty, thanks to Lavinia's motherly watchfulness and personality. The Latin state and the kingdom of his father and grandfather endured for Ascanius. I won't argue over which Ascanius this was, the son of Lavinia or an older child born to Creusa in Troy before it was burned. That Ascanius accompanied Aeneas in his travels, and the Julian family claims him as their ancestor. But who can say for sure? They're such old stories.[107]

This Ascanius, wherever he was born and whoever his mother was, was definitely the son of Aeneas. When Lavinium was flourishing with a huge population (at least for those days) and wealthy, he left the city in the care of his mother or stepmother. He founded a new city at the foot of the Alban hills, which he called "Alba Longa" because the site was stretched out long on both sides. About 30 years passed between the foundation of Lavinium and the colony at Alba Longa.

The city had grown exceptionally strong after crushing the Etruscans. The death of Aeneas, the lady regent, even the novice reign of a boy king: none of this tempted Mezentius, the Etruscans, or any other neighbors to attack. In fact, they made a peace treaty that set the river Albula, now called Tiber, as the border of Etruria and Latium.

After that, Silvius[108] the son of Ascanius was king. He happened to be born in the forest, which explains his woodsy name. His son was Aeneas Silvius, and his grandson was Latinus Silvius. Latinus Silvius established several colonies, called the Prisci Latini.[109] The name "Silvius" belonged to all the kings who ruled Alba afterwards: Alba the son of Latinus, Atys son of Alba, Capys son of Atys, Capetus son of Capys, Tiberinus son of Capetus. Tiberinus drowned while he was crossing the Albula river and gave it the name "Tiber," which endures to our day. Agrippa was Tiberinus' son, and Romulus Silvius took over the throne from his father Agrippa. He was struck by lightning and handed power down to Aventinus. Aventinus is buried on that hill which bears his name, now part of Rome. Then Proca ruled, and his sons were Amulius and Numitor.

─────────────── 2.7.2   Vergil, *Aeneid* 6.760–6.776   ───────────────

Aeneas visits the underworld and meets the ghost of Anchises, who shows him the future of Rome in a scene known as the "Parade of Heroes" (Heldenschau). Scholars have suggested that this scene is an inverted funeral procession (see **1.2**): *Aeneas is seeing the glory of his ancestors to come.*

"That young man – you see him? – who shines with a pure spear: it's his fate to hold the earthly realms next. He'll go up into the breezes of the world above first, a Trojan mixed with Italian blood. His name is Silvius, an Alban name.[110] He'll be your son, born after your death. Your wife Lavinia will deliver him in the woods, too late for your advanced age to see. He'll be a king, the parent of kings to come. Thanks to him our people will rule Alba Longa.

"Next is Procas, glory of the Trojans, and Capys and Numitor, and Aeneas Silvius, who shares your name. He'll be your equal in piety and outstanding at war, if ever he accepts the rule of Alba. What men they are! See how they show their strength! Look at the oak-leaf crowns that shade their forehead![111] These men will settle Nomentum, Gabii, the city of Fidenae, and they will set citadels on the hills of Collatia, Pometia, Castrum Inui, Bola, and Cora.[112] Lands now nameless will take these names."

2.7.3 Festus, "Silvi"

*Festus explains the name "Silvius" in greater detail. His story goes back to at least the second century BCE, and foreshadows the main myth of **chapter 3**: generational disagreement over the throne, and the importance of the woods as a sanctuary.*

The Alban kings are called SILVI after the son of Lavinia. She was pregnant when Aeneas died. Afraid that her life and the life of her unborn child were in danger, she hid in the woods[113] and gave birth. After Ascanius died, Lavinia's son was restored to the throne, beating out his brother's son Iulus. This happened when they fought with each other over the kingdom.

2.7.4 (Anonymous), *On the Origin of the Roman People* 16

This passage explains why Ascanius was concerned about his popularity after Lavinia ran away. The complimentary depiction of Ascanius/Iulus is suggestive of family history.

Lavinia was pregnant by Aeneas. But she was afraid that Ascanius would chastise her, so she fled into the woods to a man named Tyrrhus,[114] the master of her father's flocks. There she gave birth to a boy, whom she named Silvius[115] after the sylvan location. But the Latins believed that Ascanius had secretly killed her, and their belief sparked immense hatred. It grew to the point that they threatened to overcome his power by force. Ascanius tried to absolve himself by swearing that he was innocent, but he got nowhere. So he asked them to wait while he investigated. Thus he managed to break up the crowd's anger a little bit, and promised great rewards to anyone who could find Lavinia. Soon she was found. Ascanius brought her to Lavinium with her son and honored her like a mother. This treatment soon won him back the people's favor, as Gaius Caesar writes, and similarly Sextus Gellius.

2.7.5   Servius, *On the Aeneid* 6.760–6.773

*Servius comments on passage **2.7.2**. His reasoning is worth your attention; it's a helpful model for ancient historical thought.*

THAT YOUNG MAN – YOU SEE HIM? – WHO SHINES WITH HIS PURE SPEAR. Aeneas, as Cato says, took Lavinia as his wife as soon as he came to Italy. Because of this Turnus was angry, and went to war – first with Latinus, then with Aeneas, but only after he had asked Mezentius for help. Turnus himself shows this, saying "he was enough to face both Trojans and Latins."[116] But, as I said earlier, Latinus died in the first war, and Turnus and Aeneas likewise died in the second, and later Ascanius killed Mezentius and took over Laurolavinium.[117] Lavinia was worried that Ascanius would trap her and ran away to the woods, even though she was pregnant. There she hid in the house of the shepherd Tyrrhus.[118] Vergil refers to this when he says "and father Tyrrhus, whom the royal herds obey."[119] There she gave birth to Silvius.[120] Ascanius was agitated by his unpopularity. He called his stepmother out of the forest and gave her Laurolavinium, founding Alba for himself. But Ascanius died without children, so he left Silvius (who was also named Ascanius) the kingdom. So there's a mistake in Livy[121] about which Ascanius founded Alba. Later the Alban kings were all called "Silvius" after the founder of the dynasty, just as today Roman emperors are called "Augustus," or Egyptian kings "Ptolemy" [...]

   NEXT IS PROCAS: as they stood in a row, not by birth; for he was the sixth king of the Albans, and Numitor was the thirteenth. IF EVER HE SHOULD ACCEPT THE RULE OF ALBA. Obviously Aeneas Silvius. Here he shows that all the Alban kings are called "Silvius." "Should accept" from his guardian, who usurped his rule; it was only restored to him when he was 53 [...] THESE MEN WILL SETTLE NOMENTUM. The cities he lists were founded by the Alban kings and are known as the Prisci Latini; although some say that Tarquin founded Collatia.[122] Its name comes from the fact that he was proud, so he founded it from the money he had *coll*ected. But it may also be true that it was founded by the Albans and enlarged by Tarquin, as I said earlier about Tarentum, which Taras made and Phalas enlarged.[123] And even Rome is said to have been made by Romulus, although Evander founded it earlier: thus "father Evander, founder of the Roman citadel."[124]

Conclusion

The question of whether Aeneas' arrival in Italy is an "original" Italian myth or a later development is unlikely to be resolved. A better question might be "does it matter?" Given that our sources consistently tell us that Aeneas (or his son Ascanius/Iulus) came to Italy to establish a city, we should instead consider why a Trojan hero was a good choice for the founder of Roman society. As we'll see in later chapters, the myth of a Greek or Trojan hero arriving in Italy after the Trojan War is hardly unique to Rome. Such founders immediately tapped into a cross-Mediterranean historical culture, while also offering unique virtues to a given city. Aeneas, for example, was known for his *pietas*, a complex virtue that goes beyond our sense of piety (respect for the gods) to encompass respect for fellow men, duty to family, and general moral excellence. As Rome grew more powerful, this collection of virtues immediately advertised that the city stood for justice and fair play. Such virtues were especially important in comparison to some of the city founder Romulus' less admirable characteristics, as we'll see in **chapter 3**.

Although most modern scholars admit that Aeneas is a mythical figure, he was not necessarily seen as fictional to the Romans. Aeneas' adventures in Italy form part of a long line of Roman "foundations" – and he is not the first. Roman society thus claimed to be both very old and relatively new at the same time. They were old because their presence in Italy goes back to Saturn, or the mythical "golden age" of man.[125] Yet they are new because each founding figure contributes something distinctive to Roman culture and society. Roman authors thus portray their society as continually under development and adapting to changes and new stimuli. We'll notice this theme again, and some ancient authors made it explicit (Cicero, *On the State* 2.21; Livy, *From the Foundation* 2.1). Although it may seem contradictory to us, to Roman authors the idea of adaptability sat comfortably with Rome's reverence for tradition.

This last point is worth emphasizing. You may have heard Rome praised as a "melting pot," a society that was unusually open to adopting and appropriating other cultures' features. In fact, this openness is often cited as a factor in

Rome's success in maintaining a large (and expanding) empire over the course of many centuries. Integration of mythic characters and motifs was one of the many ways that Rome made itself more familiar to other cultures – and made other cultures more familiar to Rome.

Notes

1. http://ancientrome.ru/art/artworken/img.htm?id=816
2. Pompeii: http://wps.ablongman.com/wps/media/objects/13624/13951532/image s23/Fig23.7.jpg and Ara Pacis: http://web.mit.edu/course/21/21h.402/www/ara pacis/images/aeneas_scene.jpg
3. Distinct from the *Lares,* also household gods, but often used interchangeably.
4. Native deities; see **1.1** on *numina.*
5. Compare the myth of Cronus in Hesiod's *Theogony* 453–506.
6. In Latin, *latere.*
7. Italian.
8. Natives of Sicily.
9. "Whitey"; compare *Alba* Longa.
10. "Muse."
11. See **note 5**.
12. See **2.2, 6.2**.
13. Later the indigenous inhabitants of Sicily.
14. An early Greek ethnic group that has not been identified.
15. Strabo here cites Homer, *Iliad* 13.460–461.
16. Strabo here cites a line of Sophocles from a lost play.
17. The Veneto. The Eneti are Antenor's people, as the "Trojans" are Aeneas'.
18. The oracle of the tables, described by Strabo here, is related in **2.4**.
19. Homer, *Iliad* 20.300–308.
20. Italus is the eponym of Italy, as Romulus is the eponym of Rome. Leucaria's name means "snow white" in Greek. She may be the same as Alba (**2.1.6**) or relate to Alba Longa (**2.7**).
21. Usually this child was named Telegonus; see Hesiod, *Theogony* 1011–1014.
22. Diomedes had strong connections with Italy, which may be why Plutarch mentions him here; see **6.3**.
23. The Tyrrhenians are Etruscans. For the Lydian origins of the Etruscans (much debated), see Herodotus 1.94.
24. The Greek word means "strength."
25. See **note 23**.
26. See **note 20**.
27. That is, "natives" – not a very apt name for Greek settlers!
28. "Strength" in Latin; compare the Greek etymology in **note 24**.
29. See **2.1.1, 2.2**.
30. A Trojan seer who escaped the destruction of the city; Aeneas visits him in Vergil's *Aeneid* book 3.
31. Trojans.
32. Lavinia is usually an Italian: **2.1.2, 2.3.2, 2.5.1, 2.5.3, 2.5.7**.
33. See **note 28**.

34. http://shot.holycross.edu/courses/hcimgs/2003.04.0033
35. See **3.3**.
36. A similar plot occurs in the *Homeric Hymn to Hermes*; Apollo is the victim.
37. A magical number.
38. The Ara Maxima, or "Greatest Altar."
39. Propertius improves on Vergil (**2.2.1**) by giving Cacus three heads like Geryon.
40. Jupiter.
41. See **note 37**.
42. The Forum Boarium.
43. Circe.
44. Collecting herbs was a typical activity for witches in Latin literature. See (e.g.) Horace, *Satires* 1.8.
45. See **note 37**.
46. "Picus" means "woodpecker" in Latin; see **6.5.2**.
47. See **note 42**.
48. Euhemerus was a Hellenistic (late fourth century/early third century BCE) Greek philosopher who considered all myths to be legendary history.
49. "Father Finder."
50. See **note 38**.
51. See **7.1.1, 7.1.4**.
52. Compare the story of Romulus and Remus at the Lupercalia: **3.2.3**.
53. Compare the stories of Tarchon in **4.4** and Tarquin of Rome in **5.4** and **5.6**.
54. Marsyas in Greek myth is a satyr who lost a musical contest with Apollo. He had a statue in the Roman Forum; it's not clear if Solinus' Marsyas is the same.
55. See **note 38**.
56. An alternative name for Nicostrata is Carmenta/Carmentis: see **note 10**.
57. See **4.4** for myths about Tarchon.
58. See **note 23**.
59. See **2.4**.
60. Central Italy.
61. Usually the sow is white: **2.4.1, 2.4.3, 2.4.4**.
62. A reference to the Trojan War.
63. Trojans.
64. Rivers near Troy.
65. Trojans.
66. Often used interchangeably with *Penates*.
67. See **3.3–3.4**.
68. Rome's central area was marshy until the drainage projects of the sixth century; see **5.6.3**.
69. Both Aeneas and Cupid are the sons of Venus.
70. See **2.6**.
71. Possibly a reference to rituals of the *Lares* at Lavinium.
72. Some scholars believe that this line is a mistake, because the exact same line appears at *Aeneid* 3.393.
73. It was already prophesied at *Aeneid* 3.388–92, in very similar words.
74. Another name for Lavinium.
75. http://ancientrome.ru/art/artworken/img.htm?id=3005
76. Note how closely the *Odyssey* is synchronized with the adventures of Aeneas.

77. Some Roman rituals required the sacrificant to have his head covered. See **6.3.5** for a different explanation of the custom.
78. Aeneas married Latinus' daughter Lavinia.
79. Aeneas.
80. Latinus, like Aeneas, has *Penates*; thus the Latins appear to be the same as the Trojans before they are formally unified.
81. Although Mezentius' name is Etruscan in origin, the character cannot be identified with a historical figure.
82. Etruscan.
83. Compare Aeneas' *pietas*.
84. This epithet, which is applied to Hector in the *Iliad*, suggests Vergil's sympathy for Lausus.
85. This passage, with its larger-than-life heroes, recalls Homer.
86. An inversion of Homer, *Iliad* 22.
87. Turnus' sister, the nymph Juturna, was the deity of a spring in Rome.
88. Italians.
89. Evander's son and under Aeneas' protection; Turnus had killed him in *Aeneid* 10. The "charms" are *bullae*, which Roman children in Vergil's day wore as protective charms until they reached puberty.
90. The rite takes place at the Vinalia (festival of wine) according to Latin-language sources. Scholars are not sure whether Veneralia (festival of Venus) is a mistake or a purposeful change to fit the goddess honored (Aphrodite/Venus).
91. See Smith (2010) and **chapter introduction**. The identification of Ascanius and Iulus is a way to glorify the Julian family, who claimed Iulus as an ancestor.
92. Note how Servius acknowledges the co-existence of multiple variants of the story even within a single poem.
93. Vergil, *Aeneid* 6.718.
94. In the *Aeneid*, Anchises dies before Aeneas reaches Italy.
95. The foundation date of Carthage is c. 815 BCE; Aeneas' travels were over 350 years earlier.
96. Servius here differs from the Varronian dating by a century.
97. This paragraph summarizes the second half of the *Aeneid*.
98. Other authors separate the "Turnus" who lived in Aeneas' time from Turnus Herdonius, a Latin in the era of Tarquin (**5.6.2a, 5.6.2c**).
99. Another name from Ascanius/Iulus.
100. In this version, the story of Mezentius and the vintage is several years after the death of Turnus.
101. Compare the myth of the Sacred Spring: **6.5**.
102. Cythera is a name for Venus; the "Cytherian hero" is Aeneas, Venus' son.
103. A reference to Aeneas' journey to the underworld in *Aeneid* 6.
104. See **note 74**.
105. See **2.5.4, 2.5.5**.
106. A Latin ally.
107. Livy's doubts about the truth behind this mythic ancestry offer us a clue to how Romans may have understood this story.
108. Silvius means "Woodsman," which explains the etymology.
109. Literally, "Old Latins." These were Rome's earliest allies. The Latins formed a distinct and archaeologically visible ethnic group ("Latial culture").
110. See **note 108**.

111. A reference to the civic crown (*corona civica*), which was granted to any citizen who saved a fellow citizen's life in battle.
112. The Prisci Latini: **note 109** and **2.7.5**.
113. In Latin, *silvae*, explaining the name Silvian.
114. "Tuscan"; compare **note 23**.
115. See **note 108**.
116. Vergil, *Aeneid* 7.470.
117. See **note 74**.
118. See **note 114**.
119. Vergil, *Aeneid* 7.485.
120. See **note 108**.
121. See **2.7.1**; given Livy's doubts, Servius is perhaps unfairly critical.
122. See **note 109** and **5.4.1c**.
123. See **6.1.4** (Phalas); Taras appears on the city's coinage (http://numismatics.org/collection/1967.152.17).
124. Vergil, *Aeneid* 8.313.
125. Compare the Biblical Eden.

References

Bickerman, Elias J. 1952. "Origines Gentium." *Classical Philology* 47: 65–81. http://www.jstor.org/stable/267375 (accessed November 21, 2016).

Erskine, Andrew. 2001. *Troy Between Greece and Rome: Local Tradition and Imperial Power.* Oxford: Oxford University Press.

Galinsky, Karl. 1969. *Aeneas, Sicily and Rome.* Princeton, NJ: Princeton University Press.

Gruen, Erich S. 1992. "The Making of the Trojan Legend." In *Culture and National Identity in Republican Rome*, by Erich S. Gruen, 6–51. Ithaca, NY: Cornell University Press. http://www.jstor.org/stable/10.7591/j.cttq44md (accessed November 21, 2016).

Horsfall, Nicholas. 1987. "The Aeneas Legend from Homer to Vergil." In *Roman Myth and Mythography*, by Nicholas Horsfall and Jan Bremmer, 21–24. London: Institute of Classical Studies.

Smith, Christopher John. 2010. "Caesar and the Early History of Rome." In *Cesare: Precursore o Visionario?* edited by G. Urso, 249–264. Pisa: Edizione ETS.

Further Reading

Cairns, Francis. 1989. *Virgil's Augustan Epic.* Cambridge: Cambridge University Press. Analyzes Aeneas as a regal figure. Although interested in the Aeneid as a work with imperial concerns, Cairns centers those concerns on the view of kingship in Rome. He argues that Aeneas is a good king, and that this positive valuation reflects well upon Augustus. Chapters 2–4 are particularly valuable for readers of this book.

Casali, Sergio. 2010. "The Development of the Aeneas Legend." In *A Companion to Vergil's Aeneid and its Tradition*, edited by Joseph Farrell and Michael C. J. Putnam, 37–51. Malden, MA: Wiley-Blackwell. Compares Vergil's account of Aeneas in Italy with other surviving accounts of the Aeneas legend. He examines how Vergil innovated and where he chose to stick closely to Roman traditions.

Cornell, Timothy J. 1975. "Aeneas and the Twins: The Development of the Roman
    Foundation Legend." *Proceedings of the Cambridge Philological Society (New Series)*: 1–
    21. http://dx.doi.org/10.1017/S0068673500003667 (accessed November 21, 2016).
    Offers a comprehensive analysis of the varying accounts of Aeneas' arrival in Italy,
    as well as other Greek founders. He argues that these myths can be reconciled with
    the Romulus myth (**chapter 3**).
Cornell, Timothy J. 1995. *The Beginnings of Rome: Italy and Rome from the Bronze Age
    to the Punic Wars (c. 1000–264 B.C.)*. London: Routledge. Offers valuable and detailed
    historical commentary for every chapter in this book. For Aeneas, see chapter 3, espe-
    cially pages 63–68.
Perkell, Christine (ed.). 1999. *Reading Vergil's Aeneid: An Interpretive Guide*. Norman,
    OK: University of Oklahoma Press. The *Aeneid* is the most comprehensive surviv-
    ing account of Aeneas' arrival in Italy. This collection of essays offers a book-by-book
    interpretation of the poem and compares Vergil's account with what we know from
    other sources.

3

Founding Rome

Introduction

Romulus and Remus are the characters from Roman legend who have the most presence in Rome today: the twins are depicted, suckling a she-wolf, on modern-day crests of Rome. Visitors to the city will see them on trash-cans, lampposts, and even in graffiti. The story has a long history: Roman coinage with the she-wolf and twins first appeared in the third century BCE.[1] But although this myth is famous, it's also controversial.

The basic story of the city's foundation explains why. Several generations had passed after the arrival of Aeneas (**chapter 2**). The 400-year gap between the arrival of Aeneas in the twelfth century BCE and the foundation of Rome (sometime in the mid-eighth century BCE, according to most of our sources) posed a problem for writers of histories, and over time became filled with the Alban kings (**2.7**). These kings began with Ascanius and ended with the brothers Amulius and Numitor. For the most part, there are no myths about these rulers. Most scholars believe that they were a late addition to Roman myth, and had few stories because Romans did not consider them culturally significant. But like Ascanius, Amulius and Numitor are developed characters.

These brothers both inherited Alba Longa after their father's death. A variety of stories existed about how they came to split the kingdom (**3.1**), but these variants agree on certain key points. First, Amulius gained political control of the city; second, his relationship with Numitor at some point soured; and third, the brothers' quarrel eventually expanded to include Numitor's daughter, whose name was both Ilia and Rhea Silvia. Most versions of this story state that this daughter was a Vestal Virgin,[2] a religious office that required women to remain abstinent for at least 30 years.

Rhea was getting water from a well when she was raped by an unknown man. Sexual violence, while perhaps no more common in antiquity than today, was often treated less seriously – at least in legendary history. Such lack of attention to the consequences of assault is not because Romans were unconcerned about rape, although it is important to recognize that their definition was not the same as ours.[3] Instead, myths involving sexual misconduct (including, but not limited to, rape) helped introduce divine agency into the narrative. Mortals couldn't marry gods, but gods could rape and impregnate mortal women. In this way, myths introduce half-divine children (sometimes called *heroes* or *demigods*) into the world. Foundation stories in particular often begin with rape. As Jan Bremmer (1987) has argued, cities are built upon "the mother's tragedy," meaning that the founder's mother must feel the birth pains of a new civilization in a variety of ways. Yet narratives rarely focus on the struggles of the raped woman (for a partial exception, see **7.6**). Instead, they center on the child.

Rhea's story follows this pattern. She becomes pregnant and delivers twins. It is therefore clear that she has broken her vow of virginity. Although she claims that the father is Mars, Amulius punishes her by throwing her into the Tiber river, along with her newborn children. Many authors are unconcerned with Rhea's fate, although some state that she married the river god and became a deity herself. But the children are the main focus of the story. These twins, Romulus and Remus, are abandoned by the banks of the Tiber. They were hungry and crying; the noise attracted a she-wolf. This wolf, instead of attacking the children, gave them her own teats to suck on. The shepherds working nearby were amazed. One of them, Faustulus, took the twins home, and raised them with his wife, Acca Larentia. Although this story seems unlikely, it shares its basic narrative with other Mediterranean myths (comparison with Cyrus the Great of Persia comes as early as Michelet 1831, 59–61).

The twins grew up as shepherds, but somehow learned of their royal background. They got in touch with their grandfather, Numitor, and organized a coup to avenge their family. Their attack was successful: Amulius was killed in the battle, and Numitor took over the throne of Alba Longa. But Romulus' and Remus' adventures weren't done. They set out to found their own city, which was the future Rome. Soon, however, they began to fight, either over the location, the name, or who would be the actual founder of the city. To solve their argument, they took auspices, a Roman type of divination that was based on watching the flight of birds (among other things). They expected that the result would be a clear "winner": one twin would receive a successful omen, while the other would receive a negative sign. But each twin received a good omen. Romulus claimed that his were better and that the gods favored him. This is debatable, and in some narratives led to war.

In other narratives, the settlers accepted the outcome and began to build Rome. Again an argument broke out between the twins, but this time it was more serious: Remus ended up dead. Romulus buried his brother and went on building. If this behavior sounds insensitive to you, it did to many Romans as well; Romulus' reaction to his brother's death has been a serious problem in classical scholarship since antiquity. Romulus could be described in such negative terms that some scholars believe the story was invented by an anti-Roman source and accepted by the Romans out of pride or desperation (Strassburger 1968); others point out similarities to other foundation legends (Roller 1996), or change over time (ver Eecke 2008; Neel 2014); still others suggest that the foundation story was closely connected to the "Conflict of the Orders," Rome's longest internal political dispute (Wiseman 1995). Certainly the door is not closed on this major interpretive issue. The narrative that we have, however, centers on Roman themes and cultural practices (such as the auspices), even if some Romans found it distasteful. It has not been adopted wholesale from any culture; it may have been substantially adapted to fit Rome's needs.

After the city was finished, Romulus established many important laws and customs. He set up an asylum for criminals, slaves, and exiles, who would be welcomed in Rome. This asylum reinforces the idea, introduced in **chapter 2**, that Rome was a "melting pot" even from its very earliest stages. Romulus also tried to gain new citizens. The most famous example of this was the rape of the Sabine women (in this case, "rape" is used in its old-fashioned sense: these women were kidnapped and forced to marry). Neighboring cities, upset by this kidnapping, attacked Rome. This war with the Sabines included many memorable episodes, such as the taking of the spolia (**3.5.2**), the treason of Tarpeia (**7.4**), and the naming of the Lacus Curtius (**2.5.1, 8.6.1**). At the end, Romulus and the Sabine king Titus Tatius made a peace treaty and jointly ruled Rome.

At some later date, Titus Tatius died and Romulus ruled on his own. Some scholars have seen a repetition of the Romulus and Remus story here, but this parallel wasn't noted in antiquity. Instead, according to some texts, Romulus' rule became cruel and tyrannical at this point. The senators, senior statesmen whom Romulus himself had appointed, conspired to kill him. In some versions, they succeed; in others, Romulus simply dies and is deified, much like Aeneas before him. He has no children.

The Romulus story shares themes with the Aeneas legend. Both Romulus and Aeneas are the sons of a major divinity (Venus or Mars); both undergo trials to establish their city; both steal their wives (Aeneas takes Lavinia from Turnus, while Romulus marries one of the Sabine women). These similarities, while not unique to Rome, suggest that Romans considered these themes important for a foundation story. To the Romans, Romulus held continuing significance as a lawgiver, as well as founder of many city festivals, sites, and customs. But he remained only one of many founding figures. The idea that "Rome wasn't built in a day" would have been familiar to a Roman reader from at least the second century BCE onwards.

Several aspects of the Romulus story are also common to world myth. His mother's rape and subsequent murder set the stage for his later glory. His humble background – hiding the king he was and would become – is also a common feature in Greek foundation legends, as well as stories found in the Near East (Lincoln 1975 and 1976). Even the fratricide has parallels in other societies' cosmogonies (see Puhvel 1975). But it's also important to stress that Romulus is thoroughly intertwined with Roman culture. While pointing to parallels is useful and helps "fill out" the back history of the myth, it should not be substituted for trying to understand the Romulus saga in its Roman context (Beard 1993). By examining many different versions of the Romulus narrative in this chapter, you'll be able to do just that.

For Further Thought

1. How would you characterize the myth of Romulus and Remus? Does it reflect well on Roman society? Be prepared to defend your answers.

2. Are there themes in the various stories about Romulus (with or without Remus)? What about similarities between Romulus and Aeneas? What might these themes and similarities suggest about Roman culture?

3. Romulus has been called an "aetiological figure" (Pausch 2008), meaning that his life story was strongly connected with important sites and locations throughout the city. Try to imagine what the experience of walking through Rome might have been. How might you learn about and reinterpret Romulus' deeds as you interacted with the city? Can you think of any parallels in modern societies?

TEXTS
3.1 Conception, Birth, and Exposure

The contest between Amulius and Numitor for the throne sets the stage for their grandsons' attempt to rule and offers a bridge between the Alban kings (**2.7**) and the kings of Rome. It foreshadows the conflict between Romulus and Remus (**3.3–3.4**) and echoes the conflicts between Aeneas and Turnus and Ascanius and Silvius (**2.5, 2.7**). The idea of a "family curse" (**2.3.5**) can also be found in Greek myth (for example, the House of Atreus), as well as later Roman myths (the Tarquins: **5.4–5.6**). Several authors were preoccupied with the "bad" ruler, and such myths offered numerous ways to distinguish good rulership from bad.

You'll notice that the stories about the twins' birth are among the most detailed and varied myths in this book. These variants suggest the importance of the story for Roman self-definition.

3.1.1 Ennius, *Annals* 34–50

*In this fragment, Ilia wakes up from a nightmare and tells her sister and nurse about her dream. Although we can't know where this scene fit into Ennius' fragmentary poem, it seems to be early in Ilia's life. Ennius' account reveals several differences from the version we see later, including a sister, no brother, apparently no uncle, and no Alban kings (see **note 5**). But be careful: some of these differences may be due to our limited knowledge of the poem.*

Quickly, the old woman brought a lamp with her trembling hands. Weeping and frightened awake, the girl related her dream: "Eurydice,[4] my sister whom our father[5] loved, now all strength and life has left my body. An amazingly beautiful[6] man appeared to me among the peaceful willows. He grabbed me and took me to the riverbank and strange new places.[7] A little later, dear sister, I seemed to wander alone, following you slowly and looking for you, but I couldn't reach you with my heart. The ground didn't support my feet. Then our father seemed to address me out loud, in these words: 'Daughter, you must endure misfortunes. But later good fortune will return, rising from the river.'[8] So our father spoke, sister. Then immediately he sank back and didn't return to view, although I desired it in my heart. Many times I raised my hands to the blue expanse of the sky, weeping, and I called him back with loving words. Then at once sleep left me, sick at heart."

3.1.2 Livy, *From the Foundation* 1.3–1.4

*Livy continues his review of early Roman history (for the beginning, see **2.5.1** and **2.7.1**). In this section, he records the miraculous birth of the twins.*

Numitor was the older son, so he inherited the ancient kingdom of the Silvian family. But violence is stronger than a father's wishes or the respect owed to age: Amulius kicked his brother out and took the throne. He piled up crime upon crime. First he killed his brother's only son; then he chose his niece, Rhea Silvia, for a Vestal. This was an empty show of honor. Because she would have to remain a virgin, Amulius took away her hope of bearing children.

But in my opinion the beginning of so great a city, and the origin of the greatest power (second only to divine force), is owed to fate. The Vestal was assaulted and gave birth to twins. She claimed that Mars was the father of her illegitimate children, either because she really believed it or because it was more honorable to pin the blame on a god.[9] But neither gods nor men could save her or the children from the king's cruelty. He kept the priestess in chains under guard, and commanded his men to throw the children into the river. But by divine favor, the Tiber had flooded. Water stood pooled up beyond the banks, barely moving. It was impossible to reach the flowing course of the river, but they were babies – they could drown even in lazy water. At least, that was the hope of those carrying them. So they exposed the boys on a nearby floodplain, where the Ruminalis fig is today (they say it was called "Romularis" once), and left as if they had carried out the king's orders.

In those days, this area was a deserted bramble. The boys had been exposed in a basket. The story goes that when a trickle of water carried the floating basket to dry land, a thirsty she-wolf turned her wandering path out of the surrounding mountains towards the children. She offered them her pendulous teats and gently licked them clean. This was how the chief shepherd of the king, Faustulus, found them. He took the boys up to his hut to be raised by his wife Larentia.[10]

There are those who think that Larentia was called a "she-wolf" among the shepherds because she slept around. This, they say, is how the myth about the miracle got started.

3.1.3   Justin, *Epitome of Pompeius Trogus* 38.6.7–38.6.8

Mithridates, king of Pontus near the Black Sea, is giving a speech. His hostile take on Rome's myths shows how an enemy could interpret the foundation, especially the she-wolf.

"That city claims that their law is to hate all kings. For sure! Because they've had kings whose very names would make them blush: Aboriginal shepherds,[11] Sabine diviners, Corinthian exiles, or Etruscan slaves and servants.[12] The most honorable among them is the one they call 'Proud.' And even they admit that their first founders nursed at the teats of a wolf. So the entire populace has the spirit of wolves: insatiable for blood, greedy for control and wealth, and hungry for more."

3.1.4   Dionysius of Halicanassus, *Roman Antiquities* 1.76.1–1.79.3

Dionysius suggests a number of possible alternatives for the twins' birth. His narrative is elaborate, but the key elements of the narrative remain clear: the enmity of Amulius and Numitor, Ilia/Rhea's rape, and the exposure of the twins.

Amulius [...] plotted to end Numitor's family line. He did this because he feared retribution and wanted to rule forever. After he'd made this plan, he first kept his eye on Aegestus, Numitor's son, who had just reached adulthood. Amulius set an ambush in a deserted part of Aegestus' usual hunting grounds. When Aegestus went out to hunt, Amulius killed him and claimed that bandits had done it. But this establishment opinion couldn't overpower the silenced truth; despite the danger, many dared to discuss the murder. Numitor knew about it, but pretended not to; he yielded to logic, not emotion, and decided to set his anger aside for a safer time.

Amulius, seeing that the young man's death had met with no outcry, next did the following: Numitor's daughter Ilia (some writers call her Rhea Silvia) was at the ideal age for marriage. Amulius made her a priestess of Hestia, so that she couldn't marry and bear children to avenge her family. These holy maidens must remain pure and chaste for at least five[13] years, during which time they guard the everlasting flame [...] But in her fourth year Ilia was going into Ares' holy grove for pure water to use at sacrifices, and she was raped in the enclosure. Some say that the attacker was an admirer who couldn't contain his love; others say it was Amulius himself, who attacked not from desire but by design, and so dressed in armor [...]; but most say that it was the statue of the god to whom the grove was dedicated [...]

Amulius, either because he knew what had happened or because he suspected something like it, made inquiries. The girl had been missing from sacrifices for a while. Amulius kept on sending trustworthy doctors to find out why. When the women claimed that the disease was off-limits to men, Amulius made his own wife guard Ilia. This woman used her intuition to discover what had been hidden and betrayed the girl's trouble. Amulius ordered an armed guard for Ilia, since she was close to delivery and he didn't want her pregnancy to be kept secret. Then he summoned Numitor to a council meeting and informed everyone of Ilia's seduction (which had been secret up to now). He accused the girl's parents of helping her and commanded Numitor to reveal the culprit openly. Numitor replied that the whole story was news to him; he was completely innocent [...]

While they were arguing, the men assigned to guard Ilia's labor appeared and announced that she'd given birth to twin boys. Immediately Numitor said [...] that the deed was divine,[14] and begged them not to harm his blameless daughter. But to Amulius it seemed clear that some human trick had taken place: the women had supplied another baby, either with or without the guards' knowledge [...] The council, seeing that the king's mind was made up with implacable anger, made their decision as he asked. They declared that the defiled priestess must beaten with sticks and put to death, as the law required, while her children would be drowned in the river [...] Some say the girl was executed immediately; others say that she survived in a secret dungeon, which made people think she'd been killed. These authors add that Amulius' daughter begged him to save her cousin's life. They'd been raised together and were the same age, so they loved each other like sisters.[15] Amulius granted the request because she was his only daughter.

3.1.5 Dionysius of Halicanassus, *Roman Antiquities* 1.84.2–1.84.5

Some people thought the story of Mars, wolf, and salvation is ridiculous. Dionysius reports this "rational" narrative as well, aiming to explain the myth in more human terms.

They say that when Numitor learned of Ilia's pregnancy, he found other newborns and switched the babies at birth. He gave the purchased babies to the guards to take away; either he'd bribed the guards or plotted the swap with the midwives. Once Amulius had the fakes, he did away with them somehow. But Numitor gave Ilia's children to Faustulus in an effort to save them. This Faustulus was an Arcadian, descended from the men who'd come with Evander, and lived on the Palatine taking care of Amulius' sheep. His brother Faustinus, who watched Numitor's cattle near the Aventine, persuaded Faustulus to raise the children as a favor to Numitor. And the female who nursed the children at her breast was not a she-wolf, but a woman who lived with Faustulus. Her name was Larentia, but she was nicknamed "the she-wolf" because at one time she'd been a prostitute [...] When the twins could eat solids, their parents sent them to Gabii, a city near the Palatine, for a Greek education. They lived with friends of Faustulus and studied literature, music, and tactics until they reached adulthood.

3.1.6 Ovid, *Fasti* 2.383–2.420

*Unlike **3.1.1–3.1.5**, Ovid's account of the twins' birth delights in the miraculous aspects of the story. He's trying to amuse you; does it work?*

The Vestal Silvia gave birth to her divinely-conceived twins while her uncle ruled the kingdom. He ordered the newborns to be dragged out and killed in the river. What are you doing? One of those will be Romulus. His servants reluctantly carried out his orders, although they wept as they did. They brought the twins to a deserted spot. The river Albula, which got the name "Tiber" when it swallowed King Tiberinus in the waves, was luckily swollen with winter floods. Here, where the Forum is now, you could see boats bobbing;[16] so too in the valley of the Circus Maximus. When the men reached this place, they couldn't go any further. So one of them turned and said to the other, "Don't they look just like each other? Each one is *so* cute! But this one is stronger.[17] If your face reveals your parentage, if looks don't lie, I think there's a bit of the gods in *you*. But if some god *was* your father, he'd bring you help at a dangerous time like this. Your mother would help for sure, but she needs help herself. She's become a mother only to lose her children the same day. Twins you are: born together, you'll die together; together your bodies will sink beneath the waves."

He stopped talking and put the boys down on the riverbank. They both wailed identically; you'd have thought they knew exactly what was going on. The servants returned with wet cheeks.

The hollow basket lifted the boys up on top of the waves. Oh dear! Such a small boat for such great fortune! The basket pushed them into the mud near a shady wood, and gradually the waters receded. The Romularis fig (now called "Ruminalis") was there. A miracle: a she-wolf approached the exposed twins. Who would believe that a beast wouldn't harm babies? Not only did she not harm them, but she helped them out. She had recently given birth, and fed them – even though their own relatives had tried to kill them. As she stood there, she nuzzled her sweet nurslings with her tail and licked their twin bodies. You could see that they were Mars' children. They had no fear, but grabbed the teats and guzzled the milk that was meant for another.

3.1.7   Plutarch, *Life of Romulus* 2–4

Plutarch's account of the twins' birth has been interpreted as referring to an old Italian tradition (see 5.4.3b–5.4.3d). The story of Ilia is certainly unusual! Other aspects of his account fit more clearly into the traditions we've seen so far.

Some claim that [Romulus] was the son of Aeneas and Dexithea, the daughter of Phorbas,[18] that he came into Italy as a child, and that his brother was Romus. They were left to die in a basket in the flood-plains of the river. The children drifted onto the soft bank in the basket, unharmed, and from their unexpected salvation the place was called "Rome."[19] Others say Roma, the daughter of some Trojan, was married to Telemachus' son Latinus; she gave birth to Romulus. Others say Aemilia,[20] the daughter of Aeneas and Lavinia, was raped by Mars.

Some let slip entirely imaginary stories about their birth. For example, that a divine phantom appeared in the house of Tarchetius, a fierce and savage king of the Albans.[21] It took the shape of a phallus, appeared in the hearth, and remained there for many days.[22] Tarchetius sought the advice of the oracle of Tethys in Tyrrhenia.[23] The oracle said that a virgin would have to sleep with the phantom.[24] A very famous child would be born from their union, and would abound in valor, good fortune, and strength. After he heard the oracle, Tarchetius confided in one of his daughters and commanded her to sleep with the phallus. But she was too proud and sent a slave in her place. When Tarchetius found out about the switch, he was upset and sentenced both women to death. But Hestia[25] appeared to him in a dream, warning him against murder. So he commanded the women to weave a blanket while they were in jail, and said that whenever they finished, he would marry them off.

So they wove throughout the day. But each night other women unraveled the work,[26] obeying Tarchetius' command. Meanwhile the slave-woman gave birth to the twins she had conceived via the phantom. Tarchetius handed them over to a man named Teratius and told him to destroy them. Teratius brought them to the banks of a river and left them there. But a she-wolf who lived in the neighborhood offered them her teats, and many different types of birds flocked to the babies and put crumbs of food in their mouths. The animals did this until a shepherd, seeing them, was amazed and dared to come closer and rescue the children. So they were saved. When they grew up, they attacked Tarchetius and overthrew him. This is what Promathion relates in his *Italian History*.

But the story that has the greatest credibility and the most authoritative supporters is the following. Diocles of Peparethus was the first Greek to write it, and Fabius Pictor[27] followed him for the most part. There are some differences, but the basics are as follows. The kings of Alba were descended from Aeneas. Succession fell to two brothers, Numitor and Amulius. When Amulius proposed dividing their entire inheritance into two parts, the kingship and its resources or the gold from Troy, Numitor chose the kingship. So Amulius had the money, and was more powerful than Numitor because of his wealth. He easily usurped the throne. But he was afraid that Numitor's daughter would have children, so he appointed her a priestess of Hestia. This position forced her to be an unmarried virgin forever. Some authors say that her name was Ilia, while others call her Rhea or Silvia.

Not much time passed before her pregnancy was detected. Pregnancy is against the ordained law of this priesthood. The king's daughter Antho[28] begged and pleaded with her father not to do anything drastic, so Ilia wasn't killed. Instead she was kept under house arrest and didn't participate in daily life, so that Amulius would know the minute she gave birth.

She delivered twin boys, exceptionally big and attractive. And so Amulius was all the more nervous. He ordered an aide to expose the children in the river. Some say this man's name was Faustulus, but others say no, that was the man who rescued them. In any case, this aide put the newborns in a basket, set it down beside the river, and gave it a push. Seeing that the river rippled with many waves and the water was rough, he was afraid to go in himself [...]

At that point, they say that a she-wolf approached the babies as they were lying there and nursed them. A woodpecker was there, too, to help feed and guard them. These animals are considered sacred to Ares, and the Latins particularly worship and honor woodpeckers.[29] So there was some confidence in the mother's statement that the babies were Ares' sons. And yet some say that their mother was deceived in this belief, and was in fact raped by Amulius, who appeared to her with his weapons and grabbed her. Others say that the story took a mythological turn because of the name of the nurse; in Latin the word "she-wolf" (*lupa*) is ambiguous. They call female wolves "she-wolves," but the same word means "prostitute." The wife of Faustulus, who nursed the babies, was such a woman. Her name was Acca Larentia,[30] and the Romans make sacrifices to her.

——— 3.1.8 Festus, "Romulus and Remus" and "Rome" ———

Festus shows full awareness of Greek etymologies for Rome's name (2.1). He associates the etymology with the twins as well as Aeneas; compare 2.1.6 and 2.1.8.

ROMULUS and REMUS are named for their vigor: that is, their strength. Romulus named ROME after himself, but chose "Rome" rather than "Romula" because he thought that the broader meaning of the name [i.e., connecting Rome to strength] would signal a more prosperous future.

3.2 Youth of Romulus and Remus

As young men, Romulus and Remus led their own band of shepherds, which came into conflict with rival groups of herders. These raids involved theft, some violence, and eventually kidnapping. The idea that Romulus and Remus are "bandits," while surprising to a modern audience, is consistent with our evidence for Iron Age Italy (see **4.1** and **4.6** for some archaeological support). The stories about livestock rustling thus may preserve memories of early Italian social structures. These youthful bands offered quasi-military training for young men (as in Greece: see Vidal-Naquet 1998, especially pp. 129–158; Alföldi 1974, 107–150; **8.7**). The contest of the shepherds also foreshadows Romulus and Remus' desire for supremacy among their own men. This struggle will repeat itself in the myth of the foundation auspices and end in Remus' death (**3.3, 3.4**).

The conflict between Amulius' and Numitor's men distinguishes Remus from Romulus for the first time: Remus is captured, while Romulus is not. This moment of division was repeated in the yearly Lupercalia festival. The association of the twins with this festival, which took place in mid-February, is consistently noted, but not well understood. Perhaps the tale of Remus' capture was retold at the rite.

———— 3.2.1   Diodorus Siculus, *Library of History* 8.3–8.4   ————

*Diodorus related only the most important features of Roman myth. His accounts are sometimes idiosyncratic. Here, he seems to suggest that the twins were not identical (contrast **3.1.6**). The order "Remus and Romulus" is traditional (Wiseman 1995).*

Numitor was robbed of the kingship by his own brother, Amulius. He ruled the Albans. When he recognized his grandsons Remus and Romulus far beyond his hopes, he advised them to put an end to his own brother.[31] And they did. Sending for the shepherds, they rushed to the palace, forced their way through the gates, and killed those who resisted. Their final deed was killing Amulius himself.

Now these two had been exposed, and after some time had passed they grew up into young men. But they differed from each other very much in appearance and in strength. And that is how they offered safety to all the flocks, easily driving away bandits. They killed many who attacked them and took a few alive.

In rivalry over this, they began to canvass the shepherds individually and in a friendly way. Making small talk, each showed in his own way that he was moderate and sociable to anyone who needed him. So the safety of everyone lay in their hands. Most people obeyed the twins and carried out their orders, assembling in the appointed places.

3.2.2   Livy, *From the Foundation* 1.5

---

*Livy describes Remus' capture at the Lupercalia. Romulus defends himself successfully, which may hint at the idea that he is the "stronger" twin (**3.1.6**).*

The ritual was common knowledge. Some bandits, who were angry at losing plunder, ambushed the twins as they were celebrating it. Romulus was able to defend himself by force of arms, but Remus was captured and taken to King Amulius as a hostage. Their complaint was, for the most part, that Remus and his brother attacked Numitor's fields, and carried off plunder with their hand-picked band– like enemy attackers, not young shepherds. So Remus was sent to Numitor for punishment.

But even from his first encounter with them, Faustulus had hoped that his adopted children were royals. He knew about the twins who'd been exposed at the king's command, and he knew too that the time when he'd rescued his children matched closely. Still, he didn't want to reveal the matter too early, unless a good time arose or it was absolutely necessary. Necessity came first: driven by fear, he confided in Romulus.

It just so happened that Numitor had Remus under guard and heard that he had a twin brother. Comparing the prisoner's age and his attitude – hardly that of a slave – he was reminded of his grandchildren. After asking around, he was at the point of officially recognizing Remus as his grandson. So a net was woven around the king from all sides.

Romulus didn't approach the city with a pack of young men. His forces weren't strong enough for an open attack. But he told some of his shepherds to take one road, others to go a different way: at a set time they would meet at the palace to attack. Similarly, Remus gathered troops from Numitor's household and helped out. So they killed the king.

3.2.3   Ovid, *Fasti* 2.361–2.380

---

*Ovid explains the mythic history behind the Lupercalia, omitting Remus' capture. His description, especially Romulus' laugh, has caused confusion. Reconciling Ovid's version with Livy's (**3.2.2**) is impossible; you may want to consider what that impossibility suggests about Roman myth.*

A nanny-goat was sacrificed to hoofed Faunus, as usual. The crowd came when called to the scanty feast. Around noon, the priests skewered the guts with willow twigs. Romulus, his brother, and the young shepherds were exercising in the sunny field. They were playing around with poles, javelins, and slings for practice when a shepherd ran down the hill. "Romulus, Remus! Thieves are driving off the cattle!"

Putting on armor would take too long. Each one peeled off in a different direction. Remus retrieved the cattle on his way. When he got back, he took the sizzling tripe off of the skewers and crowed, "Only the winner will eat *these*!" He and the Fabii devoured the food.

Romulus arrived after a wasted effort. He saw the empty tables and bare bones. He laughed ruefully: the Fabii and Remus won, but his own Quintilii had not. When the *luperci* run without togas, they recall these events.

3.2.4   Plutarch, *Life of Romulus* 6–8

Plutarch's account of Remus' capture and the restoration of Numitor is dramatic, but inconsistent. Note especially the contradiction between Numitor's funding of the twins' education and his failure to recognize Remus – a sign that Plutarch has combined several (lost) narratives into his own.

Faustulus, Amulius' swineherd, rescued the babies and kept it a secret – at least this is what those who give the more likely accounts say. Numitor was aware of the rescue and secretly helped raise the children by sending supplies. They say that the boys learned their ABCs and other lessons that are typical for noblemen at Gabii [...][32] Indeed, their noble birth was immediately visible from their bodies, even as infants, because of their size and appearance. As they grew up, both were active and manly. They were entirely unafraid to try strange new things. But Romulus seemed a little wiser and more politic. When negotiating with his neighbors about grazing and hunting, his suggestions were those of a leader, not a follower.

That is why Romulus and Remus were adored by fellow herdsmen and people of lower status. But the twins didn't think much of the overseers, commanders, and chief shepherds of the king; they thought these men were no better than they were themselves. So they ignored their boasting and anger. They enjoyed their daily routines and their downtime like noblemen: they didn't care for free time or laziness. Instead they exercised, chased beasts and robbers, raced each other, captured thieves, and helped men who were wrongfully attacked. So they became famous for these deeds.

One day a fight broke out between the herdsmen of Numitor and those of Amulius, and some of the cattle were captured. The youths didn't hesitate to attack them or make other side run away, and they seized a large part of the herd. They weren't really concerned about irritating Numitor. Instead, they gathered together and accepted into their companionship many poor people and many slaves.[33] Thus they showed the beginnings of a courageous rebellion and spirit.

Romulus was returning from sacrifice (he was quite religious and spiritual) when Numitor's herdsmen ran into Remus, who was taking a walk with a few men. A fight broke out, and men were wounded on both sides. But Numitor's men won, and Remus was taken captive [...] Meanwhile Faustulus gathered up the basket[34] and went to Numitor, hurried and full of fear. He wanted to arrive at just the right moment.

But the guards at the palace gate doubted him, and Faustulus' confused answers to their questions raised their suspicions even more. They could see that he was hiding a basket under his cloak, too. One of them by chance had been the man who exposed the twins. Seeing the basket, he immediately recognized its bronze straps and its letters, and he took a guess at who Faustulus was. Recognizing that this was a serious matter, he went straight to tell the king and brought Faustulus for questioning.

In these desperate straits, Faustulus didn't exactly keep himself from being harassed, but he didn't spill the beans, either. He admitted that the children had been saved, but said that they were now shepherds far away from Alba. He claimed that he had come to bring the basket to Ilia, who often desired to see and touch it as firmer proof of her children. Amulius responded as men who are confused and acting with fear or anger tend to respond. He quickly sent an underling who was close to Numitor to find out whether Numitor had heard anything about the twins' survival. When the man arrived and saw that Remus was not at all in danger but was quite close to Numitor, he reaffirmed their beliefs. He strongly recommended that they lay claim to the state, and at once joined them.

The time was right, and they didn't want to delay. Romulus was already nearby, and he had with him many citizens who hated and feared Amulius. He led a large force with him, arranged in battle formation [...] Remus attacked from the inside, Romulus from the outside. The tyrant couldn't take any action or advice to save himself; all was lost and in confusion. So he was overcome and died [...]

3.3 Rome's Foundation

After killing Amulius, Romulus and Remus gave Alba to Numitor. Despite the fact that they're his heirs, they decide to found a new city. But they argue over the name and location. The logic behind this argument isn't clear to us, but it is consistent. To settle the dispute, Romulus and Remus seek divine favor through augury, a form of divination that involves watching birds. Augury was an important part of Roman public life: magistrates observed the birds before elections and battles. Romulus' success establishes him as Rome's military and religious leader. But the choice of Romulus isn't immediately obvious: augury was supposed to provide a yes-or-no answer, which should have ended the controversy immediately. Instead, sources provide us with a "contest" in which Remus sees a positive sign, followed by Romulus' even better sign. Greek versions suggest that Romulus cheated, while unorthodox variants such as Egnatius (**3.4.7**) may envision a much different struggle for power than the traditional accounts of Romulus' supremacy. As our complete accounts make clear, the preferred tradition emphasized Romulus' victory – and his ambition.

3.3.1 Ennius, *Annals* 72–91

This passage is the second long fragment from Ennius' epic (for the first, see **3.1.1**). *Ennius describes the ritual to determine the founder of the city. Auspices and augury are separate (but related) rituals; Ennius' inclusion of both is unusual, but accurate.*

Putting in great effort and desperate for kingship, they turned their attention to auspices and augury at the same time. On one hill,[35] Remus settled down to the auspices and waited by himself for a favorable bird. But blessed[36] Romulus was watching on the tall Aventine,[37] seeking the high-flying type. They were arguing over whether to call the city "Rome" or "Remora." Everyone was anxious to know which would be the leader. Their followers were waiting – like when a consul is about to give the signal and everyone eagerly looks at the gates of the track to see how soon the painted chariots will rush past the barrier. This is how the people were waiting. Fear was written all over their faces: which twin would win and gain control over the kingdom? In the meantime, the white sun set into the depths of night. Then the bright light returned, striking out with its rays. At the same time, an exceptionally lucky bird flew in from on high, far away and taking the left-hand route. At exactly the same time, the golden sun rose. A group of four consecrated birds flew down from the sky, then a second, then a third. All 12 winged their way to favorable and fortunate places. Romulus saw from this that he alone had been given a royal throne and the foundation solidified by the auspices.[38]

——————   3.3.2 Fragment of Cassius Hemina (*FRHist* 6 F14)   ——————

*Hemina's account envisions a period of peaceful joint rule between Romulus and Remus. Surprisingly, he moves the sow prodigy (**2.4.1, 2.4.3–2.4.5**) to the foundation of the city.*

The mob of shepherds, in agreement and without argument, voted authority to Romulus and Remus equally so that they could figure out the kingdom between themselves. A prodigy appeared. A sow gave birth to 30 piglets. For this reason they made a shrine.

——————   3.3.3 Diodorus Siculus, *Library of History* 8.5   ——————

Diodorus' account of the auspices, like most Greek versions, emphasizes Romulus' trickery. It centers on a cultural misunderstanding that's difficult to translate. Greeks and Romans understood their omens in entirely opposite ways. For a Roman, omens coming in from the left were favorable and omens from the right unfavorable; for a Greek, the significance was reversed. So an "omen from the right" is a bad sign – but also good, for Diodorus' Greek reader.

Romulus and Remus were watching birds to determine the founder of the city. An omen came in from the right side.[39] They say that Remus was shocked and called out to his brother. He said that often in this city good fortune would result from awkward planning.[40] For Romulus had hastily sent out his messenger and made a complete mistake about the part of the sky that concerned him. But his ignorance corrected itself.

——————   3.3.4 Cicero, *On the State* 2.4–2.5   ——————

The absence of Remus in this account is notable, but may be due to Cicero's desire to present Rome as an ideal state, without conflict. The idea that the defeat of Amulius is "documented fact" is at odds with most modern historical judgment.

When [Romulus] offered himself as their general, they overcame Alba Longa with these troops, even though it was a strong and powerful city in those days. At this point, we've come from fables to documented facts. It's said too that Romulus killed King Amulius. They also add that

after this glorious deed, Romulus for the first time considered founding
a city by auspices and establishing a state. The location of a city is a
matter which a would-be founder must consider with due diligence if
he wants his state to last. Romulus chose with unbelievably good taste.
You see, he didn't head to the sea. With his men and resources, it was
very easy to absorb the land of the Rutuli or Aborigines. He also didn't
found his city at Ostia, where many years later King Ancus established a
colony. Instead, Romulus noticed with excellent foresight that seaside
locations were not ideal for cities that had been founded for the long
haul in hope of empire. The sea is bad mainly because such cities are
not only open to many dangers but also blind [...]

3.3.5   Livy, *From the Foundation* 1.6–1.7

*Livy's account makes it clear that the twins' rivalry led to violence. The idea of
their "family curse" may originate with him.*

Once the Alban government had been returned to Numitor, desire
gripped Romulus and Remus: they wanted to found a city in the area
where they had been exposed and raised. There were very many Albans
and Latins, and then the shepherds were added to the mix, too. So
everyone easily hoped that Alba and Lavinium would become small on
account of the city that would be founded. The twins' family curse[41] –
the desire to rule – crept in among these thoughts. A shameful struggle
rose from a relatively mild beginning.

Because they were twins, it was impossible to make a decision about
who would rule on the basis of age. So it was decided that the gods who
protected those places would choose between the two, and the means
of decision would be augury. The questions: who would give his name
to the new city, and who would rule the city with absolute power once
it was founded.[42] So Romulus went to the Palatine and Remus went to
the Aventine to take auguries.

It's said that a sign came to Remus first: six vultures. But as soon as
the augury was announced, twice that number appeared to Romulus.
So each twin was hailed king by his gang of adherents. Remus claimed
that he had seen the *first* birds, while Romulus claimed that he had
seen *more*: the kingship, each said, belonged to *him*.[43] Up to this point,
they'd fought with their words; now, as their argument grew heated,
they turned to violence.[44] There, in the crowd, Remus was struck down
and died. The more common version is that Remus jumped across the
new walls to taunt his brother. At that point, angry, Romulus shouted,

"May it be the same for anyone else who jumps over my walls," and killed him.

In any case, Romulus alone gained command of the city; it was founded and named after its founder. The first place he walled was the Palatine, on which he had been reared.

------------- 3.3.6   Ovid, *Fasti* 4.809–4.826 -------------

Ovid's account glosses over any hint of discord. The foundation rite that he describes has Etruscan origins and is the first step in establishing the city's sacred boundary (pomerium). *The episode continues at **3.4.5**.*

Now Numitor's brother had paid the price and the entire crowd of shepherds was under the leadership of the twins. They agreed to gather the rustics and build walls – but which would be founder? This was in doubt. Romulus said, "There's no need to fight. Men put great faith in birds. Let's try them."

The idea seemed good. One twin climbed the rocks of the wooded Palatine; the other mounted the peak of the Aventine first thing in the morning. Remus saw six birds, but Romulus saw twice that many in a line. They stood by their agreement and Romulus had the right to rule the city.

He picked a good day to mark out the walls with his plow. The rites of Pales[45] were coming up, and this spurred on his work. He dug a ditch, threw offerings of grain into its depths, then soil from nearby territory. The ditch was filled back up with dirt; an altar was set on top of the leveled ground. A fresh fire burned on the new hearth. From that point, Romulus marked out the walls with a furrow, pressing the plow down. A white cow and a snowy bull bore the yoke.

------- 3.3.7   (Anonymous), *Vatican codex* (FGrHist 839 F1) -------

This compilation of Rome's myths should probably be dated to the mid-Principate, and it's one of the few to locate Remus' preferred foundation site.

The twins fought over the place where they would found the city. Romulus chose the Palatine, where he'd been born and raised. Remus picked a different spot, also near the Tiber – it's still called "Remoria" today. Neither of them gave way in their rivalry, so they turned the matter over to the gods.

3.4 The Death of Remus

Remus' death is one of the most problematic events in Roman myth, and potential solutions abound (see **chapter introduction**). Ancient authors differ on Romulus' responsibility for Remus' death. In general, they find the question of *why* Remus died less urgent than modern scholars, and care more about whether the death was accidental or planned (both options are common). Romulus' character changes in accordance with these judgments: authors who favor the "accident" hypothesis tend to depict a virtuous Romulus, while those who favor "murder" depict the king as an evil tyrant. Because Romulus is the first Roman, his moral character is important to Roman self-identification or foreigners' attempts to characterize the Romans as a whole. As we saw with Aeneas and Turnus (**2.5.3**), our interpretation of this single event has broad implications for how we understand the Romulus saga as a whole.

—————————— 3.4.1 Diodorus, *Library of History* 8.6 ——————————

*Diodorus' account of Remus' death, like his account of the augury (**3.3.3**), engages in wordplay and reversal. Celer, who kills Remus in this account, is the eponym of the king's bodyguard, the* celeres; *Wiseman (1995) has argued that the "fast" Celer is set in opposition to "slow" Remus, drawing on the etymologies of the two names.*

When Romulus was founding Rome, he quickly dug a ditch[46] around the Palatine. He didn't want his neighbors to attack and disrupt his plans. But Remus took his failure to win first place hard. He was jealous of his brother's good fortune. So, trailing the workers, he trash-talked their work. He claimed their ditch was narrow, and the city was in danger as a result: an enemy could easily jump across it.[47] Romulus got annoyed and said, "Tell all the citizens to take vengeance on anyone who tries to jump the ditch." And Remus again criticized the workers, saying that they had made the ditch too narrow and enemies would readily jump across it. In fact, even he could do it easily – and as he spoke, he jumped. Now to this a certain worker named Celer replied, "And I will avenge anyone who disobeys the king's command and jumps across!" As he spoke, he hoisted up his shovel and smashed it into Remus' head, killing him.

—————————— 3.4.2 Cicero, *On Duties* 3.41 ——————————

Cicero discusses deeds that are honorable (that is, good for Rome) or expedient (good for the individual). He weighs Romulus' actions as one of a series of myths *dealing with leadership. His description of Romulus is at odds with his idealized depiction in **3.3.4** (written about a decade earlier); we can also compare his account of the Republican Brutus in **8.1.1**.*

But that king who founded the city is a different story. A type of expediency drove him, since when he thought it would be better to rule alone than with his brother, he killed him. In doing so, he abandoned familial duty and human nature: he aimed for a goal that seemed expedient, but wasn't. Plus, he claimed the wall was to blame. This was a mask of honor, an improbable and unconvincing excuse. So he did wrong, regardless of whether I call him Quirinus[48] or Romulus.

3.4.3 Horace, *Epodes* 7.14–7.21

*Horace's poem, written at the height of Rome's civil wars, offers one of the most negative assessments of Remus' death to survive. He extends the motif of a "family curse" (**3.3.5**) to contemporary Romans.*

Does madness, guilt, or a stronger force drive you blind ones? Answer me! They are silent. Pale white suffuses their faces, and they gape, dumbstruck. So it is. Bitter fates spur the Romans on: the crime of a brother's death, as the cursed blood of innocent Remus flows to the earth – cursed, that is, to his descendants.

3.4.4 Dionysius of Halicanassus, *Roman Antiquities* 1.87.1–1.87.3

*Dionysius elaborates on the riot after the twins' augury (**3.3.5**). He is one of the few authors to suggest that Romulus was upset by his brother's death. This realistic detail heightens the myth's emotion and introduces the theme of (self-) sacrifice on Rome's behalf (see **8.1** and **8.6**).*

The battle was fierce, and many died on both sides. Some say Faustulus, the one who'd raised the twins, wanted to end the strife between the brothers. When he couldn't, he threw himself into the middle of the fighting, even though he was unarmed. So he sought and achieved a quick death. Some claim that the stone lion that sits in a high spot in the Roman Forum near the Rostra marks Faustulus' tomb. He was buried where he fell by those who found him. Remus also died in the battle. So Romulus won a gloomy victory through the deaths of his brother and fellow-citizens. He buried Remus at Remoria,[49] where the living Remus wanted to build his city. Romulus himself grew depressed from grief and ruminating over what had happened, and lost all interest in life. But Larentia, who'd taken him up as a newborn, raised him, and loved him like a mother, begged and urged him to get up, and Romulus was persuaded.

3.4.5 Ovid, *Fasti* 4.835–4.856

*This passage picks up on the foundation rite described in **3.3.6**. Ovid is the only author to suggest that both twins were innocent, and that Remus' death was a terrible misunderstanding. This approach fits with Ovid's general omission of conflict in the foundation myth; it's unclear if the choice is ironic.*

Jupiter signaled approval with thunder and lightning on the leftmost side.[50] The citizens were happy at the sign and laid the foundations. Soon there was a new wall. Celer hurried the work on. Romulus himself had summoned him and said: "Celer, here's your task: don't let anyone cross the walls or the ditch I dug. If anyone dares it, kill him."

Remus had no idea. He began to mock the humble walls, saying, "*These* will keep the people safe?" He didn't hesitate, but jumped across. Celer went after him with a shovel, and Remus hit the hard ground, bleeding.

When the king found out, he swallowed his rising tears and held his sorrow shut up in his chest. He didn't want to cry before the people. With a stiff upper lip, he said, "Let this be the fate of every enemy who crosses my walls."[51] But he gave his brother a funeral, and couldn't hold his tears back any longer. His hidden affection lay open to view. As his brother lay on his bier, Romulus gave his final kisses and said, "Goodbye, my brother; you were taken against my will."[52]

He oiled the limbs that were about to burn. Faustulus and Acca [Larentia] did the same – her hair was loosened in grief. Then the Romans, who hadn't yet gotten their name, wept for Remus, and the final flame was touched to his pyre as they mourned.

3.4.6 Ovid, *Fasti* 5.451–5.480

Ovid imagines that Remus returns from the grave. Although it's more typical for the unburied dead to appear in dreams, Ovid has Vergil's example to follow: in Aeneid 2, Aeneas dreams of Hector.

Remus' swiftness had been his downfall.[53] When Romulus had buried his brother in his tomb and performed the final rites, miserable Faustulus and Acca, her hair streaming, sprinkled his burned bones with their tears. Then the grieving parents went home in the early evening shadows. As they lay on their hard bed, the bloody ghost of Remus appeared to stand beside it. He seemed to speak these words in a faint whisper:

"Look at me! Half yours, half devoted to the gods. See what I am, compared to what I once was! If only *I* had seen the birds who guaranteed the kingdom, *I* would have power; *I* would be the greatest among my people. Now I'm only an empty shadow, melting into the flames of the pyre. This is the shape that is left of Remus. Poor me! Where is my father Mars? If you told us the truth, he gave us the savage teats when we were exposed. A wolf saved me, but now the hasty hand of a citizen has killed me. How funny that the animal was much kinder! Bloodthirsty Celer, I hope you give up your savage ghost and die from wounds, as I did; I hope your body is slick with blood when it goes underground. But my brother didn't want this to happen – his love for me is as great as mine for him. He did all he could when he wept over my fate. Ask him to make a festival in my honor; convince him with tears and remind him of his duties."

As he gave his last instructions, they wanted to embrace him. They stretched out their arms, but his slippery shadow escaped their grasping hands.[54] As his ghost fled, it woke them from their sleep. They went to Romulus and told him what his brother wanted. The king obeyed. He called the day "Remuria," and on that day rites are performed for ancestors.

--------- 3.4.7 (Anonymous), *The Origin of the Roman*
People 23 (Egnatius *FRHist* 101 F1) ---------

*The date and identity of Egnatius are unknown, but his account of the riot after the augury is surprisingly different from **3.3.5** and **3.4.4**. It's not clear if it was meant to be taken seriously.*

Egnatius in book 1 claims that in that struggle, not only was Remus not killed, but he even outlived Romulus.

--------- 3.4.8 Servius, *On the* Aeneid 1.276 ---------

*Servius comments on the line "Romulus will take over the people." His explanation is reminiscent of the myth of Oedipus (the plague), as well as **3.4.6**.*

TAKE OVER THE PEOPLE: As everyone knows, Remus was killed. It's agreed that after his death there was a plague. The oracles were consulted, and replied that Romulus should placate the ghost of his dead brother. So whenever Romulus gave commands, a curule chair[55] with a scepter, crown, and the other accoutrements of kingship was set up beside him. Thus they seemed to rule on equal terms, and that is why Vergil has "Remus and his brother Quirinus will give laws."[56]

3.4.9 Servius, *On the* Aeneid 6.779

*Servius comments on the line "See how twin crests stand up upon his head?" His explanation contrasts with earlier authors' preference for the wall story (**3.3.5**, **3.4.1**, **3.4.6**).*

TWIN CRESTS STAND UP ON HIS HEAD: Generally, Romulus doubled everything, so that he would seem to rule with his brother. He was afraid of the charge of murder. So he had everything in duplicate, as if he shared it with his brother.[57] And even when they took omens, Remus was on the Aventine and saw six vultures first, while Romulus was on the Palatine and saw 12, but after Remus. So they argued about founding the city, one saying that the time mattered and the other saying that the number was more important. A fight broke out in the army about the city's name, and Remus was killed by Romulus' soldiers. The idea that he was killed by his brother over walls is absurd.

3.4.10 Lydus, *On Magistrates* 1.5
(Cato *FRHist* 5 F3)

*Lydus echoes Cicero's judgment of Romulus (**3.4.2**). He adds a Greek etymology to the divine name Quirinus, deriving it from kyrios.*

So Romulus became a tyrant. First he disposed of his brother, who was older and better. He did whatever came into his head, and this is why he was called "Quirinus," like the Greek word for *lord and master*.

3.5 Wars with the Sabines

After founding the city, Romulus realized that he'd need a source of population to ensure its survival. He first started an asylum (a place of refuge for slaves and criminals), but his settlement also needed wives and children. After

Rome's neighbors refuse to marry their daughters to low-status Romans, Romulus tricks them by stealing their daughters, much as he'd stolen cattle in his youth. The women's parents retaliate with Rome's first wars.

The cities attack individually, allowing Rome to defeat them and even create military awards (the *spolia*: **3.5.2** and **3.5.5**). The final battle against the Sabines was more difficult. Several warriors distinguished themselves, including the grandfather of the future king Tullus Hostilius (**5.3**) and the Sabine Mettius Curtius, whose name survived in the Lacus Curtius in Rome's Forum ("Curtius' pool," still visible today[58]). The Sabines nearly defeat Rome thanks to female treachery (**7.4**), but the conflict is resolved through female ambassadors: the kidnapped women themselves.

The wars conclude with the Sabines and Romans joining forces. The arrival of the "Sabine women" (in fact from several cities), and later of Sabine settlers, emphasizes that Rome was built on immigration. Gary Miles (1995) also noted the close association between Roman marriage customs and the Sabine story; every Roman female was, in essence, a Sabine woman.

3.5.1   Varro, *On the Latin Language* 5.149

Varro explains the name of the Lacus Curtius. He offers three explanations, only one of which is relevant to Romulus; for the other two, see **6.1**.

Romulus with his men had attacked from the upper part of the Forum. A very brave man named Mettius Curtius – a Sabine – retreated into a swampy place that existed in the Forum at that time, before the sewers were made.[59] He made it back to his men on the Capitol, and the Lacus Curtius got its name from him.

3.5.2   Livy, *From the Foundation* 1.9–1.10, 1.12–1.13

Livy's account is relatively full of detail and features the major events of this first conflict: (1) the kidnapping; (2) early wars and the capture of the spolia; *and (3) the war with Tatius.*

The Roman state had already grown so strong that it was equal to any of the neighboring cities in war. But its preeminence was unlikely to last, because there were no women. There was thus no hope of children at home or legitimate marriage with their neighbors. On the advice of the Senate,[60] Romulus sent embassies to the neighboring peoples, asking for bonds of friendship and marriage with Rome. The Romans said that cities, like anything else, started from the lowest tier, but rose high with the help of the gods and their own virtue. It was enough to know that the gods had been present at Rome's birth; clearly, Romans didn't lack virtue. So it was no big deal to mix blood and family ties.

This speech wasn't well received anywhere. The neighboring cities disdained the Romans because they were afraid of the power growing in their midst, a threat to them and to their children. As the ambassadors were sent off, they were asked if they would open an asylum for women as well; after all, that way they could achieve marriage between equals.

The Roman youths were frustrated, and the matter was pretty clearly heading to war. The time and place were thus suitable for a trick. Romulus, hiding his irritation, busily set to work preparing rites for Neptune the horseman, which he called the "Consualia."[61] Then he invited his neighbors to come see the sights, and the Romans prepared to celebrate in the splashiest way they could. So they made the event known and anticipated far and wide.

Many people came because they were eager to see the new city. The people of Caenina, Crustumium, and Antemna came – they were the closest neighbors – and a huge crowd of Sabines with their wives and children. Everyone was welcomed hospitably into houses. When the visitors saw the location of the city, its walls and the crowded rooftops, they were amazed by how much Rome had grown in such a short time.

It was time for the show, and all attention was focused there. Then, as planned, the attack started. A signal was given and the young Romans rushed in to snatch the girls.[62] Most were taken at random by men standing close by. But some extremely beautiful women were earmarked for the chief men in the Senate. These elites sent plebeian men[63] to bring the girls home for them.

One of the women was even more beautiful than the others. They say that Thalassius picked her from the bunch. As she was being carried off, many asked where she was headed. The reply came again and again that no one could mess with Thalassius' girl, and from this cry we get our wedding cheer.[64]

Fear broke up the games. The girls' parents fled in distress, accusing the Romans of violating the laws of hospitality. They called upon the gods for help, saying that they had come to rites and games through a false treaty[65] and bad faith. The women themselves were no less outraged and no more hopeful about their future.

But Romulus himself made the rounds of the houses. He told the women about the Romans' failed embassies, and stressed that their fathers' pride was the real cause of their misfortune.[66] "But," he said, "you *will* be married, and you'll have a place in the city and its fortunes. There's nothing dearer to the human race than children. So don't be angry. Give your hearts to these men; fate has already given them your bodies. Love often springs up from wrongdoing. And so you'll enjoy better husbands; each one will take pains to fulfill your need for parents and a home, as well as performing the duties of a husband."[67]

The men added flattery to Romulus' words, excusing their actions as motivated by love and desire. Such excuses are the most effective ways to a woman's heart. Soon the women's minds were completely reconciled to their situation.

Their parents were another story. They went around their cities in rags, crying and wailing to get attention. And their unhappiness wasn't confined to their hometowns. They came from all over to gather before Titus Tatius, the king of the Sabines, who had the greatest reputation in the area. Embassies went there, too, from Caenina, Crustumium, and Antemna. These were the places which had been wronged. They thought Tatius and the Sabines moved too slowly, so the three cities made preparations for war on their own.

But even the Crustumians and the Antemnates didn't move fast enough for the Caeninenses in their white-hot rage. So they attacked the Romans on their own. Romulus appeared with his army while the men of Caenina were pillaging in small bands.[68] A quick battle proved that anger is useless without the force to back it up. The army of Caenina broke and fled; the Romans ran after them. Romulus killed their king and helped himself to the armor. Once the enemy's king was dead, their town was taken at the first attack. So the Roman army returned victorious, and Romulus himself was proud of his deeds and no less eager to show them off. So he fitted the armor of the dead enemy king to a stick made just for the purpose.[69] Then he carried the spoils[70] up the Capitol and set them down near an oak sacred to the shepherds. At the same time as he dedicated the gift, he sketched out the boundaries of a temple to Jupiter [... *Next, Rome fights and defeats Crustumium and Antemnae; fighting with the Sabines is heavy and Rome itself is threatened; see 7.4.*]

In any case, the Sabines occupied the citadel. The next day, the Roman army drew up its battle lines. It filled the area between the Palatine and Capitoline hills. The Sabines hadn't yet come down to the plain when the Romans advanced against them, spurred on by rage and the desire to retake the citadel. The top men on both sides rushed to fight: on the Sabine side Mettius Curtius, and on the Roman side Hostius Hostilius. Hostius upheld the Romans with spirit and daring from the start, but he was on a slope. When he fell, the Roman line immediately wavered and broke. Romulus himself was driven, with the crowd of fleeing soldiers, to the ancient gate of the Palatine. There he lifted his weapons to the sky and said, "Jupiter, I laid the first foundation of the city here on the Palatine by your birds' advice. Now the Sabines have possession of my citadel thanks to a crime. Between there and here, armed men have taken over the valley. Father of gods and men, you are the owner of the citadel, at least: take the terror out of the Romans and halt their awful run. I vow a temple to you as Jupiter Stator.[71] May it be a reminder to posterity that the city was saved by your help."

This was his prayer. Then, as if he knew that his prayer had been heard, he said, "Romans, Jupiter the Best and Greatest god orders us to take a stand here and keep on fighting!"

The Romans stopped as if they'd been ordered by the voice of the god himself. Romulus rushed out among the first men. Mettius Curtius, the leader of the Sabines, ran down from the citadel and drove the scattered Romans along the entire length of the Forum. He wasn't far from the Palatine gate when he shouted, "We've conquered those treacherous hosts and wimpy fighters! Now they know how different it is to kidnap girls than fight with men." As he was boasting, Romulus attacked with a knot of his fiercest soldiers. Mettius was fighting from a horse, and so he was more easily driven off. The Romans pursued him as he retreated. Meanwhile, the rest of the Roman line, bolstered by the king's bravery, routed the Sabines.

Mettius' horse was terrified by the noise of the pursuers and ran straight into a swamp.[72] The sight distracted even the Sabines, who were frightened at the danger facing such a great warrior. But he emerged to men waving and calling him, as well as the crowd's applause for his courage. The Romans and Sabines started fighting again in the valley between the two mountains, but the Roman side was stronger.

Then the Sabine women, whose wrongs had been the cause of war, dared to throw themselves in the midst of the flying spears. Their hair was streaming, their clothing torn, but their female fears had been overcome by the horrors of war. Coming in at an angle, they broke up the battle lines that were prepared to attack. They broke up the anger, too: calling to their fathers on one side, their husbands on the other, the women begged them not to defile themselves by spilling the blood of kinsmen or to curse their children with murder. They pointed out that the children of the Romans were the Sabines' grandchildren. "If having a relationship shames you, if our marriages shame you, then turn that anger against *us*. We're the cause of war; we're the reason for the wounding and murdering of our husbands and fathers. We'd rather die than live without either one of you – whether as orphans or as widows."

Their speech moved the generals and the rank-and-file. A sudden hush and silence fell over the armies, and the leaders marched out to make peace. They didn't just make peace, but they made the two cities into one whole. They shared the kingship, and brought all royal power to Rome. But the Sabines had to be given something, too. So the name "Quirites," derived from Sabine Cures,[73] was given to the doubled citizens. As a memorial of their war, they renamed the spot where Curtius had first emerged from the depths of the swamp the "Lacus Curtius," and they set up a statue of the horse in the shallows.

3.5.3 Dionysius of Halicanassus, *Roman Antiquities* 2.45.1–2.47.3

Dionysius' description of the Sabine women's plan introduces Hersilia as an older and wiser woman; other sources claim she was Romulus' wife. Either way, her plan works. The Sabine immigrants, who come from only four families, are enough to double the size of the city, emphasizing how small Rome was in its early stages.

Time was wasting. The women who were the cause of the war – born Sabine, now Roman – met separately from their husbands and made a plan together: they'd begin negotiations with both parties. The woman who proposed this plan was a Sabine noblewoman named Hersilia. Some claim that she was married, but had been taken with the other girls as if she weren't. But the more reputable sources say that she remained voluntarily with her only daughter, who'd been kidnapped.

When the women decided to go with her plan, they went to the Senate and held the floor for a long time. Each begged to be allowed to intervene with her family.[74] They claimed to have high hopes of uniting the two nations in friendship. When the Senate and king heard the women, they were overjoyed [... *The women step between the two armies, as in 3.5.2.*] After Hersilia made her plea, the women and their children all fell down at the kings' knees and didn't budge until the nearest men lifted them off the ground and promised to do they could, within reason. Then the women were escorted from the battlefield and the men held a meeting to negotiate. First they declared a ceasefire. Next, the kings declared an alliance between their cities, and they swore oaths on their agreement [...]

Most of the generals returned home with their troops, but King Tatius and three other top noblemen remained at Rome: Volesus Valerius, Tullus Tyrannius, and Mettus Curtius (the one who crossed the lake in armor). They enjoyed honors that their families possess even now. Their comrades, families, and servants remained with them, in total no fewer than the Romans.

3.5.4 Ovid, *Metamorphoses* 14.778–14.804

Ovid's account of the Romano-Sabine wars is characteristically imaginative, but also displays his knowledge of Rome's marshiness. Periodic flooding of the Forum occurred even after it was drained in the sixth century.

The children of Cures,[75] with lowered voices like silent wolves,[76] attacked. The Romans slept deeply as the enemy reached the gates, which were closed with strong bars. But Juno opened one and didn't let the hinges creak as they turned. Only Venus[77] noticed the bars of the gates yielding and would have closed them – but it's illegal for gods to interfere with the actions of gods.

Ausonian[78] naiads used to occupy the places near Janus' temple – the ones that gurgle with a cold fountain. Venus asked them to help, and her request was reasonable. The nymphs didn't delay: they called up the waters and rivulets of their stream. But the mouths of Janus didn't yet lie open, and so the waters were blocked. The flow didn't close off the road. So they put glowing sulphur under the rising stream, and they burned the dry beds with smoky pitch. The force of this – and other things as well – sent steam to the base of the fountain. Waters who vied with Alpine chill, you don't yield to those fires!

The twin gates smoke with fiery mist. The gate that had been promised to the fierce Sabines (in vain!) was blocked by the fresh flow.[79] Meanwhile the Roman soldiers threw on their armor [...] But they decided that peace could end the war. It was not fought out to the bitter end, and Tatius came to share Rome's throne.

3.5.5 Plutarch, *Life of Romulus* 16

Plutarch's version of the Sabine war includes more diplomacy. The idea that the Sabines were like the Spartans was common in Rome (6.1.6); both groups were known for being tough and living simply.

The Sabines were numerous and warlike. They lived in unwalled villages, since they were Spartan colonists; they were proud and had no fear. But they saw that they were trapped by their concern for the hostages, since they worried about their daughters' safety. So they sent an embassy to Romulus, calling for reason and moderation. They requested the return of the Sabine women and reparations for the crime. Once he did that, he could form diplomatic and personal relationships with the parents as was customary.

Romulus refused to give the women back and demanded that the Sabines recognize the marriages. So the Sabines decided to go to war and spent their time planning. But Acron, the king of Caenina, had a temper. He was a ferocious warrior and he'd suspected Romulus was shady from the get-go. This matter with the women was the last straw. Acron decided Romulus was a threat to everyone and would be intolerable unless he was punished. So he attacked with a large force.

Romulus marched out against Acron. The two sides came into one another's sight. The leaders eyed each other up and decided to duel while their armed soldiers sat still. Romulus vowed that if he won and killed Acron, he would dedicate Acron's armor to Zeus.[80] And he did win, and moreover he routed Acron's army in the fighting and captured the city of Caenina. He treated the conquered citizens well. After ordering them to destroy their own houses, he invited them to live in Rome as full citizens. Rome's growth is particularly owed to this attitude: she always laid claim to and associated with those she conquered.

Romulus considered how he could fulfill his vow to Zeus in a way that pleased the god and entertained the citizens. He cut down a huge oak tree in the Campus [Martius], shaped it into a trophy, and dressed it in Acron's armor. He was careful to tie on each piece in order. Then Romulus put on his own clothing and crowned himself with a laurel wreath. He hoisted the trophy on his right shoulder, straight and tall, and marched off singing a victory hymn[81] – the one soldiers sing in battle. His citizens welcomed him with joy and wonder.

3.5.6 Festus, "Luceres"

Some versions of the Sabine war claimed that Romulus had to call for reinforcements. Here, Festus explains how one of these armies left a permanent mark on the city.

The LUCERES are the third division of tribes made by Romulus and Titus Tatius. They're named after Lucerus,[82] the king of Ardea, who helped Romulus when he fought the Sabines.

3.5.7 Lactantius, *Divine Institutes* 2.7

The asylum was an important marker of Roman identity, since it offered a mythic reason for Rome's openness to foreigners. Lactantius' account of Rome's foundation demonstrates how an unsympathetic audience could interpret early Romans' mixed backgrounds.

When Romulus was about to found the city, he gathered together the shepherds he'd grown up with. It seemed to him that he didn't have enough of his own people to found a city, so he set up an asylum.[83] The worst men from the neighboring towns fled there, and there was no further judgment of their status. That's how he filled up his citizen list. He chose the oldest men to make up his Senate, called them "fathers," and consulted them in all matters [...] Later generations judge their decisions true and unchangeable – these decrees that a hundred old men wearing goatskins[84] made!

3.6 Death of Titus Tatius

After the war with the Sabines, Romulus and Tatius agree to rule together. It doesn't last long. The death of Titus Tatius marks a turning point in many versions of the Romulus story. Both kings are just rulers before the events that lead to Tatius' death; then Tatius, followed by Romulus, behaves more like a tyrant.

Unlike the Remus story, Romulus never bears any blame for Tatius' death. Their disagreement is often described in terms that are more favorable to Romulus than Tatius: when a group of Romans, including Tatius' relatives, behave unjustly by robbing an embassy, Tatius defends them; Romulus recommends punishment suitable for highway robbery. This difference of opinion is also a difference in outlook. Tatius focuses inward on pre-existing relationships, while Romulus looks outward for diplomatic ties. Both positions are defensible, and this myth demonstrates how such stories could be used to negotiate values.

The second failure of joint rule also points to continuing concern among the Roman elite about the appropriate exercise of power, and underlines the distinction between kingship and republic. In Republican Rome, consuls were expected to work out their differences; a monarchy needs only one king.

──────────────── 3.6.1 Cicero, *On the State* 2.14 ────────────────

*Cicero describes the good reign of Romulus. In his terms, a "good" king is marked by attention to the Senate and cooperative government. Although he clearly knows the variant in which Romulus becomes a tyrant (**3.4.2**), he omits it, perhaps for clarity or to cement Rome's positive model.*

After the death of Tatius, all power returned to Romulus. But although he and Tatius had chosen a royal council[85] – called "fathers" because they loved the people and the people loved them – Romulus ruled alone. He distributed the Romans into three tribes and 30 curiae.[86] The tribes were named after himself, Tatius, and Lucumo[87] (a companion of Romulus' who had died in the Sabine war). The curiae were named for the raped Sabine women, who had later made the speech that ended the war and led to the treaty. He did these things while Tatius was alive, but after he died Romulus paid even more attention to the authority and advice of the "fathers."

───────── 3.6.2 Livy, *From the Foundation* 1.14 ─────────

*Livy's account of Tatius' death distinguishes the Sabine king, who cares about family relationships, from Romulus, who cares about international relations. This distinction is in some ways similar to Cicero's debate on honesty vs. expediency (**3.4.1**), and points to concerns about the best way to govern.*

After several years of joint rule,[88] King Tatius' family attacked a Laurentine embassy. When the Laurentines accused them of violating international law, Tatius found his relatives' goodwill more important than his neighbors'. So he turned their punishment upon himself: as he was coming back from sacrificing in Lavinium, he was killed in an ambush. They say Romulus didn't take this as hard[89] as he should have, either because he thought their kingdom was shared under false pretenses or because he thought the murder was justified. So he didn't go to war for Tatius. But he did expiate[90] the wrong done to the ambassadors and the murder of the king, and renewed the treaty between Rome and Lavinium.

───────── 3.6.3 Dionysius of Halicanassus, ─────────
Roman Antiquities 2.52.2–2.52.5

*Dionysius elaborates on the argument between Romulus and Tatius: Romulus first hands over the bandits for punishment, despite Tatius' disapproval, and Tatius has to get them back. In the course of this raid, Tatius was killed. Dionysius also complicates the picture by stating that only some of the bandits are Tatius' relatives. The dispute is not individual relationships vs. society (contrast **3.6.1** and **3.6.2**), but whether Romans should always be defended against outsiders.*

Tatius was furious. He complained that his "fellow ruler" had wronged him by handing over these men. He was also sorry for the men who were taken away, especially one who was a relative. So immediately he

led his army at double march to help. They encountered the ambassadors on the road and freed the captives. After a short time passed, as
some say, he went with Romulus to Lavinium to sacrifice. (The kings
were required to sacrifice to their ancestral gods on behalf of the city.)
The friends and relatives of the murdered ambassadors ganged up and
attacked him at the altar using sacrificial knives and meat spits. Tatius
died [... Others] write that Tatius didn't go with Romulus or for sacrifice at all, but he went alone to persuade the victims to stop being
angry at those who had wronged them. The crowd was angry because
the perpetrators weren't given up (as Romulus and the Roman Senate
had ruled), and relatives of the dead ganged up to attack Tatius. Tatius
couldn't escape retribution and was stoned to death.

3.7 Death and Apotheosis of Romulus

The apotheosis of a city founder was fairly typical in the ancient world (compare Aeneas in **2.6**). Like Aeneas, Romulus got a new name to mark his
divine status: "Quirinus." Quirinus was probably a pre-existing god with whom
Romulus became identified; the name could also be an epithet attached to
other gods, including Mars. Its significance and etymology was debated even
in antiquity (the Sabine town of *Cures* vs. the Sabine word *curis,* spear).[91] But
myths about Quirinus are always myths about Romulus. Romans could be
called "Quirites," a word that perhaps means something like "Quirinus' people" (as "Romans" are "Romulus" people).

Despite his ascent to heaven, Romulus' death was disturbing: some authors
claimed that he was dismembered. This tradition has parallels in the Egyptian
Osiris myth, the "Orphic" myth of Dionysus, and perhaps also the historical
murder of Julius Caesar. Despite this negative tradition, the deified Romulus
continued to be honored throughout Roman antiquity.

3.7.1 Ennius, *Annals* 105–110

---

*Ennius describes the people's reaction to the death of Romulus, who's depicted
as an ideal king.*

For a long time they desired him in their hearts. During that time they
recalled him among themselves with these words: "Romulus! Divine
Romulus! What a guardian of the country the gods produced in you!
Father, progenitor, man with divine blood! You led us out into the area
of light" **[lacuna]** Romulus passed his life in the heavens with his family, the gods.

―――――――――   3.7.2   Livy, *From the Foundation* 1.15–1.16   ―――――――――

*Livy is skeptical about Romulus' deification. As a proponent of Romulus' tyran-
nical behavior, he perhaps thought that Romulus was not an appropriate choice
for a god.*

What I've related above is just about everything that Romulus accomplished as king, both at home and abroad.[92] His actions support belief
in his divine background and his divinity after death: for example, his
spirit in restoring his grandfather's kingdom, his plan to found the city,
and his desire to strengthen it in peace and in war. Indeed, the city
grew so strong from his leadership that it preserved peace for the next
40 years. But he was beloved by the people rather than by the Senate,
and he held the hearts of the soldiers far more than the rest: he had a
bodyguard[93] of 300 soldiers called "Celeres,"[94] and he kept them both
in peace and in war.

So he established these everlasting public works. When he was holding a meeting to review the army in the Campus Martius, near Goat's
Swamp, a sudden storm burst out with a great crash of thunder. A
dense cloud enveloped the king and hid him from view, and Romulus was never again seen on earth.[95] After such a violent storm, the
clear, calm sky returned, and the Roman youth settled their fears. Then
they saw that the king's seat was empty. They put some faith in the
senators who'd been standing nearby, who claimed that the king had
been swept up into the air by the storm. But all the same, for many
days a gloomy silence prevailed, as if they'd been struck by fear of
loss. Then a few made a proposal, which was universally approved:
they hailed Romulus as a god, born to a god, the king and founder of
the Roman city. With prayers, they beseeched him for peace, and they
asked that he always preserve his children with a willing and favorable
attitude.

I believe even then some people quietly made the case that the king
had been dismembered at the hands of the Senate; the story leaked out,
but only as a shadowy rumor. Admiration for Romulus and ever-present
anxiety promoted the other story. The apotheosis gained credibility
thanks to one man's advice. Proculus Julius[96] was a man to be reckoned
with, as they say, an advisor for matters big and small. Seeing that the
city was obsessed with desire for the king and angry with the Senate, he
made an announcement at a public meeting: "Citizens! Romulus, the
father of this city, suddenly appeared to me on the road this morning at
first light. He came down from the heavens. As I stood there, shivering
with fear and worshipping him and praying that I might be permitted to look at him, he said: 'go tell the Romans that the gods want my

Rome to be the chief city of the world. So they should practice military skills, and they should know and let their children know that no human power can resist Roman arms.' When he said these things, he went back into the heavens." It's amazing how much faith was put into that man's speech, and how desire for Romulus among the people and army was soothed by belief in his immortality.

———————— 3.7.3   Ovid, *Metamorphoses* 14.805–14.851 ————————

Ovid's account of Romulus' apotheosis should be compared to the parallel account of Aeneas' apotheosis (2.6.1). Ovid is atypical in that he has Romulus' wife go to the heavens with him.

You, Romulus, were giving fair laws[97] to a doubled population when Mars set aside his helmet and made the following speech to the father of gods and men: "The time has come, father, to grant the rewards you promised me. The Roman state's strong now, on firm footing. It doesn't depend on a single defender. Your grandson deserves it; take him from earth and pull him up into heaven. You once said, in council with the gods present – I took note of these sacred words and committed them to memory – 'there will be one whom you raise to the blue skies of heaven.'[98] These should be considered the best of your words!"

Omnipotent Jupiter nodded and covered the sky with dark clouds. He terrified the world with thunder and lightning. Mars felt the sure signs of the king-napping promised to him. He leaned on the bloody shaft of his spear, unafraid, and vaulted onto his harnessed horses. With a crack of the whip, he was flying forth through the air. He landed on the peak of the woody Palatine and seized the son of Ilia as he read laws to his people. Romulus' mortal body peeled away in the thin air, like a lead pellet shot from its sling tends to melt in the middle of the sky. Suddenly his appearance was godlike and more worthy of the tall couches: this is the image of the togate Quirinus.

His wife was in mourning. Regal Juno commanded Iris to go down to Hersilia on her rainbow route and relay her orders to the widow. "Wife and pride of both the Latin and (especially) the Sabine people, you truly deserved him as husband before. So stop crying; he's Quirinus now. If you want to see your husband, follow my lead [...]"

Hersilia, hardly daring to lift her eyes from awe, said: "Oh goddess (although it's not easy for me to say who you are, it's clear you're a goddess), lead on! Lead on and let me see my husband's face. If only the fates allowed me to see it once more, I'd swear I was in heaven." [... *Iris and Hersilia go outside.*] A star fell from the sky and crashed to the ground; from its light, Hersilia's hair burst into flame. Then Hersilia and the star yielded to the breezes. The founder of Rome took her up with knowing hands and changed her old name along with her body. Now she's Hora, a goddess joined to Quirinus.

Conclusion

Romulus has troubled commentators both ancient and modern, perhaps because his character is far more human than we expect from ancient heroes. He certainly has his low points: raised by a wolf, he murders (or at least is an accessory to the death of) his brother, and becomes a tyrant who's murdered in turn. He's a thief whose city grows because he allows the lowest elements of society – criminals and slaves – to gain citizen rights. He's a trickster who fools his neighbors when diplomacy doesn't work. He's a humble ruler who became known for eating turnips,[99] proverbial peasants' food, rather than the delicacies of the wealthy. But many of Romulus' negative aspects could be presented in a positive light as well. His city was truly open to anyone who wanted to work for citizenship – an appealing notion to us as well as to some Romans. He didn't set himself on a pedestal, but enjoyed the simple pleasures of ordinary Romans. He was a successful warrior who fought in the front lines, yet was also able to strategize.

Romulus' generally ambiguous character was appreciated by Roman authors, who were equally comfortable idealizing and vilifying him. Over time, most aspects of city life, customs, and culture were referred back to Romulus, so that he became the greatest of Rome's many founders. Most accounts of his life are approving, which may surprise you; remember that Romulus killed his great-uncle and perhaps his brother! Concerned about this familial violence, modern authors tend to focus more heavily on the earlier episodes of Romulus' life. Yet comparison with Greek myths can be fruitful here. Romulus is no more violent than many Greek heroes, and his family is considerably less dysfunctional than some of the cycles that were celebrated in Greece (such as the house of Atreus or the Theban cycle). In Greece, Hercules kills his children and Theseus kills his son Hippolytus – and these heroes are still accepted in Greek myth and society. Romulus' story is not so very different. In fact, as we've seen, Romulus can be distanced from his brother's death in a way that Hercules and Theseus were not.

As the founder of the city, Romulus is Rome's most common mythic figure, appearing in works of all varieties and throughout Rome's history. His character traits are those of the ideal Roman male: tough, simple, clever, god-fearing, just. He triumphs over his enemies, but he is also prepared to make peace. The importance of these qualities to Roman self-perceptions, even if those perceptions are idealized, helps explain why Romulus can seem hard to pin down.

Notes

1. http://numismatics.org/collection/1905.57.1
2. This priesthood was established by Numa (**5.2**), apparently without contradiction.
3. See **chapter 7** for more information on women in ancient Rome. "Rape" was defined not by the woman's consent *per se*, but by a combination of her consent and the consent of the male who had control of her.
4. The character Eurydice appears only in Ennius, but may relate to the "Antho" of **3.1.4** and **3.1.7**.
5. According to Servius, Ilia's father was Aeneas.
6. Anthropomorphic gods were distinguished from mere humans by their eerie beauty (compare how we might refer to movie stars as "gods").
7. A very delicate description of Ilia's first sexual encounter.
8. Some authors claimed that Ilia married the Tiber.
9. Livy again expresses his doubts about the more mythical aspects of the story; see **2.7.1 introduction**.
10. For more stories about Larentia, see **7.3**.
11. Romulus and, apparently, Remus.
12. Numa, Tarquin the Elder, and Servius Tullius; see **chapter 5**.
13. A mistake; Vestals vowed abstinence for 30 years.
14. Twin births were rare enough in antiquity that they could (apparently) be taken as shorthand for divine favor.
15. Compare Eurydice's role in **3.1.1**.
16. See **2.3.3n68**.
17. Compare the etymologies of Rome in **2.1**.
18. Perhaps the same Phorbas whose daughter is one of Achilles' captives; see Homer, *Iliad* 9.665.
19. This etymology is not clear.
20. This name change may suggest an Aemilian family myth.
21. Tarchetius is not in the Alban king list, but the name is based on an Etruscan *Tarch-* root. Compare Tarchon (**4.4**) and Tarquin (**5.4, 5.6**).
22. A similar myth was also told about the birth of Servius Tullius. See **5.4.3b–5.4.3d**.
23. "Tethys" is the Etruscan name for "Thetis," but is also a sea nymph in Greek myth. It's not clear which Plutarch means.
24. Compare **6.4.2, 6.4.4, 6.4.5**.
25. Roman Vesta; compare Rhea/Ilia's status as a Vestal Virgin.
26. Compare Penelope in the *Odyssey* (especially books 2 and 19).
27. Rome's first native historian.
28. Compare Eurydice in **3.1.1**.
29. See **2.2.5**.
30. See **7.3**.
31. Diodorus' account, which involves both twins meeting Numitor, seems different from the other accounts we have.
32. The nearby city of Gabii was, in fact, more prominent than Rome in early Italy. The city is currently undergoing excavation, with updates available at http://lapisgabinus.blogspot.com
33. Compare Romulus' asylum: **3.5.7**.

34. In which the twins had been exposed: **3.1.2, 3.1.6, 3.1.7**.
35. This line is uncertain, and it is likely that Ennius described Remus' position more precisely. The Ennian scholar Otto Skutsch (1961) suggested it should read "Murcus," part of the Aventine Hill; Romulus is seated on this hill, too. In all other accounts, the twins are on different hills (see the other passages in **3.3**).
36. "Exceptionally beautiful," the same word Ilia uses to describe Mars in **3.1.1**. Romulus' victory is foreshadowed by his similarity to the gods.
37. Usually Remus is on the Aventine, while Romulus is on the Palatine. See **note 35**.
38. The last sentence is important: the auspices establish the gods' favorable attitude towards Rome, not only Romulus.
39. That is, an unfavorable sign.
40. A pun in Greek: "righthanded fortune would result from lefthanded plans."
41. Livy refers to the power struggle between Amulius and Numitor.
42. Augury required precisely formulated questions.
43. According to Roman divination, Romulus was right: the second sign overruled the first.
44. This fight is elaborated on in **section 3.4**.
45. The Parilia, later known as "Rome's birthday."
46. Compare the rite described in **3.3.6**.
47. Bremmer (1987) suggested that Remus' death is a myth about protecting the city walls, which Diodorus seems to support.
48. Quirinus was the deified Romulus; see **3.7**.
49. See **3.3.7**.
50. See **3.3.3 introduction**.
51. An echo of **3.3.5**.
52. This line is reminiscent of Catullus 101, also about a brother's death.
53. See **3.4.1 introduction**: the idea that Remus is only successful when slow is key to Wiseman (1995)'s analysis.
54. Compare similar encounters with ghosts in *Aeneid* 6 and *Odyssey* 12.
55. The chair of Roman magistrates.
56. Vergil, *Aeneid* 1.292–293.
57. Probably a reference to the curule chair, scepter, etc. mentioned in **3.4.8**.
58. Model: http://www.digitales-forum-romanum.de/wp-content/uploads/2014/03/2-0611_KL_Lacus-Curtius_isometrisch.jpg Photo: http://www.digitales-forum-roman um.de/wp-content/uploads/2014/03/4-0611_Ruine_Lacus-Curtius.jpg
59. See **2.3.3n68**.
60. An advisory body of elders. Romulus is thought to have established the Senate early in his reign: **3.3.7**.
61. The Consualia took place in August and was still celebrated in Livy's day.
62. Republican coins show the scene: e.g., *RRC* 344/1a (about 50 years before Livy) http://numismatics.org/collection/1937.158.88
63. A similar theme appears in the story of Verginia (**7.8**).
64. "Talassio!"
65. Political differences were supposed to be set aside at international festivals in antiquity.
66. Rome made it a point to only attack in defense, even when attacking preventively. By blaming the Sabines, Romulus insists that the kidnapping is a reaction to Sabine misbehavior and therefore just, ensuring divine support.

67. Romulus' words relate to *manus* marriage, in which the bride was adopted into her husband's household. Andromache's words in Homer, *Iliad* 6.413–430 are similar.
68. Compare the shepherds' raids in **3.2**.
69. Romulus first makes a "trophy," which was a sort of scarecrow made out of enemy armor.
70. Spoils or *spolia* are the armor, weapons, and other military equipment taken from a defeated enemy, typically after death. Romulus here invents the *spolia opima*, which apparently had to be won by the commander in a duel.
71. That is, "Standstill": he keeps the Romans from running away.
72. The Lacus Curtius.
73. The Sabine city ruled by Tatius.
74. Compare the women in **8.8.2**.
75. See **note 73**.
76. Note the ironic change: usually the Romans are wolves, because of Romulus and the she-wolf.
77. Ovid plays with both the *Aeneid*'s theme of Juno's hatred for Rome, and the salvation of the city by Juno's geese (**8.10.3a–8.10.3b**).
78. Italian.
79. That is, the Sabines were unable to enter Rome's citadel due to flooding. The sulfuric water suggests hot springs.
80. Compare **2.5.4** and **2.5.5** for the theme.
81. This image, called *Romulus tropaiophorus* (carrying a trophy) is common: http://www.pompeiiinpictures.com/pompeiiinpictures/R9/9%2013%2005_files/image008.jpg
82. Called "Lucumo" or "Lycmon" in other sources: see **3.6.1, 4.6.4a, 5.4.2c**.
83. A safe haven for criminals, runaway slaves, and others no longer wanted in their home communities.
84. Note Lactantius' insistence on the primitive nature of early Rome.
85. The new Roman Senate.
86. Both are administrative divisions.
87. The Ramnes, Titienses, and Luceres; see **note 82**.
88. Between Romulus and Titus Tatius.
89. "Take it hard" is the same phrase in Latin that opens the Sabine war; at this point, that chapter in Rome's history closes.
90. Romulus thus proves himself to be dutifully religious.
91. See Dionysius of Halicarnassus 2.48.
92. The two traditional spheres of Roman civic activity, "home and abroad" provide a major organizing principle to Livy's history.
93. Associated with tyranny.
94. Compare the name of Remus' killer in **3.4.1** and **3.4.5**.
95. Compare the disappearance of Aeneas at the Numicus (**2.6**).
96. A member of the Julian family and thus a mythic relative of Julius Caesar and Augustus.
97. This reminiscence of Vergil, *Aeneid* 1.272 lets the reader know that a parallel with Aeneas is coming up.
98. A quotation of Ennius' *Annals* 54–55.
99. Lucilius fr. 1375 Krenkel: "Romulus in heaven gobbled up boiled turnips."

References

Alföldi, Andreas. 1974. *Die Struktur des voretruskischen Römerstaates*. Heidelberg: Carl Winter.

Beard, Mary. 1993. "Looking (harder) for Roman Myth: Dumézil, Declamation and the Problems of Definition." In *Mythos in mythenloser Gesellschaft: das Paradeigma Roms*, edited by Fritz Graf, 44–64. Stuttgart and Leipzig: Teubner.

Bremmer, Jan. 1987. "Romulus and Remus and the Foundation of Rome." In *Roman Myth and Mythography*, by Jan Bremmer and Nicholas Horsfall, 25–48. London: Institute of Classical Studies. http://www.rug.nl/research/portal/files/3387717/romulus.pdf (accessed November 21, 2016).

Lincoln, Bruce. 1975. "The Indo-European Myth of Creation." *History of Religions* 15: 121–145. DOI: 10.1086/462739

Lincoln, Bruce. 1976. "The Indo-European Cattle-Raiding Myth." *History of Religions* 16: 42–65. DOI: 10.1086/462755

Michelet, Jules. 1831. *Histoire romaine. 1ère partie: République*. Paris: L. Hachette. http://catalogue.bnf.fr/ark:/12148/cb32449277g (accessed November 21, 2016).

Miles, Gary B. 1995. *Livy: Reconstructing Early Rome*. Ithaca, NY: Cornell University Press.

Neel, Jaclyn. 2014. *Legendary Rivals: Collegiality and Ambition in the Tales of Early Rome*. Leiden, Brill.

Pausch, Dennis. 2008. "Der aitiologische Romulus. Historisches Interesse und literarische Form in Livius' Darstellung der Königszeit." *Hermes* 136: 38–60.

Puhvel, Jaan. 1975. "Remus et Frater." *History of Religions* 15: 146–157. DOI: 10.1086/462740

Roller, Duane W. 1996. "Euripides, Ennius, and Roman Origins." *The Ancient World* 27: 168–171.

Skutsch, Otto. 1961. "Enniana iv." *The Classical Quarterly* (New Series) 11: 252–267. DOI: http://dx.doi.org/10.1017/S0009838800015561

Strassburger, Herman. 1968. *Zur Sage von der Gründung Roms*. Heidelberg: Carl Winter.

ver Eecke, Marie. 2008. *La République et le roi: le mythe de Romulus à la fin de la République romaine. De l'archéologie à l'histoire*. Paris: de Boccard.

Vidal-Naquet, Pierre. 1998. *The Black Hunter*, tr. Andrew Szegedy-Maszak. Baltimore, MD: Johns Hopkins University Press.

Wiseman, Timothy Peter. 1995. *Remus: A Roman Legend*. Exeter: University of Exeter Press.

Further Reading

Carandini, Andrea. 2011. *Rome: Day One*, tr. Stephen Sartarelli. Princeton, NJ: Princeton University Press. Despite the title, analyzes most of the Romulus myth in a condensed study. Carandini is an archaeologist whose arguments are controversial (in brief, he argues that he has found a wall that provides evidence that the Romulus myth is largely factual). But this lavishly illustrated book is worth your time. It's aimed at a nonspecialist audience, so is missing most of the documentation you'd expect. Be prepared to question some of the author's assertions.

Dench, Emma. 2005. *Romulus' Asylum. Roman Identities from the Age of Alexander to the Age of Hadrian*. Oxford: Oxford University Press. DOI:10.1093/acprof:oso/

9780198150510.001.0001 Analyzes the various ways that Romans constructed their identity. The first two chapters, which discuss how Romans used myths to shape their place in contemporary society in Rome and with outsiders, are the most relevant for this book.

Grandazzi, Alexandre. 1997. *The Foundation of Rome: Myth and History*, tr. Jane Marie Todd. Ithaca, NY: Cornell University Press. Argues that early Roman history can be reconciled with archaeological discoveries. This book is strongly methodological, but is an immense resource for understanding the history of studying early Rome. Some readers may be put off by the dream-like prose.

Linderski, Jerzy. 2007. "Founding the City." In *Roman Questions II: Selected Papers*, by Jerzy Linderski, 1–19. Stuttgart: Franz Steiner Verlag. https://www.academia.edu/8407743/J.Linderski_Founding_the_City_Ennius_and_Romulus_on_the_Site_of_Rome._RQ_II_2007 (accessed November 21, 2016). A challenging (but worthwhile) article on the crucial bird-watching episode. Linderski is the acknowledged master of all knowledge relating to augury and auspicy, and he walks through how this particular scene worked.

Tennant, P. M. W. 1988. "The Lupercalia and the Romulus and Remus Legend." *Acta Classica* 31: 81–93. www.casa-kvsa.org.za/1988/AC31-08-Tennant.pdf (accessed November 21, 2016). Offers a solid background on the Romulus and Remus myth. The discussion focuses on the twins' birth and the potential problems with assuming Greek sources for the myth without taking Roman topography into account.

4

Images and Text

Introduction

Your first interaction with the ancient world was probably archaeological, whether you saw a Greek amphora in a museum, the Roman Forum on the cover of a history textbook, or the movie *Pompeii*. Iconographic evidence offers a valuable addition to our knowledge of myth, too. Myths are found on materials large and small, from personal articles such as perfume bottles, pottery, and hand-held mirrors to publicly viewable tombs, monuments, and sculpture. Over the past several decades, scholars have turned to such iconographic evidence as a source for novel mythic tales, and sharpened our understanding of the distinction between literary and artistic mythmaking.

Let's start by reviewing what we've learned about written myths. These myths aren't always the same story told by different authors; they can vary. Sometimes these variations are small (was Romulus' mother named Rhea or Ilia?), and sometimes they are substantial (was there one war between Trojans and Italians or three? Did Romulus kill his brother or not?). Despite these variations, the myths we've seen tend to have a structure that remains the same throughout many retellings. Jacques Poucet (1985, 238–243) has termed these structures "closed themes," while the parts that change (such as the name of Romulus' mother) are "open themes." We can think of the mythical tradition as being something like an order at a restaurant: there is a description of the food on the menu, but you can modify it in certain ways (the "open themes"), while not in others (the "closed themes"). If you ordered a hamburger, for example, you could reasonably ask the restaurant to hold the ketchup, but not to make it a turkey burger, a veggie burger, or a steak.

Early Rome: Myth and Society, A Sourcebook, First Edition. Jaclyn Neel.

Iconographic evidence is slightly different: here, the themes are harder to recognize and may not exist. There are several reasons for this difference. First, the images we see are products of a living mythic tradition on a broad social scale. The audience for an image is much broader than the audience for densely written text, because while not everyone in the ancient world could read, most of them could look. Just as importantly, most surviving myths were written down by Romans and tend to focus on Rome. As you will see further in **chapter 6**, there were many other Italian cultures in antiquity, each with their own myths. In almost every case, we know about these myths because they have some bearing on Rome (or Greece) – that is, when the myth is relevant to the author. Because we only have limited textual evidence for Italy that isn't written in Greek or Latin, we have to guess about many of the other traditions that existed in antiquity. Archaeological evidence comes from a broader cultural range, and in many cases iconography offers us our only chance to learn about non-Roman stories.

This first reason brings us to our second, which is that the myths that are illustrated aren't always the myths that exist in text. Modern scholars have only recently begun to realize how differences in medium (image vs. writing) affect how myths are retold (see Small 2003; Squire 2009). Such differences are emphasized by the working methods of ancient artisans. It is widely accepted that artisans used sketches or models to produce their images. These models would circulate and provide different workers with the same compositional scheme (as an example, let's say it's a male with a female prisoner at an altar). The basic scheme has multiple potential myths that could be attached to it; in our example, we could use the myth of Polyxena or Iphigeneia. The individual artisan could also modify this scheme, changing the gender of the prisoner, adding more prisoners, or making it an animal sacrifice. These schemes are creative and allow for flexibility, but can also be hard for modern scholars to interpret in isolation. If we go back to our original example, how might we identify the scene of the man and woman at an altar? One option could be *dress*; another is *attribute* (for example, Athena can be recognized by her aegis, and Hercules by his lionskin). But often we can't tell (we're not sure ancient viewers could, either). Sometimes, the characters in these depictions are identified with labels. In these cases, we know their names, and we can perhaps connect them to a mythic cycle. But as you will see, the iconographic version of the story can be quite different from the "known" written version.

In this chapter, we examine myths that appear in iconography, whether or not they appear in text as well. You should take advantage of the cross-referencing to the texts in other chapters to see how the iconographic characters differ from their written counterparts. Because our society tends to understand the past through words (the book you're reading is a good example), it's very easy for us to forget that other societies may not have done so. We therefore tend to privilege verbal material over visual material, and to try to explain the images in the terms of the words that survive. It's almost certain that people in antiquity did the opposite, and were much more attuned to artistic cues than we are.

Having made this observation, all of the chosen images have written material to accompany them. This admitted discrepancy should not discourage you. Examine the images on their own terms. What can you see depicted? What does it tell you? Feel free to begin with general terms ("this mirror shows a man and a woman") before moving to specifics. Once you have described as much as you can, try to piece together what it tells you. Does the clothing suggest anything about the character's social status? Does the background give clues about the location? Why might scholars think that this is a myth, rather than another form of narrative?

For Further Thought

1. What is the relationship between the iconographic versions of myths you see and read about in this chapter and the written version? (It may be easiest to start with the Labors of Hercules, available in outline at www.perseus.tufts.edu/Herakles/labors.html)

2. Consider the problems modern scholars face when dealing with a civilization that is understood primarily through its archaeological remains. What is the most difficult to deal with? Are these the same interpretive difficulties faced by scholars who deal with civilizations known primarily from words?

3. Do you think iconographic evidence for myth is more valuable than written evidence? Be prepared to defend your answer.

TEXTS[1]

4.1 Mlacuch

Hercules was known as a founder of cities. As we've seen (and will see again), a major motif in city foundation is the capture of a local woman to become the mother of the new population.[2] In the image below, we may have such a myth. Hercules perhaps kidnaps and perhaps rescues a woman in the course of one of his adventures. This scene has been connected to his argument at the shrine of the Bona Dea (**7.1.1**), or to his kidnapping of Faunus' daughter (**2.1.2**). But there is no way to connect the visual motif firmly with either myth. Some scholars have argued that rather than kidnapping the woman, Hercules is helping her. In this case, we should perhaps think of a story like Deianeira's: Hercules rescued her from the sea monster Nessus.

——————   4.1.1   Mirror of unknown provenance (possibly   ——————
                Adria), c. 500–475 BCE (London, British Museum)

http://www.britishmuseum.org/research/collection_online/collection_object_
details.aspx?objectId=466960&partId=1&images=true

The mirror depicts a man with a club, labeled "Hercle" (Hercules) hoisting a
woman labeled "Mlacuch." She is richly dressed in elaborate drapery, a narrow,
long shawl, and wears a diadem on her head. This perhaps suggests that she is
a queen or local deity. One of her arms pushes Hercules' head downwards; the
other reaches for his sword. She seems to be putting up a fight. In response,
Hercules braces one of his feet against the side of the mirror.

"Mlacuch" is an Etruscan word that appears only on this mirror. However, a
similar word appears on other mirrors featuring brides. We believe that these
scenes are non-mythical, and therefore it is possible that "Mlacuch" is not a
name, but a description of the woman in this mirror. The gesture Hercules
uses to lift Mlacuch from the waist is known from Greek abduction scenes,
which usually lead to rape or marriage and the birth of a new hero. Since
Hercules was one of the most popular founding heroes in Italy, the scene
on this mirror could be a snapshot of a foundation legend. As some scholars have argued, however, the scene is one of willing companionship. They
point out that Hercules generally treats women well, and interpret the scene as
simply erotic.

——————   4.1.2   Mirror from Vulci, fifth century BCE   ——————
                (Vatican, Museo Gregoriano Etrusco)

Atalanta and Peleus face off at Pelias' funeral.[3] He is nude, like most Greek
athletes; she is clothed lightly in a *perizoma* (shorts or a loincloth) and a cap.
In this image, she is nude on top; later imagery will add a bra. Her femininity is
marked by her covered lower body. The cap is more practical: it would prevent
her opponent from pulling her hair.

This scene appears most often on Greek vases, but the majority of such vases
have been found in Etruria. The distribution suggests that they were made with
Etruscan tastes in mind. Mirrors too display a variety of altered Greek myths
(for more examples, see van der Meer 1995). Certainly Etruscan women seem
to have led a more active life than Athenian women. Nonetheless, Atalanta
was a Greek character. She had been raised as a huntress and participated in the
hunt for the Calydonian boar.[4] In many versions of the myth, she seriously
wounded the boar and was refused the honor of the boar's hide. The story
of her wrestling match with Peleus is not very descriptive, but we know that
she won.

Because the myth of Atalanta is so well represented iconographically, it may
provide a model for Hercules and Mlacuch. Wrestling in antiquity could be
both competitive and erotic. If Atalanta is the model for Mlacuch, we could

Figure 4.1   Atalanta wrestles Peleus. Mirror, Vulci, fifth century BCE. Source: Vatican Museum inv. 12247. Photo © Vatican Museum. All rights reserved. Any reproduction, duplication, or alteration is expressly prohibited.

imagine a myth where Mlacuch competed with Hercules, either for a prize or to avoid marriage. We don't know the end of this story, and it's possible that the mirror depicts a scene in the middle, rather than its conclusion.

4.2   Hercules and Juno

Hercules had several adventures in Italy. Although Italian-made artifacts, like Greek-made artifacts, often depicted his labors, in Italy Hercules also appears in other scenes. The idea that Hercules suckled at Juno's breast to gain admission to Olympus appeared in both Etruscan and South Italian art. As you'll notice, however, different artists could approach the material in very different ways.

As a comparison, Cicero tells us about what sounds like a similar statue – not of Hercules, but of the baby Jupiter.

———— 4.2.1 Mirror of unknown provenance, fourth (?) ————
century BCE (Bologna, Museo Civico Archeologico)

Figure 4.2 Hercle suckles at Uni's breast. Mirror, fourth (?) century. Source: Bologna, Museo Civico inv. 1075. Image courtesy of the Museo Civico Archeologico di Bologna.

A woman in the center of the mirror breast-feeds a young man on the left, while a second youth watches over her shoulder. Both males are beardless, but the breast-feeding one is fleshier and perhaps younger. He barely fits within the border. Between his head and his shoulder, you can just make out the lionskin: it's Hercules. Looking carefully at his legs, you can see that his left knee is bent, and beside his straight right leg is a thin club, like a baseball bat. The woman is seated on an elaborate chair, whose armrest is visible beneath her hand. She holds out her other hand to Hercules. The man behind her has his hand on his shoulder and stands in a position similar to Hercules'. He has not been identified, but is probably one of the gods or Iolaus.

<hr>

4.2.2   Mirror from Volterra, c. 325 BCE
(Florence, Museo Archeologico Nazionale)

http://books.openedition.org/efr/docannexe/image/2741/img-16-small700.jpg

A mature and bearded Hercules nurses at the breast of Uni, the Etruscan Juno. It's time for his apotheosis. The scene takes place in the heavens, and he's watched by the gods, his new family. Behind Juno, Jupiter holds a tablet. It explains that Hercules, by nursing at Juno's breast, will become her son (and, it's implied, worthy of living with the gods). We aren't sure who the other gods are; two have been tentatively identified as Apollo (far left) and Hebe (wearing veil). Hebe will become Hercules' divine wife, so her closeness to Hercules in the mirror makes sense. However, several other mirrors depict this scene without Hebe, so her presence isn't necessary.

Above the scene, a satyr looks into a *patera*, a ritual vessel. He is probably performing a form of divination. Below is a small winged male, whose relationship with the remaining scene is unclear.

<hr>

4.2.3   Lekythos from Apulia, c. 365–350 BCE
(London, British Museum)

http://www.britishmuseum.org/research/collection_online/collection_object_details/collection_image_gallery.aspx?assetId=320621001&objectId=463602&partId=1

Hera sits on a throne, wearing an elaborate dress and jewelry. She breast-feeds the young Hercules, who wears bracelets and ankle rings, and who has a belt across one shoulder (perhaps a quiver?). Behind Hera sits Alcmene, Hercules' mother, holding a wreath; Aphrodite with Eros at her shoulder; and Iris (with wings), who faces them. In front of Hera is Athena, who holds out a bunch of flowers to Hercules.

<hr>

4.2.4   Cicero, *On Divination* 2.85

*Scenes of women suckling are relatively rare in classical art. Here, Cicero discusses an oak tree near a statue of Jupiter and Juno suckling at the breasts of Fortune. The iconography may have been similar to that of Hercules and Juno, and also recalls the divine significance of twins (**3.1**).*

Today the oak is venerated in a shrine near the statue of the baby Jupiter – the one who sits with Juno on the lap of Fortune, pawing for her breast. Mothers worship there most reverently.

4.3   Suckling Wolf

For texts related to this section, see ***3.1***.

Although the she-wolf and twins are strongly associated with Rome, animals nursing humans appear in myths throughout the Mediterranean. In Greece, for example, Zeus nursed at the teats of the goat-nymph Amalthea; in Persia, Cyrus nursed at the teats of a dog. Iconographic evidence suggests that the motif of the wolf nursing infants was known throughout central Italy. But why wolves? Scholars aren't sure. Some have connected the wolf to death, particularly in Etruria (the Etruscan word for *death* sounds similar to the Latin word for *wolf*). Others have associated the wolf with ferocity and pointed to the steady stream of wars and raids in early Italy. And others still suggest that the wolf was a common threat faced by the shepherds who feature so prominently in Italian myth.

—————   4.3.1   Stele from Felsina, late fifth century BCE   —————
(Bologna, Museo Civico Archeologico)

http://1.bp.blogspot.com/-S1vK6r3l5y0/Tkad5ATti5I/AAAAAAAAFBg/EmiHh_
GbmFU/s1600/bologna+stele.png

This funerary marker, like many others from the same **necropolis** (cemetery), is shaped like a shovel or a spoon. It has three **registers** (tiers), separated by thick bands. The top register is very narrow, with two ivy leaves. The center register has a man in a chariot, driving to the viewer's right. The horse's hooves suggest prancing, so we should perhaps think of this chariot as taking part in a procession. In the lowest register, an animal suckles a single child. This child's body faces front; he holds the animal's legs in his hands and twists his neck awkwardly to suckle. The animal has been interpreted both as a wolf (and thus similar to Romulus and Remus) and as a lion (due to its broad nose). In Etruscan art, wolves can be associated with death (see **4.5**); some scholars have suggested that this stele should therefore be interpreted as a wolf, despite the feline face.

—————   4.3.2   Mirror from Praeneste, fourth century BCE   —————
(Rome, Antiquarium Communale)

In the center of the mirror lies an animal (commonly identified as a wolf) nursing two children, who lounge with their backs to each other. While they are not in identical poses, they appear to be the same age and are acknowledged to be twins. The three figures, wolf and twins, are surrounded by rocks. Below them is another creature, which seems to be a feline rather than a wolf, which we can call a "lion." It crouches in a marshy area (there are reeds to the left of its head), which is unusual behavior for a cat.

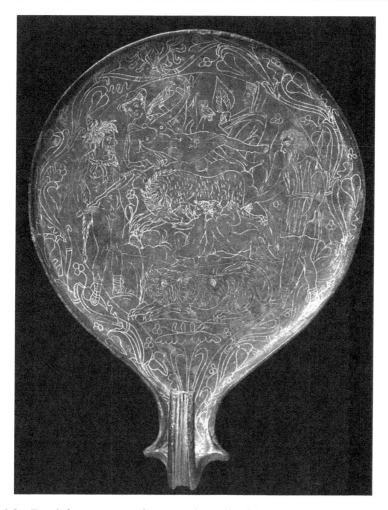

Figure 4.3 Two infants nurse at the teats of a wolf, while two men look on. Mirror from Praeneste, fourth century BCE. Source: Image © Archivio Fotografico dei Musei Capitolini and reproduced with permission of the Sovrintendenza Capitolina ai Beni Culturali – Musei Capitolini, Rome.

There is a man to either side of the wolf and twins group. The man to the left is mostly nude; he wears a goatskin cape and boots, and carries a shepherd's crook. He may have horns, and is definitely bearded. Opposite him is a man in a short tunic, wearing sandals and carrying a spear. He too has a beard, and he points to the wolf and twins, drawing the viewer's attention to the miraculous scene.

At the top of the mirror, a man wearing a hat and cape stretches out. He leans on one elbow, with his other hand touching a sickly-looking tree. The shape of this hat is called a *petasus*, which is an attribute of the god Mercury. At Mercury's shoulder is a bird, which is hard to identify but may be a wood-pecker. On the other side of the tree is another bird. This one is definitely an owl. Finally, there is a veiled woman holding a large, tear-shaped fan. Flowers grow behind her, and ivy leaves border the scene. None of the figures are labeled.

This complex mirror has been the subject of much controversy. For many years it was considered a fake because it seemed too conveniently close to the foundation myth of Rome. In the 1980s, that judgment was successfully challenged, and the mirror has been considered ancient ever since. There are two major schools of thought about what it represents. The first group considers the mirror to be the earliest surviving evidence for the Romulus and Remus myth (it is about a century older than surviving coinage: **4.3.3**). In this interpretation, the man to the left (with horns) is Faustulus, the shepherd who found the twins, or perhaps Faustinus, Faustulus' brother according to some sources. The clothed man facing him is thus either Numitor or Faustulus. The woman has been identified as Acca, Faustulus' wife and the twins' foster-mother.

The other interpretation was proposed by Peter Wiseman (1993). Wiseman argued that the first view wrongly applies written evidence to iconographic material, and suggests an interpretation that starts from the iconography and seeks a myth to match. If this methodological distinction is hard for you to grasp, don't worry: one of the criticisms of Wiseman's argument is that it's closely intertwined with literary sources, in particular Ovid.

Wiseman argues for a calendric reading of the mirror. He interprets the figure to the far left as Lupercus, whose Lupercalia festival (**3.2**) was two days before the festival of Quirinus. Quirinus was a pre-existing god who became identified with Romulus (**3.7**). Wiseman suggests that the mirror predates this identification stage, and Quirinus is the figure with a spear on the right. This leaves the twins as the explanation for the Feralia a few days later. Because the Feralia may celebrate the birth of the *Lares* (**chapter 2 introduction**), Wiseman interprets the mirror as depicting the *Lares*, rather than Romulus and Remus.

He has been challenged most often by the archaeologist Andrea Carandini, whose numerous works on Italian myth suggest a linked web of connections between the Romulus and Remus cycle and other tales. Carandini (1997) identifies the standing men as Faunus (**2.1, 5.2.3**) on the left and Latinus (**2.5.1, 2.5.6**) on the right. He further claims that the mirror itself offers an "authentic" view of all Rome's myths at once (Carandini 2012, 40). Carandini argues that Wiseman cannot explain the twin founders out of the myth; he can only add further layers of myth in.

Françoise-Hélène Massa-Pairault (2011) has recently argued that the *Lares* myth never appears on other artistic productions, while Romulus and Remus do. This type of argument is called the "argument from silence," and because we don't have every mythical illustration from antiquity, scholars usually combine this argument with alternative identifications or reasons to support their interpretations. Massa-Pairault supports her argument by referring to the importance of places and festivals to a Roman audience. In her view, the mirror combines the best points from Wiseman's and Carandini's arguments: it relates to the Lupercalia festival, but via Romulus and Remus.

The identification of the myth on this mirror continues to be debated. Because none of the figures on the mirror is labeled, there is no way to judge who is right – or if no one is right. The best option is to decide whose interpretation of the evidence is most convincing to you and be prepared to support your reasoning.

4.3.3 Silver coin from Rome, mid-third century BCE (New York, American Numismatic Society)

http://numismatics.org/collection/1944.100.15

This coin of the Roman Republic (*RRC* 20/1) has Hercules on the obverse (heads) side and the she-wolf and twins on the reverse (tails) side. Hercules is recognizable from his club (which looks like a studded collar) and lionskin (which is clasped at his throat). The she-wolf on the back twists her head backwards to lick one of the twins. Meanwhile, her tail comes between her legs to caress the other twin. The she-wolf's fur is shaggy; the wolf herself is lean and muscular, with a fierce expression.

The twins are depicted as infants with awkwardly muscled bodies. They face each other and grasp at the wolf's teats, arms crossing. Their pose is similar to the twins of the Capitoline Wolf (**4.3.4**). Below the coins is the word *Romano*, indicating that the coin was made on the authority of the Roman people.

4.3.4 "Capitoline Wolf," medieval (?) (Rome, Capitoline Museums)

http://en.museicapitolini.org/var/museicivici/storage/images/musei/musei_ capitolini/collezioni/percorsi_per_sale/appartamento_dei_conservatori/sala_ della_lupa/lupa_capitolina/11491-19-ita-IT/lupa_capitolina.jpg

The Capitoline Wolf has long been an icon of Rome. This particular example, however, may not be ancient. The twins were made in the Renaissance and added to the sculpture purposefully to call up the image of the twins Romulus and Remus. But for many years, the Wolf itself was considered a fifth-century Etruscan work of art.

When the Wolf was restored in the late 1990s, the conservator suggested that the Wolf was actually made a thousand years later. She suggested a date of c. 800 CE. Her research stirred up a great deal of controversy, with many scholars insisting that her evidence (the manufacturing technique[5]) was simply not strong enough to support her claim. Subsequent laboratory tests have been inconclusive. Right now, we don't know whether the Wolf itself is Etruscan or medieval. Even if the Wolf is ancient, however, there is no reason to assume that in antiquity she would have been associated with the twin founders of the city – especially without Romulus and Remus.

4.4 Prophets

The Etruscans were famous in antiquity for their religious knowledge and skill, particularly in divination. So it's not surprising that many of their artifacts depict scenes of prophecy. Many are unknown outside of Italy. This section centers on the founders of Etruscan prophecy, Tages and Pavatarchies. They are among the few Etruscan characters Romans took an interest in. Unlike the Vibenna brothers (**4.6**), these diviners had no relationship with Rome. Although Cicero (**4.4.3**) dismisses the myth with scorn, the Etruscans who retold these tales presumably felt differently.

──────────────── 4.4.1   Gemstone, fourth century BCE ────────────────
(Rome, Villa Giulia)

Figure 4.4   Tarchon bends over Tages as he emerges from the ground. Gemstone, fourth century BCE. Source: Villa Giulia. Image reproduced with the permission of the Ministero dei Beni e delle Attività Culturali e del Turismo – Soprintendenza Archeologia del Lazio e dell'Etruria Meridionale.

A mature man bends over to retrieve something emerging from the ground. Although the gem is damaged, you should be able to see the arm extending towards the sky. One finger points up: if you follow it, you can see a head half-buried in the ground. This is Tages, the founder of Etruscan prophecy. The bearded man bent over him is Tarchon, who recorded Tages' prophecies and spread his teachings. It's no accident that Tages appears as only a head and arm. Both are indicators of prophecy in Etruscan art (de Grummond and Simon 2009, 27–30; de Grummond 2011).

––––––––––––   4.4.2   Mirror from Tuscania, late fourth/early   ––––––––––––
third century BCE (Florence, Museo Archeologico)

http://www.tages.eu/wp-content/uploads/2012/05/IL-FEGATO-NELLO-SPECCHIO-ETRUSCO.jpg

On the mirror, a group of Etruscans consult a seer. He is the second from the right, whose foot is on a rock in traditional prophetic posture. He holds a roundish object in his hand. This is a liver, which he examines for omens in an act called *extispicy* (entrail prophecy). He's labeled *Pavatarchies*. The bearded man with a spear beside him on the far right is Vertumnus (**6.7**), an Etruscan god. On Pavatarchies' left is a woman, labeled Ucernei. Beside her, second from the left, is Aulus Tarchon; beside him is the god Rath, holding a laurel branch. In the top register is the sun chariot; in the bottom, a winged young man holds up the ground.

The name "Pavatarchies" (sometimes written as two words: *Pava Tarchies*) has been interpreted in two different ways. Most commonly, he is seen as the equivalent of Tages (**4.4.1**). If so, this mirror depicts him teaching the craft of extipicy to the watching crowd. But he has also been interpreted as a student, learning prophecy from the older and more experienced *haruspex* Aulus Tarchon (Leighton 2004, 76). We know that Aulus Tarchon is older because he has a beard, a sign of maturity, while Pavatarchies does not.

Regardless of how we interpret this mirror, it is clear that it shows a scene of prophecy. The gods' presence suggests, but cannot guarantee, that it is mythical. They may also symbolize divine control over prophetic matters, the specific gods consulted by the prophets, or a change that will happen because of the prophecy.

––––––––––––   4.4.3   Cicero, *On Divination* 2.50–2.51   ––––––––––––

Cicero's work on divination is divided into two parts: the first book defends divination, while the second decries it as false knowledge. As an augur (practicing augury, Rome's preferred form of divination), Cicero may have been especially prejudiced against Etruscan haruspicy as a competing form of expertise.

Let's examine the beginnings of haruspicy. We'll be able to judge very easily whether it has any basis. They say a man was plowing the fields around Tarquinia.[6] He'd made a rather deep furrow when all of a sudden Tages jumped up and started talking to him. This Tages, as they say in the books of the Etruscans, had boyish looks but the good sense of an older man. At the sight of him, the plowman's mouth dropped open and he let out a giant holler at the miracle. Men rushed towards him and pretty soon all Etruria swarmed towards the place. Then, when he had lots of people listening who would take down all of his words and leave them for future generations, Tages spoke for a long time. His speech forms the basis of the practice of haruspicy. Later the discipline expanded as new material was learned and fit these basics.

This is the story we get from the Etruscan diviners, who preserved these writings;[7] this is the source of their learning. Do I really need to refer to the Stoics to refute it? Could anyone be such an idiot that he believes someone plowed up a god – *or* a man? If he was a god, why did he hide himself in the ground, unlike most gods, only to be uncovered by a plow and see the light? I mean, really: couldn't a god hand down his teachings to men from a more dignified place? But if Tages was a man, how in the world could he live smothered under the dirt? And where did he learn those things he taught? But I'm even dumber than those who believe this stuff, since I've been arguing against it for this long.

─────────── 4.4.4 Livy, *From the Foundation 2.7* ───────────

*Although difficult to imagine in a modern urban environment, deep woods were sacred to the Romans. The forest was the home of Faunus (**2.1, 5.2.3**) and other deities. Livy is our sole source for this tale of the voice in the woods, but the story fits several other narratives of the prophetic head or prophetic voice (see de Grummond 2011). For the context of the prophecy, see **8.1–8.3**.*

When it came to fighting, such immense fear blanketed Tarquin and the Etruscans that the armies of Veii and of Tarquinia gave the matter up as useless. Each left for their own homes at night. They say a miracle happened at the battle: in the stillness of the next night, a huge voice boomed out of the Arsian Wood. The men believed it was the voice of Silvanus.[8] It relayed the following message: "The Etruscans lost one more man in battle, so the Romans have won the war." The men left the place after that, the Romans as victors and the Etruscans as men defeated.

──────── 4.4.5 Ovid, *Metamorphoses* 15.552–15.559 ────────

Ovid's version of Tages focuses on the surprise of the viewers, an aspect that has been emphasized when trying to identify the scene iconographically.

The news reached the nymphs, and the Amazon's son gawped too, like when the Etruscan farmer saw the divine clod of dirt in the middle of his field. It moved by itself with no help and soon took on the appearance of a man, dissolving the look of a clod. Then it opened its new mouth to relate future events. The natives called him Tages,[9] who first taught the Etruscans to read the future.

──────── 4.4.6 John Lydus, *On Omens* 3 ────────

Lydus provides more information about the transmission of Tages' teachings. He claims to have consulted Etruscan books in order to gain his knowledge.

In his writings, Tarchon relates how something amazing happened to him one day when he was plowing. Certain men suspect the ideas belong to Tages, since the book is a dialogue: Tarchon asks a question and Tages answers, like a religious devotee. Anyway, it's the sort of thing that no one's *ever* heard of happening in all recorded time. Out of the furrow a child appeared, apparently just born, but he had teeth and other indications of maturity. This child, as it seems, was Tages [...] Tarchon the elder (for there was also a younger Tarchon,[10] who commanded armies at the time of Aeneas) picked up the baby and set him down in holy places. He thought it was worthwhile to learn something about the unspeakable secrets of existence from him, and later he wrote a book based on the conversation.

4.5 Wolfman

A series of urns from Etruria and myths from southern Italy depict a "wolfman": a wolf's head with human hands and feet. The hybrid perhaps offers our first example of werewolves. Many scholars object to the identification, pointing out that the "wolfman" is clearly a man wearing a costume, much like Hercules and the lionskin. The two interpretations aren't necessarily contradictory, since a man in wolf's clothing may have been reinterpreted or misunderstood as a shape-shifter by later generations. Either way, he seems connected to ferocity and death. For the double significance of wolves in Italy, see **4.3**.

——————   4.5.1   Urn from Volterra, Hellenistic period   ——————
(Volterra, Museo Guernacci)

http://www.comune.pisa.it/gr-archeologico/musvir/urne/stofr12.htm

In the center of this relief is a wellhead with a figure springing out of it. It
has a strange head, somewhat like a dog. Similar urns tell us that it's either
a wolf or a man in a wolf's costume. He grabs a figure in front of him, who
falls to his knees helplessly. The fallen man is defended by a nude warrior
with an axe (now missing his head) and a clothed warrior with a sword.
A third, on the far right of the urn, shows us his shield, but has his sword
drawn.

The beast has a leash around his neck; the leash is held by the figure
sitting behind the well. This seated figure reclines on one elbow with his
feet pushed against the wellhead, as if he is straining to hold the beast back.
Two other figures stand on this side of the urn. One, closer to the wellhead,
holds a *patera* (a shallow dish, used for ritual purposes) above the beast. He
also has a visible sword.

Some scholars suggest that this urn, as well as several others, should be
associated with a narrative found in Pliny (**4.5.2**). In this case, we are seeing an illustration of an Etruscan myth that was retold orally, and which
Pliny wrote down. Others dismiss this idea, and suggest a mythical background with Greek parallels, such as Sisyphus capturing Thanatos (death).[11]
Finally, some scholars point to the *patera* as an indication that the scene had
religious significance. They argue that the urns depict a death ritual that
was widely practiced throughout Italy, and that the wolves should be interpreted as actors. There is as yet no consensus on how best to interpret this
iconography.

——————————   4.5.2   Pliny, *Natural History* 2.140   ——————————

*Pliny's story has parallels in works of Roman history, but he's the only one to
mention Olta. The connection with wolves is complex (and perhaps tenuous):
Olta is a monster, who must come from the underworld; the wellhead indicates
the underworld; therefore the monster can be understood as a wolf. The word
Pliny uses to describe the monster simply means "omen."*

Records remain in the annals about certain rites and prayers to collect
or cause lightning. A really old story from Etruria tells how a monster
called Olta destroyed the fields of Volsinii and attacked the city. Their
king, Porsenna, caused a thunderstorm.[12] Before him, this was often
done by Numa [...][13] Tullus Hostilius[14] was killed by lightning when
he tried to imitate Numa and made mistakes.

4.6   The Vibenna Brothers

The brothers Aulus and Caelius Vibenna offer an Etruscan comparison to Romulus and Remus or Greek brothers such as Eteocles and Polynices. These heroes seem to have been known throughout Etruria; their names and images recur in various media from different cities. We know more about them than many Etruscan figures because Caelius supposedly came to Rome to help either Romulus or Tarquin in war (**4.6.4**).

Etruscan narratives about the Vibenna brothers seem to have been quite different, and certainly less favorable to Rome. In fact, the François Tomb frescoes have been interpreted as preserving anti-Roman sentiment at a time of Roman expansion in Italy. Both sets of evidence are provided below. The literary sources fluctuate in their dating: the Vibennae appear in the early and late regal period. This is typical of Roman mythmaking, which tried to push as many events as possible back to Romulus' day or earlier.

———————   4.6.1   Frescoes from the François Tomb, Vulci,   ———————
later fourth century BCE (Rome, Villa Albani)

http://www.etruriameridionale.beniculturali.it/index.php?it/193/la-tomba-franois (diagram, images of Vibennae and Achilles)
http://www.repubblica.it/2009/06/sezioni/arte/gallerie/vulci-tomba/vulci-tomba/1.html (all)

Etruria is justly celebrated for its brilliantly painted tombs. Among the most famous of these are the painted frescoes from the François Tomb, a familial burial place in Vulci that was first excavated in the mid-nineteenth century. Several generations used this tomb, but the main burial chamber, which features floor-to-ceiling painted frescoes, has drawn the most attention. (The ceiling is painted, too, but its decorative motifs are less commonly studied.) The tomb's many labeled mythological figures are interspersed with two figures who seem to be among the deceased (Vel Saties and Arnza). Although most of the figures refer to Greek myths (such as Cassandra and Achilles), a few seem to be Roman (Camillus, for whom see **8.9** and **8.10**; Tarquin, **5.4** and **5.6**) – and one wall perhaps features a series of Etruscan heroes (including the Vibenna brothers). Going clockwise from the far left in the diagram, these scenes show Phoenix and Nestor; Eteocles killing Polynices; the sacrifice of the Trojan prisoners (across two walls); Caelius Vibenna and Mastarna; the "night attack" of three duels (between Larth Ulthes and Laris Pepathnas Velznach; Aulus Vibenna and Venthi Cau...plsachs;[15] and Rasce and Pesna Arcmsnas Svetimach); Marcus Camillus and Tarquin of Rome; Vel Saties and Arnza; a damaged panel. Unseen are Ajax and Cassandra, across from Eteocles and Polynices, and Amphiaraus and Sisyphus, across from Camillus and Tarquin.

Scholars generally agree that these disparate images share a theme. Their suggestions for what this theme is vary considerably. Some of the suggestions may co-exist (there may be more than one theme in the tomb), while others are mutually exclusive. Thus scholars have interpreted the themes as violence, designed to stand in for ritual sacrifice to the dead; cultural pride; friendship and diplomacy; and discord. There are also numerous connections between individual panels, such as the Trojan prisoners and Cassandra (both are part of the Troy cycle).

But the interpretation of the "night attack" scene has been the most disputed part of the tomb. Most scholars believe that the wall depicts an Etruscan historical narrative. Similar historical art is known from Greece and Rome, and evidence for such material is also emerging from southern Italy. Yet what is that narrative? Does it include the adjoining wall, which features Tarquin of Rome? Does it relate to our written narratives of Roman history (particularly a "negative" tradition about the capture of the city (**8.4** and **8.8.5**)), or is it independent? If it is related to Roman sources, how can that relationship be analyzed when we lack written Etruscan histories? These are some of the many questions that scholars have grappled with. While answers are not easy, there are two broad ways to interpret this difficult fresco.

One way is to include the Camillus/Tarquin wall in the "night attack" scene. Scholars interpret this combined scene as a mythicized exploit connected to the downfall of the Tarquins at Rome (**5.6.5, 7.6, 8.1–8.5**). As support, they cite the presence of Mastarna on the back wall. Mastarna, according to the speech of the emperor Claudius (**4.6.4b**), was Rome's second-to-last king; this scene shows his earlier life and adventures.

The second way is to separate the Camillus scene. Scholars don't discard Claudius' evidence, but they point out that the Etruscan and Roman evidence otherwise does not coincide. Therefore, there is no need to see the "night attack" as an attack on Rome. Instead, it could be anywhere; in fact, the other fighters in the scene are Etruscans. This group argues that the scene probably shows a mythic battle between Etruscan troops.

It seems unlikely that this debate will be decided one way or the other any time soon. However, there's other evidence (both Etruscan and Roman) that you can use to help you make up your mind about which interpretation you find more convincing.

───────────   4.6.2 Mirror from Bolsena, third century BCE   ───────────
(London, British Museum)

http://www.britishmuseum.org/collectionimages/AN00303/AN00303298_001
_l.jpg

At the center of the mirror sits the long-haired Cacu, wearing a torque and lightly draped. He holds a cithara[16] and looks at it intently. Beside him sits Artile, also lightly draped, holding a writing tablet. They're in a forest or other outdoor location. Behind the trees on either side lurk two armed men, labeled

Caele Vibenna and Aule Vibenna. Caele's head has been damaged; he has his sword drawn and holds a shield. Aule holds his shield with both hands. They seem ready to attack Cacu and Artile. Above, a satyr's head peeps down; this probably indicates a prophecy (**4.4.1 introduction**). The scene is bordered with grapevines, and a winged child runs to the right at the bottom.

The Vibenna brothers seem to be involved in the capture of a seer, an event that is known from Greek and Roman literature (**5.2.3**). Cacu's sad expression and the prophetic head suggests that he knows about the coming attack. The ambush itself is pictured on a series of urns (**4.6.3**).

—————— 4.6.3 Urn from Chiusi, second century BCE ——————
(Florence, Museo Archeologico Nazionale 74233)

Figure 4.5 Cacu is captured by the Vibenna brothers. Funerary urn, Chiusi, second century BCE. Source: Museo Archeologico Firenze inv. 74233. Image reproduced with the permission of the Polo Museale Regionale della Toscana. Reproduction in any format is prohibited.

One side of this second-century BCE funerary urn depicts the capture of Cacu by the Vibenna brothers. Cacu is the central figure with long hair. He wears a necklace of protective charms, but only a small bit of drapery covers his left leg. The Vibenna brothers hem him in from either side, wearing full armor and carrying shields. One tries to calm a rearing horse. On the far right, we see their comrade, also wearing armor; a similar character may be on the far left.

Seated on Cacu's lower left is a figure who has been interpreted as Artile. He stretches out his hand, perhaps seeking help. At the bottom, warriors on their knees holding swords have been or will be defeated.

This urn is one of several with very similar scenes coming from Chiusi and its environs. The scene seems to be a continuation of the ambush on the mirror (**4.6.2**). But who is the target of the attack: Cacu or Artile? Although arguments for both sides have been made, the majority favors Cacu. In this interpretation, Cacu is a famous seer whose knowledge of the future can help the Vibenna brothers accomplish a goal. He's not willing to share this information, so they take it by force, kidnapping Cacu and forcing him to reveal his secrets. The adventures of **4.6.2** and **4.6.3** seem to be different from that on display in **4.6.1**.

--------------------   4.6.4   Literary texts on Caelius Vibenna   --------------------

We have no written texts describing the adventures of both Vibenna brothers. Caelius was more popular among Roman authors, who considered him the eponym of the Caelian Hill. The several accounts of the Caelian's name provide some of the strongest written evidence for the adventures of the Vibenna brothers.

a. Varro, ***On the Latin Language*** **5.46**   *Varro explains the name of the Caelian Hill. Although he is unusual in setting the story under Romulus, Varro's story shares themes with later Roman myth: people who hold the high ground are trying to be king (**8.2**).*

The Caelian Hill is named for Caelius Vibenna, a noble Etruscan leader, who is said to have come with his men to help Romulus against Titus Tatius.[17] After the death of Caelius, it's said that these men went down from here into the plain, because they held a position that was too strongly fortified and they were themselves suspicious.

b. Speech of the Emperor Claudius on the Gallic Senators (*CIL* 13.1668 = *ILS* 212)   *The Emperor Claudius (r. 41–54 CE) was a noted antiquarian. In this speech, he uses mythic precedents to explain the importance of foreigners to Rome. His use of myth to defend a policy position (of allowing Gauls to enter Rome's Senate) emphasizes the importance of immigrant communities like the Sabines and Trojans to Roman life, as well as the continuing relevance of Roman myth to contemporary life. His account should be compared to **5.4.3**.*

If we follow our sources, [Servius Tullius] was born to Ocresia, a captive woman; if we follow the Etruscans, he was once the most faithful companion of Caelius Vibenna and the companion in all of his adventures. After experiencing varied fortunes, he left Etruria with all the remaining men in Caelius' army and settled on the Caelian Hill, naming it after

Caelius his leader. He then changed his name (for in Etruria he was called Mastarna) to Servius Tullius, as I have said, and Rome benefited enormously when he took the throne.

c. Tacitus, *Annals* 4.65   *Tacitus digresses from his account of a fire on the Caelian to discuss its origins. Linguistically, he seems to draw on the Emperor Claudius' version (**4.6.4b**) of the Vibenna tale, but his narrative is more like Varro's (**4.6.4a**).*

Now's a good time to add the story that that hill was long ago called "Oakville" because it was so thickly wooded. Later it was changed to "Caelian" after the Etruscan commander Caelius Vibenna. He accepted that spot from Tarquin the Elder (or some other king; authors disagree about it) when he came to help him. But the rest is clear: this large army lived in the plain as well, the one close to the Forum. These immigrants explain why it's now called the "Etruscan quarter."

d. Festus, "Etruscan Quarter"   *Festus' account of Caelius Vibenna may be the only written text from antiquity that mentions both Vibenna brothers. The manuscript has been badly damaged; although many suggestions for fixing it have been made, this translation sticks to the transmitted text.*

Many writers say that the ETRUSCAN QUARTER is named after those Etruscans who remained at Rome when King Porsenna[18] abandoned his siege. They lived in this area, which was given to them. Or because the brothers from Vulci, Caeles and [Aulus?] Vibenna,[19] whom they say King Tarquin [**lacuna**] lived in Rome. Marcus Varro says it is because they were led to the place from the Caelian Hill.

4.6.5   Literary texts on Aulus Vibenna

---

*Aulus Vibenna has a limited profile in Roman sources. His name doesn't appear until late antiquity, and then it is only as a decapitated head. But he may have been a historical figure: among other Etruscan evidence (**4.6.1–4.6.3**), there's a sixth-century bucchero cup inscribed "Aulus Vibenna dedicated me" (Heurgon 1966, 517). Although the story of the* caput Oli *is substantially fictionalized, the Capitol was a prehistoric burial ground. It's possible that Roman building crews did find human remains there.*

a. Livy, *From the Foundation* 1.55.5–1.55.6   *Livy relates the discovery of a human skull during the building of the temple of Jupiter Optimus*

*Maximus on the Capitol (**5.6.3**). Although he doesn't identify the head, that doesn't mean that the omen wasn't important: in addition to giving the Capitol its name ("head" in Latin is* caput*), the head symbolizes Rome's future prosperity.*

After they received this sign that their power would last forever, another omen followed that indicated its great size. A human head, they say, appeared as they laid the foundations of the temple. Its skull was complete. When the head had been seen, there was no doubt that it meant the citadel would be leader in world affairs.

b. Pliny, *Natural History* 28.15–16   *Pliny's account of the Etruscan seer who tries to "steal" a divine omen given to Rome has parallels in the augury of Romulus and Remus (**3.3.3**) and the king Servius Tullius (**5.5.2**). The name Olenus Calenus may be the source for Arnobius' Olus (**4.6.5c**).*

When they were digging the foundations for the sanctuary on the Tarpeian hill,[20] they found a human head. So the Romans sent an embassy to the most famous seer of Etruria about this matter. His name was Olenus Calenus, and he perceived that it was a spectacularly fortunate sign. He tried to transfer the omen to his own people by asking questions. First, he used his stick to trace the outline of the temple in the dirt before his feet and asked, "Romans, is this what you're talking about? Say this is the temple of Jupiter Best and Greatest. The head was found *here*?"

The annalists are unanimous that the fated power would have moved to Etruria if the ambassadors hadn't responded as they did (they were warned by the seer's son): "It's *not* this place. We insist that the head was found in Rome." And tradition holds that the same thing happened again when they were preparing a clay chariot for the shrine's rooftop decoration: it became life-sized in the oven.[21] And again the augury was kept in Rome.

c. Arnobius, *Against the Gentiles* 6.7   *Arnobius discusses the myths of men who are buried under shrines. His sarcastic explanation of the Capitol's eponym leaves little doubt that he knew the stories of **4.6.4**; most scholars think he also knew an older tradition about Aulus that is now lost. "Olus" and "Aulus" are different spellings of the same name.*

Is there anyone who doesn't know that the grave of Olus of Vulci is on the rulers' Capitol? I repeat: is there anyone who doesn't know that the head of a man rolled out from the depths of the foundations? It had been buried there not long before, either alone without the other limbs (as indeed some say) or with all its limbs. But if you need references,

Sammonicus, Granius, Valerianus, and Fabius will tell you whose son Aulus was, his family and his people, how he was deprived of his life and spirit by the hand of a slave, and what crime his fellow citizens accused him of, so that he was denied a place of burial in his fatherland. You'd also learn, although they pretend that they don't want to spread this rumor, what was done to his head once it had been revealed: that is, where they locked it up within the citadel in anxious obscurity, so that the secret omen stood, fixed and unmoving forever. Although it was equally likely to have been suppressed and hidden by the mists of time, the convenience of the name *caput Oli* tossed the head into the limelight and made the name and the reason for it present themselves as a permanent witness to the tale for Rome's allotted time. And the greatest city, worshipper of all divinities, was not embarrassed, when naming the temple, to name it after Olus' head, rather than Jupiter.

d. Servius, *On the* **Aeneid 8.345** *Servius comments on the line "Also Evander showed them the sacred grove of the Argiletum." He explains the name of the Argiletum, an area adjacent to the Forum.*

Some say that when the foundations of the Capitol were laid, a human head was found which was said to be Olus'. Worried by this omen, the founders sent to Etruria, to a haruspex famous at that time. Argus,[22] his son, declared that the sign had been conferred fatefully, that this place, in which the head had been found, would control the world.

4.7 Vulca of Veii

Marble was not used for building projects in early Rome. Instead, they used the far more abundant local clays. In the sixth century, Rome imported Etruscan artisans to decorate their newly-built temples. One of them became so well known that his name survived to Pliny's day, over 500 years later. Although Vulca himself may not be mythical, some of the stories associated with his artistic productions clearly are. Vulca therefore offers an example of how a historical event could become mythicized over time.

—————— 4.7.1 Statues from the Portonaccio sanctuary, ——————
Veii, c. 510 BCE (Rome, Villa Giulia)

http://www.villagiulia.beniculturali.it/index.php?it/111/veio

Several examples of Etruscan ritual terracotta statues have survived, although not from Rome. The most famous are the acroteria[23] from the temple at Veii's

Portonaccio sanctuary. They're contemporary with the statues from the Capitoline temple at Rome (**4.8.2**), so they offer a model for what Rome's statues might have looked like. The surviving statues come from the Temple of Minerva, and large-scale figures include Apollo (the famous "Aplu of Veii": http://www.apollodiveio.it/en/opera.asp), Heracles, and a woman with a child. She has been identified as Leto, Apollo's mother; as Minerva herself; and as Niobe.

These images were larger-than-life, so that from the ground they would have seemed lifelike. They originally ran along the peak of the roof, probably forming a scene from Hercules' labors. All of the surviving large terracottas are archaic in style, which means that they have round faces, almond-shaped eyes, and curly (almost ropelike) hair. They also share the "archaic smile," which is a closed-lip, contented smile that is typical of the era. The statues were all originally painted in bright colors, which are still partially visible. Apollo has gold-tinged hair, and wears a white tunic as well as a purple-bordered toga (similar to a *toga praetexta* in Rome). Hercules, meanwhile, wears his lionskin, but is otherwise nude. The woman wears a thin white dress which presses tightly against her legs. The drapery is elaborate. Unlike the men, her face is dead white. This is typical coloring for women (as opposed to men) in the Mediterranean. Both the male and the female deities are strongly muscled, which is more typical of Etruria than elsewhere.

4.7.2 Plutarch, *Life of Publicola* 13

*Plutarch's account takes place in the reign of Tarquin (**5.6**). It demonstrates the powers of the gods while foreshadowing the Etruscan conflict with Rome (**8.1–8.3**).*

While Tarquin was king and had almost completed the shrine of Capitoline Zeus, he hired some Etruscan craftsmen from Veii to make a clay statue of a chariot for the roof. Either there was an omen or he had some other reason. Not too long afterwards he was driven from the throne.[24]

The Etruscans molded the chariot and put it in the kiln. It did not react as clay usually does in the fire, contracting and settling as the moisture evaporates. Instead, it stood higher and swelled. It got to be so big, strong, and hard that it was difficult to take it out. They had to remove the roof and walls of the kiln.

Since the seers thought the chariot presented a divine sign of fortune and power among them, the people of Veii decided not to give it back to the Romans when they asked for it. They replied that the chariot belonged to the Tarquins, not those who had kicked the Tarquins out of the city.

A few days later they celebrated games on horseback. There were the usual sights and activities. But as a charioteer drove the winning chariot out of the hippodrome slowly, wearing a crown, the horses took flight, apparently at nothing (or at least nothing visible or audible). They were under the influence of some god or it was by chance. They went at full speed towards Rome, carrying the charioteer with them. Although he strained and shouted at them, it was no good. He was carried off. The horses dragged him by force all the way to the Capitoline [...] The people of Veii marveled at this event and were frightened. So they handed over the chariot to the workmen to deliver.

Conclusion

If iconographic evidence seems quite different from the myths we've seen so far, it's in part because it is: iconographic evidence comes from a range of cultures throughout Italy, while literary evidence from Italy is primarily Roman. Although we can't say for sure, it seems likely that these other societies were interested in their own city's myths, much as Romans were interested in Roman myths. The focus in each case is different, but nonetheless local.

Although various cultures supply iconographic evidence, there are still themes that appear to be shared throughout Italy. This isn't surprising: most civilizations in Italy had close contacts with both Greece and Rome, home to our literary sources, from an early date. These cultural interactions may have led to myth assimilation (gradually smoothing away the differences between different mythic cycles), adoption, or adaptation; certainly they led to myth exchange. We may see an example of that exchange in the Cacu and Vibenna mirror, which depicts a mythic scene (the capture of a prophet) known from Greek epic and Roman myths of King Numa.

Iconography also shows us myths that were important beyond the sphere of the elite. It thus helps us fill in "common knowledge" for ancient people of all social ranks, because we can learn the scenes that they'd be expected to identify. Sometimes these scenes are ambiguous, and that's okay: they might have been in antiquity, too.

Another major difference between the material in this chapter and that in the rest of this book is that most of it does not center on Rome. For this reason alone, illustrated myths, difficult as they are to grasp, are worth attention. Roman myth is fixated on the development of the city; even those myths that predate the foundation are eager to explain the establishment of customs that persist to the present day (or have been abandoned at great cost). It would be easy to imagine that all the peoples of Italy were equally interested in their home cities. The infrequent appearance of Roman myth on objects found outside the city – at least before the Principate – suggests that local mythology continued to thrive through centuries of war with Romans.

Notes

1. Live links for these images, along with some additional images, can be found at the book's website (earlyrome.omeka.net).
2. **2.5, 3.5, 7.6, 7.8.**
3. In Greek myth, Pelias was Jason's stepfather. See further http://dante.udallas.edu/hutchison/Heroes/Argonauts/pelias.htm
4. See Ovid, *Metamorphoses* 8.260–450.
5. The Capitoline Wolf was made as a single piece. Large-scale bronze statues from Greece were usually made in multiple pieces and joined together. Some scholars think that Etruscans made their large-scale bronze statues in the same way; others argue that there are not enough surviving statues for us to judge.
6. An Etruscan city.
7. Cicero probably referred to these writings in translation.
8. A woodland god often associated with Faunus.
9. "Earthy" in Greek.
10. Compare **5.4** and **5.6**, although the dates are different.
11. For another connection between wolves and demons, see **6.4.2, 6.4.4, 6.4.5.**
12. For King Porsenna, see **7.7** and **8.3**.
13. For Numa, see **5.2.3** and **5.2.5**.
14. For Tullus Hostilius, see **5.3.4**.
15. The name has been damaged in the middle.
16. A lap harp.
17. See **3.5.6** and **3.6.1**, where Caelius Vibenna's role is given to Lucumo.
18. See **7.7** and **8.3**.
19. Many scholars would like to emend the text here to read "Caeles and <Aulus> Vibenna." This would bring Festus' evidence into agreement with the François tomb frescoes (**4.6.1**). The original text includes only the letter A.
20. That is, the Capitol: see **5.6.3**.
21. Compare **4.7.2**.
22. See **4.6.5b**.
23. Decorations for the temple rooftop.
24. This dates Plutarch's story to the 510s BCE.

References

Carandini, Andrea. 1997. "Sullo specchio con lupa, Romolo e Remo. Di nuovo a proposito di T. P. Wiseman." *Ostraka* 6: 445–446.

Carandini, Andrea. 2012. *Rome: Day 1*, tr. Stephen Sartarelli. Princeton, NJ: Princeton University Press.

De Grummond, Nancy Thomson. 2011. "A Barbarian Myth? The Case of the Talking Head." In *The Barbarians of Ancient Europe*, edited by Larissa Bonfante, 313–345. Cambridge: Cambridge University Press.

De Grummond, Nancy Thomson, and Erika Simon. 2009. *The Religion of the Etruscans*. Austin, TX: University of Texas Press.

Heurgon, Jacques. 1966. "La coupe d'Aulus Vibenna." In *Mélanges d'archéologie, d'épigraphie, et d'histoire offerts à Jérôme Carcopino*, edited by Jacques Heurgon, William Seston, and Gilbert Charles-Picard, 515–528. Paris: Hachette.

Leighton, Robert. 2004. *Tarquinia: An Etruscan city*. London: Duckworth.

Massa-Pairault, Françoise-Hélène. 2011. "Romulus et Remus: réexamen du miroir de l'Antiquarium Communal." *MEFRA* 123: 505–525.

Poucet, Jacques. 1985. *Les origines de Rome*. Brussels: Publications de l'Université Saint-Louis.

Small, Jocelyn Penny. 2003. *The Parallel Worlds of Classical Art and Text*. Cambridge: Cambridge University Press.

Squire, Michael. 2009. *Image and Text in Graeco-Roman Antiquity*. Cambridge: Cambridge University Press.

van der Meer, L. Bouke. 1995. *Interpretatio etrusca: Greek Myths on Etruscan Mirrors*. Leiden: Brill.

Wiseman, Timothy Peter. 1993. "The She-wolf Mirror: an Interpretation." *PBSR* 61: 1–6.

Further Reading

Bennett, Michael J., Mario Iozzo, and Aaron Paul. 2002. *Magna Graecia*. New York: Hudson Hills. This exhibition catalogue focuses on all Greek art from south Italy and Sicily, but many of the essays discuss aspects of myth and cultural exchange. The first six chapters, which are short articles, will be more useful than the catalogue to students who are new to art history. The book covers the eighth to sixth centuries BCE.

Bonfante, Larissa. 2015. "Etruscan Mirrors and the Grave." In *L'écriture et l'espace de la mort. Épigraphie et nécropoles à l'époque préromaine*, edited by Marie-Laurence Haack. Rome, Publications de l'École française de Rome. Discusses the cultural context behind Etruscan mirrors (mostly mythical, and including a number of mirrors in this chapter). Bonfante analyzes the different ways mirrors were used in daily life and their significance in a funerary context. Online: http://books.openedition.org/efr/2741

Cherchiai, Luca, Lorena Jannelli, and Fausto Longo. 2004. *The Greek Cities of Magna Graecia and Sicily*. Los Angeles, CA: Getty Publications. Takes a city-by-city approach to the culture of Magna Graecia and Sicily from the sixth century BCE onward. The chapters are lavishly illustrated and start with the foundation myth(s) of each city; explanations of religious rites and local custom are often mythical as well.

De Grummond, Nancy Thomson. 2006. *Etruscan Myth, Sacred History and Legend*. Philadelphia, PA: University of Pennsylvania Museum. Key reading for anyone interested in learning more about the Etruscan myths in this chapter (and beyond). This book features an appendix with translations of relevant Greco-Roman material and lavish illustrations.

Holloway, R. Ross. 1994. *The Archaeology of Early Rome and Latium*. London: Routledge. While not explicitly concerned with mythic history, this book is a novice-friendly introduction to early Rome's archaeological remains. Holloway is interested in (but skeptical of) the relationship between the material evidence and written sources. Although he thinks they're largely separate, he also offers the evidence for your own evaluation.

Pallottino, Massimo. 1991. *A History of Earliest Italy*, tr. Martin Ryle and Kate Soper. Ann Arbor, MI: University of Michigan Press. Offers an in-depth examination of the non-Roman civilizations of Italy. A generation old, this book is no longer completely up-to-date. But Pallottino was an important figure in the archaeology of pre-Roman Italy, and his ideas are still worth reading. This book is a translation of a lecture series, which means that it is engaging to read, but hard to cite. You'll have to do substantial research to trace Pallottino's arguments.

5

Rome's Kings

Introduction

In previous chapters, we've seen how Romans interacted with Greek myths such as the Trojan cycle and Hercules, as well as native Italian legends such as the phallus. We've seen some of the problems faced by students of these legends, as well as by Roman authors themselves: contradictory narratives and confusion over chronology. We've also noted that Roman legends, although moving steadily towards the foundation of Rome itself, are willing to briefly focus on other locations, such as Alba Longa or Lavinium. Roman authors frequently came from such close suburbs to live in the city. Over time, just as these towns became part of Rome's territory, many local legends became incorporated into Rome's own history.

This process of growth is the focus of this chapter. As we've seen in **chapters 2** and **3**, Romans saw the city's foundation as a process of continuous development, rather than an instantaneous act. Such self-conception, while not unique to Rome, is different from many Greek foundation narratives, which credit a single founder or single group of founders with the majority of the city's customs, laws, and important sites. Yet Rome balanced the contributions of Aeneas and Romulus, as well as many other subsequent foundation figures. In fact, surviving Roman authors claim that all of their kings were founders, and that the city continued to develop after their time. In that sense, the kings did not perfect or finish Rome, but they left a legacy that contributed to the city.

Each king had a specific area of expertise. Numa was known for founding religious cults. He invented the *flamines*, *pontifex maximus*, the Vestals, and other important priesthoods, and he was interested in protecting peace.

Early Rome: Myth and Society, A Sourcebook, First Edition. Jaclyn Neel.
© 2017 John Wiley & Sons, Inc. Published 2017 by John Wiley & Sons, Inc.

He was also famous for his friendship with the nymph Egeria (**5.2.2**). Tullus Hostilius was known for his ferocity. Authors claim that he was more warlike than Romulus; his most famous act was the cruel punishment of the traitor Mettius Fufetius (**5.3.3**). Ancus Marcius was Numa's grandson, but he didn't inherit the throne. He was in many ways the most balanced king, with interests in both peace and war. He was best known for constructing the port of Ostia. Tarquin the Elder came from Etruria and had Greek connections. He engaged in many large-scale building projects, including the temple of Jupiter Optimus Maximus (**4.6.5, 4.7, 5.4.1c**). Although he had at least three of his own children, he adopted Servius Tullius (**5.5**). In an early sign of trouble for Rome's kingdom, Ancus' sons organized a plot to kill Tarquin. They succeeded, but Tarquin's wife ensured that Servius Tullius got the throne.

Servius Tullius is depicted as a new Romulus. Chosen by the gods rather than popular vote, he is a usurper: in ancient terms, a "tyrant." He organized the populace, much as Romulus had. Servius' administrative reforms are widely accepted as historical and persisted into the Republic. Because they are such a common feature of Roman civilization textbooks, they will not be treated here; a very brief summary can be found in the **note**.[1] Like Numa, Servius was friendly with a goddess (in his case, Fortuna), and like Tarquin, he died violently at the hands of his predecessor's children (**5.5.3**). This usurper, Tarquin the Proud, won the throne and became Rome's last king. Like his father, Tarquin the Proud was known for public works, including the Capitoline temple and Rome's major drainage project, the Cloaca Maxima.[2] His son Sextus was a true tyrant, as his treacherous adventure at Gabii (**5.6.2b, 5.6.2d**) and the rape of Lucretia (**7.6**) show.

As you can see, most of the city's oldest customs were traced back to the period of Rome's seven kings (including Romulus). This era is known as the Regal Period in modern scholarship. In canonical dating, these seven kings ruled from the foundation of the city in 753 BCE until the foundation of the Republic in 509. Yet this period of almost 250 years spread over only seven kings is unlikely, as was noticed even in antiquity: each king would have to rule, on average, 35 years. Such lengthy reigns aren't impossible. In modern times, the monarchs of many countries have far surpassed the 35-year mark (the most familiar examples to English-speaking students are probably the British Queens Victoria and Elizabeth II). There are also examples of considerably longer reigns from antiquity: Mithridates of Pontus, for example, ruled for almost 60 years (c. 120–63 BCE), and Bocchus of Mauretania reigned for close to 100 (c. 120–33 BCE). So why have scholars been so hesitant to believe in Rome's king list?

It's not so much the individual reigns that are unlikely, but the series of seven lengthy reigns in a row. As Timothy Cornell (1995, 121) puts it, "244 years for seven kings is without historical parallel" (sources at 423n6). Even in monarchies where one ruler is particularly long-lived, that ruler is generally balanced by shorter reigns. To make the Roman examples more suspicious, the reigns of the individual kings are roughly the same length: Romulus, 36 years;

Numa, 42 years; Tullus Hostilius, 31 years; Ancus Marcius, 24 years; Tarquin the Elder, 38 years; Servius Tullius, 44 years; and Tarquin the Proud, 25 years.

Let's compare these kings with the example of Queen Victoria. Although her reign was longer than even Servius' by two decades, the two kings immediately before her held the throne for fewer than 20 years combined. Victoria's son, who took the throne after her death, also ruled for less than a decade. In fact, if we include the six monarchs from Victoria to Elizabeth II, we find a period of approximately 180 years as of the time of writing. This list includes the two longest-reigning monarchs of British history; to match Rome's list, we would need to include a seventh with similar longevity.

Suspicions about Rome's kings date back to antiquity. Dionysius of Halicarnassus (*Roman Antiquities* 4.6–7) included a lengthy excursus explaining why Tarquin the Proud couldn't possibly be the son of Tarquin the Elder. Perhaps surprisingly, his careful calculations were largely ignored by later authors. Romans were not stupid or gullible, and we have seen that they could go to great lengths to reconcile chronology when they thought it was necessary (for example, the Alban kings: **2.7**). It seems likely, then, that the choice of seven kings was purposeful and more important than strict chronological accuracy or even realism (for a somewhat different view, students are encouraged to consult Cornell 1995, 119–127). The choice of the number seven may be related to Rome's seven hills.

The limit on the number of kings contrasts with the clear desire of members of Rome's elite to see their families appear early in Rome's history. The city's territory expanded many times over the Regal Period, and the leaders of each influx of immigrants were frequently connected to Rome's loftiest citizens. It's very likely that these migration stories were family legends (**1.2**) that were incorporated into larger-scale histories as those histories began to be written down. Although such stories could be little more than amusing or cautionary tales, over time the repetition of these narratives made the legendary ancestors significant to all Roman readers.

Romans believed that personality quirks, among other characteristics, could be inherited. Early ancestors thus provided models for family behaviors. The most famous and persistent example of such inherited qualities is the pride of the Claudii (see Skinner 1995, 19–32). This pride is apparent in the first Claudius in Rome, Attus Clausus (Livy 2.27) and persists into the Principate (the Emperor Tiberius: see Syme 1989, 84; Barrett 2004, 3–17). Although modern science suggests that personality traits are only partially heritable, Roman families seem to have combined nature and nurture quite strongly. In other words, the belief that the Claudii were proud was self-reinforcing, encouraging members of the Claudian family to act with more arrogance and self-regard than other families thought was appropriate (see Cicero, *Letters to Friends* 3.7.5). Legendary histories served as crucial tools of self-promotion and self-definition.

You may be surprised to learn that many families claimed descent from Rome's kings. Although Romans presented themselves as resistant to kingship (see Livy 2.1; **8.1–8.3**), Roman histories also emphasize the importance of these kings to Rome's historical development. As mentioned above, Romans imagined their city's foundation as a continuing process, rather than a single event. The kings formed part of that process of development, which some writers described in terms of human growth: when the city is founded, it's in its infancy. Romulus and the kings guide it through puberty, and once it's mature, the city becomes the property of the people (Cicero, *On the State* 1.39, 2.1–3, and 2.21–22; Livy 2.1). While Romans could remember their kings with gratitude as foundational figures, they didn't necessarily want new monarchs. To return to the metaphor of human development, this would be similar to a once-independent adult returning to the household rules and care of his or her parents.

The narratives in this and subsequent chapters can be difficult to grapple with. On the one hand, you are dealing with material that many modern scholars – and most ancient authors – think is historical. That is, we are moving from the realm of "myth" to that of "legendary history." Compare these stories to the tales of Romulus and Aeneas, which are generally accepted as mythical. Is there a difference in tone or plot?

Although many scholars accept some or all of these figures as historical, substantial differences of opinion remain. Some claim that all of the kings are historical figures, except Romulus. Others are more hesitant, and recognize only the last three kings (the "Tarquin dynasty") as historical. Still others accept that Rome had kings in the past, but that the kings portrayed by Roman authors are purely fictional. You should carefully read the evidence below and come to your own conclusions. Is the Regal Period elaborated? Invented? Or somewhere in between?

For Further Thought

1. A long-lived strand of historical scholarship has posited a break between the "Latin" kings (Romulus, Numa, Tullus, and Ancus) and the "Etruscan" kings (the Tarquins and Servius). Do you think that's a good description of the traditions in this chapter? If so, why? If not, what are the problems with this suggestion?

2. Early Rome relied heavily on immigrants to flourish, at least according to later Romans. What are the benefits to this vision of history? Why might it have been appealing to the authors of Roman history, especially our major sources (Livy, Dionysius, Ovid, Plutarch)? Can you find any similarities to historical Rome at a later period?

3. Many stories from the Regal Period relate terrible events, including the murder of family members, religious errors, or treachery in war. Why do you think the Romans chose to retell these stories? Similarly, why do you think Republican-era Romans chose to retain positive traditions about the kings?

TEXTS

5.1 The *Interregnum* (717–716)

After Romulus died, the new city struggled to replace him. This period without a leader became known as the *interregnum* ("time between kings") and was used whenever Rome found herself without leaders.

─────────── 5.1.1 Livy, *From the Foundation* 1.17 ───────────

Livy represents the interregnum *as a period of civic strife, first between individual senators and then between the Senate and the People. This somewhat bleak view of power is typical of his work. What does he suggest about early Roman society?*

Desire to rule and the fight for the kingship[3] turned the senators' heads. The issue didn't come down to individuals (no one was famous enough), but rather broke out in factions. The Sabines started it. They claimed that Rome hadn't had a ruler representing *their* interests since Tatius' death.[4] They'd been accepted into the city on equal terms; they wanted the next ruler to come from their own ranks. Meanwhile, the original Romans rejected a foreign king. Despite their varying opinions, everyone still wanted a *king*; they hadn't experienced sweet freedom yet. But the senators were terrified. The city had no ruler, the army lacked its commander, and the citizens were at each other's throats. What if a foreign power attacked? They decided that *some* leader was necessary, even though no one was persuaded to yield to their opponents' choice.

So the 100 senators agreed to rule jointly, forming ten groups of ten and nominating one man to be the leader of each group. Ten men were in charge at a time. Each received the royal paraphernalia and the lictors for a period of five days. After the five days were up, the power passed to the next man, rotating through all ten in turn. This period is now called the *interregnum*, because it took up the year between the kings. But at the time the plebeians[5] grumbled that they were less free than before. Under Romulus, they'd had one master; now they had a hundred![6] They vowed not to endure anything less than a king voted for and approved by themselves.

The senators could tell which way the wind was blowing. They thought it was better to offer freely what they would have to give up anyway. So they gained goodwill by entrusting the highest authority to the people, but retaining an equal amount for themselves. The senators decreed that the people could elect the king, but that the senators had to ratify the choice.

--------------------- 5.1.2   Plutarch, *Life of Numa* 2.6 ---------------------

Plutarch's vision of how the interregnum *worked is surprisingly different from Livy's.*

The 150 patricians, politically deadlocked, were afraid that partisanship would lead to chaos. The city was in crisis. They appointed one from each side to wear the royal insignia, make customary sacrifices to the gods, and conduct business for six hours each, day and night. This plan had two benefits. The equal distribution of time to each side pleased those in charge, while the constant change of power warded off popular anger. Everyone could see that the same man became king and private citizen again on the same day or night. The Romans call this method of rule *interregnum*.

5.2 Numa (716–674)

--------------------- 5.2.1   Numa's background ---------------------

After the controversy over the kingship, an offer is made to the outsider Numa. He has the virtue of being both a Sabine and a philosopher. Philosophy made him uninterested in kingship. Because heated desire for the throne was causing problems among the Roman nobility (**5.1**), Numa's utter lack of interest made him the perfect candidate. Once he became king, Numa focused on religious reforms, and most of the stories about him deal with the origins of Roman rites or priesthoods.

a. Livy, *From the Foundation* 1.18   *Livy disputes a rumor that the philosophical Numa learned from Pythagoras. This passage is useful as an example of Roman historical thinking: notice Livy's criteria for deciding what to believe.*

At the time, Numa Pompilius was famous for his justice and attention to the gods. He lived in a Sabine city, Cures.[7] He was exceptionally knowledgeable about laws (both divine and human), as far as anyone could be in those days. Some men relate the false story that the source of his knowledge was Pythagoras of Samos, because another option isn't at hand. But everyone knows that Pythagoras lived when Servius Tullius was king of Rome, more than a century later, and on the southern coast of Italy near Metapontum, Heraclea, and Croton.

b. Plutarch, *Life of Numa* 3 and 5–7   *Plutarch takes pains to describe Numa as a contemporary Roman philosopher, similar to a Stoic sage. Numa is carefully religious and moderate even before he accepts the throne.*

Numa was a nobleman in the Sabine city of Cures. The Romans took the name of this city after they were joined with the Sabines and called themselves "Quirites." Numa was the son of Pompon, a well-known man, and had three older brothers.[8] By some divine chance, he was born on the very day that Romulus founded Rome (that is, April 21). His character was naturally inclined to all virtue, and he had tamed it still more by education, perseverance, and philosophy. This included setting aside not only the hateful passions of the spirit, but also the violence and arrogance popular among barbarians.[9] He believed that it was truly manly to shut his emotions within himself by means of reason.

His beliefs led him to eliminate all luxury and expense from his home. He was a faultless judge and advisor to every citizen and stranger. He didn't allow himself free time for easy living or business: he spent his days in pious worship or logical contemplation about the nature and power of the gods. So he had such a great name and reputation that Tatius (the one who ruled in Rome with Romulus) had married his only daughter, Tatia, to Numa. So he was Tatius' son-in-law. But this marriage didn't encourage Numa to move to Rome with his father-in-law, although he respected Tatius.[10] Instead, he lived among the Sabines with his elderly father. Tatia too preferred to live in peace with her husband as a private citizen rather than in Rome with her father's honors and reputation. It is said that she died after 13 years of marriage [...]

It was no small matter, as it turns out, to persuade a man living in peace and quiet to rule a city, particularly one that had started out and for the most part grown thanks to war. In fact, it required persuasion and even begging to change his mind. Numa's father was present, as was one of his brothers, named Marcius. Numa said in front of everyone, "All life changes are difficult. But for someone who has everything he needs and is blameless in the eyes of his peers, any modification or change in habits is completely idiotic [...]"

With these words, he rejected the kingdom. The Romans rushed to appease him, begging him not to abandon them to discord and civil war. He was the only one, they explained, on whom both sides agreed. When the ambassadors were gone, Numa's father and Marcius privately tried to persuade Numa to accept this great (even divine) gift [...] As the story goes, portentous signs were added to their words, and the citizens of Cures were excited and eager. When they learned about the embassy, they begged Numa to go ahead and accept the kingship for the common good and to make the citizens more moderate. When he decided to accept, he performed sacrifices for the gods and headed to Rome. The Senate and the People met him with love and awe; the women spoke well of him, as is fitting.

5.2.2 Egeria

Friendship with deities offered one way to account for exceptionally innovative or smart ideas in antiquity. Some later Romans would also claim a special relationship with one divinity to further their political goals: for example, Sulla associated himself with Fortune. Judgments of Numa's relationship with the nymph Egeria varied: some authors considered it a divine marriage, others claimed it was mentorship, and some called it a convenient lie.

a. Livy, *From the Foundation* 1.19 *Livy is dismissive of the idea of divine-human interaction.*

Because he couldn't reach the Romans at their intellectual level without inventing some miracle, he pretended that he had nightly meetings with the goddess Egeria.

b. Plutarch, *Life of Numa* 4 *Plutarch suggests a variety of interpretations of the Egeria story. He's skeptical about a marital relationship, but is more open to human-divine interaction.*

Numa left behind the pleasures of the city. He wanted to live out in the open for the most part, wandering on his own. He passed his time in the groves of the gods, the sacred meadows, and deserted places. This habit, in no small part, led to the story about the goddess. That is, they say Numa didn't spend his life apart from men due to some sort of spiritual distress or soul-searching. Rather, he delighted in quite sacred conversation and was thought worthy of a divine spouse. He loved the goddess Egeria, taking pleasure in her company, and living with her. So he became the happiest man and wise in divine matters. All the same, it's clear that this story sounds an awful lot like the ancient myths.

5.2.3 The charm against thunder

Although Numa's reign is marked by religious innovation, the episode of Jupiter Elicius is unusual. Numa here changes his role from the philosopher and lawgiver we've seen so far to a trickster. His seemingly cavalier attitude towards the gods Faunus, Picus, and Jupiter is typical of Roman religious behavior: Romans could bargain with the gods and were willing to make hairsplitting distinctions (Watson 1992, 30–38). Both elements are on display in this myth. The ritual was referenced in **4.5.2**.

---

a. Ovid, *Fasti* 3.275–3.392   *Ovid's account combines two motifs: the tricking of the gods and the guarantee of Rome's empire.*

The goddess Egeria [...] was Numa's wife and advisor. In the beginning he decided to soften the Romans, who were too ready for war, by teaching them law and fear of the gods. He gave them laws, so that the more capable would not control everything: ancestral rites began to be celebrated without defilement. Ferocity vanished, and justice was stronger than weapons. Citizens were ashamed to raise their hands against one another. All of them had been savage. Once they saw altars, they were entirely changed, and offered wine and flour to the warm hearth.

Imagine it: the heavenly father sprinkles red flames through the clouds and pours down all the waters of heaven. These fires fall more thickly than any sent before. The king trembles and fear grabs the common people by the chest. But the goddess tells him, "Don't be too afraid! This storm can be expiated and the anger of cruel Jupiter turned aside. Picus and Faunus,[11] those spirits of Roman land, can tell you the rite of expiation. But they'll only do it if you make them. Take chains to capture them." Then she explained the trap that would catch them.

There was a grove on the Aventine, dark with oaky shadows. If you saw it, you'd say, "Some god lives in there." In the middle was grass, and a constant stream of water dripped from a rock covered with green moss. Faunus and Picus were almost the only ones to drink from it. King Numa came to this place and sacrificed a sheep at the stream. Beside it he set a cup full of fragrant wine and hid with his men in a cave. The woodland gods came to their usual stream and soothed their dry throats with lots of wine. Then they conked out. Numa came out of the cave and clamped narrow cuffs around their sleeping hands.

When they woke up, they tried to break the chains by fighting. But the harder they fought, the stronger the chains held them. Numa said, "Gods of the wood, please forgive me. If you feel sure that there's no evil in my nature, show me how to expiate the lightning."

That was what Numa said. Shaking his horns, Faunus replied, "You're asking a lot, and it's not right for you to learn from our instructions. Our powers have limits! We're rustic gods; we have power in the highlands, but Jupiter has the final say on his turf. You won't be able to turn him out of the sky on your own, but maybe you can with our help."

These were Faunus' words, and Picus' thoughts were the same. "Just free us from these chains," he said. "Jupiter will come here, lured by strong art. The cloudy Styx[12] will be my witness: I'll carry out my promise."

Numa released them from the traps. Humans can't know what they did, what spells they chanted, or with what skill they enticed Jupiter from his lofty seat; it would be wrong. But I'll tell you everything a seer's holy mouth can say. Jupiter, they called you down from heaven, and that is why even now the newer generations celebrate you and call you Jupiter Elicius.[13] It's agreed that the treetops in the Aventine grove trembled, and the ground quaked and resettled, pressed by Jupiter's weight.

The king's heart beat faster. The blood drained from his entire body, and his thick hair stood on end. When he got his breath back, he said, "King and father of the lofty gods, tell me the unfailing expiation for the lightning. If I've ever approached your altars with pure hands, if the tongue asking you is pious, grant this wish as well."

Jupiter nodded in response to this request, but he hid the truth in strange obscurity and scared Numa with ambiguous words. "Cut off a head," he said.

The king relied, "We will! We'll chop of the head of an onion dug up in my garden."

Jupiter clarified. "*Of a man.*"

Numa said, "Yes! You'll get his hair."

Jupiter demanded a life, and Numa chimed in, "Of a fish!"

Jupiter laughed, and said, "Make sure you expiate my lightning with these things, man who doesn't hesitate to bargain with gods. But as for you, I'll give you sure signs of empire tomorrow, when the sun's advanced over the entire world." Jupiter spoke, and with a huge crash of thunder he split the sky and was carried up to the heavens. He left Numa behind in awe.

The king returned rejoicing and related his deeds to the Romans. They were slow to believe him and found his words hard to trust. "But of course you'll believe me" (he said) "if events turn out as I say. So if you're here, listen up to tomorrow's news. When the sun has advanced over the entire world, Jupiter will send sure signs of empire." They left in doubt, and the promised events seemed ages away. Their faith in Numa depended on the coming day.

Early in the morning, the ground was soft, but wet with frost. The citizens lined up at the king's doorway. He came out and sat in the middle of the crowd on his maple throne. Countless men stood silently around him. The sun rose just to the horizon's edge, and their worried minds shook between hope and fear. Numa stood up and covered his head with a snow-white cloak. Then he lifted his hands, which were well-known to the gods, and said, "The time for the promised gift has come! Jupiter, make good on your promise."

As he spoke, the sun moved all the way into the sky. A heavy crash came from the northern heavens. Three times the god thundered without a cloud; three times he sent lightning bolts down. Believe what I'm about to say: it sounds incredible, but it happened. The sky began to gape open in the center. The crowd of Romans and Numa lifted their eyes. And hey! A shield dropped down, buffeted gently in a light breeze. The Romans shouted loudly enough to reach the stars.

Numa picked the gift up off of the ground before sacrificing a heifer whose neck had never felt the yoke. He called the shield an *ancile*,[14] because it was cut away on all sides, so that you could clearly see that it had no angles. Then, remembering that the fate of empire resided in this shield, Numa came up with a very clever plan. He ordered the Romans to make many shields with the same shape, so that anyone who wished to set a trap for the city would be confused.[15]

Mamurius finished off the work; it's hard to say whether he was more painstaking about his character or his craftsmanship. Numa felt generous. "Ask for a reward. If my reputation for good faith is justified, you'll get it." The Salian priests had already received their name from leaping, and also their weapons[16] and their songs to sing in specific keys. So Mamurius said, "As a prize, I want glory. Let my name echo at the end of the Salian hymn." From that point forward, the priests carried out the promised reward. In return for his work long ago, they call upon Mamurius.

b. Plutarch, *Life of Numa* 15 *Plutarch considers the capture of Faunus and Picus evidence for Numa's exceptional knowledge of religion.*

After being schooled in divine matters, the city became so submissive and so astonished by Numa's power that they were willing to accept stories that seemed impossible, like myths, and to think that nothing he did was unbelievable or impossible. For example, it is said that once he called a number of citizens to the table, which had everyday plates and very simple comfort food. As they began to eat, he commented that the goddess he was friendly with was about to visit them. All of a sudden, many luxe goblets appeared on the table, and tables heavy with delicacies and full of abundant tableware showed up too.

But what they say about his conversation with Zeus is even weirder. As the story goes, two gods, Picus and Faunus,[17] lived on the top of the Aventine. This was before it became part of the city, so people didn't live there yet. At the time, it had abundant springs and shady glens. These gods were like some sort of satyr or Pan[18] in many respects, but they were said to be masters of drugs and wise in regard to divine magic [...] The story goes that Numa subdued them by mixing wine and honey into their customary drinking water. When they were captured, they changed shape many times,[19] putting on an alien appearance that was terrifying to see.

Yet when they realized that they had been truly captured in strong and inescapable bonds, they prophesied many things that were to come in the future, and in particular they taught him a charm against lightning. This is made even now using an onion, hair, and a small fish. Some say that these deities didn't propose the charm, but they used their magic to summon Zeus.

5.2.4 Numa's descendants

A large number of Roman noble families claimed to descend from Numa or his family. In some ways, this is not surprising: Numa is the only king known for not wanting to rule. Connecting oneself with Numa was a compromise between claiming a privileged background and seeming too regal. Moreover, since Romulus died without children, it's Numa who offered Roman nobility the first opportunity to insert themselves into early Roman history – an act which some later writers found contrived. For some families, a connection with Numa may have been associated with hereditary religious offices.

Plutarch, *Life of Numa* 8 and 21   *Plutarch discusses Numa's family at both the beginning and end of his biography. In both cases, he expresses doubts about the "truth" of noble claims to descend from Numa.*

Aside from these, they stress other external signs that Numa and Pythagoras were friends.[20] First, that the Romans added Pythagoras to their list of citizens, as Epicharmus the comic poet writes in a speech for Antenor. Now Epicharmus lived long ago and had a part in Pythagoras' school. And second, that one of King Numa's four sons, Mamercus, shares a name with the son of Pythagoras. They say that the Aemilian family took their name from him once they had become patricians. This was a nickname given by the king because of his son's charm[21] and grace in speech. Finally, I've heard many Romans relate that at one time an oracle required them to dedicate statues of the smartest and the bravest Greek. The Romans set up two bronze portraits in their Forum, one of Alcibiades and the other of Pythagoras. But these matters are extremely controversial [...]

There's disagreement among historians about Numa's children and marriages. Some say that he had only one wife, Tatia, and that their only child was a single daughter named Pompilia. But others write that in addition to this daughter he had four sons: Pompon, Pinus, Calpus, and Mamercus. Each of these sons left behind a noble house and line of descent. These are as follows: the Pomponii from Pompon; the Pinarii from Pinus; the Calpurnii from Calpus; and the Mamercii from Mamercus. The last also had the *cognomen* "Reges," that is to say "kings," because of their ancestor. But a third group of historians allege that this second group is only ingratiating themselves with these families and making up false family trees from Numa's line. This third group says that Pompilia was not the daughter of Tatia, but she was born to Numa's second wife Lucretia, whom he married when he was already on the throne.

But everyone agrees that Pompilia married Marcius. Marcius was the son of that Marcius who'd encouraged Numa to take the throne.[22] He actually moved to Rome with Numa and was an honored member of his council. When Numa died, Marcius got into a fight with Hostilius about the kingship. When he lost, he starved himself to death. But his son Marcius remained in Rome with Pompilia and their son was Ancus Marcius, who ruled after Tullus Hostilius.[23]

5.2.5   Death and Books of Numa

Roman authors were less interested in Numa's peaceful death than the violent death of other kings. But the king also had an unusual burial request: his body and his books. The books of Numa were mysterious even to Romans; Livy relates that when Numa's tomb was found, there was a coffin for the books and it was empty (40.29), although they are absent from his account of Numa's reign. The account of the books' rediscovery is reminiscent of the myth of Tages (**4.4.1, 4.4.3, 4.4.5, 4.4.6**).

a. Plutarch, *Life of Numa* 22   *Plutarch's narrative suggests the importance of oral tradition in early Roman society. As it turns out, Numa may have been right (**5.3.4**).*

They didn't cremate the body. They say it's because Numa had forbidden them to do so. Instead, they made two stone coffins and set them at the foot of the Janiculum. One held the body, and the old held holy books. Numa had written these himself, like the Greek lawgivers wrote up tablets. While he was still alive, he taught the priests their contents. He produced in all of them the skill and knowledge of the rites, then ordered them to bury the books with his body. He thought Rome's secrets wouldn't be safe with soulless letters protecting them.

b. Festus, "Numa Pompilius" *Festus describes the rediscovery of Numa's books. The words in angle brackets are suggested restorations based on the passage of Augustine that follows (5.3.5c).*

They say that NUMA POMPILIUS is buried on the Janiculum. In that place <a scribe> named Terentius <was cultivating> his field <and discovered> a chest <with the books of Numa inside>.

c. Augustine, *City of God* 7.34–7.35 *Augustine explains why, from a Christian perspective, Numa's religious activity was evil. Rather than powerful, Numa's books hold perverse knowledge that doesn't deserve a place in Augustine's ideal society.*

On the contrary, we see in the work of that extremely learned Varro that the reasons behind the rites in the books of Numa Pompilius were unbearable; in fact, they weren't considered worthy of being read or known by people of religion. Instead they were hidden in the shadows [...] As you can read in that same Varro's book *On Worship,* "A certain Terentius had a farm on the Janiculum. His plowman was working near the tomb of Numa Pompilius and turned up Numa's books with the dirt. In the books were written the reasons for the rites. Terentius took the books to the praetor in Rome. When he looked at the titles, he deferred to the Senate on so important an issue. After they read the first few reasons for why each rite had been established, the senators agreed with Numa, even though he was dead. So the senators commanded the praetor to burn the books, as if they were concerned about religious consequences." [...]

That Roman king was really into divination. That's how he learned the rituals that the pontiffs have in their books and the reasons for them. Numa didn't want anyone to know these reasons, so he wrote them up when he was alone and had them buried with him when he died. In this way he ensured that they were taken away from men's notice.

5.3 Tullus Hostilius (673–642)

Hostilius was the grandson of Romulus' general Hostus Hostilius (**3.5.2**). Thus the order of Rome's four kings alternates between Latin (Romulus, Hostilius) and Sabine (Numa, Ancus); it's not clear why the Sabine element is stressed so strongly in Rome's early myths. Most of the myths about Tullus Hostilius center around war, particularly the long war with Rome's metropolis[24] Alba and its treacherous leader Mettius Fufetius.

-------------------- 5.3.1 The war with Alba breaks out --------------------

The concept of war that's similar to civil war recurs in early Roman history. The war with the Sabines is compared to war between fathers and sons; the war with Alba comes down to siblings; later wars with the Etruscans will also be compared in familial terms. The metaphor emphasizes Rome's fortune and the struggles the city overcame as it rose to power. For readers living at the time of Rome's civil wars in the first century, it was a metaphor that became all too real.

a. Livy, *From the Foundation* 1.23 *Tullus is looking for a reason to fight; the raids of Roman and Alban shepherds against each other provide an opportunity. Both sides send embassies to demand reparations, but Tullus delays the Albans until his own ambassadors are refused. Then he declares a "justified" war (see **chapter 3, note 66**).*

Back home, the Alban ambassadors delivered the king's message. Both cities prepared for all-out war. It was practically a civil war between parents and children,[25] since both cities were colonies of Troy. Lavinium was founded directly by Trojans, Alba came from Lavinium, and the Romans were descended from the Alban kings. But the fighting was less awful because of the way the war played out. There were no set battles and only the houses of one city were destroyed. Yet the result was the two populations were mixed into one.

The Albans first attacked Roman territory with a huge army. They made their camp no more than 5000 paces[26] from the city and surrounded it with a trench. This trench was called "Cluilian" after the name of Alba's king, Gaius Cluilius, for several centuries, until both the feature and the name disappeared due to age. While he was in this camp, Cluilius died. The Albans elected Mettius Fufetius dictator.[27]

Meanwhile – and particularly after the king's death – fierce Tullus repeated that the great power of the gods was seeking vengeance for this impious war, beginning from the king himself and moving against the entire Alban nation. At night he passed by the enemy's camp and marched his hostile army into Alban territory. This action roused Mettius from sitting still. He led his men as close to the enemy as he could; from there he sent an embassy to tell Tullus that they needed to talk before they could fight. If they met, he knew they'd have matters of mutual significance to discuss. Tullus agreed, but in case the talks failed he drew up his army.

b. Dionysius of Halicarnassus, *Roman Antiquities* 3.4.4–3.5.1
Dionysius' account supplies more detail about Cluilius' death and the Alban reaction to it. In doing so, he spreads the blame for warmongering among a larger segment of the Alban population. In his account, Alba is clearly in the wrong.

Cluilius made preparations for battle, planning to attack Rome's walls if necessary. When night fell, he went to sleep in his tent with his usual bodyguard. But in the morning he was found dead. There was no sign of foul play: he hadn't been strangled, poisoned, or otherwise harmed. His death surprised everyone, as one might expect. He had no pre-existing conditions. When people asked why he'd died, the more superstitious claimed he'd been killed by divine anger, since he'd stirred up an unjust and unnecessary war between metropolis and colony. But those who stood to gain financially thought they'd lost huge profits. They said that his death was the result of purely human plots and jealous rage.

———————————— 5.3.2 The Horatii and Curiatii ————————————

The major event of this war was the duel between two sets of triplets, one from each city. The choice of triplets is intriguing: such multiple births were extremely rare in antiquity, and the number three has magical qualities in many cultures. Our major sources for the duel, Livy and Dionysius, offer substantially different descriptions of the same acts. Consider the effect of Dionysius' more tragic version compared to Livy's, which suggests Roman pride. How do the authors evoke these different emotions?

a. Livy, *From the Foundation* 1.24–1.25 *Livy describes the triplets' duel, focusing primarily on the perspective of the Roman spectators.*

It just so happened that there were triplets in each army, and each trio was equal in age and strength. It's generally agreed that these were the Horatii and Curiatii. Almost no ancient event is more famous, but questions remain about even brilliant exploits: it's not clear which side each set of triplets was on. My sources aren't consistent, but the majority claim the Horatii were Romans. I'm inclined to follow this version.

The kings urged the triplets to fight, each set for his own country: whichever side was victorious would control both cities. They didn't refuse, and agreed on a time and place. Before the fight began, the Romans and the Albans made a treaty in accordance with the laws. It ensured that the people of the victorious side would rule the losing side with good grace [...]

When the treaty was finalized, the triplets took up arms in accordance with the agreement. Each side encouraged its own triplets: "Your paternal gods, your country and your parents, all citizens at home or in the army, are watching your weapons and your hands." Courageous by nature and emboldened by the voices full of encouragement, they walked into the space between the two armies. The soldiers themselves sat in front of their own camps. They had no influence over the present danger, but they worried. How could they not? The strength and luck of so few would determine who had authority over everyone. So they sat up straight at the edge of their seats, their minds working madly at the unpleasant sight.

The sign was given and the young triplets ran towards each other, swords at the ready. It was like a battle; they had the spirit of a huge army. Neither set appeared to care that their own lives were in danger, but only about their city's rule or servitude. They fought for the future fortunes of their country, not themselves. As soon as they made the first rush, their arms clattered and glinting swords shone. An immense feeling of horror enveloped the spectators. Their voices and breath dried up. Neither side was clearly winning or losing. With their hands clasped together, they at once saw not only the movement of bodies or dangerous motion of spears and shields, but bleeding wounds. Two Romans went down, one after the other, and all three Albans were wounded.

At the death of the Romans, the Alban army shouted with delight. The Roman soldiers had already lost all hope, but not all concern. They were absolutely terrified for the one Horatius left. The three Curiatii stood around him in a circle. By good fortune, he had no injuries. Although alone he wasn't at all equal to three, he knew he was a threat one-on-one. So he ran to space out his fights, thinking that his opponents would each follow as fast as his wounds allowed.

When he'd already raced some distance from the place where the fight had begun, he glanced behind him and saw the Curiatii following at large intervals. One was almost on top of him, so he turned around and jumped him. While the Alban army shouted at the Curiatii to go help their brother, Horatius had already won. With his first enemy dead, he went looking for the next fight.

The Romans helped their soldier with a roar, like men receiving an unexpected bonus. He hurried to finish off his opponent. Before the

last, who wasn't far away, could reach him, he had killed Curiatius #2.
And finally, two men faced each other in a fair fight – but they weren't
matched in hope or strength. The Roman, unharmed and encouraged
by his double victory, was ready for the third; the Alban was tired from
his wound and the run. Conquered by the defeat of his brothers before
him, he offered himself up to the victorious enemy. It wasn't a battle.
The Roman gloated. "I've killed two men for my brothers' ghosts. I offer
up the third for the sake of this war, so that Rome can rule Alba." He
plunged his sword straight down into the Alban's throat (his enemy
could barely hold up his shield) and stripped the armor from the body
as it lay there.

The Romans cheered. They welcomed Horatius gratefully. Their joy
was made greater because it had been so closely connected to fear. Each
side turned to burying their dead – but with entirely different feelings,
of course, since the Romans were increasing their sway and the Albans
were coming under foreign rule. The tombs are still there, set up in the
place where each one fell. The two Roman tombs are in one place near
Alba; the three Alban tombs are closer to Rome but spaced wide apart,
like the fight.

b. Dionysius of Halicanassus, *Roman Antiquities* 3.13.3–3.13.4
*Dionysius describes the miraculous birth of the Horatii and Curiatii. Their
unusual history makes them ideal heroes.*

The Alban leader [...] pointed out that some divine providence had
foreseen the struggle between the two cities far in advance. Each side
had champions who were excellent in war, noble in birth, handsome,
and unlike most people, since their birth was rare, surprising, and marvelous. Sicanius the Alban had married his twin daughters to Horatius
the Roman and Curiatius the Alban at the same time. Both women were
pregnant at the same time and gave birth at the same time, and each
bore male triplets. The parents considered the children a good omen
for their cities and households, so they raised the six boys together.

c. Dionysius of Halicanassus, *Roman Antiquities* 3.18.2–3.18.3
*The beginning of the duel is bittersweet, reminding readers that this war is a
family affair. The reference to religious pollution recalls both the conflict between
Romulus and Remus (3.4.3) and Greek myths like the Seven Against Thebes.*

The Alban general led out the Curiatii, while the Roman king led the
Horatii. All six had beautiful weapons and were decked out like men
marked for death. When they were near each other, they gave their
swords to their seconds. Running up to each other, they embraced, crying and calling one another sweet names. Everyone began bawling and

accused themselves and their leaders of cruelty. When they could have decided the battle with other men, they'd driven relatives to fight and brought pollution into the contest over the cities.

5.3.3 The end of the war

After the victory of Horatius, the Albans submitted to Roman power. Rome asked for military aid against the Etruscans (see **8.3** and **8.9** for further wars with Etruria). The Alban leader Mettius Fufetius agreed, but secretly allied with the Etruscans and planned to abandon Rome in the heat of battle. Instead, he double-crossed both sides and withdrew from fighting entirely. After Tullus Hostilius won the day, he called an assembly of the combined Roman and Alban troops and punished Mettius' treachery.

a. Livy, *From the Foundation* 1.28 *Not all lessons teach positive behavior. Livy retells the horrible punishment of Mettius Fufetius in order to brag about Rome's more moderate behavior in subsequent years.*

Armed centurions surrounded Mettius. The king continued as he'd begun: "I've got a very good idea that will bring blessings to the Roman people, myself, and you Albans: the entire Alban population will move to Rome. The plebeians will have citizenship; the top men will join the Senate. We'll make a single city and a single state. Before, the Alban legacy was divided between two populations. Now let it return to one."[28]

Hearing this, the Alban youths held their peace. They were unarmed and surrounded by armed men. Although their opinions varied, fear was common to all. Then Tullus continued, "Mettius Fufetius, if you'd been capable of learning good faith and how to keep a treaty, I would've forced that lesson down your throat while you were alive. But since you're beyond helping, your punishment will teach all mankind to believe that the laws that you violated should be sacred. A little earlier, you hesitated between Fidenae and Rome with two minds. Now your body will also be split in two."

With that, he brought out two chariots. He stretched Mettius out and bound him to each. Then he whipped the horses to run in opposite directions. Each chariot carried off the limbs that had been chained onto it, and Mettius was torn in two. Everyone looked away from the grisly sight. This was the first and last time that inhumane punishment was used among the Romans. Among other things, we can boast that no one is as satisfied with mild punishments as Romans are.

b. Dionysius of Halicarnassus, *Roman Antiquities* 1.34.1–1.34.4
After Alba submits to Roman rule, Tullus tries to obtain dominion over the other Latin cities as well. They refuse. The narrative foreshadows Tarquin's attempt in 5.6.2.

> Tullus asked [the Latin cities] to obey Roman orders, since the Romans had taken over Latin leadership [...] The Latin cities didn't respond individually to the ambassadors, but they met in Ferentinum and voted not to submit to Roman rule. Immediately they chose two generals [...] War between closely related peoples thus broke out.

--------------------   5.3.4   Death by lightning   --------------------

Tullus Hostilius was known for his ferocity, not religious sentiment. When he tries, in old age, to gain some of Numa's sanctity, he learns that piety requires more than show.

a. Livy, *From the Foundation* 1.31   *Livy suggests that a plague forces Tullus to change his mind about the value of religion.*

> Not long afterwards, the city was struggling with an epidemic. Although weakness became visible among the army, there was no rest from fighting on the part of a warlike king. He believed that young men were physically healthier at war than at home – until he too caught a prolonged case. Then his fierce spirit was broken along with his body. Before, he'd thought nothing was less royal than paying attention to religious rites. Suddenly he was addicted to all cults, large and small, and he filled the people with religion, too. Men all over the city looked back to the *status quo* under King Numa. They believed that a sick person had one option left: to seek peace and pardon from the gods.
>   They say that the king himself leafed through Numa's books.[29] In them, he found some secret cultic sacrifice to make to Jupiter Elicius, and he went away to perform it himself. But he didn't do it right, or wasn't paying attention. He not only didn't receive a visit from heaven, but he made Jupiter angry with his distorted religion.[30] So Tullus was struck by lightning and his house burned down.

b. Dionysius of Halicanassus, *Roman Antiquities* 3.35.1–3.35.4
This variant attributes the king's death to murder, not the gods. This account

of Ancus Marcius differs considerably from Latin accounts of the "good" Ancus,[31] and foreshadows Tarquin the Proud (5.5.3–5.5.6). Dionysius later says that he finds the story of divine vengeance more likely.

> Tullus ruled for 32 years and died when his house burned down. His wife, children, and all the rest of his household staff died in the fire, too. Some say it was struck by lightning because a god grew angry that Tullus only rarely performed sacrifice [...] But the majority think it was a human plot, and they blame Marcius, who ruled next. He was Numa's grandson and was upset at being a private citizen despite his royal blood. Seeing Tullus' family getting older, he thought it very likely that one of the children would rule if anything happened to Tullus. Mulling over these points, he conspired against the king for a long time [...] Tullus was about to perform a sacrifice at home and wanted only close friends to know. By divine chance, the sky was already overcast [...] Marcius and his friends seized the opportunity. They had swords under their cloaks as they walked through the door. They killed the king, his children, and anyone else they found, then set fire to the house. Later he claimed that lightning was the cause.

5.4 Tarquinius Priscus (616–578)

After Tullus Hostilius, Ancus Marcius (r. 641–617) took the throne. He was Numa's grandson, and some suspicions about him are clear from variant accounts of his accession (5.3.4b). His reign is the shortest of all Rome's kings, and much of it is overshadowed by the arrival of the next king, Tarquin.

With the first King Tarquin, we reach the mythic version of Etruscan influence in Rome. There's no doubt that Rome and Etruria had mutual cultural exchange from an early period; it's hard to find a time when Rome wasn't in contact with Etruria. There's little reason to believe that these contacts were due to an Etruscan ruler. Some scholars point to the monumental building projects that Tarquin is believed to have initiated, but Etruria was not the only part of Italy with monumental architecture at that date. Meanwhile, the choice of an Etruscan king as Rome expands continues the pattern of alternating a Latin king (Ancus, Servius) with a foreign king – in this case, the Greco-Etruscan Tarquins. It's likely that this pattern plays a similar role to the interpretation of Rome's foundation as a process: as Rome expands, so too do its influences and rulers. That is not to say that it's impossible that Rome had Etruscan kings; it's simply unlikely that those kings were the Tarquins we read about.

Roman authors frequently confused the deeds of the first and second Tarquin. As you will see, several of the stories that you read below will reappear in **5.6**.[32] The confusion between the two Tarquins is understandable, since ancient sources frequently refer to these kings as "Tarquin," without explaining which. A list of overlaps is in the **note**.

──────────── 5.4.1 Tanaquil and arrival in Rome ────────────

Roman accounts stress that the first Tarquin was half Greek, the son of an exile from Corinth. He thus combines two cultural debts into one: Greek birth, but Etruscan upbringing. His wife, Tanaquil, is a stereotypical Etruscan: a politically active and religiously knowledgeable woman. She plays a huge role in the Tarquins' history.

> **a. Livy, *From the Foundation* 1.34** *Livy's account of the arrival of the Tarquins repeats the theme of immigrant contributions to Roman society.*
>
> While Ancus was king, a rich and energetic man named Lucumo moved to Rome. He was spurred by the hope and (especially) the desire for great honor. This was hard to come by in Tarquinia, where he had been born to immigrants. His father was Demaratus of Corinth, who'd fled from civil war in his homeland and settled in Tarquinia. There he got married and had two sons named Lucumo and Arruns. Lucumo outlived his father and inherited all his property, while Arruns died before his father and left his widow pregnant. His father didn't outlive him long; but he didn't know that his daughter-in-law was going to have a baby, so he died without leaving his grandson anything in his will. This boy, born after his grandfather's death with no share in the property, was named "Egerius"[33] from his poverty.
>
> Lucumo, on the other hand, inherited everything. Although money had already given him attitude, he increased it by marriage to Tanaquil. Tanaquil was a high-society girl and she found it hard to marry a man of lower status. When the Etruscans rejected Lucumo as a stranger born to an exile, she couldn't contain her irritation. Forgetting the love of her fatherland that would have been in her bones if she'd seen her husband honored, she came up with the plan of moving away from Tarquinia. Rome seemed to be the best place for them. A new people, where all high status was achieved suddenly from acts of virtue – this was the place for a strong and energetic man! Tatius the Sabine had ruled Rome, and Numa from Cures followed him. Ancus, born to a Sabine mother, was noble only through Numa. She easily persuaded her husband to leave, since he wanted honor and only his mother came from Tarquinia anyway.

So they packed up their bags and moved to Rome. They'd just reached the Janiculum. There, as Lucumo was sitting in the cart with his wife, an eagle swooped down with his wings spread out. The bird lifted Lucumo's hat lightly, then flying around above the cart with a loud cry he immediately tugged it back on Lucumo's head, and flew up and away. It was like he'd been sent on a divine mission.

They say Tanaquil accepted the omen with glee. She was experienced in heavenly signs, as Etruscans generally are.[34] She hugged her husband and told him to raise his hopes high. The bird, she explained, came as a messenger from a particular part of heaven and its god. It relayed its omen by circling man's highest point – his head – lifting the item set there, and returning it as a divine gift.

They entered the city bearing these hopes and thoughts in their hearts. There the man bought a house and took the name Lucius Tarquinius Priscus.[35] His recent arrival and wealth got him noticed in Roman society, and he helped his fortune out with friendly chats, dinner parties, and any other favor he could do to win people over. Finally his reputation made it all the way to the palace. Soon after he'd been brought to the king's attention, he was generously and capably performing duties for the royal household. He attended to laws as well, so that he had an equal hand in public and private councils, war and peace. Since he'd proved his experience in all affairs, he became the guardian of the king's children upon his death.

b. Livy, *From the Foundation* 1.35   *After Ancus died, Tarquin became king and immediately went on campaigns of conquest. These campaigns made him very wealthy, and he used the wealth to fund major public works projects in Rome. The most famous of these projects is the Capitoline temple of Jupiter Optimus Maximus, whose sixth-century foundation walls are still visible today.[36] Tradition assigned this temple, variously, to Tarquin the Elder, Tarquin the Proud, and the second set of consuls. Perhaps the tradition of the long building process offered a way to convey the scale of the work to anyone who had not seen it.*

First he fought the Latins and took Apiolae, one of their towns, by storm. From that town he carried back more plunder than the limited renown of the war would suggest. He put on games that were more elaborate and more luxurious than the previous kings. That was the first time the place now called the "Circus Maximus" was marked out. He set aside space for the senators and knights to use to make themselves seats, which are called "planks." They watched from the seats, which hung between pitchforks 12 feet off the ground. The show had horses and boxers imported from Etruria. These games remained an annual ritual from that point forward; they're called either the "Roman Games" or the "Great Games."

c. Livy, *From the Foundation* 1.38 *Livy's account of the conflict with Collatia, like his account of Apiolae in 5.4.1b, has been called into question. But the monuments he refers to still stand, and most date to the sixth century* BCE.

He took the Sabine city of Collatia and the part of its territory that was closer to Rome. Egerius, the king's nephew, was left there to guard it [...] Now he also prepared to surround Rome with a stone wall,[37] which it didn't have yet. The work had already begun, but it was halted by the Sabine war. He also drained the lowest parts of the city, around the Forum and other valleys between the hills. These areas couldn't drain effectively because they were flat. He did it with a sewer[38] that led from the highest point down to the Tiber.

He also laid foundations for the shrine of Jupiter on the Capitol.[39] He had vowed this temple in war with the Sabines, and already in his mind could foresee the future size of the place to come.

5.4.2 Attus Navius

The story of Attus Navius is one of several that advertise the power of augury (Rome's preferred method of divination) over other civic, military, or political goals (for another example, see **3.3**). Attus Navius the augur was remembered both for his skill and for standing up to the king. Importantly, Tarquin cooperates – a sign that he was not as disrespectful of the gods as the later Tarquins would be.

a. Cicero, *On Divination* 1.31–1.33 *Cicero explains how Navius became famous.*

What ancient writer doesn't talk about the division of space that Attus Navius performed with his staff?[40] This was long after Romulus when the elder Tarquin was king. When Attus was a boy, he was poor and herded pigs. When one went missing (so the story goes), he vowed that if he got it back, he'd dedicate the biggest grape in the vineyard to the gods. And so, when the pig was found, he stood in the middle of the vineyard, looking south. Then he divided the vineyard into four parts.

The birds rejected three of them, but the fourth part was still left. He subdivided this part into smaller areas and found a grape of unbelievable size, as we read.

This deed became famous. All his neighbors came to him for help with their affairs, and Navius became a big name. Because of his fame, King Tarquin summoned him. To test Navius' augural ability, the king said he was thinking of something particular and wanted to know if it was possible. Navius consulted the birds and said that it was. But Tarquin said that he'd been considering whether it was possible to cut through a rock with a razor, and commanded Attus to try. So while the king and people watched, Attus carried the stone into the Comitium and sliced through it. After this deed, Tarquin consulted Attius Navius as an augur and the Roman people sought his advice in their affairs. So we learn that the stone and razor were buried in the Comitium and a stone wall was put above them.

b. Cicero, *On the Nature of the Gods* 2.9 *In this work, Cicero discussed the philosophical belief in religious rites. The period when Navius lived has changed from the passage above; does it affect how you understand the story?*

Should we scorn the staff[41] of Attus Navius, which he used to establish the boundaries of his vineyard in order to find his pig? I'd say yes, except that king Hostilius carried out great wars with the approval of Attus' auguries. But this knowledge has been lost, thanks to the negligence of our nobility.

c. Livy, *From the Foundation* 1.36 *Livy's account focuses on the contemporary memorials of Navius and the respect for augury he commanded. His story about the whetstone is similar to Cicero's, although the king's motivation is different.*

Tarquin thought that his cavalry in particular needed to be stronger. He decided to add new centuries to the three established by Romulus (the Ramnes, Titienses, and Luceres[42]), and to name them after himself. Attus Navius, the most famous augur of that time, refused. He claimed that, because Romulus had established the first set with the approval of the auspices, the number couldn't be changed or expanded unless the birds gave their approval. His words roused the king's anger. Mocking Navius' skill, they say, Tarquin said, "Okay, you prophet. Go on – ask your birds if it's possible to do what I'm thinking of right now."

Attus put the question to the birds and replied that it was indeed possible. Tarquin replied, "Well, I'd been thinking about you cutting through a flint with a razor. Here, take it – show me what the birds told you was possible." But they say Navius cut through the stone without delay.

There's a statue of Attus with his head covered in the Comitium. That's where his marvel was performed. It stands on the stairs to the left of the Senate House. Records say that the stone was also put in the same place as a memorial of his miracle for later generations. Certainly Tarquin gained such great respect for augury and augurs that afterwards nothing was done at home or in war unless it received the approval of the birds.

d. Dionysius of Halicanassus, *Roman Antiquities* 3.70.2–3.70.4
Dionysius elaborates on the discovery of Navius' talent. The division of the field parallels the actual work of augury, which divides the sky into smaller spaces for observation.

Attus' father was a poor farmer with a small lot. When he was young, Navius helped him with chores appropriate for his age, like herding pigs. One day he fell asleep, and when he woke up he couldn't find some of the pigs. He cried, afraid he'd get a beating from his father. Then, approaching a hero-shrine in the area, he asked for help locating the pigs. In return, he promised to sacrifice the biggest bunch of grapes in the area. In a few minutes he found the pigs and wanted to fulfill his vow. But he was at a loss to determine which cluster was biggest. Upset, he asked the gods to show him what he was looking for. Divine inspiration struck. He divided the vineyard into two halves and observed the birds [...] He continued this division and observation to the final vine, and there found an immense bunch of grapes, which he brought to the shrine. On the way, his father saw him and was amazed at the size of the grapes. He asked Attius where he'd found it, and the boy explained the whole story. The father rightly recognized the boy's talent for divination.

e. Dionysius of Halicanassus, *Roman Antiquities* 3.72.3–3.72.7
Dionysius' account of Attus Navius' disappearance is reminiscent of both Aeneas (2.6) and Romulus (3.7). Unlike these two founders, Attus doesn't seem to have been worshipped; the disappearance of his body may be due to his skill in divination.

When he was at the peak of his skill and had more power than other Romans, Navius suddenly disappeared. A rival envied him, an enemy plotted against him, or some other misfortune befell him. But none of his relatives could discover what happened or find the body. The Romans mourned this strange and suspicious event. The sons of Ancus Marcius took note of public opinion and blamed Tarquin [...] But Tarquin defended himself robustly and dispelled the accusation.

──────────────────── 5.4.3 The Birth of Servius Tullius ────────────────────

Servius was born in Tarquin's household. There is significant controversy, ancient and modern, about whether he was actually a slave. Some scholars find it strange that he was a slave, despite Rome's mythical open-doors policy (and first king, Romulus). They prefer to follow the emperor Claudius (**4.6.4b**) in equating him with the Etruscan warrior Mastarna. In the majority of Roman accounts, however, Servius Tullius seems more similar to Romulus or Iulus: he has strong connections with the hearth and fire, and was an exile from a young age.

a. Cicero, *On the State* 2.37 *Cicero doesn't seem to think that a slave king was a problem for Rome. Instead, Servius' innate intelligence makes him suitable for the throne. Cicero's interpretation of the "spark" is a clever twist on the more imaginative accounts that follow.*

Rumor has it that he was born to a slave of the Tarquins, who was impregnated by one of the king's clients. He was brought up among the slaves' children and served at the king's table. But there was no hiding the spark of intellect that shone out of the boy – he was *that* clever in all his duties and whenever he spoke. So Tarquin, who had young children at the time, loved Servius, and even the Roman people considered him the king's son. At Tarquin's wish, Servius learned all of the skills that Tarquin himself had learned, in accordance with the very civilized custom of the Greeks.

b. Livy, *From the Foundation* 1.39 *Livy's account emphasizes Servius' high birth, rejecting the idea that he had been born a slave. His version thus suggests that the omen of the flame confirmed, rather than instigated, belief in Servius' nobility.*

At that time a miracle occurred in the palace, amazing to see and experience. They say a boy named Servius Tullius was asleep. While many people were watching, his head caught fire.[43] The hue and cry that was raised by such a great miracle attracted the king and queen's attention. As one of the slaves was bringing water to put the fire out, the queen restrained him. Once the hullaballoo died down, she forbade them to move the boy until he got up of his own free will. Soon enough, he woke and the flame vanished.

Then Tanaquil took her husband aside for a private conversation. "See that boy, whom we're raising in such poverty? That light tells us that one day, when our affairs are precarious, he'll be a fortress to the distressed palace. So we should raise him with great affection and provide him with the opportunity to perform acts of great benefit to us and the kingdom."

From that point on, they began to think of the boy as their child and to educate him in the skills which encourage men to seek out great fortune. It was easy to do, since the gods intended it. The young man turned out to have a truly regal nature. When Tarquin was looking for a son-in-law, none of the Roman young men could compete in any way, so Servius married the king's daughter. This great honor that was given to him, whatever the motivation behind it, makes it impossible to believe that he was born to a slave and was himself a slave as a small child.[44] I am rather of the opinion of those men who say that when Corniculum was taken over, Servius Tullius the elder, who was the chief man in that city, was killed. His wife was already pregnant. She was recognized as a noblewoman among the other captives, and so the Roman queen kept her from slavery. Instead, the woman was brought to Rome and gave birth in the palace. Because Tanaquil had done her such a big favor, the two women became close friends. The Tarquins loved and respected the child, who had been raised in the house since he was small. It was his mother's misfortune – that is, that when her country was taken over she came into enemy hands – that led to the belief that he was born to a slave.

c. Ovid, *Fasti* 6.627–6.635 *Ovid suggests that Servius was a demigod, connecting him strongly with Romulus. The unusual story of the phallus is reminiscent of Plutarch's account of Romulus' birth (**3.1.7**).*

Vulcan was Servius' father and Ocresia was his mother. She was a beauty from Corniculum. When Tanaquil was performing the usual sacrifices, she told Ocresia to pour the wine on the decorated hearth. But there among the ashes was an ugly shape: a phallus! Either it was there or it seemed to be, but she thought it was actually there.[45] As commanded, she sat at the hearth and got pregnant. Servius was born from this divine seed. His father made his role known by surrounding the child's head with shimmering fire: a beanie made of flames burned around his hair.

d. Plutarch, *On the Fortune of the Romans* **9** *(Moralia* **232A–D)**
Plutarch offers several different explanations of the miracle of Servius' birth. Despite the variants, they all have the same goal of showing the Romans' good luck.

There are many other names and honors given to Fortune.[46] For the most part, these were established by Servius, since he knew that "Fortune has great influence, or rather the affairs of men are entirely due to Fortune." Servius in particular was promoted thanks to Fortune; he began as the child of a captive enemy and became king. When the Romans sacked the town of Corniculum, they took the virgin Ocresia captive. Fortune didn't hide Ocresia's appearance or her nature, so she became a royal slave, serving the king's wife Tanaquil. One of their followers – the Roman word is *client* – married her, and their child was Servius.

But some say this isn't what happened. They write that the virgin Ocresia made daily offerings to the hearth, bringing food and drink from the king's table. One day she was throwing bread into the fire as usual when suddenly the flame went out and a male sexual organ rose up out of the hearth. The terrified girl told the story only to Tanaquil. Tanaquil was smart and practical. She dressed the girl up like a bride and locked her in with the phantom, knowing that it was a god. Some say that her lover was a local hero,[47] others that it was Hephaistos. In any case, Servius was the result of their union.

When he was a baby, his head sparkled with lightning-like flames. But those who follow [Valerius] Antias disagree. They claim that when Servius' wife Gegania was dying, he lay down to rest in sadness and grief while his mother was present. As he slept, the women saw his face light up with bright fire. This was proof that he was descended from a flame, and a clear forewarning of his unexpected reign. After Tarquin's death, Tanaquil urged him to take the throne. Since he seems to have been the least eager for kingship[48] and the least regal by nature of all the kings, he was planning to abdicate. But Tanaquil didn't let him. As she was dying, it seems, she made him vow to retain power and not to betray the ancestral government of the Romans. So Servius' rule was entirely owed to Fortune, since he received it unexpectedly and was not allowed to escape the office, even though he wanted to.

5.4.4   Tarquin's Murder

You may have noticed that few Roman kings died natural deaths. Tarquin is no exception: the sources are unanimous that he was murdered. Although some suggest that he died in an Etruscan coup (**4.6.1**), it's far from certain. The jealousy of Ancus' sons fall into a typical Roman historical pattern of desire for kingship, as we have already seen with Ascanius and Silvius (**2.7**), Amulius and Numitor (**3.1**), Romulus and Remus (**3.3, 3.4**), and Tullus and Ancus (**5.3.4b**).

---

a. Livy, *From the Foundation* 1.40–1.41   *Livy's account of Tarquin's murder highlights an important problem with an elected monarchy: what happens when the princes don't become kings? This passage continues at **5.5.1a**.*

By that time, the two sons of Ancus considered it a major insult. Even earlier they'd been upset that they'd been kept off of their father's throne by the lies of their guardian. A stranger ruled Rome – not someone from a nearby city, not even an Italian! It weighed upon them more and more, and their anger increased. If the throne wouldn't come back to them even after Tarquin, if rather it would fall straight into the hands of some slave [...]! In the same city where, about a hundred years earlier, Romulus, who was the son of a god and had become a god himself, had held the throne for his brief period on earth! *This* city would be ruled by some slave, born to a slave! It would dishonor the Romans in general, but especially their family, if the throne was open to outsiders and slaves while the sons of King Ancus were perfectly healthy. They decided to repay the insult with violence. But their grievance was against Tarquin himself, not Servius; with Servius dead, Tarquin could choose any of his other brats as an heir. Besides, they thought the king would be a more serious threat if he survived to avenge the murder. For all these reasons, they plotted to kill the king.

They chose two of the fiercest shepherds for the task. Each one took the agricultural tools he was used to. In the king's courtyard they started fighting as loudly as they could, but for show. This caught the attention of all the king's attendants. When both of them called for the king and their shouts reached the inner halls of the palace, they got their wish: they were summoned to the throne. At first, each one insulted and shouted at each other. The lictors[49] forced them to be quiet and to tell their grievances in turn, calmly. One started to tell a pre-set story. As the king looked at him, turning his entire body in one direction, the other man hoisted his axe and drove it into the king's skull. Leaving the weapon in the wound, both hurried themselves out of the palace.

As Tarquin lay dying, the men in the room tried to pick him up. Meanwhile the lictors arrested the fugitives. The shouting made citizens race over, wondering what was going on. In the chaos, Tanaquil gave orders to lock down the palace and threw the bystanders out. She gathered necessities for treating the wound, ready to care diligently while hope prevailed – but if all hope was lost, she needed other options. At once she summoned Servius and showed him her husband, who by now had almost bled out. Seizing his hand, she begged him not to let his father-in-law's death go unavenged or to leave her vulnerable to her enemies.

"Servius," she said. "The throne is yours, if you're man enough to take it. It doesn't belong to those cowards who needed hired goons for this despicable crime. Lift yourself up and follow the gods. They led you this far, indicating that you would be a great man with the divine fire around your head. Now that heavenly flame calls you – now you really need to wake up! Tarquin and I ruled, even though we were foreigners; consider who you *are*, not where you came from. If you're still stunned by these sudden events, at least follow my advice."

The shouting and hammering of the crowd outside could barely be contained. Tanaquil addressed the people from the window [...] She told them to take heart, that the king was sleeping after this sudden injury. But the blade hadn't sunk far into his body, and even now he was gaining consciousness. The wound had been examined and cleaned. Everything was fine. She was sure that he'd see them himself in a few days. Meanwhile, he'd asked the people to follow Servius' orders. He, Tarquin, handed over all the duties of kingship and justice to Servius.

Servius marched out with the royal robes and lictors. Sitting on the king's chair, he decided some cases and pretended that he would consult the king about others. And so they hid the king's death for several days after he'd taken his last breath.

5.5 Servius Tullius (578–535)

Servius was, as **5.4.4a** reminds us, the first king to rule without being elected. His reign thus marks a change from elective monarchy to dynasty. Nonetheless, he was fondly remembered as a "good" king by later Romans, possibly due to his social reforms or perhaps by embodying social mobility without a threat to the *status quo*. He's credited with wanting to make Rome a republic, with substantial policy revisions that had a lasting impact, and with just rule (despite his unorthodox rise to power). His assassination led to the crisis of the monarchy.

Servius' reign recalls several previous kings. Some versions of his birth story share similarities to Romulus' (**5.4.3**), and the "Servian reforms" organize Rome's citizens much as Romulus developed the tribes and curiae (**3.5.6, 3.6.1**). His association with the goddess Fortune is similar to Numa's relationship with the nymph Egeria (**5.2.2**), and perhaps should be seen as a mark of later Romans' approval. (However, there may also be a historical basis to a tyrant claiming Fortune's support; the Pyrgi Tablets, contemporary documents from Etruria, suggest that Etruscan rulers also claimed the support of divine Fortune.) Servius' ascent to the throne shares themes with the rise of Ancus Marcius. Finally, his building projects associate him with the other two Tarquin rulers. Despite these thematic repetitions, many modern scholars think Servius truly did rule Rome.

——————— 5.5.1 Servius' ascension and Fortune ———————

As a king who had technically usurped the throne, Servius asserted his right to power in several ways. One was through claiming a special relationship with the goddess of luck.

a. Livy, *From the Foundation* 1.41–1.42: *In this passage, which continues **5.4.4a**, Livy stresses several major themes of Servius' reign: his insecurity on the throne, dynastic marriage, and the continuing problems caused by the desire to rule.*

Servius solidified his position by pretending to carry out another's instructions. But at last the death was admitted openly and mourning started in the palace.

Servius surrounded himself with a strong guard. He was the first king to rule without the vote of the people or the will of the Senate. Ancus' children heard that their henchmen had been arrested, that the king was alive, and that the fortunes of Servius had reached their peak. So they went into exile at Suessa Pometia.

Servius guarded himself with private schemes more than public ones. Worried that the children of Tarquin would bear the same resentment towards him as the children of Ancus had felt towards Tarquin, he arranged a double marriage: his daughters to the king's sons, Lucius and Arruns Tarquin. But he couldn't break fate's requirements by mortal plans, or stop resentment over the kingship from causing all sorts of hatred and treachery in his own home.

b. Dionysius of Halicarnassus, *Roman Antiquities* 4.8.2–4.8.3 *Dionysius explains how Servius consolidated his power. His description is strongly influenced by Greek ideas of tyrannical behavior, and sets up support for Tarquin's coup (**5.4.3**).*

The most powerful patricians often gathered to talk about ending Tullius' illegal rule. They decided that they'd force him to set aside the royal insignia at the next council meeting, and then they'd set up an *interregnum*, as required by law. Tullius realized what they were planning, so he focused on the people. He hoped to keep the throne by playing to the poor.

c. Ovid, *Fasti* 6.570–6.580 *Ovid explains the origin of a veiled statue in the temple of Fortune in cheerfully erotic terms. Despite what he says, there was only limited agreement about this statue in antiquity: some authors thought it portrayed Fortune herself.*

Who's that man hiding under the toga? It's Servius! We all agree on that, but not on why he's hidden. I'm not entirely sure myself. The goddess Fortune hesitantly speaks of forbidden love; as a divine being, she's ashamed to sleep with a human. But she had the hots for the king and her lust overcame her senses. For *this* man, and him alone, Lady Luck wasn't blind. At night she used to creep into his house through a small window. That's how the city gate got named Tiny Window.[50] Nowadays she's ashamed: she hides his dear face behind a veil and covers his royal features with a toga.

d. Plutarch, *Roman Questions* 36 (*Moralia* 273C) *Plutarch suggests various reasons for the name behind one of Rome's gates. One is reminiscent of Tanaquil (**5.4.4a**), while the other recalls Numa (**5.2.2**).*

Why do they call one of the gates "little window" – that's what *Fenestella* means – and why is the place next to it called the "bedroom of Fortune"? Is it because King Servius was the most fortunate man and he had the reputation of meeting Fortune? She would come to him at this window. Or is this a myth? Is it because when King Tarquin the Elder died, his wife Tanaquil, who was a clever and regal woman, addressed the people through this window? She persuaded them to make Servius the king, and so the place got its name.

5.5.2 Diana's cow

There are several variations on this story of the theft (or attempted theft) of a divine token. The motif is repeated in **4.6.5b** and **8.9.2**. Although the success of the thief varies, the message of the story remains the same in every version: Rome is meant to rule the world.

a. Livy, *From the Foundation* 1.45 *Livy's account ties the theft of Diana's cow to the wider Greek world and Servius' diplomatic contacts. Servius' skills at negotiation should be compared to the heavy-handed tactics of Tullus Hostilius (**5.3.3**) and Tarquin (**5.6.2a**, **5.6.2c**).*

At that time, the shrine of Diana at Ephesus was already famous. Rumor had it that it was made in common by the cities of Asia [Minor]. Servius praised this amazing consensus and common worship of the gods among the Latin chiefs with whom he'd already made alliances, either in his own name or in Rome's. By often repeating the same ideas, he forced the Latins to make a shrine of Roman Diana together with the Romans. It was a confession that Rome was the chief city – a status for which so many wars had been fought. Although now the issue seemed far from the minds of all the Latins due to frequent unsuccessful attempts at war, Fortune seemed to give the Sabines a chance to regain control on individual terms.

There was a cow born to one of the landowners in the Sabine territory. She was said to be amazingly big and beautiful. For many years, her horns were nailed up in the entry of Diana's shrine as a memorial to this miracle. This cow was considered a prodigy in the town (which it was), and the seers prophesied that the city whose citizen sacrificed the cow to Diana would gain supreme command.

The prophecy had reached the priest of Diana's shrine. When the first appropriate day for sacrifice appeared, the Sabine yoked the cow, led it to the shrine of Diana, and stood in front of the altar. The Roman priest was attracted by the size of the victim. Remembering the famous prophecy, he addressed the Sabine visitor: "Sir, what are you doing? Will an impure man make a sacrifice to Diana? Why don't you dip yourself in flowing water first? The Tiber flows at the bottom of the valley."

The Sabine was impressed by the requirement. He wanted to perform the rite correctly so that everything would turn out as the prophecy suggested. Immediately he went down to the Tiber, and while he was gone the Roman sacrificed the cow to Diana. In doing so, he gained immense gratitude from the king and city.

5.5.3   Death of Servius Tullius

The murder of Servius Tullius repeats many themes found in the murder of Tarquin the Elder. Some scholars have also suggested similarities with the *rex Nemorensis*, the slave priest of Diana at Nemi who was hunted and killed by his rival.

a. Livy, *From the Foundation* 1.46–1.48 *Livy's account is dramatic, but concise. He applies his theme of jealousy over the kingship to an unusual character: the king's daughter, Tullia. Compare her prominent role to the roles typically played by women in Roman myth (see **chapter 7**).*

By now, Servius' hold on the kingdom was assured beyond a doubt by squatters' rights. All the same, he kept hearing about complaints from the young Tarquin, who claimed that his reign was against the wishes of the people. So first Servius gained support among the people by distributing land that had been captured from the enemy. Only then did he dare to go before the people and ask whether they wanted or even commanded him to rule. They confirmed him on the throne with more agreement than they had ever shown in electing the earlier kings.

But the election didn't diminish Tarquin's hope of gaining the kingship. Instead, he wanted it even more. He noticed that Servius had made the distribution of land to the people despite the disapproval of the Senate,[51] and realized that this disagreement gave him a chance. He began to berate Servius among the senators and thus strengthen his position there. As a young man, he had great passion; at home, his wife Tullia encouraged his rabid thoughts.

So the Roman palace endured another tragedy. But the result was this: freedom came sooner, thanks to frustration with the kings, and the king who gained the throne through crime turned out to be the last.

This Lucius Tarquin was either the son or grandson of the elder Tarquin; there's not enough information to be sure, but most authorities say he was the son. He had a brother, Arruns Tarquin, who was kind and gentle. These two brothers, as I said before,[52] married the king's daughters, both named Tullia. The Tullias were also far different in personality. I'm sure Rome's fortune saw to it that the two siblings with criminal natures weren't joined in matrimony. That way, the city's customs were established during Servius' longer reign.

The savage Tullia felt suffocated in her marriage. Her husband showed no sign of desire or daring. She turned to the other Tarquin with the full force of her personality. She admired him, told him he was a true man, born from royal blood; she scorned her sister, who'd married a man but lacked a woman's courage. Their similarity quickly allied them, as often happens: one bad apple spoils the bunch.

But the beginning of the trouble was entirely the woman's fault. She made a habit of secret meetings with another woman's husband. In them, she didn't hesitate to spew hateful speech about her sister and her husband, his wife and brother. She even argued that it would be better if she were a virgin and he'd never married – at least that way they wouldn't be joined to their inferiors and waste away from someone else's cowardice! If only the gods had given her a husband who was worthy of her, she would have seen her father's royal power relocate to her household as soon as possible.

Her words soon inflated the young man with her bold ideas. After two funerals in quick succession, Tarquin and Tullia prepared their homes for a new marriage. Servius didn't disapprove when they got married, but he didn't approve either.

From that day forward, Tullius' old age grew more vulnerable, and his reign began to be less safe. The woman looked from one crime to the next. Night or day, she couldn't stand it if her husband rested, fearful that the previous murders would be for nothing. She didn't need a man who could be called her husband, or one whom she would silently serve. She needed a man who thought he was worthy of kingship, who remembered that he was the son of the elder Tarquin, who preferred to have a throne rather than hope for one. "If you're the man I thought I married, I'll call you my husband and my king. But if not, we've changed things for the worse. Now we're not just lazy; we're criminals! Why don't you act? You don't need to struggle for a foreign throne, like your father. You're not from Corinth or Tarquinia. Your household and native gods, the image of your father, the palace and the royal throne inside, even the Tarquin name – these all make you king and call you to power. But if you lack the courage for this, why cheat the people? Why do you let them see you as a prince? Make your way back to Tarquinia or Corinth! Go back to your roots. You're more like your brother than your father."

Harassing him with speeches like these, she goaded the young man into action. She herself couldn't rest. Tanaquil, a foreigner, had possessed such a forceful personality that she had made two kings in a row: her husband and then her son-in-law. Yet she herself, a king's daughter, had made no progress in giving the throne or taking it away!

Driven by this female fury, Tarquin made the rounds to solicit senatorial support, especially from the lesser families. He reminded them of his father's benefactions and asked for favors in return. He attracted young men with gifts. Finally, he increased his following everywhere by huge promises and reminders of the king's misdeeds. At last it seemed time to act. He rushed into the Forum, surrounded by a gang of armed men. Everyone was struck with terror as he sat himself in the king's chair in front of the Senate House and ordered heralds to summon the senators to meet with King Tarquin. They came right away. Some were in on the plot and already prepared, while others were afraid of the consequences if they didn't come. The second group was astonished by the uncomfortable novelty of the event. They thought Servius was already done for.

Tarquin started out by berating the king's lineage: he was a slave, born to a slave. After the undeserved death of Tarquin's own father, there had been no *interregnum*, as before; no public meeting had been held; Servius took the throne not by public vote, not by the Senate's authority, but thanks to a woman's gift. Born in this way, made king in this way, he was the patron of the lowest sort of men – the sort he himself came from. Because he hated other men's nobility, he had stolen land from leading men and given it to the poorest citizens. He taxed prominent citizens with all the burdensome duties that one had been commonly shared. He set up a census so that the good fortune of the wealthy would be publicized, leading to jealous grudges, and he'd made preparations to distribute their money to the neediest citizens whenever he so chose.

During this speech, Servius appeared. He'd been summoned by a frightened messenger. At once he boomed from the doorway of the Senate House, "Tarquin! What's this? What madness! How dare you call a Senate meeting when I'm alive and sit in my chair?"

Tarquin responded furiously. "It was my father's chair, and a king's son is a far better heir to it than a slave. It's bad enough that you insulted your masters for so long with mocking freedom!" As he spoke, supporters on both sides started shouting. The people rushed into the Senate House, and it became clear that the winner would rule. Then Tarquin, driven by necessity, dared to make a final push. He was much stronger, both in age and in physical power. He grabbed Servius around the waist, hoisted him up, and threw him out of the Senate House into the lower part of the Forum. As Servius tumbled down the stairs, Tarquin went back inside to assemble the Senate. The king's attendants and companions fled.

The king himself was almost dead. Without an entourage, he was dragging himself homeward when he was killed; Tarquin sent men to finish him off as he fled. It's generally thought that he committed this murder on Tullia's advice. She certainly hadn't worried about committing other crimes. It's also agreed that she came into the Forum in a cart, not at all afraid of the crowd of men. There she called her husband out of the Senate House and was the first to salute him as king. He told her to go home, away from the chaos.

[... *On the way back*] Tullia carried out a disgusting and inhuman crime. The place itself is evidence – they call it the "Cursed Quarter."[53] Maddened, driven by the angry ghosts of her sister and husband, Tullia is believed to have driven the cart across her father's body. She got some of her murdered father's blood and gore on the cart, and was herself splattered with it and infected.[54] She brought it home to hers and her husband's household gods. Their anger hurried the end of the Tarquins' reign, similar to its evil beginning.

b. Ovid, *Fasti* 6.581–6.617 *This passage continues Ovid's explanation of the veiled statue in the temple of Fortune (**5.5.1c**). Here he attributes the veil to Tullia's actions (**5.5.3a**).*

The death of peaceful king Tullius distressed the people.[55] Their grief had no limits and kept on increasing until they covered his statue by throwing togas over it.

The third possibility will take me some time to narrate. Still, I'll try to rein in my mouth. Tullia's second marriage was achieved by murder. She had a habit of goading of her husband with comments like, "What good it is to be equally guilty of our siblings' murder, you and I, if the dutiful life suits you? Better that my husband and your wife had lived, if we're too chicken to do something bigger. I offered you a dowry of my father's kingdom – *and his life*. Man up and take my wedding gift! Crime is kingly. Kill my father, take the throne, and stain our hands with paternal blood."

He was pumped by her words. Although only a private citizen, he took a seat on the lofty throne. The crowd was outraged and rushed to arm; there was blood, there was murder, and old age proved its weakness. Tarquin the Proud pried the king's scepter from his father-in-law and held it tight.

The palace was on the Esquiline. The king's dead body tumbled to the foot of the hill, getting bloodier from the rough ground. His daughter traveled through the streets, heading to her father's palace. She sat tall and vicious in her chariot. Her driver stopped short when he saw the body and burst into tears. Tullia ripped into him. "Are you going to move, or are you waiting until I give you a harsh reward for your grief? Go on, I said! Drive over his *face*! Who cares if you want to?" Here's the proof: the place is called "cursed" because of her,[56] and the deed will always weigh it down.

All the same, she dared to approach the temple that memorialized her father. You think I'm joking, but what I say *did* happen. There was a statue seated on the throne with Tullius' features. It's said this statue covered his eyes with his hand and a voice cried out "Get out of my sight! I will not see the evil face of my daughter." So the statue is covered with clothing.

5.6 Tarquin the Proud (534–509)

After killing Servius, Tarquin becomes king. He starts off on the wrong foot: despite many military successes and important public works, he's Rome's last king. This Tarquin becomes known as "The Proud," a characteristic that is common in tyrant narratives. The "pride" that Tarquin displays is a little different from the qualities you might associate with the word. In Rome, the concept is closely related to transgressing boundaries. Tarquin is "proud" because he ignores the Senate, overworks the people, and puts personal interest before

Rome's interest (compare **3.6**). These actions may be acceptable for other kings, but Roman kings are more cooperative rulers (**3.6.1**). By abandoning this model, Tarquin risks his throne.

Tarquin the Proud, as discussed in **5.4. introduction**, shares many deeds with the first Tarquin. This doubling is a feature of oral traditions. Because stories are handed down about "Tarquin," over time the specific Tarquin is lost. To compensate, the narrative becomes associated with both kings.

------------------------------ 5.6.1 Tarquin's character ------------------------------

Although this Tarquin is known as a "tyrant," you may be surprised by how mild most of his deeds are. The majority of the atrocities in his reign are committed by his relatives (wife and son). Tarquin's failure to rein in his relations, like the failure of Tatius 200 years earlier (**3.6.2, 3.6.3**), is disastrous for his rule.

a. Cicero, *On the State* 2.45 *Cicero describes Tarquin's tyrannical traits.*

[Tarquin] was already tainted from killing the fantastic king before him. The man was hardly sane. He was afraid he'd be punished for his evil deed, so he wanted everyone to be afraid of him. Giddy from riches and victory, he was gleefully extravagant. He couldn't rein in his own habits, much less the desires of his children.

b. Livy, *From the Foundation* 1.49 *This passage picks up from Livy's account of the murder of Servius (**5.5.3a**). Here he describes how Tarquin distinguished himself as a bad ruler.*

From that point forward, Lucius Tarquin began to rule. Soon he was given the nickname "The Proud," because he refused to give his father-in-law a funeral. As an excuse, he cited the example of Romulus, who had also died without being buried, and he arranged for the death of the leading senators, who (he thought) were advancing Servius' interests. Then, aware that he himself had set a bad precedent for anyone who wanted to take the kingship away from him, he surrounded himself with a thick bodyguard.[57] He had no right at all to rule except force, since he too[58] reigned without being elected or by the Senate's authority [...]

He was the first king to abandon the custom, handed down from the first kings, of consulting the Senate on every matter. He governed with the advice of his friends.[59] He started and ended war, peace, treaties, and alliances by himself as he chose, without the authority of people or Senate. In particular, he made nice with the Latins, in the belief that he'd be safer among his citizens if he was backed by foreign powers. He didn't stop at friendship with their leading men; he married into their families. Octavius Mamilius of Tusculum was by far the best of the Latins, if we can believe the report that he was descended from Ulysses and the goddess Circe.[60] Tarquin married his daughter to Mamilius, and through this marriage he gained many relatives and friends.

5.6.2 Foreign affairs

Like earlier kings, Tarquin the Proud both fights and makes alliances with nearby cities. His treatment of enemy cities is comparable to earlier kings as well. But Roman sources are eager to emphasize his cruelty towards the conquered, an aspect we saw previously with Tullus Hostilius (**5.3.3**). Tarquin's cruelty is one marker of his status as a tyrant; interestingly, so are the strengthened relationships with allies that we saw in **5.6.1**.

---

a. Livy, *From the Foundation* 1.50   *Livy's Turnus Herdonius should not be confused with Vergil's Turnus (2.5). This episode takes place in the grove of Diana; compare Servius' attempts to establish a pan-Latin sanctuary of Diana (5.5.2).*

By now Tarquin's authority among the leading Latins was established. He called them to a meeting on a set day at the Ferentine grove. He wanted to talk about next steps in matters of common interest. They gathered together at dawn in crowds; Tarquin made the meeting, but arrived a little before sunset.

The Latins discussed many things there throughout the day, holding councils on various topics. Turnus Herdonius from Aricia vehemently attacked the absent Tarquin. "It's no wonder he was given the name 'Proud' at Rome – that's what the crowd calls him, you know, even if only in whispers behind his back! Is there anything more arrogant than playing with the entire Latin nation like this? He gathered us leaders from our homes far away, but even though he called the meeting, he didn't come! He's testing our tolerance. If we tamely accept, he'll press us into service. Who can't see that he's aiming to command all Latins? Even if his own citizens thought it right to give him the throne – that is, *if* they gave it to him and he didn't take it by murder – should the Latins trust him, too? [...]"

Turnus was going on and on about these and related matters. He was treasonous, criminal, and had gained influence at home by oratorical skill. Tarquin arrived, and everyone turned to greet him. Turnus stopped talking. Since all were now silent, the men closest to Tarquin whispered that he should excuse and explain his late arrival. He said that he'd been busy settling a case between father and son. His concern over reconciling them had delayed him, and because that matter had taken up the day, he would set out what he'd planned on the next day.

They say Turnus didn't buy this excuse. He muttered that nothing could be solved more quickly or in fewer words than a case between father and son. All you had do was say "obey your father, or else." The Arician made these complains about the king and left the council.

Tarquin took the matter more seriously than he seemed to, and immediately plotted Turnus' murder. He wanted to inspire the same terror in the Latins as he had in his citizens at home. Because he couldn't kill Turnus openly by executive order, he suppressed the innocent man using a false charge. With the help of some Aricians of a different political bent, he bribed Turnus' slave to look the other way while Tarquin hid dozens of swords in his tent. Everything was done overnight. A little before daybreak, Tarquin summoned the Latin chiefs as if he were distressed about a revolt. He said that his delay on the preceding day seemed fated by divine foresight, for his own good and for the good of the Latins. He added that Turnus was rumored to be plotting Tarquin's own murder and the murder of the top Latins, with the goal of ruling the Latins himself. He would've attacked in council the previous day, but his plot was delayed. Tarquin himself was missing, and Turnus wished to kill him most of all [... *Tarquin suggests that the Latins search Turnus' tent to see if he has weapons.*][61]

The Latins went to Turnus' tent, inclined to believe Tarquin. But unless the swords were found, they planned to treat the threat as unfounded. When they reached the tent, they surrounded it with a guard and woke Turnus up. The slaves were captured as they were getting ready to fight on their master's behalf. When hidden weapons were taken out of every corner of the tent, the matter seemed exceptionally clear. Turnus was thrown into chains, and a general meeting of the Latins was called at once, in great turmoil. At the meeting, the swords were put on display. Such bitter hatred surged against Turnus that his case was decided without letting him speak. He was condemned to die in a new way: put in a basket with rocks piled up on top, he was thrown into the headwaters of the Ferentine stream and drowned.

Then Tarquin called the Latins back to the meeting. He praised them for punishing Turnus as he deserved for clearly plotting revolution and murder. Then he made a speech. Since all Latins were descended from Alba, they were bound by the treaty which all Alba had made under Tullus Hostilius – namely, to cede command to Rome with their colonies. Thus he had power over them by an ancient law. But he thought it was better for everyone to renew the treaty. Then the Latins could enjoy the good fortune of the Roman people rather than always wait for or endure the destruction of their cities or devastation of the fields, which had happened first under Ancus and then under his own father's rule. He found it quite easy to persuade the Latins, although by this treaty Rome became the supreme state. But everyone could see that the chief Latins stood by the king, while they had an immediate example of the danger that would befall anyone who disagreed. So the treaty was renewed.

b. Livy, *From the Foundation* **1.53–1.54**   *Tarquin subdued cities by war as well as by treachery. The story of Gabii's fall has clear Greek parallels (5.6.2d).*

The war that he fought with Gabii, a neighboring city, took longer than he'd expected. He had no success at all with a frontal assault, and he lost hope of besieging the city when he was forced back from the walls. So at last he attacked them in a very un-Roman way: by tricks and treachery. As if he'd abandoned the war, he pretended to occupy himself with laying the foundations of the Capitoline temple and other city projects.[62] Sextus, the youngest[63] of his three sons, fled to Gabii as part of the plan. He complained of his father's intolerable cruelty towards him: recently Tarquin had turned his arrogance away from foreigners and onto his own family. Even the company of his children irritated him, so he was making a deserted island for himself both at home and in the Senate. That way he would leave no offspring, no heir to the kingdom. He, Sextus, had escaped from his father's blows and abuse, and believed he would not be safe except among Tarquin's enemies [...] It seemed that he was ignited by anger and would move further afield unless they stopped him. So the people of Gabii took him in kindly. They told him not to be surprised that his father, in the end, acted the same way towards his children, citizens, and allies. Eventually he'd turn his cruelty upon himself, if other targets were lacking. For themselves, they were very happy that he had come to them, and they believed that with his help the war would soon move from the gates of Gabii to the walls of Rome.

     [...] Gradually he encouraged the leading men of Gabii to rebel. Sextus himself with the most zealous young men went on expeditions to scout and plunder. Sextus made all preparations to fool them in word and deed. Their faith in him increased. At last, they chose him as the leader of their war – but in vain. With the majority unaware of what was going on, a few small fights broke out between Rome and Gabii. For the most part, Gabii won. At that point, the people of Gabii, regardless of status, truly believed that Sextus Tarquin had been sent as a gift from the gods. By facing dangers and work equally, by distributing plunder generously, Sextus became so beloved among the soldiers that he was more powerful in Gabii than his father was in Rome.

At that point, when it seemed that he'd gained enough influence to try anything, he sent a messenger to his father in Rome to ask what he should do, since the gods had granted him sole power over all public affairs in Gabii. No spoken message was given to this messenger, I think because his trustworthiness was in doubt. The king, as if he were thinking, walked from the house into the garden with his son's messenger following.[64] As he was wandering around in there, silent, he knocked off the tallest heads of the poppies with his stick. The messenger got tired of asking and waiting for a reply, so he went back to Gabii with his mission incomplete. He told Sextus what he'd said and seen, but that the king had sent him with no message – whether from anger, contempt, or his usual high-handed behavior.

Sextus immediately grasped what his father meant by his silent and obscure gestures. He killed some of the leading men by denouncing them before the people; others were vulnerable to grudges on their own account.

c. Dionysius of Halicarnassus, *Roman Antiquities* 4.46.3–4.47.4
Dionysius' account of Turnus Herdonius presents him in a somewhat favorable light. In this version, the argument over sovereignty is also a dynastic struggle.

Turnus got up (this is the same man who criticized Tarquin) and wouldn't let the council agree to his rule [...] He repeated many terrible allegations against Tarquin, and finally pointed out that Tarquin ruled Rome illegally, since he hadn't received the throne from willing citizens (like the kings before him) or from the Senate. Instead, he'd strongarmed his way in and established a tyranny [... *The Latins are persuaded; Tarquin defends himself.*] "Latins, Turnus himself cleared me of these accusations he's just made when he wanted to marry my daughter. But I refused him – naturally, because who would turn down Mamilius, the best and most powerful of the Latins, as a son-in-law? Especially when the alternative lacks a family beyond his great-great-grandfather! But because I rejected him, now he accuses me."

d. Dio (Zonaras), *Roman History* 7.11   *Zonaras' account highlights the parallelism between the Greek and Roman stories of the tyrant's secret message.*

Herodotus also relates a similar story. He says that when Periander,[65] son of Cypselus, was the tyrant of Corinth, he sent a messenger to

Thrasybulus the tyrant of Miletus asking how he held his throne safely. Thrasybulus didn't respond to the messenger with words, but he walked into a field, cut off the tallest ears of wheat, and tossed them to the ground. With that, he sent the messenger on his way. The messenger returned. When Periander asked what message was sent back, the messenger said that the tyrant was crazy. He reported Thrasybulus' actions in detail, but explained that he hadn't said a word in response to the question. But Periander understood Thrasybulus' meaning. He killed all the prominent men in Corinth.

Sextus therefore did the same to the men of Gabii, killing the most powerful and distributing their property to the masses.[66] After that, some of the citizens were already out of the way; the rest were deceived and entrusted Sextus with everything. So he took possession of the city with the help of the Roman captives and deserters, who were numerous and whom he'd gathered for this purpose. And once he was in control he gave it to his father. In turn, Tarquin left the city under his son's control and went to fight others.

—————————————— 5.6.3   Building program   ——————————————

Like his father, Tarquin was associated with a number of city beautification projects, most notably the Temple of Jupiter and the Cloaca Maxima (Rome's city sewer, which drained the Forum). The Tarquins' building program has led some scholars to call sixth-century Rome "the great city of the Tarquins."

a. Livy, *From the Foundation* 1.53–1.56   *Much of Livy's material here repeats his narrative of the elder Tarquin's efforts (5.4.1b, 5.4.1c). Both the foundations of the temple and the sewer still exist in Rome today, regardless of who built them.*

Tarquin took Suessa Pometia[67] by storm. When he was dividing the plunder, it added up to 40 talents of silver. So he came up with a footprint for the temple of Jupiter that was worthy of the king of gods and men, worthy of Rome's power, and worthy of the glory of Rome itself. He set aside the money taken from the city for the purpose of building it [...] From there he turned his attention to city business. The most pressing of these was the temple of Jupiter on the Tarpeian[68] Hill, which he wanted to leave behind as a monument to his kingdom and family.

There were two Tarquin kings; the father had vowed the temple, but the son completed it.

He wanted the entire area to be Jupiter's, free from other gods' shrines. So he decided to deconsecrate all the shrines and places of worship that were already there. Some had been vowed by king Tatius when he was first fighting Romulus and subsequently consecrated and inaugurated. At the beginning of the building work, they say the gods used their divine power to indicate the great size of the city's power. Although the birds allowed all the other shrines to be deconsecrated, they did not approve the deconsecration of the shrine of Terminus the boundary stone.[69] This reply was interpreted as an omen and a sign. Only the shrine of Terminus could not be moved, and he alone among all the gods could not be called out of his sacred boundaries. So the birds indicated a firm and stable seat for Rome.

After this indication of eternal dominion was accepted, another prodigy followed, indicating the size of the empire. A human head with its skull complete is said to have appeared when the foundations of the temple were dug [...].[70]

The king was intent on completing the temple. He called craftsmen from all parts of Etruria,[71] and used not only public money but also public labor. The work was heavy and added to military service, but the plebeians complained less about building the temples of the gods with their own hands than they did later, when they were transferred to other tasks. These jobs were less elegant, but quite a bit more work. For example, they built the spectators' benches in the Circus and dug the Cloaca Maxima, a sewer to hold all the city's waste, underground. Almost no new public works can equal these two in magnificence.

b. Dionysius of Halicarnassus, *Roman Antiquities* 4.44.1   *Tarquin has standards for his workers.*

It wasn't enough to harass the plebeians illegally. He picked out loyal men who could fight well and put the rest to work building.

――――――――――――   5.6.4   Tarquin and the Sibyl   ――――――――――――

The Sibyl was the shared name of several female prophets of Apollo. The Sibyl at Cumae is most famous for her role in Vergil's *Aeneid* (book 6; **2.3.2**), but other writers told stories about her as well. One of the most famous is the Sibyl's arrival in Rome with books of prophecy, which Romans consulted and added to for generations. The original Sibylline books burned in the first century

BCE and were replaced; the replacements were destroyed in the fifth century CE, although some fragments remain. The Sibyl's cave has been identified and may be visited near Cumae.

a. Dio (Zonaras), *Roman History* 7.11   *Tarquin almost lost the Sibylline oracles in two ways: first through fire, and then through incomprehension. For Tarquin's relationship with augurs, compare **5.4.2**.*

Tarquin also procured the Sibylline oracles for the Romans, although unwillingly. Some woman, a prophetess whom they called "Sibyl," arrived in Rome with three or nine books. She offered to sell them to Tarquin and named her price. When he didn't pay attention to her, she burned either one or three of the books. And when again Tarquin dismissed her, she destroyed some of the remaining books in the same way. She would have done the same even with the last books, but the augurs forced him to buy them. So these books were saved. He bought these for the same amount that he could have paid for all of them. He gave them to two of his advisors to guard. When they couldn't fully understand what was written, he sent two men to Greece to hire expert interpreters.

b. Lactantius, *Divine Institutes* 1.6.18   *Lactantius explains the origin of the Sibylline books and relates the series of ancient priestesses called Sibyl. Many of them (not all) had individual names as well as the cult title "Sibyl."*

There were ten Sibyls, and Varro listed them all according to the authors who wrote about each one. The first was the Persian Sibyl, and Nicanor, who wrote about the deeds of Alexander, also wrote about her. The second was from Libya, as Euripides recounts in the prologue of the *Lamia*. The third was from Delphi. Chrysippus wrote about her in the book he composed about divination. The fourth was from Cimmeria in Italy. Naevius wrote about her in his poem on the Punic Wars, and Piso names her in his *Annals*. The fifth was the Erythraean Sibyl, whom Apollodorus claims was a fellow-citizen of his in Erythraea. She foretold that the Greeks would attack Troy, Troy would fall, and Homer would write a false history of the war. The sixth was the Samian Sibyl. Eratosthenes wrote that he learned about her in the old records of the Samians.

The seventh was the Cumaean Sibyl, named Amalthea, who is also named Demophile or Herophile in some sources. She brought nine books to King Tarquin the Elder[72] and offered to sell them for 300 gold coins. The king rejected the high price and mocked the woman's madness. So she burned three of them in the king's sight and asked the exact same price for the rest. Tarquin thought she was really crazy then. Again she burned three more books. When she again offered the remaining three for the same price, the king thought there was something to it. He paid for them in gold. Later their number was increased after the Capitol was restored.[73] Books were collected from all cities, both Italian and Greek, but especially Erythraea. These books were brought to Rome and they got the name "Sibylline."

The eighth Sibyl was born in the Hellespont in Trojan territory, in the area of Marpessus near the town Gergitha. Heraclides of Pontus writes that she lived in the age of Solon and Cyrus. The ninth was from Phrygia and prophesied from Ancyra. The tenth was from Tibur and was named Albunea. In Tibur she's worshipped as a goddess, near the banks of the Anio. It's said that a statue of her carrying a book in one hand was found in its waters. The Senate transferred these prophecies to the Capitol.

All of the Sibyls spoke prophecies, but especially the Cumaean Sibyl, whose books are kept secret at Rome. No one has the right to examine them except for the Fifteen Priests.

────────────────── 5.6.5 The fall of the Tarquins ──────────────────

The omen of Tarquin's downfall is dramatic, but takes a while to play out in full. The end of the dynasty is mythically guaranteed by Tullia's behavior towards her father; the omen acts as a divine warning; eventually, matters will come to a head when the family commits another crime, the rape of Lucretia (**7.6**).

---

a. Cicero, *On Divination* 1.44–1.45 *Cicero uses Tarquin's dream to discuss the powers of divination.*

But let's look a little closer to home. What about that dream of Tarquin the Proud? He himself relates it in Accius' *Brutus*:[74] "When at night I gave my body up to nighttime slumber and had soothed my weary limbs with sleep, a shepherd appeared in my dreams and drove towards me a woolly flock of amazing beauty. I chose twin rams and sacrificed the most beautiful one. Then its twin attacked with all its strength and butted me with its horns. The blow knocked me over. I lay flat on the ground, seriously injured. Looking up at the sky, I saw a great and marvelous sight: the fiery orb of the rayed sun moved backwards on a new path."

Then we see how his dream was interpreted by the prophets: "King, it's no surprise that whatever men do in life – what they think about, care about, and see, what they do and wish to do while awake – all these things appear in dreams. But in a dream like this, it's not too bold to say that these visions are a message. Beware! Someone you think is as dumb as an animal is strengthened by wisdom. He will reveal his exceptional soul and expel you from your kingdom. That is what the sun was showing you: a change in public affairs will happen very soon. May it turn out well for the people! When the powerful course changed from left to right, this is the most blessed augury that the Roman Republic will be great."[75]

b. Livy, *From the Foundation* 1.56 *In Livy's account, there is no dream. Instead, two parallel omens allow us to see the coming fall of the Tarquins: first, the snake in the column, and then its counterpart in Brutus' staff. The repetition of the omen (Brutus is the snake as well as the gold bar) helps hide the fact that we never learn the oracle's response.*

As he was doing these things, a terrible omen appeared: a snake slipped out of a wooden column. This led to a terror-stricken evacuation of the palace. The king was not so much terrified as intensely anxious. So [...] he sent two of his sons, Titus and Arruns, to [Delphi]. They traveled through lands that were, at the time, unknown,[76] and seas still more foreign. As their companion, they had Lucius Junius Brutus, the son of the king's sister Tarquinia. This young man had a very different personality than he pretended to have. When he'd heard that the leading men in the city, including his brother, had been killed by his uncle, he decided to hide any trait that could frighten the king or attract his desire. He would be safe because he was scorned; there was little protection in the law.

With this decision, he transformed himself from an active young man to faked stupidity. He allowed himself and all his possessions to become the king's property. He also didn't reject the nickname "bonehead,"[77] since he could hide his true self under the cover of the name. He waited for his opportunity; he would be the liberator of the Roman people.

Tarquin sent this Brutus to Delphi as a companion for his sons – or really as a victim for their bullying. It's said that Brutus brought a gold bar hidden within a hollow stick as a gift for Apollo. The space in the stick was made to fit the bar exactly, as an obscure symbol of his nature. After the Roman princes arrived at the oracle and carried out their father's instructions, they were overcome with desire to know which of them would be the next king of Rome. The answer came back from the depths of the cave: "Young men, whichever one of you first kisses your mother will have the greatest power in Rome."

Since Sextus had been left behind in Rome, he didn't know about the oracle and couldn't share the throne. Titus and Arruns forced everyone to keep the matter quiet. Then they drew straws to decide which of them would kiss their mother first upon arrival in Rome. But Brutus thought the Pythia's[78] oracle meant something else. As if he'd tripped and fallen, he touched his lips to the earth, the common mother of all men.

c. Dionysius of Halicanassus, *Roman Antiquities* 4.63.2–4.63.4
*Dionysius' version of the omen is significantly more violent than the others, but it's also shorter. Since Dionysius usually provides elaborate and multiple versions of events, his brevity suggests that he isn't very interested in this omen. For eagles and the Tarquins, see **5.4.1a**.*

In early spring, eagles came to a garden near the palace and made their nest at the top of a palm tree. Their unfeathered chicks were still in the nest. A crowd of vultures flew to the nest and destroyed it. They killed the chicks and drove the parents away, beating the returning eagles with their wings and pecking them. Seeing the birds, Tarquin steeled himself against fate. But he couldn't avoid his destiny.

Conclusion

Rome's kings came from all over central Italy, but you may have noticed that most of the stories about them center on Rome. This is no accident. Rome gained predominance in this part of Italy long before our sources were writing (potentially as early as the fifth century BCE, and certainly by the third). By the time these local histories were written down, they had a dual role to play: both to burnish the reputation of the locals and to provide a connection with the superpower of Rome. It's not clear that one of these two purposes was more important. Instead, different Roman authors seem to have emphasized different aspects of these tales.

But the centrality of Rome does not completely explain our lack of information about other cities. We also suffer from a loss of information. In the second and first centuries BCE, we know that there were more local histories in circulation. For example, Cato the Elder wrote a work called the *Origins*, collecting the histories of the towns around Rome itself. The surviving fragments of this work, which you've seen cited in this and earlier chapters, still offer us a valuable alternative vision of Italian history – and come from a man who benefited immensely from Rome's generous open-doors policy. Similarly, the Roman scholar Varro wrote several books on popular customs, religion, and history, which may well have included the customs of Latins in general as well as Roman material.

It may help to think about the lost material in more concrete terms. Consider the various stories you've read in this chapter and in **chapters 2** and **3**. These three chapters form the backbone of Rome's foundation story: Greek connections (via Troy, Hercules, and Evander), local connections (Romulus), and historical development (the kings). It is likely that most cities in the region once had a fully developed history, like Rome did. Although it is difficult (even impossible) to reconstruct those traditions, we should nonetheless remain aware of their existence. In later years, these towns remained proud of their local legends and heroes. We will learn more about Rome's heroes in **chapters 7** and **8**.

Notes

1. Servius divided the people into "classes" based on wealth. He established three voting assemblies, each with different political powers; for the most part, these favored the wealthy, who voted first and whose votes counted more. Servius' classes were military as well as political, and thus were subdivided into older (c. 40–60) and younger (c. 20–40) men, as well as cavalry and infantry units. While the attribution to Servius may be mythical, the class system itself was not.
2. There is historical evidence that these projects occurred in sixth-century Rome, when Tarquin the Proud lived, so the tradition may have a basis in fact. Many scholars believe that the last three kings are historical, if larger-than-life.
3. This is almost exactly the same phrase Livy uses to introduce the augury of Romulus and Remus (**3.3.5**).
4. **3.6**.
5. That is, the non-senators.
6. The plebeians grumbling is a common theme in the "Conflict of the Orders" (see **8.8**), which would last until c. 367 BCE. "Master" is a common way to describe a tyrant.
7. Also Tatius' city: **3.5.2, 3.5.4**.
8. Numa's brothers leave room for genealogical claims on the part of Rome's noble families.
9. An interesting characterization of early Romans.
10. As we saw by the terms of the peace treaty in **3.5.2, 3.5.3**, and **3.5.6**, Tatius and the Sabines were invited to Rome.
11. See **2.1** and **2.2.5**.
12. In Greek myth, a promise sworn on the underworld river Styx is unbreakable.
13. Like "elicit" in English; Jupiter Elicius was the "Summoned Jupiter."
14. An oblong shield used in the Salian dance (see end of passage). Ovid's etymology is untranslatable.
15. Numa improves on Troy, since Rome's sacred objects can't be stolen (see **chapter 2, note 22**).

16. The *anciles*.
17. See **note 11**.
18. Faunus continues to be identified with Pan in modern scholarship, and he was considered similar to Pan by Romans as well.
19. Compare the capture of Proteus in *Odyssey* 4. Menelaus gets help from a friendly goddess, as Ovid suggests Numa does in **5.2.3a**.
20. Compare Livy's doubts in **5.2.1a**.
21. Greek *aemylia*.
22. See **5.2.1b**.
23. See **5.3.4b**.
24. The metropolis, or "mother city," is a Greek term for the city a group of colonists had originally come from. Colonies and their mother cities frequently had continuing relationships, but their quality and content varied; usually they shared religious rites, language, writing styles, and political structure, and agreed not to fight each other in wars. Often they offered each other military assistance.
25. Compare the speech of the Sabine women in **3.5.2** and **3.5.3**. Wars between colony and metropolis were often seen as particularly shameful.
26. A Roman mile of 1000 paces was slightly less than a British imperial mile, so the camp was located 4.5 miles or about 7 km from Rome.
27. According to some sources, Alba had an elected government before Fufetius.
28. Livy makes a similar comment about the Sabines at **3.5.2**.
29. Compare the belief that they'd been buried in **5.2.5**.
30. It's not clear why Tullus Hostilius was trying to summon Jupiter. But compare Numa's lack of faith in books (**5.2.5a**).
31. Ennius, *Annals* 137: "After good Ancus died..."
32. Both Tarquins are named Lucius Tarquinius; both have a brother named Arruns; both have three known (that is, named) children; both were unusually dependent on their wives for political advice; both were offered the Sibylline Books (**5.6.4**); both built the Cloaca Maxima; both contributed to the building of the Circus; both used war spoils to fund the building of the temple of Jupiter Optimus Maximus (probably from the same city, Pometia: **5.4.1b, 5.4.1c, 5.6.2**); both ended their rule violently, and both were followed by a Latin ruler who was in some way imperfect (Servius was a slave, **5.4.3**; Brutus was considered an idiot, **5.6.5**).
33. "Needy."
34. See **4.4**.
35. "Priscus" means "older," and was probably added to Tarquin's name only after the second Tarquin king appeared.
36. See https://resources.oncourse.iu.edu/access/content/user/leach/www/2003/jJ.O.M. podium.jpg; for the foundation, see **4.6.5**.
37. Compare the so-called "Servian Wall," also still visible in Rome: http://www. livius.org/site/assets/files/2520/servianwall.jpg
38. The Cloaca Maxima: https://i.ytimg.com/vi/QDM-I7DG8j4/maxresdefault.jpg
39. See **note 36**.
40. The *lituus*, one of the symbols of augury.
41. See **note 40**.
42. See **3.5.6** and **3.6.1**.
43. Compare Iulus in Vergil, *Aeneid* 2.681–686.

44. Although Roman slaves could be freed, it was presumably rare for them to marry into the elite. Soon after Livy wrote this passage, the Emperor Augustus would make it illegal for the highest-class citizens to marry freed slaves.
45. Compare Livy's doubts about the birth of Romulus (**3.1.2**).
46. In this case, Plutarch clearly means Fortune as a deity, rather than a concept.
47. That is, a *Lar*: see **6.4.2, 6.4.4, 6.4.5**.
48. Compare Plutarch's account of Numa (**5.2.1b**): do you agree with his assessment here?
49. The king's entourage.
50. Others associate the name with Tanaquil's address to the people: **5.4.4a**.
51. The distribution of land was a major source of tension among the elite of second- and first-century BCE Rome.
52. **5.5.1a**.
53. The story is an aetiology of the "Cursed Quarter" (*vicus sceleratus*) in Rome.
54. Blood caused religious pollution. In this case, as in Greek tragedy, the pollution can't simply be cleaned off; Tullia's crime was too serious. So her household in general is held accountable for her actions.
55. Compare the death of Romulus in **3.7.1**.
56. See **note 53**.
57. Bodyguards were associated with tyranny.
58. That is, like Servius Tullius.
59. Councils of "friends" were typical of Hellenistic kings.
60. Probably a family legend of the Mamilii.
61. Scholars have pointed out that Livy's story implies that weapons were not allowed in the grove, making it a safe place for meetings, and that Tarquin shows his impiety by dishonoring the religious rules and bringing his own weapons.
62. See **5.4 introduction** for these projects.
63. Other sources follow Dionysius of Halicarnassus and make Sextus the oldest son.
64. This section has a Greek parallel in the tyrant Thrasybulus of Miletus.
65. The Tarquins were originally from Corinth, which may lend authenticity to the story.
66. Contrast Livy, who associates the distribution of property with Servius (**5.5.3a**).
67. Compare Apiolae in **5.4.1b**; this is a Greek word for *Pometia* and is probably the same town. Since Rome's first historians wrote in Greek, the "Pometia" story may be the later version.
68. Capitoline; see **4.6.5**.
69. Some authors include the story of Attus Navius (**5.4.2**) at this point.
70. See the story of the *caput Oli* in **4.6.5a**; it is included in Livy's original text at this point.
71. See **4.7** for one of these craftsmen.
72. Most other sources claim it was Tarquin the Proud.
73. Lactantius refers to the burning of the Capitol in 88 BCE; the books burned, too.
74. One of Cicero's favorite plays, it related the downfall of the Tarquin dynasty.
75. Compare the augury of Romulus in Ennius (**3.3.1**), which Cicero also quotes in this work.
76. An exaggeration: Livy has already told us that Tarquin's grandfather immigrated from Corinth (and this may be why Tarquin decides to seek help from Delphi).
77. "Brutus" means "dumb."
78. The priestess at Delphi.

References

Barrett, Anthony. 2004. *Livia: First Lady of Imperial Rome*. New Haven, CT: Yale University Press.

Cornell, Timothy J. 1995. *The Beginnings of Rome: Italy and Rome from the. Bronze Age to the Punic Wars (c. 1000–264 B.C.)*. London: Routledge.

Miles, Gary B. 1995. *Livy: Reconstructing Early Rome*. Ithaca, NY: Cornell University Press.

Skinner, Marilyn. 2011. *Clodia Metelli: The Tribune's Sister*. Oxford: Oxford University Press.

Syme, Ronald. 1989. *The Augustan Aristocracy*. Oxford: Oxford University Press.

Watson, Alan. 1992. *The State, Law, and Religion: Pagan Rome*. Athens, GA: University of Georgia Press.

Further Reading

Felton, D. 1998. "Advice to Tyrants: The Motif of 'Enigmatic Counsel' in Greek and Roman Texts." *Phoenix* 52: 42–54. Places the myth of Tarquin and the poppies in a broader Mediterranean context. Felton argues that the story of mysterious advice is a folkloric theme, regardless of the historicity of the Tarquins. Online: https://www.jstor.org/stable/1088244

Gantz, Timothy. 1975. "The Tarquin Dynasty." *Historia* 24: 539–554. Discusses problems with the chronology of Tarquins. Gantz argues that the Tarquins are a dynasty that marries internally to retain power. This article's family trees, outlining the relationships between Brutus and other members of the Tarquin dynasty, are immensely valuable. Online: https://www.jstor.org/stable/4435467

Koptev, Aleksandr. 2005. "'Three Brothers' at the Head of Archaic Rome: The King and His 'Consuls.'" *Historia* 54: 382–423. Although the untranslated phrases in Latin may make this article challenging, it's worth it. Koptev analyzes the Horatii and Curiatii from two angles: comparative religion and archaic Italian history. He argues that an early focus on triads develops into a focus on pairs. Online: http://www.academia.edu/1072508/_Three_Brothers_at_the_Head_of_Archaic_Rome_the_King_and_his_Consuls_in_Historia_54_2005_p._382-423

MacMullen, Ramsay. 2013. *The Earliest Romans: A Character Sketch*. Ann Arbor, MI: University of Michigan Press. Analyzes the evidence for early Rome by using character traits as a guide to Roman culture. Part 1 is most applicable to this book. MacMullen's general argument is that the historical tradition about early Rome can't be considered "history," and he uses both literary and archaeological evidence to make his case. The threads of his argument can be difficult to follow, but the summary of a great deal of evidence is very useful.

Moxon, I. S., J. D. Smart, and A. J. Woodman. 1986. *Past Perspectives: Studies in Greek and Roman Historical Writing*. Cambridge: Cambridge University Press. Although the bibliographies in this work are now out of date, the individual contributions remain valuable. In particular, Schultze's work on Dionysius introduces this Greek historian in an accessible way, while Wiseman's article (about how Romans interacted with the physical monuments of the city) and Cornell's (about how historical events became historical literature) remain strong introductions to the field.

Richardson, James H., and Federico Santangelo (eds). 2014. *The Roman Historical Tradition*. Oxford: Oxford University Press. Reprints an important selection of works on early Rome, many translated from French, German, or Italian for the first time. The articles represent a wide range of methodological perspectives and include works on the religious, political, and economic history of early Rome (both the Regal Period and early Republic).

Thomsen, Rudi. 1980. *King Servius Tullius: A Historical Synthesis*. Copenhagen: Gyldendal. Despite its age, this book is still the most substantial collection of evidence about Servius Tullius in English. Thomsen believes that Servius was a historical figure, and his argument offers a good counterweight to many of the arguments in this book.

6

Italy Outside Rome

Introduction

In chapter 6 we turn to the written myths of other Italian societies. In some ways, this means that this chapter is closely related to **chapter 4**: we are no longer interested in myths that focus on Rome. Yet in other ways, chapter 6 is quite different. As in other chapters, these myths were written down, and our knowledge of them is primarily through writing. Sometimes, these myths were written down by locals – but not always. In cases where Greek and Roman authors related the myths of foreign cities, there was usually a reason beyond mere curiosity. These external motives mean that our picture of Italian myth is partial: the stories that we know are usually the stories that were familiar or important to mainland Greece and to Rome.

While it's possible to divide Italy into subcultures by language, myths cross these boundaries. You'll notice many of the same motifs recurring in multiple stories. Nonetheless, it's helpful to remember as you read that these were distinct and heterogeneous societies with different ethnic backgrounds and relationships with Rome.

The coast of Italy was settled by Greeks starting c. 800 BCE, and there's evidence that Mycenaean traders visited the islands c. 1200 (Ridgway 1992, 3–10). So there was plenty of time for the inhabitants of these areas to learn Greek myths and teach Greeks their stories. Like Romans, the Italians of South Italy and Sicily had their own local traditions about their origins and customs. As Greeks and natives intermarried, these traditions evolved away from the myths known on the Greek mainland into new tales. We have few records of these purely local myths, but there are a variety of Greek myths which seem to

Early Rome: Myth and Society, A Sourcebook, First Edition. Jaclyn Neel.
© 2017 John Wiley & Sons, Inc. Published 2017 by John Wiley & Sons, Inc.

have been altered to fit local taste. Although the highly Hellenized residents of southern Italy and Sicily certainly knew a range of myths, in this chapter we'll focus on those that take place in Italy.

Etruscan myths are quite different. The native Etruscan material that has come down to us is almost entirely archaeological. Although Etruscans did write narratives, these have now been lost; most written evidence from Etruria comes in the form of inscriptions (on statues, mirrors, funerary urns, etc.). This writing is not necessarily representative of Etruscan literary production in antiquity. But by the turn of the first century, when our evidence for Roman myth is strongest, knowledge of Etruscan was fading. The majority of recorded Etruscan myth was written by non-Etruscans (usually Romans, but occasionally Greeks). Modern scholars hold a range of opinions about how well this Greco-Roman material represents contemporary or archaic Etruscan culture.

Finally, the myths of Latium may be the most mysterious of all. Latium was the first area to be subjected to Roman expansion. As a result, most of their written mythological production took place under Roman control. We know the names of many local gods and heroes, but often nothing else. Additionally, since Rome was a part of Latium, it's difficult to determine whether Latin myths and Roman myths shared the same themes, or whether (and how) they were different.

The myths of this chapter, although coming from different parts of Italy, share some common points. The most common thread is that many of them are foundation myths for a particular city. Foundation myths have been extensively analyzed by scholars interested in Greek colonization, both in Italy and elsewhere. These scholars argue that Greek foundation myths seek to rationalize new parts of the world by assimilating the inhabitants to known players in the Greek mythic universe. For example, such myths were used to connect Italians to mainland Greece via Evander of Arcadia (**2.1.1, 2.1.2, 2.1.6, 2.1.8, 2.2.2, 2.2.4–2.2.8**). Other major figures were Hercules, who traveled across the Mediterranean to perform his labors, and the heroes of the Trojan War, who frequently got lost on their way home. In Italy, Persephone offered another important link to the Greek mainland. Several authors maintained that she was kidnapped by Hades in Sicily, and various locations were associated with that myth.

Foundation myths are a common aspect of Greek mythological production, but they also helped non-Greek societies identify themselves with nearby non-Greek neighbors. When such myths aren't explicitly about foundations, they're called "kinship" myths. Kinship myths offer a way for cities to link themselves to other cities using myth. A foundation myth is a subtype of kinship myth that connects a new city to its metropolis. A kinship myth can take place at any point in the city's history, not just the foundation, and it can connect any number of cities with bonds of mythic kinship (such as "descent from Hercules"), not just a colony with its metropolis. These two types of myth aren't mutually exclusive, and most cities would have had myths that served both functions.

Latium, Etruria, and southern Italy gradually came under Roman power. It was a long process, beginning in the fifth century and fully completed only at the beginning of the Principate. Roman myth reflects this, with the city's kings fighting Etruscan and Latin cities yearly (see **chapter 5** for Rome's first major conquests in Latium, and **chapter 8** for Rome's first major conquests in Etruria). The harsh fighting in some cases led to the loss of native myths, which now appear only in tantalizing references. Many of the themes will nonetheless be familiar to you: traveling Hercules, nymphs, and local heroes. Others have no precise parallels. It is up to you to weigh the stories and their sources carefully: what can these myths tell us about local civilizations?

For Further Thought

1. Are the myths of southern Italy, Etruria, and Latium more similar to Rome than different in terms of how they adapt Greek and local history? Be prepared to defend your answer, including any differences you see between the mythic cycles of these three cultures.

2. This chapter offers a rare example of a non-Roman Italian relating his own local myths (Diodorus Siculus, speaking of Sicily). How would you characterize these stories in relation to the others you've read? In relation to Diodorus' non-Sicilian narratives? (Compare his accounts of Rome in **3.2.1** and **3.3.3**.)

3. Are there common themes in the Etruscan myths you've encountered in this chapter? What do these themes suggest about Etruscan society? Be prepared to answer the same questions about Latium and southern Italy.

TEXTS

6.1   Greek Founders in Italy

Rome's substantial foundation tradition provides the bulk of material in **chapters 2** and **3**. We can study it because it survives in detail. Other Italian foundation myths are alluded to only in brief terms. Although many are somewhat similar to Rome's foundation legend, others are quite different.

Like the Roman foundation stories, these myths were once substantially more detailed and connected a city to the Greek mythic universe. Over time and in the words of different mythographers, these myths would have varied. We only rarely have access to variant narratives; sometimes, that variant comes from the metropolis itself. What might that suggest about the relationship between a colony and its homeland?

—— 6.1.1   Diodorus Siculus, *Library of History* 5.15.1–5.15.6 ——

According to Diodorus, Sardinia has Greek roots. Archaeological investigations on the island confirm that it had an early Greek settlement.

The island called Sardinia is close by. In size it's quite close to Sicily, but it's inhabited by barbarians named "Iolaeans" who think they are descended from Thespian settlers under Iolaus. At the time when Hercules completed his famous labors, he had many children with the daughters of Thespius. Hercules sent them to Sardinia at the advice of an oracle. He sent a worthy force of Greeks and barbarians with them to settle the place. Their leader was Iolaus, Hercules' nephew, who captured the area and founded noteworthy cities in it. He divided the country into lots and distributed them to the people, whom he called "Iolaeans" after himself. He also built gymnasia, temples to the gods, and everything else that makes life pleasant.[1] These have remained as memorials of him to the present day. In fact the very beautiful plains are called "Iolaiea" after him, and the people who now occupy the land are also named for Iolaus.

The oracle about the settlement claimed that those who had a share in the colony would retain their freedom forever. And the oracle has, surprisingly, turned out to be correct so far: the natives have preserved their autonomy unshaken [... *despite attempts at conquest on the part of the Carthaginians and Romans*]. But returning to ancient times, Iolaos settled the colony and returned to Greece, but the descendants of the Thespians remained on the island for many generations. Finally they crossed to Italy and settled in the area around Cumae. Those who remained went barbarian and were ruled by the best of the natives as leaders. So they preserved their freedom down to our day.

————— 6.1.2   Ovid, *Metamorphoses* 15.7–15.57 —————

The Metamorphoses *is concerned with myths about changing shape. The majority of myths take place in Greece, but the last three books feature Italian myths. In this passage, Ovid finds a clever way to include the foundation myth of the Greek city of Croton (where Pythagoras lived) into his account of king Numa (5.2.1).*

Numa's love of science drove him to leave his country behind and visit Croton. He asked who had founded this Greek city on the coast of Italy. One of the older inhabitants, who clearly knew his history, replied: "The son of Jupiter,[2] they say, was rich with cattle. He traveled from the Ocean along the Lacinian shore,[3] a fortunate path. As his herd grazed in the sweet grasses, the hero himself entered the friendly home of great Croton and refreshed himself from his long labors. After resting, he departed and promised, "This place will be a city when your grandchildren grow old." His words came true thanks to Myscellus, son of Alemon of Argos. The gods preferred him to any other man of his time. Hercules hung above him while he was deep in sleep, and said: "Get up! Abandon your ancestral home. Go and look for the distant Aesar's[4] rocky shores." And he made many terrible threats if Myscellus didn't obey. But after the god and the dream disappeared at the same time, Myscellus woke up and mulled over his vision. For a long time he struggled with himself. A god told him to leave, but the laws forbade it under pain of death; it was wrong to want to leave your country.

The bright sun hid his shining head in the ocean and the star-strewn night lifted its head up. The god seemed to approach Myscellus once again with the same warnings, but threatened more serious consequences if he didn't obey. Myscellus was scared, but prepared to emigrate to new locales. The rumor was whispered throughout the city: he was accused of flouting the laws. As the first day of the trial drew to a close, the crime was tried and proved without a witness. The defendant, dressed in rags, lifted his face and hands to the gods above. "Bring help, I beg you, Hercules! You encouraged my crime."

It was an old custom for the jury to use black and white pebbles: the black condemned the defendant, the white absolved him. At this trial, the sentence that passed was disappointing. Every marker dropped into the unforgiving urn was dark! But when it was overturned and spilled out its stones to be counted, each one had changed from black to white. This brilliant justice from Hercules' divine power let Myscellus off the hook. He thanked his patron deity and set sail when the winds were favorable.

He sailed the Ionian Sea past Salentine Neretum, Sybaris, Spartan Tarentum, the gulf of Siris, Crimisa, and the Iapygian fields.[5] He'd scarcely passed through the lands that faced the sea when he hit upon the fated mouth of the Aesar River. Not far away was a mound that buried the holy bones of Croton[6] with dirt. As ordered, he founded a city there and took its name from the tomb."

6.1.3   Strabo, *Geography* 6.1.3   ───────

Strabo offers a bare-bones account of several foundation myths. His list suggests the number of cities that could be attached to a single founder, an important relationship for kinship myth.

Petelia is considered the metropolis of the Lucanians and they've inhabited it well enough until now. It was founded by Philoctetes when he fled Meliboea due to civil strife. The city was naturally well-fortified; yet the Samnites once had to build a fort against the Thurians. Ancient Crimessa is nearby, and was also founded by Philoctetes. Apollodorus in his books *On Ships* recalls that some say that Philoctetes arrived in Croton before he colonized Cape Crimessa and also the city Chone beyond it. From this city the natives are called Chonians. Some of Philoctetes' men set out to Sicily and founded Egesta near Eryx.

──────   6.1.4   Pausanias, *Description of Greece* 10.10.6–10.10.8   ──────

Pausanias' tale of the foundation of Tarentum possesses the key elements of a Greek colonization myth. A single founder receives an oracle to settle elsewhere, fights the natives, and ultimately rules them.

The Lacedaimonians settled Tarentum. Phalanthus of Sparta was the founder. An oracle came to him from Delphi as he was setting out to found his colony; it said that when rain fell on him from a clear sky, he would settle a city and territory. So he immediately beached his ships in Italy, although he hadn't reviewed the oracle privately or shared it with any of the interpreters. Although he won wars against the barbarians, he didn't take their cities or gain land. So he remembered the oracle. He thought the gods' words were impossible: how could there be rain when the sky was clear and blue? His wife[7] had followed him from their homeland. Seeing that he was discouraged, she cheered him up in several ways. In particular, she put his head on her knees and plucked out the lice. And because she loved her husband, her tears welled up as she looked at him, with his hard work coming to nothing. Her tears flowed in streams. When they rained down on Phalanthus' head, he understood the oracle: the woman's name was Skye. So the next night, he took Tarentum, the biggest and most prosperous city on the coast, from the barbarians.

They say that Taras was a hero,[8] the son of Poseidon and a local nymph. After the hero died, the city and the river were named after him.

──────   6.1.5   Justin, *Epitome of Trogus* 20.1.6–20.2.1   ──────

Justin explains the background of Greek cities in Italy. You may recognize some of the founders.

Many cities still show traces of Greek customs, even after so long. For example, the Etruscans who now occupy the shores of the Etruscan Sea came from Lydia;[9] the Eneti,[10] who (as we see) now inhabit the Adriatic, came from Troy. Antenor was their leader. And Adria is a Greek city. It's also very close to the Illyrian Sea, and in fact the sea is called "Adriatic" after the city.

   After Troy's destruction, Diomedes founded Arpi, since he was ship-wrecked in that place. Pisa, in Liguria, also had Greek founders. Among the Etruscans, Tarquinia was founded by Thessalians, as was Spina in Umbria. Perusia too was founded by Achaeans. Do I need to mention Caere, or the Latin populations who are descended from Aeneas? Are the Falisci not descended from the Chalcidians? Are Nola and Abella not their colonies? What about all of Campania, Bruttium, or the Sabine lands? the Samnites? Can we accept that Tarentum was set-tled by Lacedaimonians, called Spurii? They say Thurii was founded by Philoctetes, and there is a monument there visible even today; likewise the arrows of Hercules, fateful to Troy, are in the temple of Apollo. The people of Metapontum also show off artifacts in their temple of Min-erva: for example, the tools with which Epeos their founder made the Trojan horse. Because of this Greek background, that entire part of Italy is named "Greater Greece" [Magna Graecia].

——————   6.1.6   Servius, *On the* Aeneid 8.637–8.638   ——————
(Hyginus *FRHist* 63 F9)

*Not all Greek founders settled in Magna Graecia. Here Servius comments on Vergil's description of the Sabine women (see **3.5**).*

The Sabines draw their lineage from the Lacedaimonians [...] In partic-ular, they descend from Sabus, who came from Persia through Sparta and arrived in Italy. After driving the Siculi out, he owned the Sabine territory.

6.2 Hercules

Hercules (**2.2, 4.1, 4.2**) was one of Greece's greatest heroes. He traveled all over the world, was generally benevolent, and occasionally had accidents that endeared him to mere mortals (a familiar joke in Greece centered on muscu-lar Hercules' constant hunger). So it's not surprising that many cities in Italy claimed that Hercules visited them. Although we know most about Rome's claim to Hercules, we also have substantial evidence for Hercules outside of Rome. The literary evidence comes from Sicily. Diodorus Siculus' local legend is surprisingly similar to Rome's, and may suggest that cities in Italy competed over their Herculean credentials.

For his tenth labor, Hercules traveled from Greece to the Straits of Gibraltar (the 'Pillars of Hercules' in antiquity) and across to Spain, where he stole the cattle of Geryon. This was a popular topic of Greek vase painting (over 100 examples survive). On his way back to Greece, he drove the cattle through Italy, encountering many populations. The most elaborate story of Hercules we have involves his fight with the monster Cacus around Rome (**2.2.1–2.2.3, 2.2.6–2.2.8**). Despite the similarities of name, it's unlikely that Cacus and Cacu (**4.6.2–4.6.3**) are related (for a contrasting view, see Small 1982).

——————— 6.2.1 Stesichorus, *Geryoneis* fr. 12 Curtis ———————

*This fragmentary poem is the oldest surviving account of Hercules' battle with Geryon. Only major lacunae are marked in the text. In this passage, Hercules and Geryon duel. Compare the duel to Cacus (**2.2.1–2.2.3, 2.2.6, 2.2.8**).*

[Geryon] divided it in his mind **[lacuna]** it seemed to him much more clever **[lacuna]** to make war stealthily against a powerful man **[lacuna]** on the one hand, he thought up bitter destruction for him. Geryon held a shield against the son of Zeus.[11] **[lacuna]** and now Hercules took up his sword and knocked the helmet from Geryon's head. The horsehair helmet made a loud noise and immediately rolled away onto the ground...

With death around his head, stained with blood **[lacuna]** and bile, with the pain of the man-destroying, many-necked Hydra. Silently and cunningly, he fixed it in his forehead. He sliced through flesh and bone, carrying out divine fate. The arrow held course straight to the very top of his head. It stained his torso and gory limbs with purple blood. Geryon drooped his head, as when a poppy, ashamed of its soft body, suddenly sheds its petals.

—— 6.2.2 Diodorus Siculus, *Library of History* 4.22.5–4.24.4 ——

Diodorus describes local myths about Hercules as he moves south through Italy. This excerpt traces his journey through Campania and Sicily, ending with the local Hercules myth of Diodorus' own city.

When [Hercules] arrived at the border between Rhegium and Locri, he took a rest from the fatigue of walking. They say that he was bothered by the cicadas and begged the gods to make the annoyance disappear. And because of his piety, the gods confirmed his prayer.[12] Not only did they make them disappear at that time, but forever afterwards there haven't been cicadas there [...]

After this he traveled through the plains of Leontini and marveled at the beauty of the place. He had goodwill towards those men who honored him, so he left behind undying memorials of his presence there. And something special happened near the city of Agyrium.[13] He was honored here as an equal to the Olympian gods with panegyric and elaborate sacrifices. Although he had never before permitted such sacrifices, this time for the first time he approved. Some god gave him indications of his immortality. For example, there was a rocky path not far from the city. His cows left footprints in it just like it were made of wax. And so did Hercules himself [...] He declared that the cows' hoofprints that were imprinted on the road should be named after him, and he set up a precinct for the hero Geryon, which is honored by the natives even now. And he also made a sizeable precinct to Iolaus his nephew, who shared his journey. He established honors and sacrifices for him to be performed each year, which are preserved even now. Everyone who lives in the city from the moment of his birth takes care of his hair for Iolaus, until the time when they deliver it to the god in expensive sacrifices.

6.3 Diomedes in Italy

Diomedes was a Greek hero of the Trojan War. Like Hercules and Odysseus, he was credited with extensive travels. In most accounts, he never made it home to Greece. He married a local woman in Italy and had several sons, who likewise became founders of cities.

――――― 6.3.1   Vergil, *Aeneid* 11.225–11.230 and 11.243–11.278   ―――――

As the Latins lose ground in the war against Aeneas (2.5), they seek a proven ally: the Greek war hero Diomedes, who has moved to Italy. In the passage below, the embassy sent to get Diomedes' help make their report, interrupting a heated war council.

Then came the icing on the cake. In the middle of the commotion and the angry mob, the embassy brought the reply from the great city of Diomedes. Their message wasn't hopeful: all the expense of their important mission did no good. Gifts, gold, and great prayers had gained nothing; Diomedes said that the Latins should seek other allies, or make peace with the Trojan king. [...]

"Citizens, we saw Diomedes and the Argive camps and we overcame all the misfortunes we encountered on the road. We shook the hand that destroyed Ilium.[14] That conqueror founded the city Argyrippa, named after his father's race, in the Iapygian territory of Mount Garganus. After we arrived, we were allowed to speak openly, as much as we wanted. We brought out the gifts and related our name and country, the people we're fighting, and why we had come. When Diomedes heard it all, he replied placidly as follows:

"'Ancient Ausonians,[15] you are a fortunate people, living in Saturn's domains.[16] What fate has riled up your quiet men and persuaded you to initiate wars? It's unlike you. All of us who desolated Troy's fields with our swords have paid for it – unspeakable punishments throughout the world, every penalty for evil. Even Priam could pity us. Ignoring what we endured fighting under the high walls [...], even now omens follow me, horrible to see. Like when my lost companions took to the sky with wings. Turned into birds, they wandered around rivers and filled up the cliffs with their panicked voices. Gods, such terrible punishments! From the time when I went crazy and attacked a goddess with my sword, when I wounded Venus with my defiled hand, I've had nothing to hope for – except that it would end. So please, don't encourage me to join this fight.' "

—— 6.3.2 Ovid, *Metamorphoses* 14.449–14.482 and 14.505–14.511 ——

Ovid recounts Diomedes' sufferings in Italy after the Trojan War.

Aeneas gained the palace and daughter[17] of Faunus' son Latinus, but not without a fight. The fierce nation started the war because Turnus was angry over his broken engagement; all Etruria rushed to Latium. For a long time each side strove to win a difficult victory through unending war. Both sides gained strength from external forces, and many men guarded the camps, both Rutulians and Trojans. Aeneas didn't reach the walls of Evander in vain, although Venulus had no luck at the city of Diomedes the refugee.[18] Diomedes indeed had already established immense walls under Iapygian Daunus; he farmed the fields he'd gained from his dowry. But after Venulus carried out Turnus' orders by asking for help, the Aetolian hero[19] made excuses about his military might. He didn't want to commit himself to war, much less his father-in-law's citizens; in fact, most of the populace had no weapons.

"I don't want you to think I made up excuses. Although my bitter sorrows are roused by your request, I'll bear the memories. After lofty

Ilium[20] burned and Troy trembled from the Greek flames, the hero Ajax raped a virgin priestess.[21] Only he *deserved* to be punished – and he was – but we all got a share. We Greeks were scattered and dragged by the winds through hostile waters; we endured thunder, dark skies, rain – all the anger of the sky and sea; we coped with the rocks of Caphareus, which tear ships to pieces. I won't keep you by relating my sad misfortunes one by one. Even Priam would have wept for us. The care of armored Minerva saved me [...]

"As my men marveled, they took on the same avian look. The greater number of my soldiers flew up and surrounded the boat, flapping their wings. If you want to know the species – well, not white swans, but like them. Now I'm Iapygian Daunus' son-in-law. I can barely keep this place and its dry fields with so few men."

6.3.3 Strabo, *Geography* 5.1.9

Strabo relates some of the myths surrounding Diomedes in northern Italy.

The Eneti[22] are supposed to have granted certain honors to Diomedes. For example, they sacrifice a white horse to him, and they point to two groves he founded: one sacred to Hera of Argos, the other to Artemis of Aetolia. They claim that the wild animals in these groves are tame. Wolves and deer interact peacefully. When men enter and pet them, they sit still and enjoy it; even if the animals are being chased by dogs, the hunt ends when they enter the grove. And they say that some guy who always bailed men out (so often that he was mocked for it) stumbled across some hunters who had a wolf caught in their nets. As they were kidding around, he promised to pay for whatever damage the wolf did in return for their promise to set it free from the net. When the wolf was let go, it collected a beautiful herd of wild horses and led them to the stable of the man who had made the promise. He accepted them as a gift and branded them with the sign of a wolf.

6.3.4 Strabo, *Geography* 6.3.9

In this passage, Strabo relates the traditions about Diomedes from southern Italy.

Once Canusium and Argyrippa were the biggest cities of Italy, which is clear from their walls, but now Argyrippa is quite small. It was originally named Argos Hippion, then Argyrippa, and now Arpi. They say that Diomedes founded both, and they point to several indications of his rule in these places. For example, there's the plain of Diomedes, as well as ancient statues in the shrine of Athena in Luceria (in fact it began as an ancient Daunian city, but now it's fallen into rough times). There are also two islands called "Diomedean" in the nearby sea. One of them is habitable, but the other, they say, is uninhabited. Diomedes disappeared and his companions were turned into birds there. And even now, they say, these birds have held out and live a human life: accustomed to orderly meals and calm people, while running from criminals and murderers.

They say that Diomedes also tried to dig a canal [near Cape Garganon] to the sea, but he left it half-finished. While he was engaged in digging (and other deeds as well), he was called back home and died. This is one story about him. A second is that he remained in that place until he died, a third story is the one I already mentioned about disappearing on the island, and the fourth, if anyone is really interested, is the story told by the Eneti. And they talk about his death in their territory, I guess, although they refer to it as apotheosis.

6.3.5 Servius, *On the* Aeneid 2.166

*Vergil described how Odysseus and Diomedes stole the Palladium, Troy's sacred statue of Minerva; Servius explains how the Greeks tried to return it. Compare the similar aetiology in **2.4.5**.*

Diomedes tried to present the Palladium to Aeneas when he was traveling through Calabria. But since Aeneas was sacrificing with his head covered, he had looked away. So a certain Nautes took the statue, which is why the rites of Minerva are conducted by the Nautii, not the Julii.

6.4 Myths of Locri

Outside of Rome, there are few Italian cities for which we have even one detailed myth. But we know three about Locri: the miraculous cicadas, the boxer Euthymus' fight with a ghost (the Hero of Temesa), and the appearance of the divine twins Castor and Pollux during the long war between Locri and Croton in the south of Italy. Modern scholars and ancient authors agreed that the main battle of this war, which took place at the Sagra river, was suspiciously similar to the Roman battle of Regillus (**8.5**).

—— 6.4.1 Diodorus Siculus, *Library of History* 8.32.1–8.32.2   ——

Diodorus' account of the Sagra is brief, but valuable. He is among the earliest writers to mention this war. The account repeats earlier Greek themes of Spartan warriors refusing to leave Sparta (Herodotus 6.106).

The Locrians sent an embassy to Sparta seeking military aid. The Lacedaimonians, hearing about the size of Croton's army, pretended that religion kept them home. They replied that the Locrians could take the Dioscuri as allies, as if the gods were their only salvation. The ambassadors accepted this help, either due to divine foresight or because they took the words as a sign. They obtained good omens and set up couches of the Dioscuri on their ships, and so sailed home.

—————————— 6.4.2 Strabo, *Geography* 6.1.5   ——————

The story of the Hero of Temesa connects to several mythic themes. The Hero himself is part of Odysseus' crew, and thus ties Temesa into the nostos *tradition. His conflict with the locals may mythicize memories of colonization, and the dedication of a virgin recalls the phallus in the hearth (**3.1.7, 5.4.3**).*

After Laos, the first city is Temesa in Bruttium (now called Tempsa.) It was founded by Ausonians,[23] but later occupied by the Aetolians with Thoas. The Bruttii threw them out, and were conquered by Hannibal and the Romans. The heroon near Temesa is covered with wild olives and dedicated to Polites, Odysseus' companion. He was lured to his death by the barbarians and became very angry. The people who live there pay him tribute in accordance with some oracle, and so there's a saying about mean people: they have the Hero of Temesa at their backs.
    The men of Locri Epizephyrii captured this city. They tell a story about Euthymus, a boxer who fought the Hero. When he won, he forced the Hero to release his countrymen from the tribute.

—————————— 6.4.3 Strabo, *Geography* 6.1.9–6.1.10   ——————

The story of the cicadas' divide between Rhegium and Locri offers an enduring symbol of the cities' conflict.

The cicadas here are notable, because they chirp in Locrian fields, but they're silent in Rhegium. The locals think it's probably because the land is thickly shaded, so that the insects are moist and can't rub their skin. But on the other side they bake in the sun until they are dry and hard, so their voice comes out naturally.

In Locri they display a statue of Eunomus the musician with a cicada sitting on his lyre. Timaeus[24] says that once at the Pythian games[25] he competed against Ariston of Rhegium, and they argued about the vote. Ariston claimed that the people of Delphi should act in his favor, since his ancestors were Apollo's priests and his colony was sent out from Delphi. But Eunomus claimed that he shouldn't share the victory because they were competing over songs, and among the Rhegians even the cicadas were silent, although normally they were the loudest creatures on earth. So although Ariston was the favorite and hoped to win, Eunomos won and put up the statue I've mentioned in his hometown. This happened because in the contest one of his strings broke. A cicada appeared and filled in the tune with his chirping [...]

[At the Sagra], there's an altar to the Dioscuri in the place where 10,000 Locrian and Rhegian troops attacked 130,000 men of Croton and won. From this victory, they say, came the proverb "truer than events at the Sagra" which is said to disbelievers. Some say that the proverb came about because the battle was the same day as the Olympic games started, and an announcement came to Olympia about what had occurred in Italy. And quickly it was discovered that the message was true.

─────── 6.4.4   Pausanias, *Description of Greece* 6.6.4–6.6.11 ───────

*Pausanias' account of the Hero of Temesa refers to a monument whose imagery may recall Olta (**4.5**). Many scholars disagree with the comparison; what do you think?*

Euthymus was born in Locri in Italy, and he had some land near Cape Zephyrus. His father was, officially, Astykles – but his neighbors claimed it was really the Caecinus river. This river divides Locri and Rhegium and brings forth the miracle of the cicadas. That is, the cicadas on the Locrian side of the Caecinus sing, like other cicadas do. But if you cross the Caecinus, none of the cicadas in Rhegium makes a sound. So Euthymus was said to be the son of this river [...]

When Odysseus was wandering after the fall of Troy, they say, he was carried by the wind to many cities in Italy and Sicily. And in particular his ships landed at Temesa. While he was there, one of the sailors got hammered and raped a girl, and he was stoned to death by the townsmen for the crime. Odysseus indeed didn't think much about the man's death and sailed away. But the ghost of the man who'd been stoned never stopped killing the people in Temesa and he attacked everyone, regardless of age. It reached the point where the entire population was set to run away from Italy, but the Pythia wouldn't allow them to leave Temesa. She commanded them to supplicate the Hero, set aside a sacred space for him, and build a temple there. They would also have to give him the most beautiful girl in Temesa every single year as a wife.

They carried out the god's commands, and the ghost didn't bother them anymore. But Euthymus learned about what was going on. He had come to Temesa at the very moment when they were making the yearly ritual. He wanted to enter the shrine, and there he saw the girl. As soon as he saw her, he felt pity, then love. The girl swore up and down that she'd marry him if he saved her. Euthymus got ready and waited for the ghost's attack. And he won the fight. The Hero was driven from the land and hid himself in the depths of the sea. Then Euthymus had a wonderful wedding with all the men whose freedom from the ghost was ensured.

I've also heard another story about Euthymus: that he reached a very old age and escaped death again[26] somehow. *[There's a painting of]* the city of Temesa and the hero-shrine. In this place was the ghost that Euthymus expelled. He had strange, black skin and his entire appearance was most frightening. He was wearing clothing made of wolfskin, and the name "Wolfie" was written on the painting.

6.4.5   Aelian, Historical Factoids 8.18

Aelian explains how Euthymus died. His disappearance in the river echoes the myths of several other Italian figures (2.6, 7.2.3).

Euthymus of Locri was a good fighter among the Italians. He was confident in his incredibly strong body. The people of Locri show off a rock, extremely large, that he picked up and put in front of his doors.[27] He also forced the Hero of Temesa to stop making the Temesans pay tribute. He came into his shrine, which was off-limits to most people, fought with him, and forced him to repay more than what he'd already taken. Then the saying that they had about the Hero died out. It used to be said about people who made useless profits; they'd say that the Hero of Temesa would come get them.

They say the same Euthymus went to the Caecinus river, which flows past the city of Locri, and disappeared.

—————— 6.4.6 Justin, *Epitome of Trogus* 20.2.9–20.3.9 ——————

This version of the Sagra is similar to the story of Mezentius and the vintage (**2.5.4, 2.5.5, 2.5.7**).

The people of Croton made war against Locri. Terrified at the prospect, the Locrians ran to the Spartans in supplication and begged for help. The Spartans thought the trip was too far for their army, and told the Locrians to get help from Castor and Pollux. The legates didn't reject their ally's advice. They went to a nearby temple, made a sacrifice, and begged the gods for help. The omens seemed favorable. Since they'd gotten what they wanted (in their view), they were as happy as if they were sailing away with the gods themselves. They put divine couches on their ship and set off with favorable omens. They brought home comfort instead of military aid.

When the people of Croton learned about this affair, they sent an embassy to the Delphic oracle, praying for an easy victory and favorable outcome in the war. The reply came that they would conquer their enemy with vows, not weapons. So they promised a tenth of the spoils from the war to Apollo. But the Locrians found out about the oracle and their enemies' vow. They vowed a ninth of the spoils and kept the matter quiet, so they couldn't be conquered with [new] vows.

When they marched out in formation, the people of Croton had 120,000 armed men. The Locrians only had 15,000. Looking at their small numbers, they lost all hope and agreed to face certain death. Each soldier gained courage from desperation: as long as they took a few with them, they thought they'd die in victory. But while they were trying to die gloriously, they managed to win. And the very reason for their victory was that they'd lost hope. While the Locrians were fighting, an eagle was never far from their line and flew around them in circles for a very long time, until they had won. Two young men were seen fighting on the sides, wearing different armor from everyone else. They were unbelievably big, with white horses and red cloaks. After the fighting ended, they were never seen again.

6.5 The "Sacred Spring"

According to Roman legend, Romulus and Remus founded Rome partly to deal with excess population in Alba (**3.2, 3.3**). Ancient sources attribute similar customs to other Italian cities. In a "Sacred Spring," men born in a given year would leave home to settle elsewhere. There are some historical records for the practice (**6.5.3**), but these are late and may represent false "revivals" of a non-existent tradition, much like the Scottish tartans revived in the nineteenth century. The rituals involved in a "Sacred Spring" remain mysterious, but the rationale is similar to Greek colonization.

6.5.1 Dionysius of Halicanassus, *Roman Antiquities* 1.16.1–1.16.5

Dionysius explains the Sacred Spring as a reason for migration throughout Italian history.

The Aborigines were said to have made their home in these lands [...]
But first a group of consecrated youths left. These were a few men seeking a new life, driven out by their parents. They'd been chosen by an ancient customs which I've learned many Greeks and barbarians[28] alike use. Whenever [an] experience, good or bad, forced the city to become smaller, they consecrated all the men born in one year to one of the gods, gave them weapons, and sent them away [...] And since those who leave never return to their fatherland, if they don't found a new city, they make a home by alliance or war. The god to whom they were consecrated when they were driven out seems to guide them for the most part [...] The Aborigines consecrated those born that year to one of the gods, and when the children grew to adulthood they left to found a colony.

6.5.2 Strabo, *Geography* 5.4.2

Some scholars consider Strabo's description of a "spirit animal" (the woodpecker) part of the Sacred Spring ritual.

The Picentine area is part of Umbria, between the cities of Ariminum and Ancona. The Picentines started out from Sabine territory with a woodpecker as guide. They got their name from the woodpecker, which is "picus" in their language.[29] They think woodpeckers are sacred to Ares.

6.5.3 Festus, "Mamertini"

The Mamertines are the most famous example of a Sacred Spring: their name derives from the god Mars. These central Italians did immigrate to Sicily, but it's not clear that their move was due to a Sacred Spring.

The MAMERTINES are named from the following circumstance. When a serious epidemic fell upon all of Samnium, Sthennius Mettius their leader called a meeting of his citizens. He explained that Apollo had appeared to him as he slept and warned him that, if they wanted to be free of this curse, they had to vow a Sacred Spring. That is, they had to sacrifice anything born in the previous year to Apollo. When this was done, the disease went away, but returned 20 years later. And when asked again, Apollo responded that they hadn't completed the vow, because the humans hadn't been sacrificed. But if they exiled those men, they would definitely be freed from this disastrous illness. So the Samnites ordered them to leave their country.

6.6   Caeculus of Praeneste

The tale of Caeculus, the founder of Praeneste, shares several themes with the Roman foundation myth. These similarities may explain why Roman authors retold his story. Caeculus was conceived by a god in a supernatural manner (compare **3.1** and **5.4.3**) and was exposed by his family because of his illegitimate birth. But he was rescued and reared. As an adult, he led a band of cattle rustlers and perhaps staged his own abduction of local women. Because Praeneste is close to Rome, these common themes suggest culturally important values for founders in this part of Italy.

6.6.1   Festus, "Caeculus"

Festus connects the story of Caeculus to a Roman elite family. From him, we can see that immigrating nobles brought their myths to Rome with them.

CAECULUS founded Praeneste. Some think that the Caecilian family, a group of Roman nobles, are descended from him. Others say they are descended from Caecades the Trojan, a companion of Aeneas.

6.6.2   Tertullian, *To the Gentiles* 2.15

Tertullian mocks the gods of the non-Christian world. He claims that gods should deliver blessings, and connects Caeculus with losing vision.

For example, Viduus is the god who bereaves the body of its spirit – you condemn him, because he's not allowed a shrine within the walls. It's the same with Caeculus, who steals the sight from eyes, and Orbana, who makes seeds sterile. Even death is a goddess.

--------------- 6.6.3   Servius, *On the* Aeneid 7.678 ---------------

Servius explains the lines "The founder of Praeneste was there too. Caeculus was the son of Vulcan, a king among rustic herds. He'd been found in the hearth – at least, that's what generations of men have believed" (Aeneid 7.678–680).

THE FOUNDER OF PRAENESTE WAS THERE TOO. Praeneste is not far from Rome. The name comes from *oak trees* in Greek,[30] because oaks are very common there. They call their priests "pontifex" and worship the Indigetes,[31] like at Rome. They also have two brothers who are called demigods there. Once their sister was sitting beside the hearth when a spark leapt out and struck her womb.[32] They say that she conceived a child from this incident. Later she gave birth to a boy near the temple of Jupiter and abandoned him there. It was not far from a stream. Girls coming to collect water found him beside the fire and picked him up. Because he was found near a fire, he was called the son of Vulcan. But the name "Caeculus"[33] is because his eyes were rather small, as if he was often squinting in smoke.

After he'd collected a group of people and spent a while as a petty criminal, he founded the city of Praeneste in the hills. He invited the neighboring populations to a festival and urged them to live in his city. To glorify himself, he spread the rumor that he was the son of Vulcan. Because no one believed him, Caeculus called on Vulcan to prove that he was the son of a god. At that point the entire meeting of people was surrounded by flames. Frightened by the sight, they all at once admitted and believed that Caeculus was the son of Vulcan.

6.7   Pomona and Vertumnus

The Etruscan Vertumnus, like the Greek Proteus, was a shape-shifting god. But while Proteus was associated with the sea and its changing tides, Vertumnus was associated with the land and seasonal changes.

--------------- 6.7.1   Propertius 4.2 ---------------

Propertius' poem glorifies Vertumnus' abilities. The speaker is the god himself, probably in the form of a cult statue.

Hey you – the one gaping at my figure – why stare at so many forms in one body? Learn about the ancestral markers of the god Vertumnus. I'm an Etruscan, born and bred. I'm not ashamed to have deserted Volsinii in battle.[34] This crew pleases me, and I don't need an ivory shrine to be happy. It's enough for me to see the Roman Forum [...] Because we receive fruits of the changing seasons, immediately you think it's a rite of Vertumnus. My early grapes ripen to purple clusters, and my wheat-sheaf hair explodes with sticky fruit. Here you see sweet cherries, there the fall plums, and mulberries that sunburn on a hot day. The grafter has fulfilled his vow with a crown of fruit; the pear tree has apples on its added branch.

You're a pain, lying rumor. I have another proof of my name. Just believe a god when he tells his own story. My spirit is ready for every shape. Turn me into whatever you want: I'll be beautiful. Drape me in Coan[35] silk and I'll become your willing mistress – but no one would claim I'm not a man when I wear a toga. Give me a pitchfork, push a straw hat on my shoulders, and you'll swear that I cut my grains by hand.[36] Once I picked up weapons – I remember that I was praised for it [...]

Do I even need to add my greatest glory? Should I talk about the best gifts of gardens left in my hands? A glassy cucumber, squash with swollen belly, and a cabbage swaddled in hay mark me out. There's no flower gasping for water in the meadow that wouldn't droop becomingly when it's placed on my brow.

As for my name, my native tongue gave it to me from the fact that I alone can change into every shape. And you, Rome, distributed rewards to my Etruscans; that's why today the Etruscan Quarter has its name.[37] There was a time when Lycomedeius came with his comrades-in-arms and crushed the Sabine soldiers of fierce Tatius.[38] I saw the battle-lines pass by and the spears fall. I saw the enemy turn their backs in shameful flight. Father of the gods, make sure that the Roman crowd wearing their togas march before my feet forever.

----------- 6.7.2   Ovid, *Metamorphoses* 14.623–14.697 -----------

Only Ovid includes this charming love story between god and goddess. The association of gardener and shape-shifter may be an intentional echo of Propertius' description of Vertumnus as a cornucopia.

None of the Latin hamadryads could garden as carefully as [Pomona], and no one was more focused on the fruit of trees. This is how she got her name, which means "Apple-girl": she didn't care for woods or rivers, but she loved the countryside and branches heavy with pleasant fruit [...] This was her love, this was her passion – she didn't care about sex. In fact, fearing violence from her neighbors, she closed off her orchard from the inside. She didn't let men in; she avoided them. None of them could make her do it. Not Satyrs, not young men who were good at dancing, not Pans with their pinecone garlands or Silvanus who always acted younger than he was, not even Priapus who scares off thieves with his phallus– *ahem*, his pitchfork. They had no power. But Vertumnus conquered them all with love and no one is happier than he and Pomona.

Often he came in the costume of a tough farmhand with ears of barley in his basket – the spitting image of a farmhand, too. Often with garlands of hay on his temples, he could be seen flipping the new-cut grass. Often he toted cattle prods in his callused hand – you'd swear he'd just unyoked his tired bulls. Give him a knife, and he's a pruner or a trimmer of vines. Mounted on a ladder, you'd think he was picking apples. With a sword he's a soldier, but he's a fisherman once he picks up a net. And finally, the master of disguise obtained entry and was captivated by seeing Pomona's beauty.

He had a brightly-colored scarf around his temples and leaned on a stick. Gray streaks ran through his hair: he seemed to be an old woman. He came into the well cared-for garden and admired the fruits. "How much better this is!" he said, and gave a few kisses in praise. No *real* old woman had ever given kisses like those! He settled down on an uneven pile of dirt and looked up at the branches that were bent over with the weight of fall fruits. A lovely elm faced shiny grapes. After he approved of both plants equally, he said, "If the trunk stood alone without the vines, it would have nothing desirable but its leaves. And the vine needs the elm that it's grafted to; if they weren't attached, it would slump on the ground. But you're not impressed by the example set by the tree. You run from men's beds and you have no desire to marry [...] If you were smart, you'd want to make a good match for yourself. You should listen to an old woman. I love you more than all those guys, more even than you'd believe. Reject regular marriage and choose Vertumnus as the companion of your bed! I'll give you this pledge of faith on his behalf: he doesn't know himself better than I know him,[39] and he's never wandered here and there to see the world. He farms only here. And he's not like most suitors, who fall in love at first sight every day. You're his first and last passion. He'll be devoted to just you for years and years."

Conclusion

The myths of central and southern Italy (and to a lesser extent, those of Etruria) occupy an unusual position between Roman and Greek tales. We hear about them from a variety of sources, most of which casually refer to myths that are no longer known. Our sources expect their readers to know the details, or to be able to find them. As modern readers, we often can't. We get an idea of what we've lost from the works of Diodorus Siculus and Servius. Diodorus is proud to tell the Greek-speaking world about the culture and myths of his native city and their neighbors, and gives us valuable details about the customs of Sicily and southern Italy. Servius, in turn, attempts to fill in the cultural background of Vergil's *Aeneid* for students who know basic Greek myths but were less well-informed about the culture of pre-Roman Italy.

Yet even the assumption that these myths were known can be valuable to us. They tell us that the myths of Latium, Etruria, and southern Italy slowly became integrated into the mythic universe of Rome and the Greek mainland. The cities of Italy share certain motifs that helped them establish ties of kinship and diplomacy – or rivalry – with each other. For example, many cities could boast that they were visited by Hercules, Odysseus or Diomedes, or a Trojan hero such as Aeneas and Antenor. They may have debated which city hosted the hero first, or simply agreed to disagree. Most cities also had a local founder or hero, whose adventures predated the Greeks' arrival. Local heroes tended to cluster around identifiable features in the landscape: rivers, mountains, or forests that were unusual in some way and therefore seemed divine.

You may have noticed that these motifs sound very similar to the myths of another city: Rome. It's not accidental. Although Roman myths are by far the most numerous because of Rome's position of dominance in the Mediter-ranean, the stories themselves are very typical of Italian legend. This cultural *koine*, or common ground, was part of what helped Rome succeed as an empire.

Notes

1. For a Greek, these are the markers of civilization.
2. Hercules; compare **2.2.1–2.2.4, 2.2.6–2.2.8**.
3. Lacinia was a headland near Croton.
4. The Aesar is a river in southern Italy.
5. All in southern Italy.
6. The city of Croton, like many Greek colonies, had two founders: a local hero and a Greek colonist. See **6.1.4**.
7. Greek colonists sometimes came with women, but often the groups were male-only.
8. Taras, the local hero, in fact appears on the city's coinage: http://numismatics.org/collection/1967.152.17
9. This was the hypothesis of Herodotus (see 1.94); it was disputed in antiquity (Dionysius of Halicarnassus 1.28) and remains contentious, despite several DNA studies.
10. The Venetians: **2.1.4** and Livy 1.1.
11. Hercules.
12. See **6.4.3** and **6.4.5**.
13. Diodorus' hometown.

14. Troy.
15. Italians.
16. See **2.1**.
17. Lavinia; see **2.3.2, 2.5.1, 2.5.3, 2.7**.
18. See **6.3.1**.
19. Diomedes.
20. See **note 15**.
21. Cassandra; see **2.3.1, 4.1.1**.
22. See **note 10**. The Eneti were famous for horse-breeding in antiquity, and Diomedes was also a horseman (see Homer, *Iliad* 5 and 23).
23. Italians.
24. Timaeus of Tauromenium was a Sicilian historian.
25. Games in honor of Apollo; the story can be dated to the sixth century BCE.
26. The Hero is equated with death.
27. Compare Vergil's account of Hercules and Cacus (**2.2.2**), or the Cyclops in Homer, *Odyssey* 9.240.
28. See **8.10.1b** for an example of the Gauls.
29. See **2.2.5** and **5.2.3**.
30. *Prinoi.*
31. Plural of Indiges; see **2.6**.
32. Compare **3.1.7** and **5.4.3c–5.4.3d**.
33. "Squinty" or "a bit blind."
34. That is, abandoned his Etruscan city for Rome; compare **8.9.2**.
35. Silk from the island of Cos was famous and almost sheer.
36. Compare the appearance of Vertumnus in **6.7.2**.
37. The Etruscan Quarter; contrast **4.6.4**.
38. Lycomedeius is probably another name for Lucumon, the ally of Romulus; see **3.5.6, 3.6.1**, and **4.6.4**.
39. This ironic statement (Vertumnus is speaking) is common in disguise narratives; see **8.6.2**.

References

Ridgway, David. 1992. *The First Western Greeks*. Cambridge: Cambridge University Press.
Small, Jocelyn Penny. 1982. *Cacus and Marsyas in Etrusco-Roman Legend*. Princeton, NJ: Princeton University Press.

Further Reading

Bradley, Guy J., Elena Isayev, and Corinna Riva. 2007. *Ancient Italy: Regions without Boundaries*. Liverpool: Liverpool University Press. Offers chapters devoted to the cultures of individual Italian societies, organized by region. The authors offer a helpful historical background to the myths highlighted in this chapter (as well as **chapter 4**). The material evidence is well-presented, and the discussion of cultural exchange is excellent.

Dougherty, Carol. 1993. *The Poetics of Colonization: From City to Text in Ancient Greece*. Oxford: Oxford University Press. Establishes a pattern in the foundation myths of Greek colonies, with a particular focus on the archaic period. The book needs to be read as a whole to be fully appreciated, and the topics are occasionally difficult to understand because of their complexity. But students who are interested in Greek colonization will find their effort rewarded.

Erskine, Andrew. 2005. "Unity and Identity: Shaping the Past in the Greek Mediterranean." In *Cultural Borrowings and Ethnic Appropriations in Antiquity,* edited by Erich S. Gruen, 121–136. Stuttgart: Franz Steiner Verlag. Examines the Greek foundations in southern Italy in particular. He argues that Greek foundation myths serve two purposes: to make a community of Greek and non-Greek populations, and to connect that community to the Greek world as a whole.

MacSweeney, Naoíse (ed). 2014. *Foundation Myths in Ancient Societies: Dialogues and Discourses*. Philadelphia, PA: University of Pennsylvania Press. Offers a general introduction to foundation myths as a way for ancient societies to construct their ethnic identity. The chapters feature individual case studies from around the Mediterranean; only two (Donnellan and Squire) center on Italy. The comparative approach is a helpful way to place these Italian stories in a broader context, as they would have been in antiquity.

Patterson, Lee. 2010. *Kinship Myth in Ancient Greece*. Austin, TX: University of Texas Press. Despite being focused on the eastern Mediterranean, this book is valuable as one of the few undergraduate-friendly works on kinship diplomacy. Patterson analyzes how Greeks used myth to construct diplomatic relationships, while questioning the extent to which belief in these myths was important to diplomatic success.

7

Rome's Women

Introduction

You may be surprised to find that women receive their own chapter in this book. In Greek myth, women play an essential (if limited) role as the mothers of heroes, damsels in distress, and schemers. But Roman myths are mainly about men. The role of women in crucial cycles, like the foundation myths of Romulus and Aeneas, is small. Lavinia, the "love interest" of the second half of the *Aeneid*, doesn't have a speaking role; the most important female in Romulus' myth is the she-wolf. It's useful to gather the myths that do give women a prominent role in one place, because these myths help us determine expectations for real-life Roman women.

Women in Roman myth tend to fall into two categories. One category deals with the divine: goddesses, nymphs, semi-divine women, or mortals who catch the eye of roving gods. Stories like these tend to be quite similar to Greek myths on the same themes, although the women involved have strong ties to Italy. We've in fact already seen some examples: in **2.3** and **5.6.4**, we met the Sibyl; in **3.1**, we read about Rhea Silvia's rape by Mars; and in **5.2.2** and **5.5.1**, we learned about the goddesses Egeria and Fortuna.

The other category falls more on the "legendary" side of the spectrum. These myths are stories of real (or realistic) women who handle exceptional circumstances in a memorable way. These women are usually unmarried teenagers. Some of them behave more like men. They're remembered for military participation, or for their exceptional courage in warfare. Such stories capitalize on the blurry line between men and women before puberty. But even more Roman myths center on concerns about these women's fidelity. The stories question

Early Rome: Myth and Society, A Sourcebook, First Edition. Jaclyn Neel.

women's loyalty to Rome or to their families, and suggest that female sexuality needs to be guarded. Scholars have used these themes to argue both that myths echo the constrained lives of Roman women, and that they reflect the freedom of Roman women (relative to their Greek peers) and male concerns about that freedom.

To better understand how the same myths can support these opposing interpretations, we must examine the typical life of an elite Roman woman. In **1.2**, you were introduced to *exempla*, or stories designed to teach a moral lesson. What lessons could a Roman woman learn from these myths?

It's unlikely that most female readers would strongly identify with the female warriors in these narratives. These women don't reproduce societal expectations about how women should behave, and would seem appropriate only in their mythic contexts. (Similarly, we don't expect to meet real wizards or superheroes, but can enjoy stories about them.) An elite Roman woman would be educated, at least to a certain level, with her brother(s) if she had any. In her teens, she would gain the status of a *virgo*: a female person old enough to marry, but not married yet. The *virgo* had a different position in society than either the prepubescent girl or the married woman. A *virgo* was vulnerable, since her reputation depended on her good behavior. But in myth, she was able to move in society more freely than a married woman (contrast the similar stories of the *virgo* Verginia and the married Lucretia (**7.6, 7.8**): Verginia is able to travel outside her home to school with her nurse to protect her, while Lucretia stays at home with her slaves). It's no accident that the moral of both stories is the same: myths taught women how to behave at different ages.

These lessons could take various forms. Some women, like Lucretia, are active participants in their own fate. Others, like Verginia, are passive. Such differences suggest that, while women had a limited number of options for good behavior, they could achieve the end result through different means. We could interpret the similar stories of Lucretia and Verginia as offering a Roman woman two possible avenues for dealing with unwanted male attention.

Another possible interpretation is to oppose women's lives to those of the male authors of our narratives. Elite Roman women got married in their late teens and at the wishes of their parents. In early Roman history, these marriages would be *manus* marriages (see **3.5.2n67**), a custom that persisted among some noble families throughout Roman history. In a *manus* marriage, the woman transitioned from her birth family to her husband's family. Men, in contrast, typically remained in their birth households for life. Even men who were adopted by another family proudly retained the name of both adoptive and birth father (for example, the conqueror of Carthage L. *Cornelius* Scipio *Aemilianus*).

Girls in their twenties in particular were at a time of transition as they went from their own household to that of their husband. This change roused suspicions about their loyalty, which helps explain why mythical women betray their family for their husband (or desired husband). Such betrayals represented a real fear on the part of those retelling such narratives, as women occupied a space between two households. In this case, the myth provides an example of bad behavior, and the mythical women are duly punished to discourage contemporary Romans from imitating them.

Over time, *manus* marriages became less frequent and women remained part of their parents' family forever. This transition is not clearly marked in mythic narratives, but we can imagine that it would have increased anxieties about women betraying their husbands. Instead of the woman gradually transitioning to her new household, she remains an interloper from another family. This status is particularly marked because of the Roman practice of guardianship (*tutela*), which ensured that most women, as well as all children, legally remained under adult male supervision. In the eyes of the law, women were children for life, despite their biological age. Guardians could marry off or force the divorce of mature women, redistribute their property, or bar them from other personal interactions. (Although scholars hold varying views on the historical realities of *tutela* in the late Republic and Principate, in Roman myth the practice exists and is strictly maintained.)

As we will see, *tutela* deprived women of agency when they were under threat, and empowered their guardians to take extreme measures. In fact, many stories about Roman women can be seen as a failure of *tutela*, or lessons aimed at teaching men how to react when the wrong person attempts to exercise power over their women. The "wrong" person can be a man outside the family (**7.6, 7.8**), a family member (**7.5**), or even the woman herself (**7.4**). Myths like these reinforce the right of male relatives to control female behavior.

Sandra Joshel (1992) has argued that the stories of Roman women reveal them to be "catalysts" for male action. As catalysts, the women have to suffer some wrong, typically a form of violence. Although Joshel's argument is primarily concerned with women of the early Republic, whose stories you'll read in this chapter, it shares many features with Bremmer's concept of the "mother's tragedy" in earlier mythic cycles (**chapter 3 introduction**).

The interpretations above are primarily centered on elite Roman women. So are most myths, although there are a few exceptions. In Rome, female slaves had considerably more freedom of movement, although they also had many fewer rights. This combination put them in a more vulnerable position physically, which is rarely the subject of Roman mythic narratives. But it also made the stories of their loyalty to Rome more remarkable. Roman authors consistently depict elite and non-elite women's acceptance of a *status quo* in which their lives were less important than a man's. But because they were less important, they were not expected to be as heroic. The rewards for good behavior, in myth and perhaps in life, were great, regardless of gender or status.

For Further Thought

1. Is there a difference in how women are presented as we move closer to the Republic? Why do you think that might be the case?

2. Do you think a Roman woman would agree with these depictions? Why or why not?

3. What do these myths tell you about a woman's value to Roman society? And if you were a Roman woman reading them, how would you behave?

TEXTS

7.1   The Bona Dea

The Bona Dea was a goddess whose rites were celebrated both publicly and privately. In private worship, it seems that the cult was open to everyone. The state ritual was limited to elite women, however, which made men curious (and maybe also suspicious) about what went on there. The most famous result of this curiosity took place in 62 BCE, when the roguish nobleman Publius Clodius Pulcher dressed up in women's clothing and went to the ritual. He was put on trial for sacrilege, and the rites had to be repeated.

Because of its secrecy, we know little about the ritual. Myths offer limited information. Authors agree that the Bona Dea was related to Faunus (**2.1, 5.2.3**), and that part of the ritual involved abstaining from alcohol. Most focus on explaining men's exclusion from the cult and the deity's vague name (the "good goddess").

─────────────── 7.1.1   Propertius 4.9.21–4.9.70 ───────────────

*Propertius' account of the Bona Dea focuses on the exclusion of men from the cult and Hercules' revenge. He suggests that the ritual makes all Romans similar to the locked-out lover of Roman elegy: the women are having fun inside, but they want nothing to do with men. This passage continues **2.2.3**.*

Hercules spoke, but thirst twisted his dry palate. The fertile land didn't offer water at all. But far away he heard girls laughing behind walls, where the trees formed a grove in a shadowy circle. This place and its sacred waters were devoted to a goddess: the rites couldn't be opened to any man without penalty. The secluded gates were draped in red garlands; the crumbling house shone with scented fire. Poplars decorated the shrine with long fronds and covered the singing birds with many shadows.

Hercules ran here with dust collecting in his dry beard and lay before the gates. His words were somewhat pathetic for a god: "I beg you, whoever's playing in the sacred cave of the grove, open your hospitable shrine to a weary man. I'm looking for a spring and this place echoes with the sound of water – a cupped hand filled with water would be enough! Did you hear about the man who took the weight of the world on his shoulders?[1] That's me; everyone calls me Hercules. Who hasn't heard about the brave acts of my club? [...] If my appearance or my shaggy lionskin or my hair that was burned white by the Libyan sun scares anyone, I myself have performed servile duties in a Carthaginian dress and I spun my daily wool on a Lydian wheel. A soft bra bound my hairy chest and I was a fully equipped girl, with hard hands."

That was Hercules' speech. But the kind priestess whose gray hair was bound with a red ribbon answered: "Guest, spare your eyes and leave this grove; its rules must be honored. Go on, get away, and leave these gates safely as you depart. The altar worshipped in this secluded house is forbidden to men by sacred law. Beware! It takes revenge. Pallas[2] set aside the Gorgon to wash her strong body. The seer Tiresias saw her, to his cost.[3] I hope the gods will give you other springs. These pools flow for girls only, set aside in a secret stream."

So the old woman said her piece. Hercules slammed the dark gates with his shoulders; the closed door couldn't endure his angry thirst. But after he'd conquered his burning thirst by drinking up the river, he enacted grim laws with his now-wet lips. "This corner of the world welcomed me as I fulfill my fate: *this* land barely cracked open for me when I was tired. So the new altar I dedicated when I found my herds, the Ara Maxima[4] – the altar made the greatest[5] by these hands – it will *never* be open to women for worship. Let Hercules' thirst be forever avenged!"

7.1.2 Tertullian, *To the Gentiles* 2.9

Tertullian is unimpressed by reports of the Bona Dea's virtue.

If Faunus' daughter excelled so much in female virtue that she refused to be in men's company, either she was uncivilized or ugly (and knew it!) or ashamed of her crazy daddy. How much worthier Penelope was than Bona Dea! She protected her chastity when she was besieged by all those nasty suitors, and did it with a smile.

7.1.3 Lactantius, *Divine Institutes* 1.22.9

Lactantius explains that worship of the Bona Dea is foolish, despite her virtue.

Faunus established pagan rites in Latium, or rather his grandfather Saturn did;[6] and he honored Picus his father among the gods,[7] as well as Fatua Fauna his sister, and he also married the same woman. As Gabius

Bassus relates, she was named "Fatua" because she used to tell women their *fates*, just as Faunus did for men. Varro writes that her virtue was so great that no man saw her while she lived – except her husband – and no man heard her name. So women sacrifice to her in the open, and call her "Bona Dea." And Sextus Clodius in his Greek book says she was the wife of Faunus. He adds that she once drank a bottle of wine in secret, because it was against the customary ideals of good behavior under the kings. Since she'd gotten drunk, her husband beat her with myrtle rods until she died. But later he regretted what he'd done and couldn't bear how much he missed her. So he gave her divine honors, and in her rites he used a covered jug of wine. So Faunus left no small mistake to posterity, although those who are clever can see through it. For example, Lucilius mocks the idiocy of men who believe that statues are gods in his poems.

───────── 7.1.4 Macrobius, *Saturnalia* 1.12.24–1.12.28 ─────────

Macrobius offers a series of erudite interpretations of the Bona Dea. Some of his explanations may preserve knowledge of the public ritual.

Several say she is the daughter of Faunus, who rejected her father's desires when he fell in love with her. She resisted his desire even when she was dead drunk from wine. For that, he beat her with myrtle rods. But they believe her father transformed himself into a snake and thus slept with his daughter.[8] As proofs of all these tales they say that it's forbidden to have myrtle branches in her shrine, that vines grow out of her head because her father tried his best to deceive her with them, that wine can't be brought into her temple or even mentioned by its usual name (the vessel that holds wine is covered up and called "honeypot," and the wine itself is called "milk") and that the snakes appearing in her temple are neither afraid nor terrifying [...]

She's called in Greek the Womanly Goddess, whom Varro relates is the daughter of Faunus and so chaste that she never left the woman's area of the house, nor was her name ever heard in public. She never even saw or was seen by a man, and that's why no men can enter her temple. Also women in Italy can't become involved with the rites for Hercules, because when Hercules was leading the cattle of Geryon through the fields of Italy, he got thirsty.[9] A woman told him that she couldn't offer him water, because the day was a festival for the goddess of women and men were religiously barred from taking part in the feast. And this is why Hercules hated the rite and commanded Potitius and Pinarius, the guardians of his shrine, not to allow female participation.

7.2 Women of the *Aeneid*

The events of epic poetry typically center around men. But Vergil includes several female characters in his *Aeneid*. The most famous character is Dido, the queen of Carthage who kills herself when Aeneas leaves her for Italy. Vergil is interested in Dido herself; Ovid related the adventures of her sister Anna, who's largely ignored in Vergil's story.

Once in Italy, Aeneas marries Lavinia (**2.5.1, 2.5.3, 2.5.7, 2.7**), but other mythical women inhabit Latium. The female warrior Camilla bears many similarities to Greek Amazons, and may have been a Vergilian addition to Roman mythmaking. She joins the Latin side with her own band of hand-picked fighters and proves that female leadership can be equal to Turnus' male leadership (but not Aeneas': the distinction is important). Her role in the second half of the *Aeneid* thus parallels Dido's in the first half.

--------- 7.2.1 Vergil, *Aeneid* 11.498–11.583 ---------

Vergil describes Camilla's background and courage. Try to imagine the scene from a Roman perspective: what does Camilla's offer suggest about Turnus' army?

Camilla ran into him on his way, accompanied by her Volscian troops. The princess jumped from her horse at the very gates; her entire company copied her. Leaving their horses behind, they switched to walking. Then she said, "Turnus, if you believe that the brave are worthy, I'm bold enough to join you. I promise to fight Aeneas' army and to march against the Etruscan cavalry alone. Let me test the dangers of war in the first rush, while you stay with the infantry at the city and guard the walls."

In response, Turnus fixed his gaze on the fierce female. "Girl,[10] pride of Italy, what thanks or repayment can I offer? Sharing the work with me – your spirit's beyond all gratitude [...]"

Meanwhile, among the gods, Diana was speaking sadly with swift Opis, one of the virgin comrades of her sacred band. "Girl, the war has come to fierce Camilla. She bears our weapons in vain, though she's dear to me beyond all others. This love of mine isn't new; sudden tenderness moves my spirit.

"Metabus was exiled from his kingdom, Privernum, due to his unpopularity and arrogance [...] Imagine the Amasenus river flooding, blocking his flight. So much rain had burst through the clouds that it foamed at its tall banks. He was ready to swim across, but love for the child made him hesitate: he was worried about his bundle of joy. As his thoughts darted in every direction, he suddenly decided on this plan: as a warrior, he carried a huge spear in his strong hand. It was solid, knotty wood, dried out and strong. He wound his daughter in cork bark, fully enclosing her limbs, and bound her to his spear (it was more convenient for throwing). Then, hoisting the stick in his huge hand, he turned to the sky, saying, "Kind daughter of Leto,[11] inhabitant of the woods, I beg you: as a father, I dedicate my child to your service. Holding your spear, she flees the enemy to you first: a suppliant rushing through the air. Accept on my witness, goddess, your child, who is now sent off on doubtful breezes." He spoke and, drawing back his arm, hurled the spear. The waves crashed, and poor Camilla flew across the swift waters on the whistling weapon [...]

"Metabus raised his daughter among bushes and the frightening bogs, suckling horses' teats and wild milk, milking udders with tender lips [...] In vain many mothers in Etruscan towns wished to have her as a daughter-in-law; she was content to love her spears and virginity forever."

7.2.2   Vergil, *Aeneid* 11.799–11.819

Despite Camilla's unconventional upbringing, she retains female faults. Arruns, an Etruscan, manages to kill her while her attention is occupied by sparkly Trojan armor (for the theme, see 7.4).

Arruns sent his spear through the air; it buzzed as it flew. All the Volscians turned their fierce thoughts to the queen, and looked her way. But she paid no attention to the breeze or the noise, and didn't notice the spear falling from the sky. Then it thudded into her, driving deep below her exposed breast, and finally stopped to suckle her virgin blood.

Frightened, her companions rushed up and lifted their queen as she crumpled to the ground. Arruns, terrified beyond everyone else, also fled. His happiness was mixed with fear [...]

Camilla was dying. She tugged at the spear, but its iron point stood deeply wedged in her rib bones. Bloodless, she sank down, her cold eyelids sliding down with death.

7.2.3   Ovid, *Fasti* 3.559–3.694

Ovid takes advantage of the similar sound of Anna and the Latin word for year (annus) to revisit the life of Dido's sister. Suggesting multiple aetiologies for a single festival is typical of Ovid.

Anna was forced out of her home. Crying, she left her sister's walls behind [...] She got herself a fleet and companions for the journey.

Looking back at the walls her sweet sister had made, she slid along the calm waters. There's a fertile island near sterile Cosyra. Melite[12] is its name, pounded by the waves of the Libyan gulf. She made for it, trusting in her longstanding friendship with the king, Battus. He was filthy rich. After he'd heard about what had happened to both sisters, he said, "Although my country is small, it's yours." He would've kept his word to his death, if he hadn't been afraid of Pygmalion's[13] soldiers.

Two years passed, and the third was coming along. It was time for exiled Anna to look for a new home. Her brother showed up looking for a fight, and the king hated weapons. "We don't do war. Run away while you're safe." She took the advice and ran, trusting her ship to the wind and waves. The Mediterranean wasn't nearly as cruel as her brother. [*A storm blows Anna to Latium.*]

Trusty Aeneas already ruled the place and Latinus' daughter.[14] He'd joined the two peoples together. With only Achates[15] as his companion, he took a private stroll barefoot on the land he'd received as dowry. He saw Anna walking, but couldn't believe it was her: why would *she* come to Latium?! Aeneas kept his thoughts to himself, but Achates was louder: "It's Anna!" he shouted.

At her name, she lifted her head. *Oh no! What should I do? Could I run? Maybe the earth will swallow me up.* She could see her poor sister's ghost before her eyes. But Aeneas could tell, and spoke to the frightened girl. He was crying too, moved by the reminder of Dido. "Anna [...], whether you came here to our country on purpose or a god brought you here, you're welcome in my kingdom. I'm thankful to you for many things, and I have quite a few debts to Dido; you'll be honored for your own sake and your sister's."

She believed him when he said these things – not that she had any other hope – and explained her own travels. As she entered the palace in her Carthaginian clothes, Aeneas began to speak. The rest of the crowd was silent. "Lavinia, my wife, I'm bringing this woman here for a good reason. I accepted her help when I was shipwrecked. She was born in Tyre and had a kingdom on the coast of Libya. So I hope you'll love you like a dear sister."

Lavinia made all the promises he asked and silently fought down the unfounded pain in her heart. She pretended that she wasn't furious. When she saw Anna being given many gifts before her eyes, she was sure that just as many were sent secretly. She couldn't *quite* decide what to do [...] but she hated Anna intensely, prepared a trap, and wanted death to come with a vengeance.

Night came. Dido seemed to stand before her sister's bed. She oozed blood from her filthy hair. "Run away!" she said. "Don't hesitate. Escape from this ill-omened roof." With her words, a breeze slammed the squeaking door.

Anna jumped out of bed and at once threw herself out of the small window and onto the ground. Fear itself made her bold. She ran, blind with terror, like a deer frightened by the sound of wolves. Her unbelted tunic hid her as she ran. It's thought that the horned river-god Numicius snatched her up in his welcoming waves[16] and hid her in his swamps. Meanwhile, men looked for her through the fields with loud shouts. They saw signs she'd passed, including her footprints. The footprints led to the shore, and there were traces all the way to the waves. The river, fully aware of what was happening, held his peace. She herself appeared to say, "I am a nymph of the peaceful Numicius; because I hide in the river all year, I'm called Anna Perenna [...]"

Another story has also come to our attention, and it's not that different from the truth. A long time ago, before the plebeians had tribunes to guard them, they seceded and camped on the Sacred Mount.[17] Soon they lacked the one thing they'd taken with them: food and bread fit for men to eat. An old woman named Anna lived in the suburb of Bovillae. She was poor, but very eager to please. With a light scarf tied around her gray hair, she rolled rough cakes with a trembling hand and distributed them, still steaming, to the people every morning. Her generosity was well-received by the people. When peace was made with the patricians, they set up a memorial to Perenna, because she had brought them aid when they needed it.

Now all that's left for me to explain is why the girls sing dirty songs [on her holiday]. They gather around and sing songs that are quite naughty. When Anna had just been made a goddess, Mars tugged her aside and made a plea. "You're worshipped in my month. I shared my days with you. I have great hopes that you'll repay the favor. I've been destroyed by love for Minerva – one armor-toting god burns for another! For a long time, I've nursed this wound. We two have such similar interests. See to it that we come together as one. You're a nice old lady. The job suits you."[18]

Anna pulled the god's leg with an empty promise. She led him on, constantly dragging out his stupid hope with uncertain delays. Whenever he asked how it was going (which was often), she said, "I'm doing what you told me. She's won over. She just surrendered herself to your wishes."

He was in love, so he believed her and prepared for his wedding night. Anna was brought in, with her face veiled like a bride. Mars got ready to smother her with kisses – but then saw that it was Anna! Shame and anger swept over the god at the trick. The new goddess laughed at the lover of her friend Minerva and nothing made Venus like her more than this escapade.

―――――――――――   7.2.4   Servius, *On the* Aeneid 4.682   ―――――――――――

Servius suggests a surprising change: Anna, not Dido, was in love. Vergil's line is in a speech of Anna's; it reads, "Sister, you've killed yourself and me."

YOU'VE KILLED YOURSELF AND ME. Varro says that Anna, not Dido, loved Aeneas so much that she threw herself on the pyre and died.

7.3   Acca Larentia

Acca Larentia may be the result of combining two earlier myths. We've already encountered one Larentia: she raised the twins Romulus and Remus (**3.1, 3.4.5, 3.4.6**). As the foster-mother of Romulus, her myth became the focus of an imperial-era cult (the Arval Brothers). But a separate myth connects her to Hercules. The two versions can't be reconciled, both for reasons of chronology and sense. The association is perhaps due to the fact that in both tales, Acca is a prostitute – a status rare enough in myth to force the identification.

―――――――――――   7.3.1   Plutarch, *Life of Romulus* 5   ―――――――――――

Plutarch differentiates the two Larentias. He apparently liked this story; he retells it in almost the same words in Roman Questions *35.*

They honor a different Larentia for the following reason. The custodian at Hercules' temple was wandering around – at leisure, as it seems. He offered to dice with the god, and they agreed that if he won, he would get something nice from the god, while if he lost he would offer Hercules a lavish meal and a beautiful woman to sleep with. With the terms set, the god and his custodian threw the dice. As it turned out, the watchman was defeated. He wanted to keep his end of the bargain and stick to the terms of the agreement. So he cooked up a feast for the god and paid Larentia, a beautiful call girl who would later become famous, to entertain the god in the shrine on the couch he'd prepared. After the feast they locked the doors, and the god actually had his way with her. And indeed they say that the god enjoyed her company and at dawn ordered her to walk to the Forum, greet the first man she met, and make him her companion. She met one of the citizens, Tarutius, who was elderly and rich enough but had no wife or children. He recognized[19] and cherished Larentia, and when he died he made her heir to his many luxurious possessions. In her will, she gave most of this property to the Roman people.

-------------------- 7.3.2 Aulus Gellius, *Attic Nights* 7.7 --------------------

Gellius equates the two Larentias, but supplies two different explanations of her honors. One explains a festival, the other a priesthood.

Acca Larentia, on the other hand, was a common prostitute and had earned a heap of money in the business. In her will, she made either king Romulus (as [Valerius] Antias writes in his history) or the Roman people (as some others say) heir to all her possessions. In return for this benefaction, the *flamen Quirinalis*[20] performed a public sacrifice for her and a feast day in her name was added to the calendar. But Sabinus Masurius in his first book of *Memoirs* says that some writers of history make Acca Larentia the nurse of Romulus, and he follows them. "That woman," he says, "had 12 sons, but one died. Romulus offered himself to Acca as a son in the boy's place, and he called the other 11 brothers "Arval Brethren." From that time onwards, the college of Arval Brethren has remained 12 in number, and their priesthood is marked out by a crown of grain and white ribbons."

-------------------- 7.3.3 Tertullian, *To the Gentiles* 2.10 --------------------

Tertullian is scandalized by the Romans' apparent pride in worshipping a prostitute. Take note of how a Christian author adapts the myth to his monotheistic point of view.

Let's hurry on to worse examples. Your authors aren't ashamed of Larentina[21] – you flaunt her openly. This whore is worthy of honor either because she was the nurse of Romulus (and called a "she-wolf" *because* she was a whore) or because she was Hercules' girlfriend, and now he's dead – oops, I mean now he's a god.
    They say that his temple custodian was amusing himself by playing dice in the temple. He was playing solo and wanted a partner. Since he didn't have one, he said one side was Hercules' and the other side was his own. And so he started the game on the following terms: if he himself won, he'd buy himself a nice dinner and a hooker from Hercules' cash stores. But if "Hercules" won – meaning the other side of his own game – he'd do the same "for the god." "Hercules" won – a worthy new labor! The custodian made "Hercules'" dinner and procured him the whore Larentina. **[lacuna]** Larentina slept by herself in the shrine. This woman, who came from a pimp's palace, claimed that she had been busy with dreams of Hercules. It's possible that she could have felt it in

her dream while she mulled it over.[22] First thing in the morning she left the shrine. A young man she met, a *third* Hercules[23] as they say, fell in love with her... [*The rest is fragmentary.*]

———————— 7.3.4 Macrobius, *Saturnalia* 1.10.16–1.10.17 ————————
(Cato *FRHist* 5 F16; Macer *FRHist* 27 F2)

Macrobius cites two early authors for the two variants of Acca Larentia's myth.

Cato says that Larentia got rich from her profession, which was prostitution. After she died, she left her [extensive] lands to the Roman people. They honored her with an incredible tomb and annual mourning rites. But Macer in the first book of his histories claims that Acca Larentia was the wife of Faustulus and the nurse of Romulus and Remus. When Romulus was king, she got married to a rich Etruscan, Carutius. Her wealth was increased by inheriting his, and later she left her money to Romulus, because she raised him.

7.4 Tarpeia

The girl Tarpeia was the subject of much dispute in antiquity. Authors were divided on whether she had betrayed or tried to save Rome, whether she was Roman or Sabine, and whether she was a demigod or human. But everyone agreed that Tarpeia was the eponym of the Tarpeian rock and hill (the hill was later renamed the Capitol). Tarpeia's story seems to encapsulate the worries that teenage girls caused Roman men: their desires (for money, for sex, for fame) might destroy the city. But it's wise to remember that some versions of the myth glorified her as a heroine, rather than remembering her as a traitor. This is probably the reason behind her appearance on public art.[24]

———————— 7.4.1 Varro, *On the Latin Language* 5.41 ————————

Varro explains the continuing significance of Tarpeia.

In front of [the Capitoline temple] there's a crag named "Tarpeian" after the Vestal Virgin Tarpeia, who was killed there when the Sabines buried her under their weapons. Because this cliff is called the "Tarpeian rock" even now, a memory of her name remains.

---------------------- 7.4.2 Livy, *From the Foundation* 1.11 ----------------------

This passage continues **3.5.2**. *By having Tarpeia meet Tatius while she gets sacred water, Livy also ties her story to Rhea's (***3.1.4***). He's careful not to name Tarpeia; he doesn't want to celebrate her treacherous behavior.*

War broke out again, this time with the Sabines. It was much more serious than previous wars. The Sabines *planned*. They didn't act irrationally out of anger or greed, and they didn't show off before they attacked.

They also threw in a trick. Spurius Tarpeius commanded Rome's stronghold. Tatius ran into his daughter when she was outside collecting holy water. He bribed the girl to let the enemy soldiers into the citadel. After she let them in, they killed her by burying her with their shields. Either they killed her so it would look like the citadel had been taken by storm, or they wanted to make an example of her, warning others not to trust traitors. Some add the story that the Sabines used to wear heavy golden armbands on their left arm and sparkly rings that were very beautiful. So the girl asked them to give her what they had on their left hands.[25] Instead of gold, they showered her with their shields. There are those who say that when she made the deal for what was on their left arms, she actually meant the weapons. The Sabines thought she was acting deceitfully and so she paid the price.

---------------------- 7.4.3 Propertius 4.4.15–4.4.94 ----------------------

Propertius tells the story of Tarpeia from her point of view. Although Tara Welch (2005) has suggested that Propertius makes us sympathize with Tarpeia, the end of the poem sounds a traditional note.

Tarpeia poured fresh water as a sacrifice to the goddess. A clay pot pressed the crown of her head and hurried her on. Can one death be enough for the terrible girl who wished to violate your flames, Vesta? She saw Tatius doing practice drills on the sandy plains, raising his painted shield above his yellow-crested helmet. As she gawked at the king's face and his royal weapons, she forgot she held the urn. It fell out of her hand. She pretended several times that the innocent moon had sent an omen telling her to wash her hair in the river. She often brought silver lilies to the kindly nymphs, begging them not to let Romulus' spear mar Tatius' face. Tarpeia mounted the cloudy Capitol in the early mist and sat down. Her arms bled from the brambles, and she cried her heart out – but Jupiter (her neighbor) was hardly sympathetic.

"Campfires, army tents, and Sabine weapons – beautiful to *my* eyes. If only I could sit under your conquering gods as a captive! That is, *if* as a captive I could gaze at my darling Tatius. Seeya, Roman hills, Rome, and even Vesta, blushing at my lust! Your horse will bring my love back to the camp [...]

"The triumphal toga suits you. It doesn't look right on that man who lacked a mother's care, who suckled at the tough teats of a savage wolf. I'd wander in your palace as a guest or your queen; by betraying Rome, I'd bring you a good dowry. If that's not enough, the raped Sabine women need avenging: take *me*! That way, your revenge is tit-for-tat. I could put an end to the drawn-up battle lines.[26] Draw up a treaty on my wedding dress. Play the wedding march! Trumpeter, shush your fierce tune! Believe me, our marriage night will soften *your* spear [...]"

There was a festival in the city [...] Romulus decreed that the guards could give themselves up to partying. The camps lay silent; even the horns stopped. Tarpeia realized that this was her chance to welcome the enemy. She made a deal: her city for her crush. The hill was hard to climb and empty from the festival. Without delay, the barking dogs were silenced by the sword. Everything was cloaked in sleep; Jupiter alone decided to pay attention to punishment.[27]

She betrayed the firmly-set gates and her sleeping country in exchange for the wedding day she wanted. But Tatius didn't honor traitors, even when they were on his side. He said, "Get married – and mount *this* royal bed!" As he spoke, his men piled up their weapons on her body. Virgin, this was a dowry fit for your priesthood. The Tarpeian mountain gets its name from its general, as is fitting: guardian, fate has unjustly rewarded you.

––––––– 7.4.4 Dionysius of Halicarnassus, *Roman Antiquities* –––––––
2.38.3 and 2.40.1–2.40.3

Dionysius relates a version of the story in which Tarpeia is a heroine. The sources he cites include the earliest Roman historians, indicating long-term debates about how to remember Tarpeia.

According to Fabius and Cincius, desire for the bracelets and rings on the Sabines' left arms seized Tarpeia [...] But Lucius Piso, a reliable source, says she was eager to perform a noble deed and hand over the enemy to her fellow-citizens bereft of armor. [...*Tarpeia contacts Tatius and makes a deal on one of these two terms; the Sabines enter the Capitol and prepare to settle up.*]

Piso says that the Sabines were ready to give her their jewelry, but Tarpeia demanded their shields instead. At this treachery, Tatius was filled with fury, but found a way to avoid breaking their agreement. He decided to give her the weapons as she'd asked, but in such a way that she'd never be able to use them. Immediately he hoisted his shield and threw it on top of the girl as hard as he could. He commanded the others to do the same. Pelted from all sides, Tarpeia fell due to the number and strength of the blows; she died buried by shields. But those following Fabius claim that the deceit was on the Sabines' side. When it was time to deliver Tarpeia's gold per the agreement, they were grouchy at the price and threw their shields at her, as if they had promised to give her these when they had sworn.

The version of Piso seems more likely to be true. For there where she fell she was honored with a tomb set on the most sacred hill of the city, and the Romans make liquid sacrifices each year (as Piso writes). No one (neither those who were betrayed nor those who killed her) would be likely to do that if she had died betraying her country to the enemy.

7.4.5   Plutarch, *Life of Romulus* 17

*Plutarch suggests a number of variant stories, including one account in which Tarpeia's treachery takes place in 390 rather than c. 750 BCE (see **8.10** for context).*

The Sabines chose Tatius as their leader and went to war with Rome. The city was hard to get at because the hill now called "Capitol" offered an excellent natural defense. Tarpeius was its guard, not the girl Tarpeia (as some say, as if Romulus was a dimwit). Tarpeia was the general's daughter. She betrayed the citadel to the Sabines because she wanted the gold bracelets she saw them wearing, and as a price for her treachery she asked them to give her "what they wore on their left arms." Tatius made the deal. At night she opened a single gate and let the Sabines in [...] Tatius, remembering their agreement, told the Sabines not to begrudge her anything that they bore on their left arms. And he was the first to tear off his armband along with his shield and throw them down on her. The others all followed his lead. She was struck by the gold and buried under the shields, and died from their number and weight.

Tarpeius too was arrested and banished for treachery by Romulus, as Juba says Galba Sulpicius claimed. And other stories are told about Tarpeia, some unlikely – for example, that she was the daughter of Tatius the Sabine leader, and she was forced to live with Romulus. Such men (including Antigonos) claim that she did and suffered these things at her father's will. And Simylos the poet is completely nuts, because he thinks Tarpeia betrayed the Capitol not to the Sabines, but to the Gauls. He claims she was in love with their king.

7.5 Horatia

The story of Horatia picks up on the duel of the Horatii and Curiatii in **5.3.2**. Like the myth of Tarpeia, the myth of Horatia reveals anxieties about female loyalty: will women be faithful to Rome, or will they go over to the enemy? But Horatia's tale also raises questions about who ought to be the ultimate judge of a woman's conduct: her family or the community. The decision at her brother's trial establishes that a woman's family has the right to police her behavior, and depends heavily on their father's evidence. As the *paterfamilias*, he has the "right of life or death" over all of his children. While this right was rarely, if ever, exercised in historical Rome, in mythical Rome it features in several myths of childrens' misbehavior (see also **7.8, 8.1.3, 8.1.4**).

————————— 7.5.1 Livy, *From the Foundation* 1.26 —————————

Livy's account of the events immediately following the duel between the Horatii and Curiatii show how dedicated Romans were to their national heroes. The question of who Horatia "belongs" to (her own family, or her spouse-to-be) is highlighted in the narrative.

Horatius was walking in front, carrying the triplets' spoils in front of him. His young sister, who was engaged to one of the Curiatii, met him at the Porta Capena. She recognized the cape she'd made for her fiancé on her brother's shoulders. She undid her hair and, crying, called out the name of her dead fiancé. Her brother's fierce temper was roused: his sister mourned his victory while the public celebrated! He drew his sword and stabbed the girl. He also reproached her, saying: "Get out of here with your love for your fiancé! What bad timing! You've forgotten your dead brothers and your living one, and you've forgotten your country. May every Roman woman who mourns the enemy end up like you!"[28]

This act seemed awful to the senators and people, but Horatius' recent honors stood in contrast to the crime. Even so, they arrested him and brought him before the king. [...*There's a public trial.*]

Publius Horatius the father moved men most in this trial. He insisted that his daughter deserved to die; if she hadn't, he himself would have punished his son, as was his right.[29] Then he begged the jury not to leave him childless, when just a few days earlier they had seen him with several children. Among these pleas, the old man embraced his son and pointed out the armor taken from the Curiatii [...]

The people couldn't bear it. Not the father's tears; not Horatius' spirit that was a match for every danger. They acquitted him not so much because his cause was just as because they admired his macho behavior. But because they thought such an obvious murder required expiation, they ordered the father to purify the son at public expense.[30] So he made the expiation with particular sacrifices that have been handed down through the Horatian family.[31] He set a beam across the road and sent the youth underneath it with his head covered, as if he were sent under the yoke. And his beam remains in this city today; it's kept up at public expense and called the "Sister's Beam."

------ 7.5.2 Dionysius of Halicanassus, *Roman Antiquities* ------
3.21.2–3.21.3

Dionysius' description of Horatius' thought process indicates the high standards for Roman women.

As Horatius approached the gates, he saw a crowd of citizens pouring from the city, and his sister in particular running out in front to meet him. As soon as he saw her, he was dismayed that a girl of marriage-able age would leave her chores at her mother's side *and* put herself among an unknown crowd. After considering many unlikely reasons, finally he decided on the one that was both likely and generous: she longed to be the first to greet her brother who'd survived and hear about the virtues of her dead siblings from his own lips. So she'd over-looked proper behavior, since she was only female. But she'd dared to go out onto the unfamiliar roads because of her overpowering love for one of her *cousins*, not her brothers. She'd been engaged to this relative and had secretly hidden her love. But when she heard someone com-ing from the camp with news about the battle, she couldn't hold back anymore.

7.6 Lucretia

The story of Lucretia provides the strongest example of a woman as catalyst to male action. Lucretia was a Roman wife whose virtue was famous. After she was raped by prince Sextus Tarquin, she committed suicide; her reasoning was both shame and to avoid being an *exemplum* of bad behavior. Her body was the rallying cry for the expulsion of the Tarquins (see **5.6.5** and **8.1–8.5**). Her long-term visibility stands in sharp contrast to her virtue and secluded lifestyle. Like many of the other Roman women we've read about so far, the myth of Lucretia gains power in part because her actions are unexpected – and show a boldness of spirit that Romans considered masculine. Indeed, Lucretia's actions are idealized throughout the entire episode.

———————— 7.6.1 Livy, *From the Foundation* 1.57–1.60 ————————

The story of Lucretia is strategically placed at the end of Livy's first book and marks the transition between the Regal Period and Republic.

The Rutuli possessed the city of Ardea.[32] The people were exceptionally rich for that time and place. This very wealth was the reason for the war: the Roman king [Tarquin the Proud] had used up his money on public works, and he was eager to get richer and to win over popular opinion with the spoils of war. The people hated him above all because of his arrogance, but also because he had humiliated them by making them work as apprentice craftsmen and had them doing slaves' work for so long.[33]

They tried to capture Ardea in a single attack, but it didn't work. So they besieged the city to pressure them into surrender. In the permanent camps, the troops were relatively free to come and go, as is appropriate in a war that was more time-consuming than difficult. The noblemen were given this privilege more than the soldiers. The king's sons even amused themselves with the occasional feast or party.

One night they were drinking heavily at Sextus Tarquin's tent. Collatinus Tarquin, the son of Egerius,[34] was dining there too. The conversation rolled around to women. Everyone praised his own wife to the skies. Their argument got heated. At that point, Collatinus said that they didn't need to argue; in a few hours they'd know how much his Lucretia outshone other women in virtue. "We're young and energetic; why don't we hop onto our horses and pay a visit? We can judge our wives' character while we're there. The best basis for judgment is how they react when their husbands come unexpectedly."

They were drunk. All agreed: "Great idea! Let's go!" They flew off to Rome on quick horses. When they arrived, shadows were just starting to stretch out. They went on from there to Collatia, where they found Lucretia acting completely differently from the royal daughters-in-law. The men saw the princesses passing the time in feasting and indulging themselves with their friends.[35] Lucretia, on the other hand, was working late. She sat in the middle of her patio, spinning wool[36] by lamplight with her slave-women.

Lucretia won this contest of women. Her husband approached and the Tarquins were kindly welcomed. The victorious Collatinus cheerily invited the royal youths inside. There an evil desire took hold of Sextus Tarquin: he wanted to rape Lucretia, aroused by her beauty and her obvious virtue.

Then the young men returned to the camps, their nighttime games over.

A few days later, Sextus Tarquin went to Collatia with a single companion. Collatinus didn't know about it. Lucretia welcomed him warmly, with no idea what he was planning. After dinner, she brought him to the guest room. Then, burning with love, after he was sure enough that it was safe around him and everyone was asleep, he drew his sword and crept towards the sleeping Lucretia. He held her down with his left hand and said, "Be quiet, Lucretia. It's me, Sextus Tarquin. My sword's in my hand; one sound and you die."

The woman was startled awake. She saw that she had no escape; death was looming. Then Tarquin began to confess his love for her. He begged, mixing threats with pleas. He did everything he could do to turn her womanly heart in his favor. When he saw that she remained stubborn and even fear of death didn't budge her, he added public shame to fear. He threatened to kill a slave and set him next to her dead body, naked. Then he would claim that he had killed her for the worst kind of adultery.[37] Fear of dishonor conquered her stubborn chastity, almost as if he'd won by force. Tarquin raped her and left feeling heady.

Lucretia was devastated by so great a crime. She sent messengers to her father in Rome and her husband in Ardea, asking each to come with one trusted friend. Quick action was needed, because something awful had happened. Spurius Lucretius[38] came with Publius Valerius, son of Volesus.[39] Collatinus came with Lucius Junius Brutus;[40] they'd been traveling to Rome together when they'd met the messenger.

They found Lucretia sitting despondently in the bedroom. She started crying at her family's arrival. When her husband asked, "Is everything okay?" she answered "No! What could be 'okay' for a woman when her honor is lost? Collatinus, there are traces of another man in your bed. But only my body has been tarnished. My mind is innocent; my death will prove it. Give me your hand and promise that the culprit will be punished. It's Sextus Tarquin. Last night he brutally repaid our hospitality: he was armed and had his way with me. His pleasure destroyed me – and if you're all men, it will destroy him, too."

Each in turn gave his promise. They tried to comfort the distressed woman by transferring the blame from the one who was forced to the one who carried out the crime. They assured her that minds did wrong, not bodies, and that without consent she bore no guilt.

Lucretia replied, "You'll make sure he gets what he deserves. As for me – even if I'm free from blame, I don't release myself from punishment. No unchaste woman will live by citing my *exemplum*."[41] She'd hidden a knife under her clothing; now she plunged it into her heart. Falling forward onto the wound, she collapsed, dying. Her husband and father gasped.

While they were distracted with grief, Brutus pulled the knife from Lucretia's chest. He held it before his eyes while it dripped with blood. "I swear by this blood – most chaste of all before the prince harmed it – and with the gods as my witnesses, I will force out Lucius Tarquin the Proud, his evil wife, and all of his children. I'll do it by fire, by sword, by whatever means I can. And I won't allow them, or anyone else, to rule Rome!"

Then he gave the knife in turn to Collatinus, Lucretius, and Valerius. They gaped at the miraculous new spirit that had taken over Brutus' chest. They swore like he told them to, and all their grief turned to anger. Then they followed Brutus, their leader, in calling for the king to be expelled.

Lucretia's body was carried out of the house to the Forum. Men rushed out at the amazing novelty (as it seemed) and enormity of the crime. Each complained about the king's evils and outrages against himself. The father's grief moved them. But Brutus told them to stop whining [... *They march to Rome.*]

Brutus riled up the crowd. He drove them to take power from the king and ordered them to exile Tarquin, his wife, and their children. A handful of young men grabbed their weapons and went with Brutus to rouse the army encamped at Ardea against the king. Command in Rome was left to Lucretius, the royal deputy. In the confusion, Tullia fled from the palace. Men and women cursed her wherever she went and called down her father's avenging ghost.

When these events were announced in the camp, the king was anxious about the rebellion. He rushed to Rome to settle the riots [...] Tarquin found the doors closed to him. His people told him to go into exile. The soldiers in camp happily accepted a liberator for the city and booted the king's sons out. Two followed their father into exile in Caere, an Etruscan city. But Sextus Tarquin went to Gabii, as if it was his own kingdom.[42] There he encountered men eager to repay old grudges for the murder and pillaging he'd committed in the city. They killed him.

7.6.2 Ovid, *Fasti* 2.725–2.852

---

*Although Ovid borrows heavily from **7.6.1**, his version of Lucretia's rape is more cynical. He mocks Lucretia's famous chastity by imagining her as a typical lovesick woman, in love with her far-away husband.*

The young Tarquin welcomed his comrades with feasts and strong wine. One of them was made emcee for the night. He said, "While Ardea keeps us here engaged in a slow war and we can't bring our weapons home to our ancestral gods, do our wives feel a sense of duty or concern for us, like we feel for them?"

Each guest praised his own wife. Their arguments got more and more heated as their tongues and hearts glowed from lots of wine. Collatinus lurched upright and said, "We don't need words![43] Believe their actions. The night is young. Let's get on our horses and ride to the city." The plan was decided and the men threw bridles on their horses. The horses carried their masters to the royal palace first. There was no guard in the hall. See what they found? The princess' neck dripped with garlands and she was up late, hitting the wine.[44] From there it was a short trip to Lucretia. She had wicker baskets and raw wool in front of her bed. Her slave-girls spun their daily ration by a small light. She spoke to them in tender tones. "Now hurry up, girls. As soon as I make it into a cloak, I'll send it to my husband. What have you heard [about the war]? Whenever I picture him fighting, an icy chill takes hold of my heart." She broke down in tears and threw aside the thread she'd begun, burying her face in her lap. The pose suited her; so did her virtue and her tears. Her beauty was equal to her emotions, and worthy of her.

"Don't worry, I'm home!" Collatinus shouted. Lucretia sprang to life and draped herself around her husband's neck – a loving weight, for sure. Meanwhile the prince caught a maddening fever. He was crazy and captured by blind love. Her shape? Perfect. Snow-white skin? He liked it. The blond hair? Her inborn charm? Her words, her voice, her loyalty? Everything pleased him. He wanted her all the more because he didn't have a chance.

Just then birdsong signaled the arrival of day. The young men returned to their camps. Tarquin made his way back distracted by the vision of the woman he'd left behind. As he remembered her, she delighted him even more. The way she sat, the way she dressed, the way she wove her wool; the way her hair lay on her neck, her look, her words, her skin, her face, her beautiful lips...! [...]Aroused by the prod of wrongful love, he plotted a frightening attack against her innocent bed. "The outcome isn't clear. We'll have to dare the utmost!" he said. "Let her see me! Chance and God help the daring. I took Gabii by daring, too." Saying these things to himself, he strapped on his sword and urged his horse onward.

The bronze gates of Collatia let him in just as the sun was setting. An enemy disguised as a guest entered Collatinus' inner sanctum. He was welcomed warmly; he was family.[45] What a mistake on her part! Unaware of his plans, the unfortunate hostess prepared dinner for her guest. He ate her food, and it was time for bed.

Night came, and there was no light in the entire house. He got up and took his sword from its gilded sheath. He crept into your bedroom, chaste bride. As he pushed her into bed, the king's son said, "Lucretia, I have my sword – and I am Tarquin."

She said nothing. She had no voice or power to speak, or even any thought in her entire body. She just trembled, like a small lamb who strayed from its pens and got cornered by a dangerous wolf. What could she do? Fight? A woman who tries to fight will be overcome. Shout? But the sword in his hand forbade it. Run? His hand pushed against her chest, the first time she'd been touched by another man.[46] Her hostile lover wooed her with begging, bribes, and threats. But nothing could change her mind. "It's no use," he said. "I'll kill you and claim you deserved it. I'm the adulterer, but I'll swear on the stand that it was you. And I'll kill one of your slaves and say that I caught you with him."

She gave in, conquered by fear of a bad reputation. Conqueror, why are you happy? Your victory will destroy you. It's sad, isn't it, how much a single night cost your kingdom?

Soon it was morning. She sat with unbrushed hair, like a mother about to go to her son's funeral, and called her old father and faithful husband from the camps. Each came without delay. When they saw her, they asked why she was sad, whose funeral she was preparing, and what evil had befallen her. For a long time she was silent and hid her burning face in her clothing. Tears flowed like the waters of a winter spring. First her father, then her spouse wiped away her tears and begged her to tell them what was wrong. They cried, too, terrified with blind fear. Three times she tried to speak; three times she stopped still.[47] The fourth time she didn't even dare to lift her eyes. "Do I owe Tarquin this, too?" she said. "Do I have to speak? Poor me! Do I have to relate my shame?" She told what she could and left the rest unspoken. She cried, and her wifely cheeks burned red.

Her father and her husband excused her; she'd been forced. But she said, "You can forgive me; I don't forgive myself." Without delay, she stabbed herself in the chest with a hidden blade, and fell, bleeding, at her father's feet. Even as she died, she took care to collapse chastely; even as she died, chastity mattered. Think of her husband and father collapsing over her body, groaning over their shared loss; they don't care what they look like.

Brutus was there. His spirit proved that his name was a lie.[48] He grabbed the blade stuck in the half-living body. As he clutched the knife, still dripping with noble blood, he made a fearless speech with menacing words [...]

The wife with manly courage was brought out to her funeral, accompanied by tears and grudges. The gaping wound was open for all to sec. Brutus gathered the Romans with a shout and told them about the king's heinous crimes. Tarquin fled with his children; the consul received annual authority; that was the last day of the kingdom.

7.7   Cloelia

The story of Cloelia revisits the masculine woman motif we saw in Camilla (**7.2.1, 7.2.2**). Cloelia was one of a number of youths in the early Republic who acted with particular heroism; she was the only woman.[49] The tale takes place after the expulsion of the Tarquins (**5.6.5, 7.6, 8.1–8.3**), when Rome is at war with the Etruscan king Porsenna. The two armies make a truce and Rome provides hostages. Cloelia escapes with some other hostages (all female). Porsenna's angry at first and demands them back. But thanks to the good faith of the Romans, when the hostages are returned, Porsenna allows them to release several more hostages. The episode leads to an alliance with Porsenna (the Tarquins continue fighting).

Cloelia's story may have its origin in a mysterious female statue in the Roman Forum. Not knowing why a woman would be honored with a statue on horseback, Romans came up with the idea of a female hero in the early Republic. The story may also be connected to the family legends of the Cloelian house, and variants naming Valeria (**7.7.2, 7.7.3**) suggest that other families had similar myths. Modern scholars have noted that it's rare for an unmarried woman, like Cloelia, to engage in such virtuous behavior. Yet it is also possible that Cloelia's unmarried state is what enables her to act like a man, since she isn't tied down to a husband.

───────────   7.7.1   Livy, *From the Foundation* 2.13   ───────────

Livy's account lauds Cloelia as the most courageous of the three canonical heroes of the early Republic.

At that time, virtue was so esteemed that even a woman was roused to act in the public interest. The teenage hostage Cloelia managed to elude the guards. The Etruscan camp was pitched not far from the shores of the Tiber; she led a band of girls across the river. They swam away as the enemy threw their spears. So she returned all the captives safely to their relatives in Rome. When this was announced to king Porsenna, at first he was furious and sent speakers to Rome to demand the hostage Cloelia – the others were hardly worth it. But then his anger turned to admiration. He said that her deed was greater than Cocles' or Mucius',[50] and if she weren't returned to him as a hostage in some way, he would consider the treaty broken; but if she was handed over, he'd return her to her relatives untouched and unviolated. Both sides kept faith. The Romans returned their hostages in accordance with the peace treaty, and the girl's masculine courage was not only guarded but even honored by the Etruscan king. He praised her and said that he would give her a selection of the hostages to do whatever she wanted with. The hostages were paraded out; tradition says that she chose young boys, influenced both by female delicacy and by the consensus of the hostages. That is, she thought it best to free from the enemy those whose age made them most vulnerable to abuse.[51] With peace restored, the Romans honored this novel female courage with a new dedication: an equestrian statue.

7.7.2 Pliny, *Natural History* 34.29

Pliny is less impressed by Cloelia's deeds, since he knows alternative traditions.

Piso says the statue of Cloelia was set up by those who were hostages with her and whom Porsenna returned to their families because he admired her. Annius Fetialis has a different opinion. He says it was a statue of Valeria, the daughter of Publicola the consul [...] This Valeria, he says, was the only one who fled and swam across the Tiber. The other hostages sent to Porsenna were killed by the treachery of Tarquin.

7.7.3 Plutarch, *Life of Publicola* 19

Plutarch suggests that there were multiple heroines among the hostages. Notice Publicola's reaction to Cloelia's return. What does this suggest about female behavior?

Some say that one of them, named Cloelia, rode a horse across the stream, urging the other girls on and giving them courage. When they arrived safely before Publicola, he didn't gape at them and he wasn't happy. Instead he was concerned that Porsenna would seem more true to his word than the Romans. He also worried that the girls' audacity would give Porsenna a reason to punish the Romans. So he at once gathered them and sent them back to Porsenna.

When Tarquin's supporters realized what had gone on, they set up an ambush for the girls. Since there were a lot of men, they hoped to capture the girls. But the Romans fought them off all the same, and the daughter of Publicola, Valeria, hurried through the crowds of fighters and escaped. Three of her servants escaped with her and they were safe.

The other girls were in danger, since they were mixed up with warriors. But Arruns the son of Porsenna noticed the trouble and quickly came to the rescue. Putting the enemy to flight, he saved the Romans [...]

A statue of a girl on horseback lies on the Via Sacra towards the Palatine. Some say it is not Cloelia, but Valeria.

7.8 Verginia

The story of Verginia is known almost entirely from Livy. Although the events he describes took place a century later than the rape of Lucretia, the moral is almost the same. This lengthy episode has been significantly excerpted; a brief summary follows. Rome's kings have been exiled and the city is governed by a council of ten men (the Decemvirs). One of them, Appius Claudius, falls in love with the *virgo* Verginia. He comes up with an elaborate scheme to get her: one of his underlings (clients) claims that Verginia is his slave and takes the girl to court; there's a delay while her father is brought in from the army; finally, Appius sits in judgment on his own case and declares that the girl is in fact a slave and is no longer under her father's authority. The decision that Verginia is a slave leaves her physically vulnerable to Appius' client. Rather than give his daughter up, her father kills her.

In Livy's retelling, the kings and Decemvirs lose power for the same reason: because one bad apple can't control himself around women. It's perhaps not a coincidence that the Claudii, like the Tarquins, were known for their pride. One of the ways that this pride manifests itself is by usurping authority over a Roman man's possession: his daughter. The strikingly similarities between Lucretia and Verginia suggest an ongoing concern about women's bodies (if not women's safety) on the part of the Roman elite.

—————— 7.8.1 Livy, *From the Foundation* 3.44–3.48 ——————

Livy starts his Verginia narrative with an explicit reminder of Lucretia to make sure that you understand the parallelism.

Next up was another crime in the city. It started with sexual desire, in the end no less disgusting than the lust that drove the Tarquins from the city and kingdom – I mean the rape and death of Lucretia. The result was the same: the end of the kings, the end of the Decemvirs. And it was for the same reason, too.

Appius Claudius the Decemvir was overcome with longing. He wanted to rape a plebeian[52] girl. Her father, Lucius Verginius, was a general at the Algidus; he was a man of high birth and exemplary behavior at home and in the field. His wife had been the same and raised their children in an appropriate manner. The daughter, Verginia, was engaged to the tribune Lucius Icilius [...]

Appius was crazy for this girl, who had grown up to be outstandingly beautiful. He began to solicit her with bribes and hope, and after he observed that his attempts were fenced out by her virtue, he turned his mind to overcoming her by cruel and arrogant force.[53] He turned the business over to Marcus Claudius, one of his clients.[54] The plan was to publicly declare that the girl was a slave, and not to give her up to the freedom desired by her friends when they demanded their rights. Because the girl's father was out of town, Appius thought he could get away with this crime.

The Decemvir's agent of lust laid hands on the girl as she was coming into the Forum – in those days, school was held in the shops – and claimed she was his slave, born to his slave-woman. So he ordered her to follow him; if she resisted, he said, he'd drag her off by force. Terrified, the girl stood gaping. Meanwhile, her loyal nurse's shouts for help gathered a crowd [...] The impostor[55] said that there was no need for a commotion, since he was prepared to assert his claims legally rather than violently. He called the girl to court [... *Appius judges the case and says Verginius must return from war to defend his claim; until then, he says Marcus Claudius can take Verginia. But the bystanders force him to reconsider because of her age. She goes home and her father returns for the trial.*]

Verginius in beggar's clothing arrived in the Forum. He led his daughter, dressed the same way; a mass of supporters and a crowd of respectably married women came with them. He walked around and asked men for their support [...*in the upcoming trial. But Appius judges in favor of his client, as expected. Verginius asks permission to say goodbye to his daughter before she's taken away forever.*]

The request was granted. Verginius took his daughter and his nurse aside to the shops near the shrine of Cloacina – the ones called New Shops now. There he seized a knife from a butcher and said, "My daughter, I'm giving you freedom in the only way I can." Then he stabbed the girl in the chest. Looking back at the judge's bench, he said, "Appius Claudius, this blood is on your head – I curse you with it!"

Appius, alerted by the shout that arose at so desperate an act, ordered his men to arrest Verginius. Verginius managed to cut a path with his sword through to his crowd of supporters. Then he made it safely to the gates and escaped.

Icilius and Numitorius[56] lifted up the lifeless body and showed it to the people.[57] They bemoaned the crime of Appius, the girl's unlucky beauty, and the father's last resort. The wives followed them, moaning [...] The men's attention was devoted to outrage over public affairs [...*leading to the downfall of the Decemvirs*].

7.9 Slave-women and the Nonae Caprotinae

Although most Roman narratives of heroism focus on the elite, occasionally Romans admitted that non-elites performed acts of heroism, too. The following accounts of heroic slaves offer an aetiology for the strange rituals of the Nonae Caprotinae (the "goat days" of July). In this ritual, men run away and shout each other's names. A separate aetiology connects the rite to Romulus' apotheosis (Romulization: see **1.2**). The two aetiologies are mutually exclusive, but are often retold together.

The version related here focuses on slave-women immediately after the Gallic Sack (**8.10**). The slaves take the place of elite women in a reversal of the Sabine women myth (**3.5**). Modern scholars have noted dramatic elements to the story, as well as elements of reversal (not only women playing the heroic roles of men, but slave-women dressing as freed women). They suggest that this myth helped strengthen the normal gender and class roles in Roman society.

—————————— 7.9.1   Plutarch, *Life of Camillus* 33 ——————————

The Latins are threatening to besiege Rome unless the Romans send them wives. Slaves offer to go instead, preserving elite women's chastity. Plutarch's account focuses on the military results of the slaves' actions. Compare the use of female slaves' bodies in this narrative to the stories of free women in the rest of the chapter. What does this tell you about expectations for women of different social status?

They say that the Latins sent free girls and women to the Romans and asked them to send their women in return. Either this was a pretext or they really wanted to intermarry with the Romans again as they had in the city's early years. The Romans had no idea what to do. They hated the idea of war when they hadn't at all recovered their strength or become settled. Also, they were suspicious that the request for women was in fact a demand for hostages, called "matrimony" for appearances.

A slave-woman named Tutula – or as some say, Philotis[58] – advised the leading men to send her instead, accompanied by other slave-women who were particularly pretty and looked like freeborn ladies. They would be dressed as well-born brides. She promised that she would see to the rest. The men were persuaded to send as many girls as she thought would be necessary, to dress them in finery and gold, and to hand them over to the Latins, who were encamped not far from the city. At night, the other women filched their enemies' daggers. Meanwhile, Tutula or Philotis climbed a huge fig-tree and hung a lantern facing Rome, while she stretched out her cloak behind. This was the agreement between her and Rome's leaders, although no one else knew about it. And that's why a crowd of soldiers made their way out of the city, with their generals urging them on, calling to each other and keeping order with difficulty.

When they arrived at the enemy palisades, the Latins weren't expecting them and remained asleep. The Romans took the camp and killed most of the Latins. And this occurred in the month of July at the Nonae Caprotinae, when now they hold a festival to recall the deed.

——————— 7.9.2   Pseudo-Plutarch, *Lesser Parallels* 313a   ———————

Pseudo-Plutarch changes the ethnicity and names of all involved, but the story is clearly the same. In this version, the women don't act voluntarily. How does that affect your understanding of the story?

Atepomarus the king of the Gauls was fighting the Romans. He said that he wouldn't leave the country until they gave him their wives for companions. As a trick, the Romans sent their slave-girls instead. The barbarians[59] wore themselves out by having endless sex with the slaves. Then they went to sleep. Rhetana (the whole plot was her idea) shimmied up a wild fig to the wall and informed the consuls. They marched out to battle and conquered the Gauls. This is why the Romans celebrate the festival of the slaves.

Conclusion

Many Roman myths about women center on sex. The Camillas and Cloelias of Roman myth, who function almost as equals to the men they meet, are rare; variations of the love story gone wrong are relatively frequent. We see women who fall in love with inappropriate men (Tarpeia), men who fall in love with inappropriate women (Lucretia, Verginia), and comic (or tragic) mistakes about love (Anna). The theme is not surprising: the myths we have were written by Greek and Roman men, and elite men in antiquity were concerned about controlling access to female bodies.

But saying that men chose the narratives about myth doesn't mean that these myths were meaningless to Roman women. The myths may, in fact, have been *more* significant to these women because they provided models to imitate and avoid in their daily life. Many women may have sympathized with Tarpeia, who longed for something (whether precious gems or a man) she could not have; they surely worried about their relatives in combat, like Horatia or Ovid's Lucretia; and many may have felt torn between the interests of their birth and marital households, which plays a role in most of these stories. Readers male and female may not have noticed the underlying societal expectations of these myths, such as Ovid's casual comment that women who fight an assailant are bound to fail (**7.6.2**), or the general consensus that Cloelia was brave primarily because courage of any sort wasn't expected in a girl (**7.7**). Similarly, they may not have noticed the stereotypes about women that cross the boundaries of time and space: that women are obsessed with jewelry, for example (**7.2.2, 7.2.3, 7.4**), or that alcohol gets women into trouble (**7.1.3, 7.1.4, 7.6**). But these stereotypes offer us important clues about Roman cultural attitudes towards women.

Some modern scholars have argued that women were able to play only limited roles in ancient Roman society, based on the myths that were told about them. You can compare these expectations for women in myth to the expectations of men you've seen in other chapters. Were the expectations for women lower, or only different? And are there any "Roman" themes that men and women share?

Notes

1. Hercules chooses a selection of his labors to highlight.
2. The reference is to Athena; the "Gorgon" is her breastplate.
3. He went blind. That's why the priestess tells Hercules to "spare his eyes" at the beginning of her speech.
4. **2.2.2** and **2.2.6–2.2.8** suggest different aetiologies for this altar.
5. "Ara Maxima" means "greatest altar" in Latin.
6. See **2.1**.
7. See **2.2.5**.
8. A similar story is told about Alexander the Great's birth: Plutarch, *Alexander* 2 and Pausanias 4.14.7–4.14.8.
9. See **7.1.1**.
10. The word is *virgo*, for which see **chapter introduction**.
11. Diana.
12. Melite is modern Malta; Cosyra is Pantellaria.
13. Pygmalion is Anna's brother. They had a family feud.
14. See **2.5**.
15. Aeneas' friend in the *Aeneid*.
16. Ovid inverts the disappearance of Aeneas in **2.6**.
17. See **8.8.1**.
18. Compare Vertumnus' disguise in **6.7.2**.
19. The Greek word means "know" – in this case, it may be in the Biblical sense of "slept with" (and perhaps married).
20. Priest of the deified Romulus.
21. Christian writers, possibly relying on Tertullian, consistently call Larentia "Larentina."
22. Tertullian doesn't shy away from sexual innuendo.

23. Great men in antiquity could be called a "second" Hercules; a "third" Hercules is third-rate.
24. For example, the Basilica Aemilia frieze (http://www.ilgiornaledellarte.com/immagini/IMG20100408180513904_900_700.jpeg) and coins, both Republican-era (http://numismatics.org/collection/1987.26.59) and Augustan-era (http://numismatics.org/collection/1937.158.379).
25. Compare **7.2.2**.
26. For the story, see **3.5.2** and **3.5.3**.
27. Compare Juno in **8.10.3**.
28. An echo of Romulus' words to Remus in **3.3.5** and **3.4.5**.
29. As *paterfamilias*.
30. Even though this crime appears to be a private matter, the expiation and symbol of the crime (the beam) are publicly funded.
31. An indication that the story may be Horatian family lore.
32. Compare Aeneas' enemy Turnus (**2.5**).
33. See **5.6.3**.
34. See **5.4.1a** for the relationship between Egerius and the royal Tarquins; Egerius had been left in charge of Collatia in **5.4.1b**. "Collatinus" means "from Collatia."
35. Compare the famous painted tombs of Tarquinia (for example, http://www.artic.edu/aic/collections/citi/resources/_JaharisLaunchPad/RS3A_Tomb_of_Leopards.jpg or https://classconnection.s3.amazonaws.com/139/flashcards/1167139/jpg/tomb1330510875569.jpg)
36. A key virtue of the Roman wife, "spinning wool" appears on tombstones from all eras.
37. Adultery with a slave would be extremely shameful for a woman of Lucretia's high status.
38. Lucretia's father, who has not been introduced in the narrative; Roman readers would realize that he was her father because she has the female version of his name.
39. Later named Publicola; see **8.2**.
40. The same Brutus as **5.6.5**.
41. See **1.2** for the important role played by *exempla*. Lucretia is painfully aware that her survival would set a precedent for adultery.
42. Compare Sextus' adventures in Gabii in **5.6.2b** and **5.6.2d**.
43. Compare Ovid's account of the augury content between Romulus and Remus (**3.3.6**), using the same phrase.
44. See **note 35**.
45. See **note 34**.
46. That is, anyone besides her husband.
47. A magical number.
48. "Brutus" means "fool."
49. Compare Cocles and Scaevola in **8.3**; they're typically associated with Cloelia.
50. See **8.3**.
51. Sexual abuse was even more shaming to a Roman elite male than to a female. The myth of Cloelia is one of the few examples we have of the dangers facing prisoners of war (Walker 2005).
52. This story takes place during the Conflict of the Orders (**8.8**), a struggle for plebeian rights; there is class conflict as well as gender conflict in this story.

53. Cruelty and arrogance are markers of tyrannical behavior.
54. "Clients" were lower-status citizens bound to elite Romans by various ties, most notably service. Appius' client is in a difficult position: he can't really say no.
55. Marcus Claudius.
56. A friend of the family.
57. Compare Brutus' actions with Lucretia (**7.6.1**).
58. Tutula (*tutela*) means "guardianship"; "Philotis" means "Lovey." The latter is a more likely slave name.
59. In the Greek sense of "foreigners," but in context perhaps also in our sense of "outrageous."

References

Joshel, Sandra. 1992. "The Body Female and the Body Politic." In *Pornography and Representation in Greece and Rome*, edited by Amy Richlin, 112–130. Oxford: Oxford University Press.

Walker, Cheryl. 2005. *Hostages in Republican Rome*. Cambridge, MA: Center for Hellenic Studies. http://chs.harvard.edu/CHS/article/display/5571 (accessed November 23, 2016).

Welch, Tara S. 2005. *The Elegiac Cityscape: Propertius and the Meaning of Roman Monuments*. Columbus, OH: Ohio State University Press.

Further Reading

Claassen, Jo-Marie. 1998. "The Familiar Other: The Pivotal Role of Women in Livy's Narrative of Political Development in Early Rome." *Acta Classica* 41: 71–103. www.casa-kvsa.org.za/1998/AC41-02-Claassen.pdf (accessed November 23, 2016). Provides an extensive backgrounder on Roman historiography and some aspects of gender studies. Claassen's methods are easy to follow, and her list of women in Livy is helpful for student research.

Kampen, Natalie. 1991. "The Reliefs of the Basilica Aemilia: A Redating." *Klio* 73: 448–458. DOI: 10.1524/klio.1991.73.73.448 Argues that the Tarpeia iconography of the Basilica Aemilia reliefs (**note 24**) must be understood in the context of the Augustan moral reforms. Kampen ties this publicly visible relief to the changing (and perhaps regressive) conception of appropriate female behavior in the early Principate.

Michels, Agnes Kirsopp. 1951. "The Drama of the Tarquins." *Latomus* 10: 13–24. http://www.jstor.org/stable/41516814 (accessed December 4, 2016). Analyzes the Tarquin regime as a dramatic trilogy revolving around three women: Tanaquil, Tullia, and Lucretia. There is some untranslated Latin, but it's not necessary for comprehension. Michels' argument about the dramatic transmission of Roman history has been slow to gain favor, but many scholars now believe that Roman cultural knowledge may have been transmitted through plays.

Russell, Brigette Ford. 2003. "Wine, Women, and the Polis: Gender and the Formation of the City-State in Archaic Rome." *Greece & Rome* 50: 77–84. https://www.jstor.org/stable/3567821 (accessed November 23, 2016). Discusses Roman attitudes to wine. Based on the myths of Bona Dea, Lucretia, and others, Russell argues that wine was

associated with loss of self-control. Yet this is at odds with contemporary archaeological evidence for both men and women drinking. Russell argues that the myths,
particularly the wife contest in the Lucretia tale, provide evidence for societal change.

Small, Jocelyn Penny. 1976. "The Death of Lucretia." *Americal Journal of Archaeology* 80:
349–360. http://www.jstor.org/stable/503575 (accessed November 23, 2016). Analyzes the scenes on several Etruscan urns as images of the death of Lucretia. Although
Small's argument has not found widespread favor, the article offers an interesting link
between the material in this chapter and in **chapter 4**.

Welch, Tara S. 2012. "Perspectives On and Of Livy's Tarpeia." *EuGeStA* 2: 169–
200. http://eugesta.recherche.univ-lille3.fr/revue/eng/issues/issue-2-2012/ (accessed
November 23, 2016). Analyzes Livy's Tarpeia narrative in comparison with other
mythical women, notably Horatia. Welch argues that Livy uses women to symbolize
Roman expansion: as women change households, nearby cities become Roman. But
unlike *exempla*, where moral judgment is meant to be clear, Livy's narrative allows
the reader to choose whether these female behaviors are good or bad.

8

Rome's Heroes

Introduction

After the death of Lucretia (**7.6**), Rome went to war with its kings. Tarquin fled to his Latin allies, particularly the Etruscan king Porsenna (who besieged Rome) and the Cumaean tyrant Aristodemus. The aged king eventually died in Cumae, but his sons kept up the fight until the Tarquins suffered a decisive defeat at the Battle of Lake Regillus, several years after the rape of Lucretia. During this time, the Romans slowly established the consular system that would remain in place for the majority of the Republic. The first chaotic year provides a glimpse of how the process probably worked: five consuls (due to death and exile), treason, and war.

The stories in this chapter are about the foundation of the Republic, and so are foundation legends of a sort. Brutus was honored as a founder, just as the kings were; in fact, his statue joined the statues of the first six kings on the Capitoline (Tarquin the Proud was left out). As Livy tells us (*From the Foundation* 2.1), every king added something to the city: Romulus built the city itself, Numa gave it religion, Tullus Hostilius added Alba, Ancus Marcius added Ostia (Rome's port), Tarquin the Elder built the temple of Jupiter, Servius Tullius organized the people into centuries, and Brutus gave Rome its freedom.

As we've seen, Roman authors appreciated that the city was constantly evolving. These changes provided strength, rather than weakness: the city was powerful because its "constitution" was flexible. This flexibility was especially apparent in the early years of the Republic, which tested out several forms of government before eventually settling on two consuls; it's likely that the Republican system we recognize wasn't fully in place before the fourth century BCE.[1] We've seen some of these other types already: for example, in

Early Rome: Myth and Society, A Sourcebook, First Edition. Jaclyn Neel.
© 2017 John Wiley & Sons, Inc. Published 2017 by John Wiley & Sons, Inc.

the story of Verginia (**7.8**), the city is controlled by the Decemvirs, ten men who were elected to codify the city's laws. Verginia's fate eventually led the Romans to abandon this experiment, and the concept of government by two consuls (with the occasional emergency rule of a single dictator) became the standard.

Ancient authors generally present this early period as series of foundations. After Brutus establishes the Republic, other key players establish important offices, customs, and rituals. These myths stem from *exempla*, a concept that was defined briefly in **1.2**. As Matthew Roller (2004) has argued, an *exemplum* can be distinguished from other praiseworthy deeds because it is both *noticed* and *replicable*: the act of doing good in itself is not an *exemplum*, but when that good deed is recognized and repeated, it is.

Exemplary acts are characteristic of the early Republic. They can be of positive, negative, or dubious value to Rome. A positive *exemplum* embodies a virtue that should be cultivated, while a negative *exemplum* suggests traits to avoid. The Roman hero Camillus, for example, provides a positive *exemplum* of mercy when he frees the children of Falerii (**8.9.3**); he offers a negative *exemplum* of tyrannical excess when he triumphs with white horses (**8.10.4**). As you see, ancient sources can use the same figure as both a positive and a negative *exemplum*: context (and authorial commentary) determines how to interpret the action.

Many of the stories that have come down to us relate the exemplary deeds of individual families. Some of these families, such as the patrician Claudii, remained important until the imperial era: Rome's first imperial dynasty, the Julio-Claudians, was a branch of this ancient house. Other families gradually faded from importance. The hero Cincinnatus' line had largely disappeared by the late Republic, although other branches of his family endured. Even when the family had mostly died out, the stories of the heroes continued to be retold; however, it seems that Romans were quite eager to attach their names to heroes of the past. The orator Cicero's friend Atticus, for example, wrote histories of noble families (Nepos, *Life of Atticus* 18), and Cicero suggested that some of his friends added heroes to their family trees (Cicero, *Brutus* 62).

No doubt this embellishment was partly attractive because prominent families wanted to claim a longstanding connection to the city. Rome, as a traditional society, valued the old more than the new. But a connection to a positive *exemplum* had another benefit. Romans believed that personality traits were heritable, much like physical traits (see **chapter 5 introduction**). Families could therefore gain and reinforce their reputation through mythology. Just as stories about Romulus told all Romans who they were and how they ought to behave, stories about individual families taught the elite about their past and expected behaviors.

The focus on foundations and families means that this chapter covers a lot of ground: about a century of Roman history. There are many more tales that could be told, including lengthier versions of almost all the myths that are presented. If you'd like to learn more about this period, Livy is the natural starting point; Greek authors such as Dionysius, Dio, and Plutarch are also helpful. In selecting the myths for this chapter in particular, the goal has been coherence rather than completeness: all myths emphasize the central lesson of "Rome first." You shouldn't be misled into thinking that's the only theme of the early Republic (although it is probably the most important one): think back to **7.6–7.9**, which take place in the same period.

This chapter, and the book as a whole, ends with the Gallic sack of Rome (c. 390 BCE). Although there are many potential endpoints to Rome's legendary history, the sack is compelling for a few reasons. One is practical: oral histories have been found to be accurate for a period of approximately six generations, or between one and two centuries. Because the earliest Roman histories were written in the third century BCE, the fourth-century sack lies at the edge of the period that was most likely to be exaggerated into legend. Another reason is that Greek and Roman authors consistently state that Rome's records were destroyed in the sack (see **1.5**), and therefore they had less information to work with for this earlier period. They responded by assimilating the Gallic sack to earlier episodes of Roman history – or maybe it was the other way around (Romulization (**1.2**); contrast Richardson 2012). Some ancient authors also saw the Gallic sack as a major turning point: Livy, for example, ended his fifth book with the Gauls, and marks a new phase of Rome's history in book six.[2] Not all authors agreed that the sack was a turning point, however; the Greek Dionysius set the limit of early Roman history a century later, during the war with Pyrrhus of Epirus (c. 280–275). But surviving Roman authors do not, on the whole, treat the episode of the Gallic sack with the same level of trust as they treat later, more clearly documented conflicts, such as the Punic Wars. There is, therefore, some justification in the sources for treating this episode with caution – but it is also important to remember that ancient authors did not openly question the sack.

Despite the Romans' faith in the story, scholars hold varying opinions on the historicity and severity of the sack (Cornell 1995, 313–322; Holloway 1994, 1–13). Parallels with Romulus' war against the Sabines are suspicious, and have been recognized since antiquity (see Plutarch, *Life of Romulus* 17). But while *Romans* did not write down their histories until many years after the Gallic sack, several contemporary or near-contemporary Greek sources record wars in central Italy at this time (**8.10.2c**). These histories, preserved in later authors, provide the most compelling evidence for the historicity of the Gallic sack. Continuing archaeological discoveries in Rome may shed more light on this question in the future.

The somewhat arbitrary nature of historical periodization (where we set the beginnings and ends of eras) can be both frustrating and vague. Modern historians hold a variety of opinions on when Rome's "mythic" history ends. As you read, you may find yourself disagreeing about this book's choice. You may also find yourself noticing similarities between the stories in this chapter and the stories of Rome's kings. If so, well done: you're on your way to mastering one method of studying early Rome.

For Further Thought

1. The concept of a "foundation legend" was very flexible in Rome. Why do you think the Romans conceived of their city as constantly evolving? How might that help them distinguish themselves from their neighbors? How might it contribute to a sense of civic solidarity?

2. What is the value of an *exemplum*? Why do you think Romans had so many at this period in their history?

3. Family histories are an important source of material in the early Republic. What does that suggest about how Romans transmitted historical information? How does this idea complicate our understanding of early Republican history?

TEXTS

8.1 Brutus

As the founder of the new government, Brutus had many responsibilities – including punishing traitors who preferred the Tarquins. His loyalty to Rome was tested several times, but two occasions in particular stand out: the banishment of Lucretia's husband Collatinus, and the execution of his own sons. Roman authors could connect these stories closely or separate them. Livy and Dionysius approach the narratives in very different ways. For Livy, Brutus retains his exemplary stature as Rome's new founder; Dionysius is less sure about the value of some Roman customs. Both authors place the Tarquins' attempt to return to Rome in the background.

——————————————— 8.1.1 Cicero, *On Duties* 3.40 ———————————————

*Cicero discusses the difficulty of determining whether deeds are performed for the common good or for self-promotion. He uses Brutus and Romulus as contrasting examples; compare his judgment of Rome's founder in **3.4.2**.*

When Brutus took power away from his colleague Collatinus, it may seem that he was acting unjustly. After all, Collatinus had been his comrade and ally in expelling the kings. But when the leading men had undertaken this plan to eliminate the family of Tarquin the Proud, the name "Tarquin," and the memory of his kingship, protecting the country was a priority. The choice was so clear that even Collatinus himself had to agree.

8.1.2 Livy, *From the Foundation* 2.2

Despite his hostility to the Tarquins, Lucretia's husband is deemed unfit for Rome because of his name. The story inverts the immigration motif, as Collatinus leaves the city in order to help it grow.

Perhaps our Republic's founders took their protective stance too far in unimportant matters. For one of the consuls had a name that was despicable to the city, even though he had done no other wrong. Word had it that the Tarquins were too comfortable with kingship. Tarquin the Elder started them off; then Servius Tullius ruled; despite the intervening years, Tarquin the Proud had not forgotten the throne, even when it was held by another. He'd used violent crime to claim it as if it was his birthright. Now, with Tarquin gone, Collatinus had power! The Tarquins didn't know how to live as private citizens. The name displeased the people; it endangered their freedom.

Beginning from a few agitated men, the speech gradually spread across the city. Since they were riled up with suspicion, Brutus called the people to an assembly [...] "Lucius Tarquinius, remove our fear. We're aware, we admit that you expelled the kings. Finish your good deed and remove their name. I promise the citizens won't just repay you for your property; they'll pay it back with interest, in whatever way it's lacking. Leave as a friend; free the city from a fear (even a silly one); this way they'll be convinced that the kingdom has left with the Tarquins."

At first his fellow consul was speechless from sudden and unexpected shock [... *but eventually*] Collatinus conceded, overcome by the consensus of the citizens. He was afraid that once he was a private citizen,[3] the request would recur – and that at that point, his property would be seized and further shame would befall him. So he abdicated the consulship, transferred all of his positions to Lavinium, and left Rome.

8.1.3 Livy, *From the Foundation* 2.4–2.5

A Roman father had the right to punish his misbehaving children in any way, including death. Brutus sets the standard for all future Roman fathers by ensuring that his love of Rome comes first, even before his love for his own children. When his sons are discovered conspiring to bring back the Tarquins, he presides over their execution.

The conspiracy was first entrusted to the Vitellii and Aquilii, both sets of brothers. The Vitellii's sister was married to the consul Brutus, and already they had two children from the marriage, Titus and

Tiberius. The boys were admitted into their uncles' conspiratorial mob. Meanwhile many other noble youths were adopted into the conspiracy, but their names have been lost over the course of time. [...*The Tarquins send an embassy to Rome asking for the return of their possessions. While the people consider the proposal, the ambassadors seek support among the Roman nobility.*]

The day before the Tarquins' envoys were supposed to leave, they happened to dine with the Vitellii. In the privacy of home, the conspirators discussed many plans about the new conspiracy, as often happens. One of their slaves by chance overheard their conversation. He'd already suspected that something was going on, but he'd been waiting for an opportunity to intercept the letters (which would prove his case) from the envoys and give them to the authorities. After he'd seen the letters exchanged, he brought the matter to the consuls [...]

The traitors were condemned and handed over for punishment. The event was watched more intently because it was the responsibility of the consul father to condemn his children. Fortune made Brutus carry out a punishment that he should never have had to see. The noblest young men stood tied to stakes, but everyone turned their eyes towards the consul's sons, as if the rest were nobodies. They pitied them not because of the pain of their punishment, but because of the crime that caused it. In the very same year that the country had been liberated, when their own father had freed it, when the consular office was born in the Junian household, plus the senators, plebs, everything human or divine that was Roman – in *that* year, those boys had gotten it into their heads to betray city, father, and all affairs of state to that proud man, the former king, in his unhappy exile.

The consuls filed into their seats and sent lictors to carry out the penalty. They lashed the naked prisoners with their sticks and then cut their heads off with the axes.[4] The entire time, the father kept his face and gaze fixed on the sight, with his paternal feelings obvious during the display of public duty. After the guilty had been punished, in order to set a positive example for those who stopped crimes, public money was given to the informer as a reward; he was also given freedom and citizenship.

— 8.1.4 Dionysius of Halicarnassus, *Roman Antiquities* 5.8.1–5.11.2 —

Dionysius, unlike Livy, strongly intertwines the punishment of Brutus' sons with the expulsion of Collatinus. This excerpted passage begins after Brutus has learned of his sons' conspiracy. In Dionysius' narrative, Collatinus' nephews are involved, too – but Collatinus is more forgiving.

The Romans think that Brutus' actions after that were amazingly noble. But I'm afraid that Greeks will find them incredibly cruel [...] He told his sons to speak up if they had anything to say. But neither of them dared to boldly deny [the conspiracy]; instead, they wept, making their guilt clear. After a few minutes, Brutus stood up. He ordered everyone to be quiet, and they waited to learn what he'd do. The consul announced that he condemned his sons to death. In response, everyone protested that such an excellent man didn't deserve to see his children die [...] Brutus told the lictors to take the young men away. Crying, they pleaded with him, using loving words. Everyone was shocked when Brutus seemed to ignore the citizens' requests and his sons' tears.

They were more shocked when he didn't moderate their punishment at all: he didn't take them aside out of everyone's sight for execution, nor did he leave the Forum to avoid seeing them killed. He didn't let them escape their lot without the full force of shame; he scrupulously observed every custom about punishing traitors. The youths were whipped in public and beheaded. Brutus watched it all. The most amazing thing is that he didn't avert his eyes or tear up [... *Collatinus' nephews are next.*]

Brutus ordered the lictors to drag them off to execution, unless they wanted to defend themselves. But Collatinus told them to wait a few minutes so he could speak with his colleague. Drawing Brutus aside, he pleaded his nephews' cause at length [...] But Brutus refused to show mercy or even delay the trials (Collatinus' last resort). He swore up and down that he would execute them all on that very day.

Collatinus was at his wits' end, since all his proposals had failed. "Fine!" he said. "Since you're wrongfully harsh, *I* pardon them. After all, I have the same authority as you."

Brutus replied harshly. "Over my dead body! Collatinus, you can free traitors – but you'll pay the price soon." [... *Brutus calls an assembly and denounces Collatinus before the people. The passage picks up at the end of his speech.*]

"Collatinus, you're stripped of office. Exile yourself to a different city. Citizens, it's time to vote. Form your blocs right now and decide if I'm right. But hear me out: either he'll be your consul or I will."

Collatinus shouted protests as Brutus spoke. He called Brutus a treacherous backstabber [...] The people were furious and didn't want to hear his defense or pleas. They clamored to vote. Spurius Lucretius, Collatinus' father-in-law, was more cautious. He feared that Collatinus would be violently removed from office and from Rome. He asked permission to speak. The people respected him... [*The remainder of the story follows **8.1.1**].*

8.2 Publicola

Rome went through several consuls in its first year as a Republic. Publius Valerius Publicola (**7.6.1**) replaced Collatinus, but his motives and loyalty to the Republic were also questioned. The *exemplum* of Publicola's house shows us that regal behavior took many forms, and underlines the importance of a physical home to elite identity. When Publicola's house is at the top of the hill, he's imagined to be lording it over the other Romans; when he sets it at the base of the hill, he's one of them. Unlike Collatinus, whose name is imagined as an unchangeable part of his identity, Publicola can move his house and prove that Rome is more important to him than power.

——————— 8.2.1 Livy, *From the Foundation 2.7–2.8* ———————

The site of a house in ancient Rome was a marker of wealth and class identity. In this passage, Livy explains how Publicola's lofty house gets him into hot water. The narrative begins after Brutus has died in battle against the Tarquins, leaving Publicola as the only consul.

A rumor started that Valerius wanted to be king, since he hadn't chosen a colleague to replace Brutus and he was building a house on top of the Velia – a citadel in a tall, protected spot would be impossible to attack. The report distressed the consul, since the people believed he was acting shamefully. He called a public meeting and climbed up the speaker's platform with the *fasces*[5] lowered. The sight pleased the crowd, since they saw that the symbols of sovereignty yielded to them – an admission that the people had more authority and greater power than the consul [...]

"Do you suspect *me* of aiming to be king? I'm his fiercest enemy! If I wanted to live on the Capitoline, on the citadel itself, should I believe that my fellow-citizens would be afraid of me? Is my reputation so worthless to you? Does your trust rely on such weak foundations that where I live matters more than who I am? Romans, my house won't stand in the way of your freedom [...]"

Immediately all of the building material was moved below the Velia. The house was built on the lowest part of cliff where the shrine of Vica Pota now stands. Next the consul passed laws that not only absolved him from the suspicion of kingship but actually changed opinions completely: he was now seen as democratic.[6] So he was given the name "Publicola."[7]

8.2.2 Plutarch, *Life of Publicola* 1–2

*Plutarch's idea of Publicola's character is more typical of what we know about Roman elites. Although he accepts that he might not be the best man for a given job, his pride is hurt when he feels that he's been passed over. In this respect, Publicola is a model for Coriolanus (**8.8.3**, **8.8.4**) and eventually Julius Caesar.*

When Lucius Brutus had undertaken the revolution, he came to Valerius first. Brutus found Valerius extremely eager and helpful in expelling the kings. So long as the people seemed likely to elect a single general in place of the king, Valerius was happy to let Brutus take the lead in governance, since he'd been the leader in securing freedom. But when the people were unhappy with the name of monarchy and it seemed preferable to share supreme power, they suggested that two men should put themselves forward in an election. Valerius hoped to be chosen to rule with Brutus, but he failed completely. For Tarquinius Collatinus, the husband of Lucretia, was elected as the second consul, against Brutus' wishes. He was as noble as Valerius, but the powerful citizens feared the kings, who were plotting even from outside and softening the city's resolve. So these men preferred the man who was most intensely hostile to the Tarquins as a leader, since he wouldn't give in.

Valerius was furious: because he personally hadn't suffered at the hands of the tyrants, he wasn't trusted to do anything at all for his country! He left the Senate and refused to address the assembly. He completely gave up his public activities, which gave the majority a valid reason to fear that he would join the kings out of anger, and thus overturn the city and its constitution while they were still in a precarious state.

8.2.3 Plutarch, *Life of Publicola* 10

Plutarch's version of the story about Publicola's house makes the social value of Roman houses explicit. In this anecdote Publicola's behavior is more in line with what's expected of an ideal statesman.

When he heard at great length from many friends that he was making a mistake by building such a lofty house, he wasn't itching for a fight or angry. Immediately he gathered many craftsmen and tore down his house that night, razing the entire thing to the very foundations. When day came, the Romans saw and crowded together. They rejoiced and marveled at the man's great heart on the one hand, but they were sad about the house, too.

-------------------------- 8.2.4 *Lapis Satricanus (CIL I² 2832a)* --------------------------

This sixth-century inscription[8] from the Latin town of Satricum may offer proof of Publicola's existence.

The companions of Publius Valesios[9] dedicated this to Mamers.[10]

8.3 The War with Porsenna

When Brutus died, the Romans fought their way to victory over the Tarquins. But the Tarquins weren't ready to give up. With an ally, the Etruscan king Porsenna, they attacked Rome. As Rome fought Porsenna, several individuals rose to prominence for their heroism. Three in particular became exemplary for displaying immense courage in battle. We've seen one, the teenage Cloelia, in **7.7**. The other two were men: the experienced soldier Horatius Cocles and the would-be assassin Mucius Scaevola.

-------------------------- 8.3.1 Livy, *From the Foundation 2.10* --------------------------

Livy's version of the Cocles story is brief, but satisfying. He introduces a theme that will become increasingly important to his history: the single savior of Rome. Although Rome's new government was oligarchic, opportunities existed for great men to excel – provided that they realize their role is temporary.

When the enemy was close, the farmers left their fields for the city voluntarily; they surrounded the city itself with a guard. Some spots seemed safe because of the walls, others because the Tiber blocked the way. Even so, the wooden bridge nearly gave the enemy a way in, if not for a single man: Horatius Cocles. Rome's fortune put him on guard that day. He was stationed at the bridge when the Janiculum was captured in a sudden attack. He saw the enemy soldiers racing down from there quickly, while his own side dropped their weapons and abandoned formation in a frightened crowd. He scolded the individuals he met, blocking their way, and [...] told them to destroy the bridge: with swords, with fire, with anything they had. Meanwhile, he would face the enemy onslaught as well as a single fighter could.

He hurried to the bridge to meet the first onslaught. Standing out among the clearly visible backs of men fleeing battle, he turned his arms to fight at close quarters. The enemy stopped to stare at his amazing audacity. But two others felt shame, too. Their names were Spurius Larcius and Titus Herminius, both noble by birth and in deed. They helped Horatius hold off the first rush of danger, and for a little while the fighting was extremely heavy. Then, when only a small part of the bridge remained, he forced even these companions to return to safety.

Meanwhile, those who were cutting the bridge down called all three back. Horatius swept his eyes menacingly across the Etruscans in the front lines. First he challenged them to duels, then taunted them. He called them slaves of proud kings, who had come to a foreign war without thinking of their own freedom. They hesitated for a while. Each looked at his neighbor, expecting someone else to start the fight. Finally shame provoked the battle line into motion, and with a shout they threw their spears from all directions at a single enemy. All of the missiles stuck in his lifted shield, but he was no less resolute as he blocked the bridge with his legs straddled wide.

Soon they tried to push him away with an attack. At the same time, the broken bridge crashed down and the Romans shouted. The work had been completed with quick readiness. The Etruscans stopped the attack in sudden fear. Cocles said, "Holy Father Tiber, I beg you, accept these arms and this soldier in favorable waters." Armed as he was, he jumped into the Tiber and swam unharmed across the river to his men, despite the many spears falling around him. This daring deed has earned more fame than belief among posterity.

––––––––––   8.3.2   Livy, *From the Foundation* 2.12–2.13   ––––––––––

Another of Rome's early heroes was the young nobleman Gaius Mucius, who went on a daring assassination attempt against the Etruscan king Porsenna. When his attempt failed, Mucius mutilated himself by holding his hand in the fire rather than reveal information that could endanger the city's safety. From that point forward, he was known as "Lefty" (Scaevola), a name that persisted among Rome's elite until the early Principate.

Mucius set out with his sword hidden in his clothing. When he reached Porsenna's camp, he stood in a packed crowd near the king's tribunal. Porsenna was distributing pay to his soldiers with a scribe sitting next to him. Both king and scribe wore nearly identical clothing, hard at work as the soldiers approached *en masse*. Mucius was nervous about recognizing which was Porsenna: he'd never seen the king, and he wasn't sure which one was which. Rashly, he let fortune be his guide: he killed the scribe instead of the king.

As he hurried from there through the frightened crowd, he tried to carve his own path with his sword. A throng of people gathered, alerted by the noise. The king's retainers caught Mucius and dragged him back to the king's tribunal.

Amid such great threats to his life, he was awe-inspiring rather than afraid. "I'm a Roman," he said, "a citizen. Gaius Mucius is my name. I came here as an enemy, to kill an enemy. My mind's equally prepared to murder and to die. It's a Roman trait to act and endure bravely. And don't think I'm the only one to have this attitude! There's a long line of men seeking the same honor. So prepare yourself for this struggle, if that's your choice: you'll fight for your life one hour at a time, since you'll have an armed enemy at the palace gate. We young Roman men declare war against you. You don't have to worry about troop formation or combat. The contest will be between you alone and us, one by one."

The king burned with anger and shook with fear at the danger. Menacingly, Porsenna ordered his men to surround Mucius with flames unless he revealed what treacherous threats to the king's life lay behind his cryptic words. At that, Mucius said, "You'll see for yourself that we Romans don't value our bodies when we're faced with great glory." With these words, he thrust his right hand into the fire that had been lit for sacrifice.

Mucius acted like his mind was totally separate from his senses while he burned. Porsenna was astonished at the amazing sight. He jumped up from his seat and ordered the young man to be removed from the altars. "Get away from here," he said. "You've carried out a greater crime against yourself than against me. I'd praise you if you showed this courage for my country's benefit. As it is, I dismiss you as a free man, unharmed and unviolated,[11] by the law of war."

Then Mucius, as if returning the favor, said, "Since you respect courage, for your kindness I'll give you information; you'd never have gotten it with threats. Three hundred young Romans, the cream of the crop, have taken an oath to come against you in this way. My lot shook out first. The rest will follow in turn, until fortune yields the opportunity against you."

Mucius was dismissed. Afterwards, he had the name "Scaevola" added to his name, because of the damage to his right hand. Ambassadors from Porsenna followed him to Rome. The near escape from the first danger troubled the king. It seemed that nothing had protected him beyond his assassin's mistake, so he'd have to face as many threats as there were surviving conspirators. And so he offered a peace treaty to Rome.

8.3.3   Plutarch, *Life of Publicola* 16

Plutarch offers a rational explanation for Cocles' name.

Horatius had received the name Cocles because he'd lost one of his eyes in battle, or (as some say) because his nose was so short and flat that he seemed to have nothing between his eyes; also his eyebrows ran together. So many wanted to call him "Cyclops," but by a slip of the tongue he was called "Cocles" by most men. In any case, this man stood in front of the bridge and resisted the enemy until his men cut down the bridge behind him. Then he threw himself into the river with his armor and swam until he reached the opposite riverbank. On the way an Etruscan spear wounded him in the buttocks. Publicola was in awe of his courage and immediately commanded every Roman to provide him with a day's rations. He also gave him as much land as a man could plow in one day.

8.3.4   Pseudo-Plutarch, *Lesser Parallels*
(*Moralia* 305F–306A)

Pseudo-Plutarch's version of the Mucius story suggests the quiet wit of the Spartans.

Porsenna the king of the Etruscans was fighting the Romans and camped near the river Tiber. Taking a moderate store of grain from the Romans, he wore them down with famine. The council was in turmoil, but Mucius, a young nobleman, took 400 age-mates from the senatorial class in everyday clothing and led them across the river. Seeing the king's bodyguard offering rations to the generals, he mistook him for Porsenna and killed him. He was brought before the king and put his right hand into the fire. Covering up his pain with good spirits and a smile, he said "Barbarian, I'm free, even if you don't wish it. Know that there are 400 men against you in this camp, and we're all looking to kill you." The king was frightened and made a treaty with the Romans.

8.4   Porsenna Captures Rome?

One strand of the historical tradition, known only from imperial-era sources, suggests that Livy was mistaken about Rome's glorious defeat of Porsenna (**7.7, 8.3**). In this alternative tradition, Rome was in fact defeated in battle against the Tarquins and their allies. The idea isn't impossible: compare **7.4, 8.8.5, 8.10.2** and **8.10.3**. The circumstances surrounding the capture of the city are unclear, but many scholars believe they are more historically plausible than the patriotic legends of Porsenna's defeat (see Cornell 1995, 215–226).

————————— 8.4.1 Dionysius of Halicarnassus, —————————
Roman Antiquities 5.34.1–5.34.4

*Dionysius' account follows directly on his version of the Cloelia narrative (largely repeated by Plutarch in **7.7.3**). He compares the continuing tyrannical behavior of the Tarquins to the good king Porsenna.*

Porsenna was outraged by the king's treatment of the Roman hostages, and called the Etruscans to a meeting. He explained that the Romans had asked him to moderate their dispute with Tarquin, but before he'd been able to make up his mind, the former kings had tried to break the truce by illegally attacking the inviolable hostages and ambassadors. So he thought that the Romans had been right to kick them out, and he himself planned to end his friendship with the Tarquins and their ally Mamilius.[12] [...] Then he held a meeting with the Roman ambassadors about peace and friendship, and they swore a treaty. Porsenna gave them a gift to take back to the city: all of the hostages without ransom.

————————— 8.4.2 Tacitus, *Histories* 3.72 —————————

Tacitus relates the burning of the Capitol in the first century CE to the threats facing the city in its earliest history.

This was the most grievous and disgusting deed to happen to the Roman people from the city's foundation onwards. Without external enemies, when the gods favored us – if our behavior had let them – the seat of Jupiter Optimus Maximus, founded as a pledge of empire in a spot established by the ancestors and our auspices, was set on fire. This deed, which neither Porsenna, when the city was given up, nor the Gauls,[13] when it was captured, dared to do, was accomplished by the madness of the foremost citizens.

8.5 The Battle at Lake Regillus

At the Battle of Regillus, the new Roman Republic finally defeated the forces of Tarquin. According to the stories later generations told about the battle, they had divine aid: the twins Castor and Pollux. Ancient authors, as well as modern scholars, have noted the similarities between Regillus and the Battle of the Sagra (**6.4.1, 6.4.3, 6.4.6**). Such parallelism is not unusual in ancient histories, but modern scholars have disagreed about the best way to interpret it. Some argue that the repetition suggests that one of the tales is invented (usually the Roman version), while others see it as important evidence for different ways of understanding the past. The second option makes no claims about the *accuracy* of such legends.

8.5.1   Cicero, *On the Nature of the Gods* 2.6

Cicero uses a historical example to prove that the gods exist in this dialogue on religion and philosophy.

This doesn't happen by accident or by chance, but because the gods were present (as they often are) and made their power known. One example was during the Latin war, when Aulus Postumius the dictator was fighting with Octavius Mamilius of Tusculum at Lake Regillus. Castor and Pollux appeared on horseback, fighting with our troops.

8.5.2   Livy, *From the Foundation* 2.20

Unlike other sources, Livy omits the supernatural appearance of Castor and Pollux. In his retelling, Rome's success at Regillus was due to Roman military virtue, not divine aid.

As the exiles approached the Roman line, Titus Herminius, a Roman legate, saw them. Among the troops he recognized Mamilius, whose clothes and weapons stood out, and attacked with even greater power than the Master of Horse had used when he'd engaged the enemy leader in battle a little earlier. His achievement was to kill Mamilius with a single blow to the side. But as he was stripping the corpse of its armor, Herminius himself was struck by a javelin. He was carried back to the camp as a victor, but died during medical treatment.

   The dictator rushed to the cavalry, begging them to fight on foot – the infantry, he claimed, was by now exhausted. The men obeyed [...] Then at last the Latins were driven back and the defeated line gave way. The cavalry mounted their horses in order to pursue the enemy, and the infantry followed them. They say that on the spot the dictator vowed to build a shrine to Castor, neglecting neither divine nor human aid. He also announced rewards for the troops.

8.5.3   Dionysius of Halicarnassus, *Roman Antiquities* 6.13.1–6.13.4

*Dionysius provides a compromise between **8.5.1** and **8.5.2**. He not only connects the appearance of the gods to the battle, but also to the foundation of the Temple of Castor in the Roman Forum.*

In this battle, they say, a vision appeared to Postumius the dictator and his men: two men on horseback, immense and exceptionally beautiful compared to typical humans. They were just at the edge of manhood. They led the Roman cavalry charge at breakneck speed and struck the Latins with their spears. After the Latins fled and their camp was ransacked, it was late afternoon; the battle ended. That same afternoon, two young men are said to have appeared in the Roman Forum. They were the same age, very tall and handsome, and wore military gear. Their faces wore a grim battle mask, and their horses dripped with sweat. Each of them let their horses drink and washed off in the fountain [...] Many people surrounded them and asked if they'd brought news. The two men told them about the battle and that the Romans won. After they left the Forum, they were never seen again, although a search was made [...] There are many indications in Rome of this miraculous and unexpected epiphany. For example, there's the temple to the Dioscuri,[14] which was built in the Forum at the spot where they'd been seen.

8.6   Stories of Self-Sacrifice for Rome

The Roman Republic strongly valued civic service – up to and including death. We have already seen that the early months of the Republic were marked by heroic deeds. This heroism continued after the city's government stabilized. The stories in this section cannot always be assigned a secure date, but they provide *exempla* of bravery in the service of the state.

8.6.1   Varro, *On the Latin Language* 5.148 and 5.150

*Varro offers three separate explanations for the name of the Lacus Curtius in the Roman Forum. The first appeared as **3.5.1**; the other two relate the name to the self-sacrifice of a Roman citizen.*

It's agreed that the Lacus Curtius in the Forum is named after Curtius, but there are three traditions about him [...] Procilius claims that the earth gaped open there and the matter was referred to the haruspices by

senatorial decree. The response came: the god Manius(?)[15] was seeking
a sacrifice that had been neglected. His demand was that the strongest
citizen should be sent down into the pit. So a certain Curtius, a brave
man, jumped onto his horse wearing armor and turned towards the
temple of Concordia. Then he rushed at it with his horse. The hole
closed over him and his body was buried at the god's will. It remains as
a memorial to his people.

But Cornelius and Lutatius write that the spot was hit by lightning
and fenced in by order of the Senate. This was done by Curtius in his
consulship, the one who had Marcus Genucius as his colleague, and so
the place was called "Curtius."

─────────── 8.6.2 Ovid, *Metamorphoses* 15.565–15.621 ───────────

*The unusual story of Cipus' horns is similar to many other myths that relate the
importance of prioritizing Rome over oneself.*

Or when Cipus saw his horns in running water (and believe me, he saw
them). He thought his eyes were playing tricks on him, and kept on
touching his fingers to his head to feel what he saw. Finally he stopped
blaming his eyes and didn't resist any longer. Like a victor leaving a
conquered enemy, he lifted his eyes and arms to the sky and said, "Gods,
I'm not sure what this terrible sign means. But if it's a sign of good
fortune, let it be good for the country and for the Roman people. If it's
bad, let it be bad just for me."

He tried to appease the gods by burning brilliant green tufts of grass
and fragrant herbs on the altar. He offered a goblet of wine and a slaughtered sheep. Then he examined the quivering organs to see what they
suggested. An Etruscan haruspex examined them, too. He saw important undertakings in store, but the message wasn't clear. When he lifted
his sharp eyes from the sheep's insides to Cipus' horns, he said, "Greetings, king! Cipus, this place will give you and your horns a citadel. Just
don't wait – hurry through the gates that lie open for you. This is what
the fates command. You'll be received in the city as king and you'll have
power for good, safe on your throne."

Cipus made his way back and turned his horned head away from
the city walls. "Dear gods, keep all these prophecies far, far away from
here! I'll live out my life as an exile long before the Capitol sees me as a
king." Right away he called a meeting of the people and distinguished
Senate. But first he covered his horns with peaceful laurel and stood on
a rampart made by a strong soldier. He prayed to the ancient gods in
the customary way and started his speech.

"There's one man here who will be king if you don't drive him out of the city. I won't name him, but I'll give you a hint: he has horns on his head! The augur foretold that if he enters Rome, he'll enslave the city. He could have burst through the open doors, but I stood in his way, even though I'm closer to him than anyone else.[16] Romans, keep this man out of your city. If he's worthy, cuff him in heavy chains; if not, end your fear by killing the tyrant!"

As a pine grove rustles when the bitter wind blows through, or like a river rushes when you hear it from far away, so the people murmured. But one cry rang out through the words of the people echoing in confusion: "Who is it?" And they looked at each other's foreheads to find the horns.

At once Cipus said to them, "The one you're looking for is ... *me!*" As the people protested, he took off the garland and showed them the two horns on his forehead. Everyone looked down and groaned. They didn't want to see the warning sign on the head of that deserving man. Who could believe it? They couldn't bear to let him go without honor, so they replaced the festive crown. Cipus, since you're forbidden from entering the city, the senators gave you a different honor: as much land in the countryside as you and your ox could plow in a day. The Romans sculpted the horns on the bronze gatepost, a memento of the amazing change for all time.

8.7 The 306 Fabii

Unlike the stories of individual self-sacrifice for Rome, the legend of the 306 Fabii relates the sacrifice of an entire family. As we saw in the myths about Brutus and Publicola (**8.1, 8.2**), such "family legends" easily moved into mainstream city history. Since the first native Roman historian was a Fabius (Pictor), we can speculate that the heroic 306 Fabii were among the first additions to the city's official record.

The number of Fabii and their total destruction is reminiscent of the 300 Spartans at Thermopylae. Although the narrative is different, scholars have suggested that historical patterning is at work here, much as it was in the story of Regillus (**8.5**). But the story is not merely imported into Rome. The Fabii connect to several important themes of this period, some of which are clearly historical. For example, their deaths are aetiological, explaining one of the "black days" (*dies atri*) in the Roman calendar; they foreshadow Rome's loss to the Gauls at the Allia on the same black day (**8.10.1–8.10.2a**); and they fit seamlessly into Rome's ongoing struggles with the Etruscan city of Veii (**8.9**). The story thus reinforces a cyclical view of history, in which past events tend to repeat themselves; a student of history needs only to recognize the pattern and learn from what happened earlier to avoid the same mistakes.

8.7.1   Livy, *From the Foundation* 2.48–2.50

Livy's dramatic and emotionally charged version of the Fabian legend focuses on elite contributions to Roman welfare. The Fabii, a prominent family that in Livy's day was in decline, are shown at their most glorious. Elsewhere in his history, Livy lists the many leading men produced by the Fabian family; here he recounts the house's fall in the early fifth century BCE.

Veii, a constant rather than serious threat, was annoying the Romans more than endangering them. They could never be neglected or stopped. So the Fabii approached the Senate. The consul spoke on behalf of his family: "Senators, as you know, the war with Veii requires a standing garrison, but not a large force. You can look after other wars; let us handle Veii. We'll ensure that Rome's sovereignty is safe there. We're offering to wage war at private expense – a family affair, so to speak. The state will lose no money or manpower in this arena."

Immense thanks were forthcoming [...] The news flowed through the whole city, and the Fabii were praised to the skies. A single family was bearing the city's burden [...]

The next day [...] 306 soldiers, all patricians, all from the same family, none of whom you'd disdain as a leader, outstanding on any occasion, came before the Senate. The strength of that single family threatened to take on the bothersome people of Veii. An entourage of relatives and companions followed them. Their minds roiled with no humdrum hopes or cares, but giant ones. Members of the public followed too, spurred by anxiety and gaping with admiration and goodwill. [... *The Fabii leave Rome and make camp near the Cremera river. They have a series of skirmishes with the people of Veii, in which the Romans do quite well.*]

At first the people of Veii took the Roman victories quite hard. But their bitterness led them to devise a plan for capturing their fierce enemy through trickery. They gloated as the daring of the Fabii increased with each success. So sometimes they drove cattle into Fabian territory to be taken, as if it were by accident. Local rustics abandoned their fields to be pillaged, and reserve troops who'd been sent in to guard the people retreated from fake fear more often than real concern. Soon the Fabii thought so little of their opponents that they couldn't believe their own Roman men would ever be defeated – at any place or time. Their confidence led them to rustle some cattle they'd seen far away from the Cremera, despite the armed enemy troops that were visible here and there across the intervening space.

When they flooded out on their unwise journey, they passed by ambushes set up on the very road around them. They split up into many directions to retrieve the cattle, which had scattered (as they often do when terrified). Suddenly, the men of Veii bolted out of their hiding-places: enemies were in front of them and on all sides. At first the noise surrounding them was terrifying; then spears began to fall from all directions [...] Eventually, the enemy proved superior. The Fabii were all killed and the garrison was stormed. It's basically agreed that 306 men died, but one Fabius was left behind because of his age – he was practically a boy. This child was the root of the Fabian family, which would often be Rome's greatest[17] aid in peace and war.

8.7.2   Dionysius of Halicarnassus, *Roman Antiquities* 9.22.2–9.22.5

Dionysius expresses skepticism about the miraculous survival of one child.

It's impossible that all of the Fabii who went to the fort had no wives and no children. Archaic laws forced men to marry when they came of age, and Romans raise all of their children. Surely the Fabian clan alone would not break this law [... *Dionysius elaborates on the reasons why the story is unlikely.*] Since I have examined the story and determined that it isn't true, here's the truth: I believe that only one child survived from the three brothers Caeso, Quintus, and Marcus – the ones who were consuls seven times in a row. This child was the son of Marcus, and he was said to be the sole descendant of the Fabian house.

8.7.3   Ovid, *Fasti* 2.213–2.242

Like Livy's account, Ovid's version focuses on the important role that the Fabii would play in Roman history. The story may in part honor Ovid's friend Paullus Fabius Maximus, a contemporary member of the Fabian family.

When the people of Veii realized that they couldn't conquer honestly, they planned treacherous ambush. There was an open space enclosed by hills and hilly forests that shelter predators. They left a few men and scattered cattle in the middle, while the main body of men lurked in the dense bushes. Imagine it: the Fabii fill the valley [...] Excellence falls to trickery. From all sides, enemies leap into the open plain and occupy it. What could a few brave men do against so many thousands? What was left for them in their need? A boar driven far from the woods by swift dogs scatters them with his thunderous snorts, but he's still doomed to die. Likewise, the Fabii don't die unavenged; they give and receive wounds in turn.

A single day sent all the Fabians to war; a single day destroyed those who'd been sent. But it's likely that the gods themselves made sure that the line of Hercules[18] would continue. A single boy, too young to bear arms, remained in the Fabian house – so that you, Maximus, could one day be born to save the state by delaying.[19]

8.7.4   Festus, "Cursed Gate"

Festus explains how 306 men could have so much success against an army.

The "CURSED" GATE [...] got this nickname because 306 Fabii passed through it with 5000 clients to fight the Etruscans. All of them were killed at the Cremera.

8.8   The Conflict of the Orders

Strife between patricians and plebeians broke out almost immediately after the final defeat of the Tarquins and lasted well into the historical period. The Conflict (or Struggle) of the Orders lasted over a century, from the early fifth century until at least the Licinian-Sextian Rogations of 367 BCE allowed plebeians to become consul.[20]

Patrician-plebeian conflicts in ancient sources are marked by stereotypical behaviors on both sides. The plebeians stubbornly refuse to do what the Senate wants (sometimes with justice), and either retreat ("secede") outside of the city or threaten to do so. Meanwhile, the patricians cling to their ancestral privileges and frequently seem tyrannical – that is, they treat the plebeians as inferior, despite having equal rights. The categories of "plebeian" and "patrician" are tricky to navigate and often seem interchangeable with "rich" and "poor." Certainly this division was not valid when our authors were writing; scholars debate whether it ever was.

8.8.1   Livy, *From the Foundation* 2.32

Menenius Agrippa is a relatively unknown figure whose major appearance is in this episode. His job is to reconcile the seceded plebeians to the Senate. The parable of the body relies on the metaphor of the body politic to justify the role of the Roman Senate.

Menenius Agrippa was eloquent, and the plebs liked him because he'd risen from plebeian status. They let him into their camp, and he is said to have told the following hoary, homely tale – and nothing else.

"Once upon a time, human body parts didn't agree as they do now. Instead, each organ did its own thing and spoke for itself. Every organ resented the stomach: it enjoyed all the fruits of their efforts and attention, but sat in torso, doing nothing and having a good time. So they agreed on a plan: the hand wouldn't carry food to the mouth, the mouth wouldn't open if it was offered anything, the teeth wouldn't chomp, and so on. Although they wanted to teach the stomach a lesson by starving it, each organ and indeed the whole body reached a dangerous state of emaciation from their anger. So it became clear that the stomach's duty wasn't useless, and it wasn't just fed: it gave all the organs a way to survive and thrive by consuming food and distributing strong blood evenly through the veins."

So Agrippa compared the internal strife of the body to the plebs' anger at the senators and changed their minds.

8.8.2   Livy, *From the Foundation* 2.35–2.41

Livy's account of Rome's hero-gone-bad Coriolanus is lengthy and was well adapted by Shakespeare. Coriolanus is a patrician of immense military talent whose pride hinders his ability to effectively govern his city – a complete contrast to Menenius Agrippa (8.8.1), whose parable immediately precedes this story. Coriolanus' revenge on his own city offers a lesson of how a nobleman shouldn't behave. The passage opens with Coriolanus' trial for unreasonable behavior against the plebeians.

When the day of the trial came, Coriolanus did not appear. The plebeians remained angry, and condemned him in his absence. He went into exile among the Volsci, bitterly vowing revenge against Rome.

When he arrived, the Volsci welcomed him warmly. They grew friendlier by the day as Coriolanus' anger with the Romans grew. His complaints and threats became more frequent. He was staying with Attius Tullius, at that time the most distinguished of the Volsci. Tullius had always been a threat to Rome; now, the old enemy and the new joined forces and plotted war against Rome [... *Rome is holding a large festival. Many Volscians attend, and Attius Tullius tells the consuls that they are planning an attack like the Rape of the Sabine Women (3.5). In reality, this information is false and the first step in Coriolanus' plan for revenge.*]

The consuls took their information to the Senate as questionable intel from a secure source. As usual, the source held greater authority than the facts, and the Senate chose to act from an abundance of caution.

They issued orders to remove the Volsci from the city. Heralds went to tell them to leave before nightfall. The visitors were terrified and ran to retrieve their belongings. But as they were leaving, they got mad. They were being kicked out like infectious criminals from the festivities, from the games, from essentially the meeting of gods and men!

As they were marching almost continuously, they encountered Tullius at the Ferentine river. He'd gone on ahead, and as the leading men passed him, grumbling and frustrated, he took each one aside [... *Tullius encourages the Volscians to go to war in revenge. He and Coriolanus have joint command of the Volscian army, and Coriolanus successfully defeats Rome in several battles, reconquering territory he'd gained for Rome a few years earlier. The Romans try to make him stop.*]

The men sent to win Coriolanus over to peace received a sharp reply. He offered two options: (a) give the Volsci their territory and talk diplomacy; or (b) enjoy the war. He said that he remembered that his fellow-citizens had hurt him and his hosts had helped him; his job was to prove that he was furious, not depressed, because of his exile. When the ambassadors tried again, they weren't allowed to enter the camp.

It's said that priests in their ritual clothing went to beg at the enemy camp, too, to no avail. But then the wives of Rome went *en masse* to Veturia, the mother of Coriolanus, and Volumnia, his wife. I haven't figured out whether these women were sent by the public or just spurred on by their female fear, but they definitely achieved their aim: both Veturia, who was very old, and Volumnia with their two sons, set out for the enemy camp. [*Their arrival is announced.*]

Coriolanus jumped up like a madman and seized his mother in a bear hug. Veturia turned away in anger and said, "Please. Before I am embraced, let me know: have I come to an enemy or a son? Am I a mother or a captive in your camp? Have I lived so long for this – that I see you an exile and then an enemy? How wretched my old age has become! Can you truly attack the land that raised and fed you? Although you arrived with hostile intent, surely your anger departed when you crossed the border! When Rome was in sight, didn't you think '*my house and home are within those walls, and so are my mother, wife, and children*'? I wish I hadn't given birth to you! [...]"

At last Coriolanus broke down. He hugged his family, sent them home, and moved the camp away from the city. History records that Coriolanus died, overcome by the Volscians' ill-will when their army had left Roman territory. But the account of his death varies. Fabius, by far the oldest authority, records that Coriolanus lived to advanced age; the aged Coriolanus would often say that exile was much more painful to an old man.

---------- 8.8.3 Livy, *From the Foundation* 3.26 and 3.29 ----------

The Roman nobleman Cincinnatus exemplified devotion to the Republic. He was forced out of the city when his son Kaeso was fined and exiled for unruly behavior. The fine was so steep that Cincinnatus was left penniless. But Cincinnatus' services were too valuable to be lost, and Rome recalled him as dictator for external wars and internal strife. Many Romans served as dictator in this period; Cincinnatus is famous not for his conduct in office, but for preferring humble life on his farm to the supreme military command of the Roman army.

Anyone who thinks money is everything – or that honor and virtue are nothing without wealth – has to hear this. The sole hope of the Roman empire, Lucius Quinctius [Cincinnatus], was at that time farming four acres across the Tiber – the place is now called the Quinctian Meadows, opposite the docks. His farm had all his attention; whether he was plowing or digging a ditch isn't clear, but everyone agrees that he was working.[21] The senatorial representatives met him there and they exchanged greetings. Then the representatives asked him to put on his toga in order to hear the Senate's commands – "and may they benefit you as well as Rome!"

Cincinnatus was shocked, and asked, "Is everything okay?" He told his wife Racilia to get his toga out of their cottage right away. Meanwhile, he washed off his sweat and dirt. When he stepped forward in formal attire, the legates congratulated him and addressed him as "dictator" [... *Cincinnatus returns to Rome, where he is greeted warmly by the patricians and sullenly by the plebeians. He quickly defeats the enemy, rebukes the consuls, and gets revenge for his son's exile.*] Although he'd been given a six-month term, Cincinnatus resigned as dictator on his sixteenth day.

---------- 8.8.4 Dionysius of Halicarnassus, ----------
Roman Antiquities 8.57.1–8.59.1

*Dionysius details the gory death of Coriolanus. The passage begins soon after he's agreed to leave Rome's territory (**8.8.2**). Coriolanus disbands his army and distributes plunder to his men.*

The army that had shared his struggles came home loaded with gold. They were quite happy to end the war. They liked Coriolanus and thought he deserved forgiveness [...] But the young men who'd remained in the cities were jealous of the veterans' rewards and felt deprived of seeing Rome's self-esteem crushed. So they turned against Coriolanus bitterly [...] Tullus Attius[22] in particular spurred on their anger. He'd collected a large following in every city, and he'd been obviously jealous of Coriolanus for a long time. He'd decided to kill him [...]

Tullus prepared his followers to take the lead in a criminal act. They came to the Forum. From the *rostra,* Tullus accused Coriolanus at great length and urged the people to take away all his authority if he didn't give it up willingly. Coriolanus then rose to make his defense. A huge racket came from Tullus' crowd of hecklers and drowned out his words. Then Tullus' men shouted, "Hit him! Strike!" The boldest circled around and stoned him to death.

--------- 8.8.5   Dionysius of Halicarnassus, ---------
Roman Antiquities 10.14.1–10.15.2

During the Conflict of the Orders, internal strife occasionally threatened Roman security. Dionysius recounts the capture of the Capitol by Sabine troops (compare **7.4**, **8.4**, **8.10**). *After several days, the Romans are rescued by allies from the Latin city of Tusculum.*

A Sabine man named Appius Herdonius decided to destroy Rome's power. He was a rich nobleman who planned either to establish a tyranny with himself as the leader or to give power to the Sabine nation – or maybe just to become notorious. He shared his plan with many of his friends and explained how he would capture the city. Since the idea seemed good to them, he gathered his bravest slaves and dependents. Soon he had a band of about 4000 men, supplied with weapons, food, and other wartime necessities. They boarded skiffs and sailed down the Tiber to Rome [...] It was the middle of the night, and the whole city was asleep. With the quiet darkness to help, Herdonius quickly helped his men off the boats and through an unlocked gate. (One of the holy gates near the Capitol, which locals call the Porta Carmentalis, is always open, thanks to an oracle.) He and his troops climbed up the Capitoline and captured the citadel [...]

His plan, after he captured the most strategic locations, was to announce to exiles and slaves that they'd be welcomed as free men. He also intended to offer money to the poor, and to share the plunder with other disaffected citizens who were happy to see a change in government due to their jealousy or hatred of the leading men [... *Dionysius explains that Herdonius' calculations were based on the idea that the split between patricians and plebeians was irreconcilable.*] But as it turned out, his plan completely missed the mark. Slaves didn't desert to him; exiles didn't come, either; men who had no public voice or private property didn't sell out the public for their own gain. His allies didn't have enough time to prepare for war, because it was all over in three or four days. But the Romans were terrified into utter chaos.

8.9   Camillus and Veii

The decade-long war with Veii is explicitly modeled on Troy (Livy 5.4), with a major difference: although descended from the besieged Trojans, the Romans attack Veii. Veii's defeat in 396 BCE established Rome as a major power in Italy, although Romans continued to fight significant wars with their neighbors. But much as the Greek heroes suffered on their way home from Troy, the Romans suffer from their defeat of Veii: they are attacked by the Gauls (**8.10**).

The major hero of both the capture of Veii and the Gallic sack, Camillus, has been the subject of much study. Hailed as the second founder of the city (**8.10.4**), he's in many ways a more virtuous Romulus: a good soldier and statesman, he was exiled from Rome only to return for its salvation. Because Camillus' adventures explicitly refer back to Rome's two foundation legends of Aeneas and Romulus (**chapters 2** and **3**), he represents one possible end to Rome's legendary history.

Camillus' story spans all of Livy's fifth book and part of the sixth, and was a common reference point for Cicero; Camillus himself was one of the few[23] early Romans to receive a Plutarchian biography. As a result, we know more about Camillus than about many other early Roman figures. But Camillus is, in many ways, a flat character; he can be counted on to do the right thing. His virtuous depiction is problematized by the frescoes of the François Tomb (**4.6.1**), which *may* depict him in a less favorable light – but no negative qualities are on display in the written source material. His relatively colorless personality has led many scholars to believe that Camillus is entirely fictional.

───────────────   8.9.1   Livy, *From the Foundation* 5.15   ───────────────

Rome had been fighting Veii off and on for years before the siege. As nearby cities begin to fall to Roman power, omens trouble the Roman people: in particular, the Alban lake's water level rises. The capture of the seer and the omen that predicts the city's fall are both paralleled in the Troy narrative,[24] as well as the iconography of Cacu (4.6.2, 4.6.3).

An old Veientine man was sent by fate as an interpreter. While the Roman and Etruscan soldiers jeered in their guardposts, he chanted like a prophet: "Until the water is drained from the Alban lake, Rome will never conquer Veii." At first his words were scorned as random, but then people started repeating them [...] When a religiously-inclined Roman soldier heard that the old man was a prophet, he went to talk to him, as if he wanted to ask about expiating a private omen.[25] Since they were both far away from their comrades and unarmed, the old man wasn't afraid. But the young Roman was strong; he grabbed the weak old man in sight of everyone and brought him over to his own camp. The Etruscans were in an uproar.

Meanwhile, the old man was brought to the commander, then sent to the Senate in Rome [... *He said*] that when the Alban lake flooded, the Romans would defeat Veii if they drained it correctly. But before that, Veii's gods would not desert its walls. Then he explained the ritual for draining the lake.

8.9.2   Livy, *From the Foundation* 5.19–5.22

Between internal dissent and some military missteps, Rome is less sure of its ability to defeat Veii. Meanwhile, word comes that other Etruscan cities are rallying to help Veii, despite wars with the Gauls. At this point, the Romans appoint a dictator to ensure that they win.

Once the Latin festival and the games had been re-celebrated and the water from the Alban lake drawn off onto the fields, fate came for Veii. And so they named a leader who'd been divinely chosen to destroy that city and save Rome: Marcus Furius Camillus [...] They began a tunnel into the enemy's citadel, which was exceptionally long, hard work. To make sure that the labor wasn't interrupted and that same men wouldn't get burned out by constant toil underground, he divided the workers into six units and assigned each unit to work a six-hour shift. So they worked without stopping to create a passage to Veii's citadel [... *Soon it's ready.*]

Camillus attacked the city from all sides, so that the Veientines wouldn't notice the looming danger from the tunnel. The people of Veii had no idea that they had been betrayed by both local prophets and foreign oracles, or that their protecting gods had been called to share in the spoils and lured from their city to new temples in Rome; they had no idea that this was their last day, much less that their walls had been breached by a tunnel and that soon their stronghold would be full of enemy soldiers. No, they ran to the walls, each man armed and prepared to defend himself, wondering why, after so many days sitting quietly in the camp, the Romans now decided to attack so suddenly and forcefully.

At this point, a myth is added. While the king of Veii was sacrificing, the Roman soldiers heard a voice echo in the tunnel. It was a prophet telling him that whoever cut the entrails from the victim would win the war. The Romans quickly jumped out, snatched the entrails, and brought them to Camillus.[26] In such old matters, I think it's enough to accept the parts that seem like the truth as true; this story is more appropriate for dramatic performance than belief. But it's not worth the effort to confirm or refute it. [*Veii falls.*]

Once the personal property had been removed from Veii, the Romans turned to the gods' votives and statues. These were carried off respectfully, not as plunder. Young men were selected from the body of soldiers to carry Queen Juno to Rome. They washed their bodies squeaky clean and dressed in white, then entered Juno's temple reverently. They stretched out their hands in religious devotion, since in Etruria only priests from certain families are permitted to touch Juno. Then one of them, either inspired by the gods or as a stupid joke, said, "Juno, do you want to go to Rome?" The rest shouted that the goddess did.

A myth is added to the story at this point. It says that the goddess' voice was also heard saying that she did want to go. Certainly they moved the statue[27] with little effort using rollers; she was light and easy to move.

8.9.3   Plutarch, *Life of Camillus* 10–11

The successful campaign against Veii demonstrates Camillus' military skill, but he was also capable of mercy. The story of the treacherous Schoolmaster of Falerii shows Camillus' good faith: he was unwilling to take advantage of his enemies, even when presented with the ideal opportunity. The Etruscan city Falerii was allied to Veii; Rome besieged it, too.

The people of Falerii had so much faith in the strength of their walls on all sides that the siege didn't concern them very much. Except for the guards on the walls themselves, the citizens wandered around the city in civilian gear and the children even went to school. Their teacher took them outside of the city for nature walks and exercise [...] But he plotted to betray the city to the Romans using the children. Every day he took them outside, at first staying close to the walls and bringing them back in when they'd finished their exercise. Then he gradually led them further and further, encouraging them to feel entirely fearless. Finally, he reached the Roman sentries with his charges, handed them over, and demanded to see Camillus.

When he entered Camillus' tent, the teacher stood in the middle and explained his thinking. Although he was a teacher, he preferred to gain Camillus' goodwill than to do the right thing. So he was delivering the

city to Camillus by delivering its children. The plan seemed atrocious to
Camillus as he listened. He announced to everyone there, "War's hell:
terribly unjust and violent. But even in war there are ground rules, and
good men follow them. Winning isn't worth it if we have to accept
favors from evil men who spurn the gods. A real general relies on his
soldiers' skill, not others' crimes." Then he ordered his aides to tear off
the teacher's cloak,[28] bind the man's hands behind him, and give the
children sticks and whips so that they could punish their teacher as
they chased him back to the city.

The Faliscans[29] had just discovered the teacher's treachery. Of course,
the entire city was filled with grief over the catastrophe. Men and
women rushed to the walls and the gates without thinking. There they
saw the children driving back the teacher, who was naked, bound, and
being beaten. They called Camillus their savior, their father, and their
god.

8.10 The Gallic Sack

Gauls were always frightening to the Romans. According to ancient authors,
the Gallic sack (c. 390 BCE) was Rome's first major catastrophe. It is one of
the few conflicts that took place on Roman soil, and ancient authors attribute
Rome's lack of early records and chaotic street plan (very different from later
cities' grids) to the destruction and quick reconstruction of the city (**8.10.3a;**
Plutarch, *Numa* 9). As a major siege narrative, the Gallic sack shares several
similarities with the legends of the Sabine attack on Rome (**3.5**) and provided
a framework for the historical war with Hannibal (218–201 BCE).

Although this conflict was not long, its history is somewhat complicated.
The Gauls, who lived in what is now northern Italy, had been attacking the
cities of Etruria periodically for several years (**8.9.2 introduction, 8.10.1a–
8.10.1c**). At first, this distracted Etruscans from war with Rome, and was con-
ceivably one of the reasons for Rome's success against Veii (**8.9.2**).

—————————   8.10.1 War breaks out   —————————

When the Gauls attacked Clusium, one of Rome's allies, Rome had to respond.
After some Roman ambassadors took part in a skirmish, the Gauls attacked.
The ill-fated battle of the Allia broke the Roman army, which retreated to the
recently conquered city of Veii.

a. Livy, *From the Foundation* 5.36–5.37 *Livy explains how the war
began. The Gauls are recurring bogeymen of book 5, and have been consistently
harassing cities in Etruria. Romans send assistance to their ally Clusium.*

It was a moderate embassy, or would have been if the envoys had been reasonable. But they acted more like Gauls than Romans [... *The Gauls demand some Clusine territory in exchange for leaving; the Romans scoff.*] The Romans asked by what law the Gauls were claiming land from its owners and threatening them, and furthermore what the Gauls wanted in Etruria. The Gauls replied that their law was war, and that brave men owned everything. Tempers flared on both sides, and they all seized their weapons. A scuffle broke out. Even the ambassadors took up arms, in contravention of international law.

From that point on, Rome's fate was sealed. It couldn't be kept secret that three of Rome's noblest and bravest young men were fighting under the Etruscan banner. Their military skill distinguished them from the natives. Also, Quintus Fabius left the line to attack a Gallic lieutenant who was making a savage rush on the Etruscan standards. The Roman threw his spear into the Gaul's side and killed him. While he was stripping his enemy, the Gauls recognized him, and the whisper ran through the entire line: *The Roman ambassador killed him.* From that point forward, the Gauls stopped being angry at the people of Clusium. They retreated, yelling threats at the Romans. [... *The Gauls send ambassadors to Rome demanding reparations; the Romans refuse.*]

In the meantime, the Gauls discovered that the Romans had *honored* these men who had violated international law, and had moreover rejected the embassy. Burning with anger – it's an ethnic trait – they quickly took up the standards and marched to war. As cities perceived them swiftly passing by, they panicked and rushed to arm themselves; farmers fled their fields. But wherever they went, the Gauls shouted that they were headed to Rome. Their cavalry and foot, in loose battle formation, spread out over a huge amount of space. But although the report and messengers from Clusium and then other cities had arrived first, the Gauls were so quick that most Romans were terrified. The army was gathered quickly and barely made it 11 miles out of Rome.

b. Plutarch, *Life of Camillus* 15 *Plutarch romanticizes the outbreak of the war. In doing so, he connects the Gallic conflict with several other myths: the "Sacred Spring," in which a culture's youth are forced to leave their homeland in search of prosperity (6.5); the early history of the Tarquins (5.4.1); and the siege of Rome by the Sabines (3.5, 7.4). This collapse of the two threats to the Capitol – under Romulus and under Camillus – reinforces the idea that Camillus was Rome's "new founder."*

The Gauls are a subgroup of the Celts who are believed to have left their homeland when their population grew. Since their homeland couldn't feed them, they were seeking a new place to settle. There were thousands of them – for the most part young men, but also many women and children [... *They scattered to many lands, but decided to seek out the place that produced wine.*] The man who introduced them to wine and encouraged them to Italy in particular was Arruns the Etruscan, an unfortunate nobleman but not evil. He was the guardian of a fantastically rich and attractive orphan named Lucumo. Lucumo had lived with Arruns since childhood; when he grew up, he didn't leave, but pretended to enjoy Arruns' company. In reality, he was having an affair with Arruns' wife, and for a long time they kept it a secret. But finally, their emotions overcame them. They could no longer resist their desires or hide their passion. So Lucumo tried to steal the woman openly. Arruns sued him, but lost due to Lucumo's wealth and many friends. He left his city. When he heard about the Gallic emigration, he joined them and led their army to Italy.

c. Plutarch, *Life of Camillus* 18   *Plutarch blames the war on Rome's non-elite citizens, echoing a common ancient opinion: the people can't be trusted to know what's good for them.*

The Senate entrusted the matter to the people. All of the priests agreed that the Fabii should be condemned, but the people scorned the gods and flouted their priests. Rather than punish Fabius, he and his brothers were made military tribunes.[30] When the Gauls learned about what had happened, they were outraged. They marched with all haste in military formation. Their numbers, elaborate armor, power, and emotion struck everyone they met with fear. The locals expected that the Gauls would destroy their land right away and cities next. But no: the Gauls didn't touch them or take anything from the fields. As they passed by the cities, they shouted that they were marching to Rome, and their war was with Rome alone; the other cities were their friends.

d. Dio (Zonaras), *Roman History* 2.153–2.154   *This account of the outbreak of the Gallic war picks up on the theme of the heavenly voice (4.4.4).*

The gods are said to have warned the Romans of the Gauls' approach. Marcus Caedicius was walking at night when he heard a voice say, "The Gauls are coming!" He relayed the message to the Senate and people, but they laughed and jeered at the story – until the Gauls made it known that they were nearby. Then the armies marched out in all haste but with no order. They were shamefully defeated. Many men were killed in battle; many were taken and killed as they ran away; and a really large number were shoved into the Tiber and drowned. The rest escaped, some to Rome and others elsewhere.

8.10.2 The siege

With their army in Veii, the Romans were nearly defenseless. They retreated to their citadel on the Capitoline Hill, and allowed the Gauls to take over the rest of the city. Some of Rome's most venerable citizens died heroically rather than retreat (**8.10.2a**). The Gauls easily sacked and burned the abandoned city and set up a camp to besiege the citadel.

a. Livy, *From the Foundation* 5.39–5.41 *This passage continues* **8.10.1a**. *The battle at the Allia results in a resounding Gallic victory. Most soldiers retreat to the nearby city of Veii. The Gauls are shocked, but soon march on Rome, which is largely undefended.*

But the citizens who were in Rome that night and the next day proved that they were completely different from those who had fled so shamefully at the Allia. The tiny garrison that had been left at Rome had no hope of being able to defend the city. So they decided that the young men of military age, their wives and children, and the healthiest senators would retreat to the citadel on the Capitol with their weapons and provisions. Entrenched there, they could defend their gods, citizens, and Rome's reputation. The *flamen* and Vestals carried the city's sacred objects away from the anticipated killing and burning; the rites would not be abandoned while anyone was alive to perform them. As long as the citadel and Capitol where the gods lived, the Senate in charge of public affairs, and the young troops survived the coming destruction of the city, it would be easy to dismiss the loss of the old men left in the city. They were close to death already [...]

Many women followed their families to the citadel. No one asked them to come, but no one forbade them; it was too cruel, even if it was useful to the fighters to have fewer civilians. A crowd of mostly plebeians streamed out of the city and made a beeline for the Janiculum. A small hill like the Capitol couldn't hold them all, and there wasn't enough food. From the Janiculum, some slipped off to the country, others to nearby cities. They had no leader or plan. It was every man for himself, since no one had hope for the city.

Meanwhile, the *Flamen Quirinalis* and the Vestal Virgins were considering which of their sacred objects they had to bring with them and which could be left behind. They couldn't take them all, even though they pushed aside all concern for their private property. They also weren't sure where the most secure hiding place would be. Finally they decided to bury the items in jars in a shrine near the flamen's house – the place where spitting is now a religious offense. They divided the rest amongst themselves and took the road which passes the Pons Sublicius towards the Janiculum. They were on the slope when Lucius

Albinius,[31] a plebeian, saw them. He was driving a wagon with his wife and children among the crowd of civilians who were leaving the city. He thought that the divide between human and divine affairs ought to be maintained: it was awful that the city's priests and sacred objects were on foot while he and his family were on wheels. So he told his wife and children to get down, set the Vestals and their relics on the wagon, and drove off to Caere by the route they chose.

Meanwhile, everything that could be done to guard the citadel in such circumstances was complete. A group of old men went home to face the arriving enemy; their minds were set on death. Those who had held a curule magistracy wished to die in the trappings of their former fortunes, honors, and virtues. They wore their finest clothing, suitable for triumphal chariots, and sat on ivory chairs in the middle of their doorways [...]

The Gauls had enjoyed a peaceful night and were now refreshed. They hadn't fought hard in battle, and they weren't planning to take the city by brute force. So the next day they sauntered in without anger [...] They gaped at the patricians as if they were sacred images until one of them touched Marcus Papirius' beard – a long beard, as was typical in those days. Papirius lifted his ivory scepter and clocked the Gaul on the head. This angered them all and was the beginning of the mass murder. Papirius died first; then all the others were slaughtered in their seats. After the leading men were killed, they moved to the masses; finally, the Gauls stripped the valuables from the houses and set fire to all the buildings.

b. Strabo, *Geography* 5.2.3 *Strabo protests that Rome has forgotten how her allies helped her during the Gallic sack.*

When the Gauls captured Rome, the Caeretans fell upon them in the Sabine country and made them retreat, and they took back the Romans' ransom from the unhappy Gauls. And in addition to this, they saved the Romans who fled to them, as well as the eternal flame and priestesses of Vesta. Now the Romans, thanks to some worthless leaders they had at the time, don't remember much about the Caeretans' services to the city.

c. Plutarch, *Life of Camillus* 22 (Aristotle *FGrHist* 840 F23) *Plutarch criticizes some of the earliest information on the Gallic sack. Aristotle's discussion of Rome is otherwise lost; see **8.10.2a** for a possible explanation of his evidence.*

Aristotle the philosopher had clearly heard an accurate report of the sack of the city by the Celts. He says the savior was Lucius. But Camillus' name was Marcus, not Lucius.

8.10.3 War ends

After a lengthy siege, the Romans managed to send out a messenger to the army in Veii. This messenger asked Camillus, in exile after being falsely charged with fiscal malfeasance, to lead the army to Rome's assistance. Camillus eventually agreed; meanwhile, the Gauls noticed the messenger returning to Rome and attacked with full force. The sacred geese of Juno alerted the Romans to their approach, and the attack was stopped by the heroic actions of Manlius Capitolinus.

Yet the siege continued. Finally, the Romans decided to pay the Gauls to leave. The Gauls were weighing out the gold when Camillus arrived with the Roman army, attacked, and defeated them.

a. Diodorus Siculus, *Library of History* **14.116.5–14.116.9**
Diodorus is one of the earliest sources to survive with a nearly complete narrative. Although most of his information is similar to that which we receive in later authors, some of the individual quirks may look back to an earlier version of events. In this excerpt, the Romans have been defeated by the Gauls at the Allia and are now besieged on the Capitol.

The Celts saw fresh footsteps from the man who had climbed up the back side of the Capitol. They made a plan to ascend the same cliff at night. It was the middle of the night; the guards were negligent because the place was so secure. Some of the Celts started up the cliff. Although they escaped the guards' notice, Hera's sacred geese[32] (who lived on the Capitol) saw the men climbing and started to honk. The guards rushed over, and the Celts were too terrified to move. One notable man, Marcus Mallius,[33] ran to help and cut off one of the Celts' hands with his sword. Then he struck the Celt's chest with his shield and hurled him off the rock. The second climber died in the same way. The others quickly tried to run – but since they were on a sheer cliff, all fell to their deaths. That's why, when the Romans sent ambassadors to resolve the conflict, the Celts were persuaded to take 1000 pounds of gold in exchange for leaving Rome and its territory. The Romans, since their houses were rubble and many citizens had died, gave the survivors permission to rebuild wherever they wanted [...] Since each man built his home in the place he chose, the city's streets turned out narrow and winding. Even later on, as the city grew larger, they couldn't make the streets straight [...]

b. Livy, *From the Foundation* **5.46–5.47**   *Romans believed that respect for the gods was crucial to their success in war. This belief appears several times in the sack narrative. During the siege, one Fabius shows his piety*

*by walking through the massed Gauls to complete a required ritual. Mean-
while, the Gauls prepare to attack, but are stopped by a timely warning
from Juno.*

At Rome, meanwhile, the siege continued slowly. Both sides were quiet;
the Gauls were mainly interested in keeping the Romans penned in.
Suddenly one of the Roman soldiers gained the admiration of both his
fellow-citizens and the Gauls. The Fabii had a family ritual that had to
be carried out on the Quirinal Hill. To carry it out, Gaius Fabius Dorsuo
put on the formal Gabine toga[34] and descended from the Capitol with
his sacred objects in his hands. He walked calmly and quietly through
the enemy ranks and reached the Quirinal, where he dutifully carried
out his rites; then he came back to Rome at a steady pace, just as calmly.
[*The Senate agrees to recall Camillus and makes him dictator. When a messenger is sent out of the city, the Gauls notice; see* **8.10.3a**.]

On a dimly-lit night the Gauls sent one unarmed man to test the
route. Then the rest followed, passing weapons along steep parts,
pulling or supporting their comrades in turn, and tugging each other
along as the place required. They reached the hilltop so silently that
the guards didn't notice them, and even the dogs, who usually bark at
night, didn't wake up.

But Juno's sacred geese noticed. The Romans hadn't eaten them, even
though they desperately lacked food. This turned out to be very lucky,
because their honking and flapping woke up Marcus Manlius, who had
been consul three times and was an outstanding warrior. He grabbed his
weapons and called his fellow-soldiers to arms. While the others hesitated, he whacked a Gaul who'd reached the summit with his shield and
threw him off the cliff. This Gaul fell backwards on the Gauls behind
him, knocking some down. Manlius killed the others, who were hang-
ing onto the rocks with their bare hands, terrified, their weapons lost.

Now the Romans rallied and threw spears and rocks to push back the
enemy. The entire venture was lost and the soldiers fell headlong to the
base of the Capitol.

c. Plutarch, *Life of Camillus* **28**   *Plutarch and Livy offer nearly identical
accounts of the Gallic sack in many places. The final defeat of the Gauls is one of
them. Both authors attribute the Romans' victory to illness in the Gallic camps,
to Camillus, and to the* hubris *– pride that offends the gods – of the Gallic leader
Brennus.*

At this point, it looked grim for the Gauls. They needed supplies, but
they were too afraid of Camillus to forage. Disease crept in from the
number of dead bodies, since they were camped in Rome's ruins. The

deep piles of ash, which were easily vaporized in the dry and putrid air thanks to the winds and burning pyres, made it hard to breathe and harmed their health. The change in climate exacerbated their illness. They'd left a cool and shady land with easy escape from Mother Nature, and come to lowlands whose climate varied strangely as fall approached. They'd also sat at ease for a long time before the Capitoline; at this point, the siege had lasted seven months. So the effects of disease in the camp were immense; they couldn't even bury the dead, because too many were dying.

But it wasn't any better for the besieged Romans. They were *hungry* and, with no idea of how Camillus was faring, disheartened. No one could check in with him because the Gauls kept the city under close watch. Since both sides were in desperate straits, they proposed a compromise. At first the scouts negotiated; then the leading men decided that Sulpicius, a Roman military tribune, should meet with Brennus [the chieftain of the Gauls]. They came to the following terms: the Romans would pay 1000 pounds of gold, and the Gauls would leave immediately.

They swore an oath to abide by these terms, and the Romans brought out the gold. But the Gauls cheated, first secretly snatching coins and then openly weighing down one side of the scale. The Romans were furious. But Brennus, laughing triumphantly, tore off his sword and scabbard, and tossed them on the balance. When Sulpicius found out, he asked, "What was that for?"

Brennus replied, "Salt in your wounds[35] – what else?" This reply immediately became proverbial. But the Romans were angrier. Some thought they should immediately take the gold away and remain under siege. Others encouraged them to put up with this small injustice. It wasn't shameful to give *more*; it was shameful that they were paying the Gauls to leave in the first place! But it had to be done.

8.10.4 Aftermath

After the total destruction of the Gallic army, Camillus returned to Rome in triumph.

a. Diodorus Siculus, *Library of History* 14.117.5–14.117.6 *This early account already betrays inconsistencies about Camillus: was he an ideal hero or did he push the boundaries of what Romans would accept?*

As the Gauls were leaving Rome, they attacked Rome's ally Veascum. Camillus attacked them, killed most, and seized their possessions. There he found the gold that the Gauls had taken from Rome and almost everything that had been looted from the defeated city. Although he accomplished these great deeds, the tribunes held their grudge and he didn't triumph. But some say that Camillus celebrated a triumph over the Etruscans. He drove a chariot with four white horses, and for this reason he received a hefty fine from the people two years later.

b. Livy, *From the Foundation* 49 *Livy's passage picks up immediately after Brennus' cheating (**8.10.3c**) and explains how Camillus saves the city. Camillus' argument is legally true, but might raise your eyebrows: is he acting in good faith from a modern perspective? Certainly the Romans thought he was a hero, and he celebrates a grand triumph. There are significant parallels in Livy's description of Camillus' triumph and the final years of Julius Caesar.*

Neither divine nor human effort would allow the Romans to live with the shame of having purchased their freedom. The dictator arrived before the unspeakable transaction was complete, and gave orders to take the gold away. He also told the Gauls to get out. When they resisted, citing the treaty, Camillus said that there was no "treaty": he was the dictator, and this agreement had been made without orders by lower-ranking magistrates. He ended by warning the Gauls to prepare for battle [...]

The Gauls were terrified by this new development. They snatched their weapons and made a rush at the Romans with anger but no plan. Now the tables were turned: divine aid and human skill were helping Rome. So in the first rush, the Gauls were scattered as quickly and completely as they'd defeated the Romans at the Allia. In another battle at the eighth milestone on the road to Gabii, where they'd regrouped, the victory was finalized. Camillus still led the army. His destruction of the Gauls was complete: their camp was taken and not even a messenger was left alive. The dictator had won back his country from the enemy. He returned in triumph to the city; along with the soldiers' jokes that are typically tossed around, they called him "Romulus," "father of the country," and "second founder of the city"[36] – and the praise rang true.

Conclusion

The stories of the early Republic offer a far wider cast of characters than the stories of the kings. As Rome adjusted to a new form of government, its leading families gained an enduring legacy. Indeed, one of the major arguments in favor of the historical accuracy of some early Republican legends is that the family later died out (and so had no need to invent stories to promote its ancestors). But we also know that Romans such as Cicero could and did mock these family legends as self-serving fictions. Similarly, authors like Livy and Dionysius openly question some of the information that they relate. The challenge for any historian of the early Republic is determining a method that can be used on all of these stories and applying it consistently, regardless of apparent truth or fiction.

The many tales in this chapter share a few basic themes that continue to resonate in later Roman history. We can postulate that these themes represent the most important lessons ancient authors wanted their readers to learn from these tales. The first, and arguably most important, theme is the concept of putting the city before oneself. It is difficult to imagine a Roman hero who does not share this trait; we see it in the stories of Brutus, Scaevola, Cocles, Publicola, Cincinnatus, Camillus, the Fabii, and many others. This concept of "self-sacrifice" does not need to extend to actual death; the main lesson is that the community's interests ought to hold more weight than personal interest. In a fiercely competitive culture, as ancient Rome certainly was, this reminder to put Rome first acted as security against the rise of a new dynasty of kings, and was successful for centuries.

Another major theme is military valor. Rome was constantly at war, often on several fronts at once. With so many conflicts, survival depended on fighting fiercely and running calculated risks to win your battle. We see examples of this quality in the stories of war with the Tarquins, as well as Camillus' daring attack on the Gauls. We also see Roman bravery in tales of military failure, such as the 306 Fabii. The reactions of the crowd to the deeds of the protagonists offer us a guide to how readers are supposed to feel (see Feldherr 1998): proud, exhilarated, and determined to follow in the footsteps of these great men.

Closely connected to the theme of valor is that of clemency towards the defeated enemy. Although Romans certainly identified themselves as a martial state, they did not see themselves as cruel. Offering mercy to the defeated gained goodwill; offering protection to defenseless neighbors (in exchange for land or soldiers) gained an empire. The good treatment (in Roman eyes) of defeated or potentially defeated communities continued to be the cornerstone of Roman military policy for the rest of its existence, and forms the basis of what we term "Roman imperialism." This continuity suggests that Rome's myths continued to be effective teaching tools for generations of future generals, governors, and even emperors.

Notes

1. See Cornell 1995, 218–239 for historical comparanda in Italy; pp. 218–276 are largely devoted to the establishment of the Republican system.
2. Compare Livy's description of the new foundation of Rome at **2.1** with its new era in **6.1**.
3. That is, when his year in office was finished.
4. The lictors carry the *fasces* as a symbol of the consulship (previously the symbol of the kings): two axes wrapped in a bundle of sticks.

5. See **note 4**.
6. Or "popular," in the sense of having the people's interests at heart.
7. Publicola is often translated as "friend of the people," but perhaps "guardian of the public interest" would be more accurate.
8. Images are available at http://lila.sns.it/mnamon/index.php?page=Esempi&id=17 &lang=en
9. That is, Valerius.
10. That is, Mars.
11. Compare Porsenna's similar words in **7.7.1**.
12. See **5.6.2a** and **5.6.2c**.
13. See **8.10**.
14. The Temple of Castor (and Pollux) survives in the Roman Forum today. It is most recognizable by its three columns: http://sights.seindal.dk/img/orig/8317.jpg
15. The god's name is uncertain; the *di Manes* were underworld spirits.
16. Compare Vertumnus in **6.7.2**.
17. Livy here refers to Fabius Maximus Cunctator, who was Rome's general against Hannibal for many years in the third century. "Maximus" means "greatest"; Livy's pun on the name is typical of ancient aetiology.
18. The Fabian family traced their family back to Hercules.
19. See **note 17**; Ovid adds a pun on Fabius' *cognomen* Cunctator, "the delayer," as well.
20. The period of the Conflict of the Orders is debated, a topic that cannot be detailed here; see *CAH*[2] 7.336–346; Feig Vishnia 1996; Lintott 1999.
21. A sign of poverty; well-off Romans had slaves for hard labor.
22. Attius Tullius in **8.8.2**.
23. The others are Romulus, Numa, Publicola, and Coriolanus.
24. By Helenus and the Palladium: Apollodorus' *Library* 5.9–10.
25. Roman religion recognized two types of divinely-sent sign: public (which related to state matters) and private (which did not). Ambiguous signs could be reported to the Senate for consideration.
26. Compare the cow in **5.5.2**.
27. See **4.9** for images from Veii's sanctuaries.
28. A mark of shame and loss of citizenship.
29. People of Falerii.
30. For a brief period in Rome's early history, consuls were not in charge of the state. Instead, the Romans elected four to six "military tribunes" with similar powers. Modern scholars have often understood the military tribunate as evidence for the gradual development of the Roman Republican system. If so, the appearance of this office may suggest the age of this story: this type of tribune disappeared in the fourth century BCE. See **chapter introduction**.
31. Possibly the Lucius of **8.10.2c**.
32. Compare the failure of Tarpeia's plan in **7.4**.
33. This is the Manlius Capitolinus of later sources. He is later accused of trying to become king and executed; see Livy 6.1–20.
34. The Gabine toga (or more accurately, "Gabine cincture") was a specific way of wearing a toga. Compared to normal Roman toga habits, the Gabine toga left the arms and legs free to move.
35. Plutarch is translating Livy's famous phrase *vae victis*! In Latin, the phrase literally means "woe to the conquered."

36. Livy's description of this triumph, more than Plutarch's parallel version, suggests what we know of Julius Caesar's triumph in 46 BCE. The idea of being a "new Romulus" is older than Caesar, but how much older is debatable.

References

Cornell, Timothy J. 1995. *The Beginnings of Rome: Italy and Rome from the Bronze Age to the Punic Wars (c. 1000–264 B.C.).* London: Routledge.

Feig Vishnia, Rachel. 1996. *State, Society and Popular Leaders in Mid-Republican Rome 241–167 BC.* London: Routledge.

Feldherr, Andrew. 1998. *Spectacle and Society in Livy's History.* Berkeley, CA: University of California Press. http://ark.cdlib.org/ark:/13030/ft1g500491/ (accessed November 23, 2016).

Holloway, R. Ross. 1994. *The Archaeology of Early Rome and Latium.* London: Routledge.

Lintott, Andrew. 1999. *The Constitution of the Roman Republic.* Oxford: Oxford University Press.

Richardson, James H. 2012. *The Fabii and the Gauls.* Stuttgart: Franz Steiner Verlag.

Roller, Matthew. 2004. "Exemplarity in Roman Culture: The Cases of Horatius Cocles and Cloelia." *Classical Philology* 99: 1–56. http://www.jstor.org/stable/10.1086/423674 (accessed November 23, 2016).

Wiseman, Timothy Peter. 1998. "The Roman Republic: Year One." *Greece & Rome* 45: 19–26. http://www.jstor.org/stable/643205 (accessed November 23, 2016).

Further Reading

Bauman, R. A. 1966. "The Abdication of 'Collatinus.'" *Acta Classica* 9: 129–141. http://www.jstor.org/stable/24591249 (accessed November 23, 2016). Analyzes the development of a consul abdicating office in Roman history. The argument is primarily legal-constitutional; Bauman sets the debate in the political context of the first century BCE.

Bridgman, Timothy P. 2003. "The 'Gallic Disaster': Did Dionysius I of Syracuse Order It?" *Proceedings of the Harvard Celtic Colloquium* 23: 40–51. http://www.jstor.org/stable/25660726 (accessed November 23, 2016). Offers an easily readable discussion of the Gallic sack in the context of the politics of the fifth and fourth centuries BCE. Bridgman's hypothesis that a Sicilian tyrant masterminded the Gallic sack has not found acceptance among classicists. But he provides an interesting view of the Gauls from a different disciplinary standpoint.

Forsythe, Gary. 2005 *A Critical History of Early Rome.* Berkeley, CA: University of California Press. Puts forward a controversial re-examination of many early Roman legends. Forsythe tries to establish a history of the city's early years by integrating legendary material with archaeological evidence and historical theory. His chapters 6–8 are most relevant to this chapter.

Gaertner, Jan Felix. 2008. "Livy's Camillus and the Political Discourse of the Late Republic." *The Journal of Roman Studies* 98: 27–52. http://www.jstor.org/stable/20430664 (accessed November 23, 2016). Examines various aspects of the Camillus tale and suggests two major versions followed by different sources. For advanced students only; good introduction to source criticism.

Kraus, Christina S. 1994. "'No Second Troy': *Topoi* and Refoundation in Livy, Book V." *Transactions of the American Philological Association* 124: 267–289. http://www.jstor.org/stable/284293 (accessed November 23, 2016). Analyzes Livy's use of the Trojan War narrative as a metaphor and structuring principle. Kraus is particularly interested in the Veii and Gallic sack narratives, and suggests that Livy retells the story with variations to indicate that history is both cyclical (it repeats itself), but not inevitable (there may be different winners and losers).

Rosenberger, Veit. 2003. "The Gallic Disaster." *The Classical World* 96: 365–373. http://www.jstor.org/stable/4352787 (accessed November 23, 2016). Analyzes Roman attitudes towards Gaul after the Gallic sack. He argues that, although historians assume that Romans were terrified of Gauls, the place of Gaul in Roman culture is more complex.

9

Conclusion

Derivative. Uncreative. "Copied." In the past, scholars were quick to dismiss Roman mythical production in favor of the kaleidoscope of Greek myth. In their eyes, Greeks were artists; Romans were lawyers and politicians, whose gifts to the world lay in constitutions, not legends. Since Greek myth was clearly superior to Roman cultural production, Romans adopted these foreign tales as their own. More recently, scholars have questioned those assertions, and suggested that Rome "creatively adapted" Greek myth from a variety of sources.

You may wonder whether there's a difference between "adaptation" and "adoption." After all, isn't taking bits and pieces from several sources still derivative and unoriginal? The problem lies in equating these concepts. Many modern works are "derivative" or "adaptations," including famous classics. Shakespeare's *Julius Caesar*, which some of you might have read in school, is an adaptation of Plutarch's biography of the same man. Yet few people deny that Shakespeare was creative!

It might help to think of a few modern examples. The book and movie *Bridget Jones' Diary* is a contemporary adaptation of the nineteenth-century novel *Pride and Prejudice*. Its author, Helen Fielding, has admitted that the basic characters and plot are based on Austen's novel – but there are still substantial differences in character and how the story is told (BBC 2013). In Austen's novel, for example, the plot unfolds from an omniscient third-person perspective (that is, the narrator is the novelist herself, who offers commentary on her creation from a distant and all-knowing perspective). But Bridget Jones tells her own story in Fielding's novel, using a series of diary entries to describe her search for Mr. Right. Another difference can be found in relationships of secondary characters to the protagonist. Austen's protagonist, Elizabeth Bennet,

Early Rome: Myth and Society, A Sourcebook, First Edition. Jaclyn Neel.
© 2017 John Wiley & Sons, Inc. Published 2017 by John Wiley & Sons, Inc.

is a relatively elite woman whose closest confidante is her sister (although Elizabeth's neighbor Charlotte is also a close friend). Bridget, in contrast, has no siblings; she shares her travails with her friends. Bridget also works for a living, and has a much wider social circle in London than Elizabeth in her small town. Although it is possible to list other differences between the two novels, this selection should give a sense of how it is possible to change a narrative creatively. Similarly, when Italian authors retell a mythic plot that is known from an earlier Greek source, they creatively adapt it to fit their own cultural context. We saw examples of such adaptation in **chapter 2**. Aeneas begins as a Homeric hero, but in Roman hands he establishes important religious and cultural norms. Aeneas began the custom of sacrificing with a veiled head (**2.4.5, 6.3.5**), and almost every author mentions that he carried the *Lares* or *Penates*, domestic gods that were worshipped in every Roman household.

Not all adaptations are based on the full original plot. The popular movie *Frozen* was originally based on *The Snow Queen*, a fairy tale by Hans Christian Andersen. The Andersen original has a long and involved plot, unlike the relatively simple story of the Disney movie. It is a love story between two neighbors (a boy and a girl) that unfolds over several years. The boy is kidnapped by the Snow Queen, and the girl goes on a quest to find him. There is a strong religious component to the story, and it is ultimately a quest narrative. While the Snow Queen is important, she is not the main character. In contrast, the movie *Frozen* centers on the "snow queen": Elsa, the girl whose magical powers act as a curse because she can't control them. She runs away from home to avoid harming her family or kingdom. There is still a quest narrative, as Elsa's younger sister Anna tries to lure her back to the kingdom. But it is a story about familial bonds, rather than romantic love, and religion is absent from the plot. The movie's creators chose to focus on a small subsection of the Andersen tale (the idea of a "snow queen" and a quest to return a beloved childhood companion) and elaborated it into a full-length plot. We can see a similar type of adaptation in the many Italian versions of *nostoi* (**2.2–2.5, 6.1–6.3**).

Perhaps the best example of adapting source material to a new culture is found on the small screen. The TV series "The Office" started in the UK, but has been produced in the US and several countries around the world (including France, Germany, and Canada). Although the basic plot of the series is the same – it's a sitcom about working in an office – there are differences in plot and characterization designed to match the office culture of the country in which it is produced. The industry changes (in the UK, a paper company; in Germany, insurance brokers). The cast of characters changes (in Germany and Canada, there are no accountants; the US version features more employee turnover than other iterations of the series). Through these different versions, viewers can see a basic concept being adapted to different cultural norms (similar to "the labors of Hercules": **2.2, 4.1, 4.2, 6.2**). This process of adaptation makes each version of the TV show its own entity – in fact, the UK version flopped in France, while the French adaptation was a hit (Schillinger 2006). Similarly,

Roman myths might have points of contact with Greek myths, but they are altered enough to make them worth study in their own right.

You may have noticed as you read the chapters in this book that "myth" wasn't its own genre in antiquity. Greeks and Romans used myths as a framework for understanding the world around them. The city and the world at large could be mapped out through mythic heroes; common customs had their roots in mythic adventures; even individual behaviors could be traced back to mythic ancestors. Understanding Rome's myths is a way to better understanding Roman literature, history, and culture. You now have the tools to do that.

References

Schillinger, Liesl. "Foreign Office." *Slate*, September 2006: http://www.slate.com/articles/arts/television/2006/09/foreign_office.single.html

"Interview with Helen Fielding." *BBC Radio*. 28 January 2014. https://web.archive.org/web/*/http://www.bbc.com/news/entertainment-arts-2120495

Appendix 1
Author Biographies

*indicates authors whose works are now mostly fragmentary.

*Accius (second/first century BCE) was a Roman playwright. He wrote on Greek and Roman myths and history.

Aelian (third century CE) was a Roman author who wrote on a variety of topics, in both poetry and prose. His work is so varied that it is difficult to describe; some scholars think his works are collections of culturally important anecdotes.

*Agathocles of Cyzicus (fourth century BCE?) wrote local histories.

*Alcimus (fourth century BCE) was a historian from Sicily.

*Annius Fetialis (first century CE?) was a Roman historian.

*Antigonus (third century BCE) wrote both biographies and collections of marvels.

*Apollodorus is probably a reference to the second-century BCE scholar.

*Apollodorus of Erythrae wrote sometime between the third and first centuries BCE.

Aristotle the philosopher (fourth century BCE) tutored Alexander the Great. Many of his writings on diverse topics survive; he mentions Rome only briefly.

*Ateius (first century BCE) was a freed slave from Athens; he wrote at least one historical work.

Early Rome: Myth and Society, A Sourcebook, First Edition. Jaclyn Neel.
© 2017 John Wiley & Sons, Inc. Published 2017 by John Wiley & Sons, Inc.

Augustine (fourth/fifth century CE) was bishop of Hippo in northern Africa. He wrote numerous works, including several books against non-Christian beliefs. His work *On the City of God* was written in the early fifth century and is our greatest source for the Republican antiquarian **Varro**'s work on religion.

Aulus Gellius (second century CE) was the Roman author of a miscellany called the *Athenian Nights*. We know little about his life. His book embraces a wide variety of disciplines, but without a clear ordering principle beyond "learned information."

***Caesar** (first century BCE) was an antiquarian. His *praenomen* was Lucius; Gaius (**2.7.4**) is a mistake.

Calpurnius Piso (second century BCE) was a Roman historian. His work seems to promote Roman morals, as befits a *censor.*

***Caltinus** has not been identified by modern scholars. The name may be a mistake for the Hellenistic Sicilian historian Callias.

Cassius Hemina (second century BCE) was a Roman historian. His history covered the foundation myths until (probably) the Third Punic War. His work was especially rich in religious detail, which later antiquarians mined; very little of it survives.

***Cato** the Elder (third/second century BCE) was a Roman politician. He was the first member of his family to achieve the office of consul, one of the two heads of state. Cato was famous for stern morals in virtually every aspect of his life. His work *Origins* retold the foundation myths of Italian cities; unlike previous Roman historians, who wrote in Greek, Cato used his native Latin.

***Cephalon of Gergitha** was a Hellenistic author; the name is a pseudonym.

Cicero (106–43 BCE) was a Roman orator and politician. After a successful legal career, he was the first member of his family to reach the consulship. His political career was marked by highs and lows; in the low periods, he wrote books on oratory and statesmanship. The work *On the State* was written in the late 50s; *On the Nature of the Gods* and *On Duties* in the mid-40s. Cicero was murdered in the turbulent months that followed Caesar's assassination.

***Cincius Alimentus** (late third century BCE) was a Roman historian writing in Greek.

***Clinias** has not been identified by modern scholars.

***Cornelius** has not been securely identified.

Dio (Cassius)/Zonaras (second–third century CE/twelfth century CE) was a Roman senator. He wrote a history of Rome from Aeneas to his own day. Dio's history is preserved in excerpts by several authors. This book uses excerpts from Zonaras, a Byzantine monk.

*Diocles of Peparethus (fourth/third century BCE) wrote the earliest known history of Rome.

Diodorus Siculus (first century BCE) wrote a universal history in Greek, examining the history of the Mediterranean basin from the mythical period to his own day. Only 15 complete books survive out of an original 40; the rest are fragmentary. Diodorus' work was, by necessity, brief and selective, but heavily researched and easy to follow. He seems to have written between c. 60 and c. 36 BCE.

Dionysius of Halicarnassus (first century BCE) tutored Roman noblemen in the early Principate. He wrote about rhetoric as well as Rome's mythic history; the *Roman Antiquities* was at least partially complete c. 7 BCE. It covered the period from Aeneas to the First Punic War (c. 1200–264 BCE) and aimed to show that Rome was a Greek city. Of the original 20 books, the first ten survive complete and the second ten are fragmentary.

*Domitius has not been identified by modern scholars.

*Egnatius has not been identified by modern scholars

*Ennius (third/second century BCE) came from southern Italy; his generation was the first to be under Roman rule. He was connected to many politically important families of his day, and received Roman citizenship in 184 BCE. His poem *Annals* related Roman history in epic verse for the first time.

*Eratosthenes was a scholar who lived in the third century BCE. He wrote a variety of works, including geography and a world chronology.

Euripides (fifth century BCE) was an Athenian playwright. His plays are considered intensely psychological.

*Fabius Pictor (third/second century BCE) was the first Roman historian. His history was written in Greek. He was a member of the elite Fabian family, but we know few personal details. According to **Dionysius of Halicarnassus**, Fabius related the foundation myths in great detail, but aside from that focused on contemporary events.

Festus (second century CE) compiled a dictionary-encyclopedia of Roman customs. His work was based on a similar (but considerably longer) work by an Augustan-era antiquarian named Verrius Flaccus. The only surviving copy of the book has been damaged, which is why there are so many *lacunae* (gaps in the manuscript). The capitalized letters in the translation indicate dictionary headwords.

*Gabius Bassus was an author of the Late Republic.

*Galitas (third century BCE?) wrote a history of Rome in Greek.

*Granius Licinianus (second century CE) was a Roman historian.

Hemina *see* **Cassius Hemina**.

*Heraclides Lembos (second century BCE) was a Greek historian and philosopher.

*Heraclides Ponticus (first century CE) was a scholar living in Rome.

Herodotus (fifth century BCE), the "father of history," was from the Greek city of Halicarnassus in Asia Minor. His work *Histories* is primarily concerned with the Greco-Persian wars of the early fifth century, but includes a selection of other myths.

Homer (eighth century BCE?) composed the *Iliad* and the *Odyssey*. The works were written down in the Hellenistic period.

Horace (first century BCE) was a Roman poet. In the civil wars of the first century BCE, Horace chose the wrong side. He was later pardoned. His work encompassed a variety of genres, but generally had a philosophical bent.

Hyginus was a freed slave living under Augustus (27 BCE–14 CE). His works on astronomy and myth survive.

*Juba (first century BCE/CE) was the king of Mauretania. He wrote several works of scholarship in Greek.

John Lydus (sixth century CE) was a public official in Constantinople. He was fluent in both Greek and Latin, which allowed him to write a series of antiquarian works about Roman religion and customs. It is not clear whether he was Christian, but most scholars assume that he was.

Justin *see* **Pompeius Trogus**.

Lactantius (third/fourth century CE) was a Christian apologist from North Africa. He studied rhetoric as a young man and put this rhetorical background to use in his religious and philosophical writings. Later Christian doctrine considered his views heretical. The *Divine Institutes,* which criticizes Greco-Roman culture in comparison to Christianity, was completed shortly before his death in 325.

*Licinius Macer (first century BCE) retold early Roman history from a Euhemeristic and seemingly populist perspective.

Livy (first century BCE) was a Roman historian from Padua. His massive work *From the Foundation of the City* was an annalistic history of Rome from Aeneas to Livy's own time. Of the original 142 books, only 35 remain complete; all of the material about early Rome survives in full. The popularity of *From the Foundation* gradually led to the loss of earlier Republican historians, whose less-complete histories stopped being copied.

*Lucilius (second century BCE) was a Latin satirist.

*Lutatius (first century BCE?) may have been a freed slave and historian.

Lycophron (date unknown) is the author of the poem *Alexandra*, one of the earliest Greek works to acknowledge Rome's importance. Major debates about his life exist: suggestions for dating the *Alexandra* range from the fourth century to c. 200 BCE. The strong presence of Rome in the poem is more consistent with Rome's power in a later period.

Macrobius (early fifth century CE) can't be securely identified, but was probably a high-ranking official in Rome. His major work, the *Saturnalia*, was an antiquarian collection in the form of a dialogue. It focuses heavily on old-fashioned Roman traditions, suggesting that the author was not an adherent of the rising Christian religion.

*Naevius (third century BCE) came from central Italy. He wrote primarily drama, including plays and an epic poem dealing with Roman history (including the myths of Aeneas and Romulus).

On the Origin of the Roman People is a work of unknown authorship. It probably dates to the fourth century CE. Its first half seems to use a Republican-era commentary on Vergil (similar to **Servius**); the second half cites more questionable authorities. The authenticity of these citations has been questioned.

Ovid (first century BCE/CE) was a Roman poet of the early Principate. His work encompassed several genres, but had two broad themes: love poetry and myth. Roman myth appears in several of Ovid's works, but is the focus of the *Fasti*, a poem about the Roman calendar, and the last books of the *Metamorphoses*.

Pausanias (second century CE) wrote a guide to Greece. He traveled widely and recorded the famous sights of the places he visited, retelling the myths associated with them. Although he did not visit Italy, he relates several myths from the Greek cities of Magna Graecia.

*Piso *see* **Calpurnius Piso**.

Pliny the Elder (first century CE) was the author of a wide-ranging encyclopedia, the *Natural History*. This work encompassed insights from many different subdisciplines of the natural and social sciences. Although not explicitly intended as a mythological work, the *Natural History* includes much material that we consider mythical.

Plutarch (first/early second century CE) was a Greek author of wide-ranging interests. He was well-connected among the Roman elite and seems to have known Latin; he wrote works on Roman and Greek myth, religion, and history.

Pompeius Trogus/Justin (first century CE/ late fourth century CE) wrote a universal history under Augustus. Pompeius Trogus himself was a Gaul whose family received Roman citizenship in the first century BCE. His work proceeded from East to West in chronological order. It survives only in the abridgement (epitome) written by Justin. Unusually for an epitomator, Justin extracted large portions of Trogus' original work, probably including the portions on early Roman history.

*Procilius (first century BCE) was a Roman antiquarian.

*Promathion (third century BCE) was a Greek historian.

Propertius (first century BCE) came from Umbria. Like many wealthy Romans of his era, he was caught in the turbulent circumstances of Rome's civil wars. His poetry is primarily elegiac love poetry, but in book 4 of his work he turns his attention to Roman myth as well.

*Sabinus Masurius was a lawyer in the reign of Tiberius (14–37 CE).

*Sammonicus (second/third century CE) was a Roman antiquarian.

Servius (auctus) (fourth century CE/seventh century CE) wrote a commentary on Vergil's *Aeneid* for Roman schoolchildren. The text has been passed down to us in two parts: the first is attributed to Servius, probably written c. 400, and seems to be an abridged version of an earlier commentary with some of Servius' own additions. The author of the second part is unknown, but was probably writing in the early seventh century CE. This anonymous author drew on both Servius and Servius' sources to construct his commentary. This book does not distinguish between the two authors. The capitalized letters in the translation indicate quotations from Vergil.

*Sextus Clodius was a Sicilian rhetorician of the first century BCE.

*Sextus Gellius is probably a mistaken reference to Gnaeus Gellius, a second-century BCE Roman historian.

*Simylos was a Hellenistic-era Greek poet.

Solinus (third/fourth century CE) was the writer of a varied work called the *Collected Tales*. He related myths, cultural traditions, and other information. The work is organized geographically, and the section on Italy provides valuable information on city founders. Little is known of Solinus outside of his book.

*Stesichorus (sixth century BCE) was a Greek lyric poet from Sicily. He wrote a series of mythological works, which are mostly lost. The longest surviving fragments have been found on papyri. Although most of Stesichorus' poems center on Greek mythic cycles, his recounting of Hercules' struggle against Geryon (the *Geryoneis*) deals with events that took place in the western Mediterranean.

Strabo (first century BCE/CE) was a Greek writer of the early Roman Principate. He wrote a work of history (now mostly lost) and a *Geography* of the Roman empire (mostly complete). The *Geography* draws in many cases upon first-hand knowledge of people and customs, and is intended as a practical guide to the traditions and peoples of the known world, including their myths.

Suetonius (second century CE) was an imperial biographer.

*Sulpicius Galba (first century BCE/CE) was a Roman historian.

Tertullian (second/third century CE) was a Christian from North Africa. He received a complete Roman education, and was able to use his detailed knowledge of Roman culture and traditions to promote the superiority of Christianity in numerous works.

Tibullus (first century BCE) was a Roman poet. We don't know much about his life. Several of his poems allude to myths.

Timaeus (fourth/third century BCE) was a Greek historian from Sicily. He wrote a massive history of the western Greek world, including Rome, from its mythical beginnings to his own day. This work is now mostly lost.

*Valerius Antias (c. 80–60 BCE) was a historian and major source for Livy. Scholars suspect that he integrated Valerian family myths into his work.

Varro (first century BCE) was an immensely learned scholar of the late Republic. He wrote on a variety of topics, from farming to satire to linguistics; his output included both creative works and practical manuals. More than 60 titles are known, many of which are now lost.

Vergil (first century BCE) wrote Rome's national epic, the *Aeneid*, as well as other poems. He was closely connected with the imperial household, and recited portions of the *Aeneid* to the emperor's family. The poem became a school text, learned by every educated Roman; graffiti from Pompeii suggest its pervasive influence.

Zonaras *see* **Dio (Cassius).**

Appendix 2

Greek Mythical Characters

Achilles was the greatest Greek warrior of the **Trojan War** and one of the protagonists of Homer's *Iliad*. He died at Troy.

Aeneas was the son of the goddess Venus (**Aphrodite**) and mortal **Anchises**. A minor character in the *Iliad*, he later rose to prominence as one of the few characters to escape **Troy**. Romans believed he settled in Italy.

Agamemnon was the commander of the Greek troops at **Troy**.

The lesser **Ajax** was a Greek warrior at **Troy**. He raped **Cassandra**, the priestess of Apollo, when the city was captured; this act brought divine vengeance.

Alcmena was the mortal mother of **Hercules**.

Anchises was a Trojan. Elderly at the time of the **Trojan War**, he escaped the city's destruction with his son **Aeneas**. In most narratives, he dies before reaching Italy.

Atalanta was known for her hunting ability. She almost killed the Calydonian Boar and received a reward. She also defeated her male opponent, **Peleus**, in a wrestling match.

Cassandra was a Trojan princess and prophet of **Apollo**. She predicted Troy's destruction. When the city fell, she was raped by Ajax and became **Agamemnon's** slave. She died when he returned to Greece.

Castor and Pollux were the twin brothers of **Helen**. Pollux was divine, but Castor was mortal. When Castor died, Pollux offered to share his divine status. The twins were models of fraternal affection.

Early Rome: Myth and Society, A Sourcebook, First Edition. Jaclyn Neel.
© 2017 John Wiley & Sons, Inc. Published 2017 by John Wiley & Sons, Inc.

Circe was both a goddess and a witch who turned humans into animals. She kept **Odysseus** trapped on her island for several months.

Cronus was the king of the gods until **Zeus** defeated him. He's associated with a "golden age" of simplicity and abundance. Roman authors call him Saturn.

The **Cyclops** was a one-eyed monster who lived in Sicily. Odysseus meets him in *Odyssey* 9.

The **Dactyloi** were spirits who guarded baby **Zeus** from **Cronus**. Cronus swallowed his children so that they couldn't overthrow him. Zeus was hidden until he was old enough to challenge his father.

Dardanus was the ancestor of the Trojan people.

Deianeira was **Hercules'** last wife. He saved her when she was attacked by **Nessus**. Nessus claimed that his blood was a love potion, and Deianeira saved it; when she thought Hercules had fallen in love with another woman, she put the blood on his shirt. It burned Hercules to death.

Dido was both queen and founder of Carthage. She'd emigrated from Phoenicia when her brother **Pygmalion** wanted to kill her.

Diomedes was a Greek warrior during the **Trojan War**. He was one of the best fighters. He and Odysseus had several adventures. Because Diomedes wounded **Aphrodite**, he wasn't allowed to return to Greece. He settled in Italy.

Emathion is the name of several characters in Greek myth. In context, this Emathion is probably one of the Trojan princes.

Eteocles and his brother **Polynices** fought and died over the sovereignty of Thebes. Their story made up part of the **Theban Cycle**.

Geryon was a three-bodied monster who lived in the western Mediterranean. **Hercules** fought him for his cattle.

Hebe was the divine wife of **Hercules**.

Hector was the leading warrior of **Troy** and one of the protagonists of the Iliad. He was killed by **Achilles**.

Helen was the wife of **Menelaus**. The **Trojan War** began when she was kidnapped by **Paris**.

Helenus was a Trojan prince and prophet. He escaped **Troy** and settled in Epirus.

Hercules was the son of **Zeus** and **Alcmena**. **Hera** hated him because of Zeus' adultery and made him go crazy. After killing his wife Megara and their children, the madness disappeared. To be released from the pollution of killing his family, Hercules had to fulfill many Labors (first 10, then 12). The Labors are

Hercules' most famous deeds, but he had many other adventures throughout the Mediterranean.

Hippolytus was **Theseus'** son. His stepmother, Phaedra, falsely accused him of raping her. Theseus threw him out and cursed him. When Hippolytus left the house, he was killed. The story is the subject of Euripides' *Hippolytus*.

The **House of Atreus** was at the center of a Greek mythic cycle involving family strife, including multiple murders. **Agamemnon** and **Menelaus** were Atreus' sons.

Iolaus was **Hercules'** brother or nephew and accompanied him on many adventures.

Iphigeneia was **Agamemnon**'s daughter. She was sacrificed before the expedition to **Troy**; in revenge, her mother killed **Agamemnon** when he returned.

Iris was a minor goddess who acted as a messenger for the **12 Olympians**. She takes the form of a rainbow.

Leto was the mother of **Apollo** and **Artemis**.

Marsyas was a **satyr** who challenged **Apollo** to a music contest. When he lost, Apollo skinned him alive.

Menelaus was a Greek warrior at **Troy**. His wife **Helen** was the cause of the war.

Nessus was a centaur. He tried to kidnap **Hercules'** wife **Deianeira** and Hercules killed him.

Nestor was the oldest Greek warrior at **Troy**. He was known for his wisdom.

Niobe had 12 children. When she bragged that she was better than **Leto** because she'd had more children, **Apollo** and **Artemis** killed them all.

Nostos (pl. *nostoi*) *see* **Trojan War**.

Odysseus was a Greek warrior at **Troy**. He was known for his strategy. He and **Diomedes** had several adventures. His journey back from Troy is recounted in Homer's *Odyssey*.

The **12 Olympians** were the major gods of the Greek pantheon. See **Appendix 3**.

Pallas is another name for **Athena**.

Pan was a minor god who lived in the countryside. He oversaw herding and hunting, among other rural matters. He is depicted as part **satyr**.

Paris, also known as Alexander, was a Trojan prince. He kidnapped **Helen**, leading to the outbreak of the **Trojan War**. He killed **Achilles** by shooting him in the heel.

Peleus was the mortal husband of **Thetis** and father of **Achilles**. Before his marriage, he lost a wrestling match to **Atalanta** (among other misadventures).

Pelias was a king of Iolcus. When he died, his son held funeral games; **Peleus** and **Atalanta** wrestled there.

Penelope was **Odysseus'** wife. She waited 20 years for his return without remarrying, despite many suitors.

Philoctetes was wounded on the way to **Troy**. The festering wound smelled so bad that the Greeks abandoned him on an island. **Helenus** prophesied that his arrows were needed to take Troy, so **Odysseus** and **Diomedes** brought him back.

Phoebus is another name for **Apollo**.

Phoenix was **Achilles'** tutor and a Greek warrior at **Troy**.

Pollux *see* **Castor and Pollux**.

Polynices and his brother **Eteocles** fought and died over the sovereignty of Thebes. Their story made up part of the **Theban Cycle**.

Polyxena was a Trojan princess who was sacrificed at **Achilles'** tomb.

Satyrs are goatlike deities of the countryside. They often accompany **Pan**.

Sisyphus was a king of Corinth who was known for his intelligence. He managed to capture the god of death, but was punished for this deed.

Telemachus was the son of **Odysseus** and **Penelope**. In some authors, he married **Circe** after Odysseus' death.

Telephus was a son of **Hercules**; he was exposed by his mother and survived by suckling at a deer. He later led the Greeks to **Troy**, but didn't fight there.

The **Theban Cycle** is a series of myths set in and around the Boeotian city of Thebes. They revolve around sovereignty of the city. Some of the tales are retold in Aeschylus' *Seven Against Thebes* and Sophocles' *Oedipus Rex*, *Antigone*, and *Oedipus at Colonus*, among others.

Theseus was the king of Athens and one of its founders. He had many adventures, including kidnapping **Helen**, killing the Minotaur, and fighting the Amazons. He cursed his son, **Hippolytus**, causing his death.

Thetis was a nymph and the mother of **Achilles**. She prophesied that he would live a long but boring life or a short but glorious one. The *Iliad* centers around Achilles' choice to live gloriously.

Tiresias was a prophet. When he accidentally saw **Athena** naked, she made him go blind.

The **Trojan War** was a decade-long conflict between Greeks and Trojans. The war was the subject of numerous Greek and Roman plays, poems, and prose works. The Greeks defeated the Trojans. Afterwards, a few Trojans escaped to nearby (or distant) cities, while the Greeks went home. Their ***nostoi*** provided additional material, since Greek leaders often struggled to make their way back.

Troy *see* **Trojan War**.

Appendix 3

Greek and Roman Gods

By the time of our sources, Greek and Roman gods were assimilated to each other in myths. The table indicates the Greek name for the Roman god and vice-versa.

Greek to Roman

Aphrodite	Venus
Apollo	Apollo
Ares	Mars
Artemis	Diana
Athena	Minerva
Cronus	Saturn
Eros	Cupid
Hera	Juno
Hermes	Mercury
Hestia	Vesta
Zeus	Jupiter

Roman to Greek

Apollo	Apollo
Cupid	Eros
Diana	Artemis
Juno	Hera
Jupiter	Zeus
Mars	Ares
Mercury	Hermes
Minerva	Athena
Saturn	Cronus
Venus	Aphrodite
Vesta	Hestia

Early Rome: Myth and Society, A Sourcebook, First Edition. Jaclyn Neel.
© 2017 John Wiley & Sons, Inc. Published 2017 by John Wiley & Sons, Inc.

Index

Early Rome: Myth and Society, A Sourcebook, First Edition. Jaclyn Neel.
© 2017 John Wiley & Sons, Inc. Published 2017 by John Wiley & Sons, Inc.